THE CONURBATIONS
OF GREAT BRITAIN

The Conurbations of Great Britain

by

T. W. FREEMAN

Reader in Economic Geography in the
University of Manchester

with a chapter on
THE SCOTTISH CONURBATIONS

by
CATHERINE P. SNODGRASS

MANCHESTER UNIVERSITY PRESS

Published by the University at
THE UNIVERSITY PRESS
16–324, Oxford Road, Manchester, 13
1959

TO THE MEMORY OF

C. B. FAWCETT

and

ALAN B. OGILVIE

Printed in Great Britain by Butler & Tanner Ltd., Frome and London

PREFACE

FEW people who love English would regard the word 'conurbation' as a musical addition to the language. Apart from the difficulty of finding an alternative, the word by its very ugliness bears witness to the problems raised by the fusion of one town into another through industrialization and especially through the re-housing of millions of people during the past forty years. This is a study of a nation of townspeople, and of people living primarily in large towns. Those who teach geography in British universities find that many of their students have an innate understanding of industry, of towns, perhaps of economic and social problems inherent in a commercial and manufacturing nation. To many such students, rural life is something remote from experience, though the countryside is visited during holidays or at weekends. Excellent work has been done in schools for many years by organized walking tours, journeys or visits to field study centres; and some university teachers are grateful for the provision of students trained to face the physical hardships of rural field work, even if they appear to have learned little else. While it is important to realize that Britain remains dominantly rural, and that the prosperity of farming should be assured by the needs of the townspeople, there is a need for continued study of our towns, if only because they are changing perpetually and must change in the future.

From choice, this book deals exclusively with the major conurbations of Britain, and with minor conurbations of 50,000 or more people, following the usage of Professor C. B. Fawcett who gave form and direction to the stimulating ideas of Sir Patrick Geddes on this theme. The section on Scotland has been written by my friend Dr. Catherine P. Snodgrass, who from 1936 to 1956 served on the staff of the Geography Department in Edinburgh University and wrote some distinguished articles on Scottish farming as well as the East Lothian volume of the *Third Statistical Account of Scotland*. It was good to find an author who is a loyal daughter of Scotland, knowing both its urban and rural life intimately. All the conurbations have something in common, yet all are different. One would perhaps argue that the economic history of Birmingham and the Black Country has been more fortunate than that of Tyneside; one could compare the effects of deepening the Clyde with similar efforts—made at the eleventh hour—on the Tyne. Opportunities of expansion have been available but some have been seized and some have not. Creations largely (but by no means exclusively) of the last hundred years, these conurbations are reacting in varying ways to the challenge of the present changing times. Some appear to have reached a state of stability, some are threatened with decline, and others have a pulsating vitality hard to control. There is always the salutary thought that the boom area of today may be the depression area of tomorrow, for the Victorian idea of continuing progress everywhere is false. New sources of power, automation, the expansion of air services, changes in demand, all offer new opportunities and problems that must affect the distribution of the industrial population.

In each chapter some consideration is given to the administrative units of the conurbations. Much excellent work has been done on the structure of local government but little has been said on the definition of administrative units in relation to the distribution of population. The major conurbations as entities have been reasonably well defined in the 1951 Census, with one serious exception, Greater London. As always in British life, historical circumstance has remained a powerful influence, crystallized at least partially in strong local feelings that are not to be despised. Inevitably this book rests statistically on the 1951 Census. But there are clear signs that the total population of Great Britain is still increasing, though not everywhere, and if by any chance a later edition is called for after 1961 it may be possible to note how far current trends, of expansion, stability or contraction, have been maintained. The aim has been to shed some light on the distribution of the town population in the nineteen-fifties, rather than to prophesy, or to give any kind of directive for planners. But the study of current trends in economic and social geography has obvious relevance to our time—as to any other time, not least because such trends are revealed in the changing face of Britain. Twenty years from now the distribution of our population will be considerably changed: so too, one hopes, will our towns.

During the past nine years, many Honours and some post-graduate students in Manchester University have written theses on industrial towns of England, especially Lancashire, and thanks are given to them not only for the use of their unpublished work but for the stimulus of their interest and—in some cases—enthusiasm. Other theses include a group concerning the Rhondda valleys by three Welsh students who were in Manchester at the same time. The debt to various published sources must be made clear: in an age when some geographers, and more non-geographers, appear to think that work 10,000 miles from home is inevitably more useful than study of the land near at hand, it is a pleasure to acknowledge the usefulness of the local journal, the *East Midland Geographer*. In time there may be other such journals: France has a dozen or so.

Many friends have helped in the production of this book. Numerous requests were made to town clerks for assistance and all were answered, in some cases with an invitation to visit the town for an interview. Similarly housing managers, planners or medical officers of health, gave interesting information that would be worthy of wider circulation. Indeed, one problem has been the extent of the material available. The maps have been drawn by Miss E. A. Lowcock and the manuscript was typed (and in places tactfully edited) by Mrs. Kirkman, who as Miss P. M. Billington, B.A., was the friend of all the university geographers in Manchester for eleven years to 1958. The kindly guidance of Mr. T. L. Jones, B.A., has been available once more. But the final word must be given to the Honours students who by their attention and apparent interest, and in some cases by their own thesis work, have led me to 'think on these things'. Manchester's students, or some of them, have shown a refreshingly critical attitude to authorities, and a desire to investigate the situation for themselves—and it has been good to be with them.

T. W. FREEMAN

May, 1958

A NOTE ON SOURCES AND MAPS

OF the basic sources used in this work, the most significant is the Census volumes published every ten years, together with Ordnance Survey and other maps. The debt to economic historians is obvious and various local studies in geography have been used with profit. For each conurbation a series of administrative maps from 1888 to the present has been given; and it has also been possible to include similar maps for some of the smaller conurbations and towns. Many other towns are at least as interesting as those illustrated here but a selection had to be made. Local studies of towns in journals are far fewer than one might wish but the annual British Association Scientific Surveys have helped to fill what is commonly called a 'long-felt want' though they are of varied quality. The British Museum's rich map collection has been especially useful for the numerous privately-printed maps: the B.M. numbers have been given to help other workers. Where collieries have been shown on the maps, the information is drawn from the *Guide to the Coalfields*, 1957, ed. R. H. Walkerdine and E. G. Corbin, published by the Colliery Guardian, London, which has admirable maps and statistical material.

CONTENTS

LIST OF TABLES

LIST OF MAPS

CHAPTER 1

A NATION OF TOWNSPEOPLE

NEVER in history has there been a civilization so thoroughly of the town as that of modern Britain. Of every ten people in England and Wales, eight live in towns and four live in one of the six major conurbations, or groups of towns, now officially recognized to exist: in Scotland also more than four-fifths of the population live in towns. The recognition of conurbations as a feature of modern industrialized society was largely due to Patrick Geddes, though in passing one may note that contiguous towns, 'twin-towns', 'twin-cities', have long existed apart for various reasons, not least the barrier of a river or a belt of marshland. London-Southwark, Manchester-Salford, Newcastle-Gateshead, Runcorn-Widnes, Minneapolis-St. Paul are clear examples, of which some have been studied in terms of their site, situation, relationship and functions, in some cases complete with the pseudo-scientific jargon that one notes in a recent title, 'The C . . . -Q . . . symbiosis—a study in urban mutualism'.

The Definition of Conurbations

The word 'conurbation', though unmusical to the ear and of Latin (rather than Greek) extraction, is not jargon. It was apparently inspired by a contemplation of Lancashire: '. . . here', said Geddes, 'far more than Lancashire realizes, is growing up another Greater London as it were—a city-region of which Liverpool is the sea-port and Manchester the market, now with its canal port also; while Oldham and many other factory towns, more accurately called "factory districts", are the workshops'.[1] In short, Geddes saw the whole of South Lancashire as a human region largely urban in character. He continues, speaking of its towns: 'Constellations we cannot call them; conglomerations is, alas, nearer the mark, but it may sound inappropriate, what of "Conurbations"?'[2] These were conceived by Geddes on a broad scale, for he gives as other examples the Sheffield district and the South Wales coalfield (or 'Waleston'), neither of which received official approval in the 1951 Census which reserves the term 'conurbation' for the major examples only. The definition of Greater London and 'Midlandton' given by Geddes is similar to that used in the Census—though the latter is called the

1

West Midlands. In Scotland, Geddes foresaw the development of a continuously-settled industrialized region extending from the Clyde to the Forth, of which Greater Glasgow was only a part.[3] Having distinguished seven 'conurbations' outside Greater London, Geddes comments that each corresponds broadly to the area of a coalfield and forms 'a new Heptarchy, which has been growing up naturally, yet almost unconsciously to politicians, beneath our existing, our traditional political and administrative network . . .' [4] And the suggestion follows that the existing town and county councils could hardly deal with many of the problems common to such areas of interlocking towns and industrial villages—many of which were amorphous.

C. B. Fawcett's conception of a conurbation was more rigid than that of Geddes.[5] It was taken in 'the strict sense of a continuously urban area: i.e. a conurbation is an area occupied by a continuous series of dwellings, factories and other buildings, harbours and docks, urban parks and playing fields, etc., which are not separated from one another by rural land, though in many cases in this country such an urban area includes enclaves of rural land which is still in agricultural occupation'. In fact there may be within a conurbation area some agricultural land of high value and some areas of intensive production, such as the glasshouse belt of the Lea valley in London or the small area to the southwest of Leeds which is intensively used for rhubarb cultivation. But these are enclaves, perhaps all the more worthy of preservation because they are enclaves. Parks, playing fields and other public and private open spaces belong more specifically to the towns themselves. In central Scotland, for example, Fawcett mentioned Clydeside as a conurbation, Geddes the entire industrial area: Geddes viewed industrial districts as a sociological factor in Great Britain, and his chosen areas corresponded fairly closely with those having more than 600 people to the square mile, a density that can hardly be achieved under a solely agricultural way of life in Britain.

In the mid-twentieth century the word 'conurbation' has become respectable in Britain for it appears in the 1951 Census and in other government publications. In 1957, however, a government spokesman avoided the word by speaking of 'special review areas'. There is no such thing as a 'typical' conurbation; they do not everywhere consist of a number of well-integrated towns but rather of a series of sprawling industrial areas tied for social purposes into administrative parcels labelled urban districts and municipal boroughs in England. It is not always so: within the industrial areas of the land, some places have become well-developed towns having good shopping centres, strong markets, excellent commercial and professional facilities and a varying range of intellectual activities. The 'dark galaxy of towns' that—according to Patrick Geddes[6]—forms the industrial West Riding, is not merely that; for some of its centres are both commercially and intellectually seething with vitality. This is not the view of the more visionary planners who regard industrial areas as the epitome of all that is worst in our civilization, but rather an evaluation of the brighter side of life in areas admittedly lacking in external charm and grace.

The Origin and Development of Conurbations

Conurbations normally consist of a congeries of industrial towns, though they may include places which are primarily commercial or residential. These towns may have a strongly-marked local individuality, as in the Manchester conurbation, where Bolton, Bury, Oldham, Rochdale, Ashton-under-Lyne, Stockport and several other places are all clearly-marked industrial and market centres rather than suburbs of Manchester. They have in fact their own suburbs, some of which interlock with those of Manchester and other towns. And here one may consider the process by which a conurbation develops. On the 1848 Ordnance Survey map, there was a line of houses along the 8 miles of road from Manchester to Oldham, and along the canal a short distance away there were numerous mills. The fusion of towns had begun: for example three separate towns, Ashton, Hyde and Dukinfield, had a continuous line of buildings on the roads between them. 'Ribbon development' was already rampant, especially along main roads which had houses, shops and inns, though behind these ribbons of settlement there was generally open country.

Incipient conurbations were clearly seen in the industrial north by the middle of the nineteenth century along some of the turnpike roads with mills beside the canals and canalized rivers. Once transport became swifter, the possibilities of town expansion were vastly increased. The horse omnibus and the private carriage made residence 2–5 miles from a town centre possible for the wealthier sections of society who could afford the costs and the travelling time and did not need to be at work by 6 a.m. The industrial masses were housed beside their work and the factory proprietors who built cottages were normally regarded as benefactors. In other words, the residential suburb grew, generally beside some old village a few miles from the centre of a town. Hampstead, Highgate, Clapham and many other London examples could be given, with countless others in the provinces: inspection of Fig. 29 will show that around Manchester such places as Fallowfield, Withington and Didsbury were outlying villages already partly suburban by the middle of the nineteenth century. Many such places had—happily still have—some pleasant early nineteenth century houses, and there too the wealthier merchants and manufacturers built spacious houses in their own grounds, so expressing the wish of many British townsmen—to create the illusion that they are living in the country, or immediately beside it. And these suburbs expanded, both outwards into the rural area and inwards towards the towns from which they had drawn their inhabitants. In many cases the suburbs became strong social and shopping centres, having a vigorous local life centred on a variety of clubs and churches—in fact, the elements of a 'neighbourhood unit'.[7]

Even before the railway age, the outward movement of population from central town areas was marked, but it was a mere ripple compared with what was to come in the twentieth century. And the main effect of the building of railways was to open industrial towns to trade more and more through the years, with the result that the towns expanded by adding new factories and new streets of workers' houses with smaller areas of middle-class houses, located generally on the fringe of the towns when they were built, or convenient to some railway station having a good service to town. Not always were the railways concerned primarily with suburban traffic: the lines to Euston, for example (p. 40), were at first used almost exclusively for long-distance transport. On the other hand, some of the lines serving east London made possible the growth of vast workers' dormitories by providing cheap workmen's tickets for travellers from Walthamstow, Tottenham and the East End. And similar cases could be given in the provinces: when railways were built from Manchester into the Cheshire lowland and the Pennines, suburban growth followed as much as 10 miles from the city, and as Merseyside acquired its ferries from the eighteen-twenties and its railways twenty years later, so the Wirral peninsula was opened to suburban settlement. And in time areas beyond the older industrial ports and towns were themselves industrialized, for example, in Birkenhead, which grew from a hamlet to a large industrial town when provided with steam ferries and a railway line to London.

Trams replaced horse buses during the last forty years of the nineteenth century, but not everywhere. It was now possible for people to live farther from their work, but a half-hour journey generally covered only about 6 miles, commonly less, except in cities where the trams were laid on special sleeper-based tracks. Acceleration came with the motor-bus services developed from c. 1910; for a half-hour journey might now cover 7 miles or even more in the case of the express bus services characteristic of some towns. Without such travel facilities, it would have been impossible to contemplate such re-housing schemes as Wythenshawe, Manchester, at its furthest extent 10 miles from the city centre, where 85,000 people depend almost entirely on bus transport. Accelerated tram services, bus services, and suburban railway lines, especially those electrified in the major cities, all made possible the phenomenal outward spread of the population in the provincial and Scottish conurbations during the inter-war period. And along with these came the private car whose owner could drive into town or to a convenient suburban railway station as he wished. Similarly, bus services fed the trains with passengers.

Every conurbation showed these features in varying degrees during the inter-war period, but London most of all. The efficiency of the London Passenger Transport Board made possible this dispersion on a scale not seen before, for almost as soon as a new underground station was built, a new suburb grew around it. And the willingness to travel long distances made the separation of home and workplace a feature of the lives of millions. This was not normally measured in distances, but rather in time and cost, and especially time, as commonly rents and rates are cheaper away from the inner areas of London. Nevertheless this was no new thing, merely an old phenomenon seen in a more intensive form. And what one has seen so far is presumably only the beginning of an outward spread of population by which all the congested housing areas of our cities will be removed, and their inhabitants settled in flats at a far lower density per acre, or in new housing areas of a type all too familiar.

Withdrawal of the population from the inner parts of cities is a phenomenon now more than a century old. It was first noted in the city of London early in the nineteenth century (see pp. 31–5), as houses were pulled down to provide sites for new roads, offices and commercial premises. The first clear signs in the larger provincial towns came in 1841–1851, for example in Birmingham (p. 82), Glasgow (p. 318), Manchester (p. 138), Leeds (p. 172) and

B

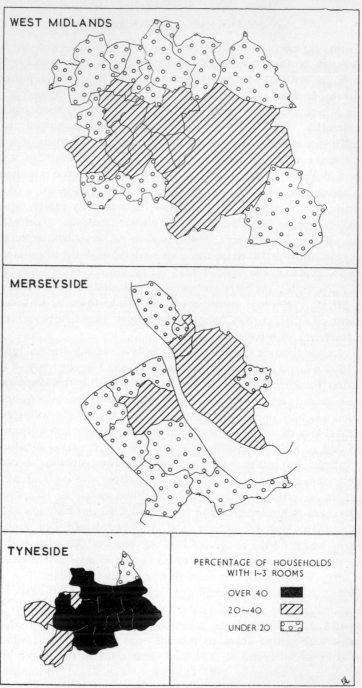

FIG. 1. PERCENTAGE OF HOUSEHOLDS IN 3 ROOMS OR LESS, WEST MIDLANDS, MERSEYSIDE AND TYNESIDE CONURBATIONS

Liverpool (p. 109). The central parts of towns were needed for railways, factories, warehouses, shopping streets and roads and the first slum clearance was achieved by the commercial expansion of the big towns. Slum clearance as a matter of deliberate social policy came much later and little was done until the last twenty years of the nineteenth century. For one reason or another, first the areas in the centres of towns, and then those in the middle belt began to decline in numbers; and many places that were sharply increasing some fifty years ago are now losing population. And nowhere is this more dramatically seen than in the county of London, which lost over a million people between 1931 and 1951.[8] Unfortunately this inevitable change has left deep if temporary scars on many of our cities, where property sinks into a decrepit state in areas to be cleared. All acquainted with major British cities will realize the relevance of the phrase 'the blighted belt',[9] generally found between the centre and the suburbs: prosperity and squalor are apparently not incompatibles.

The re-housing of people from slum property—not to mention the vast areas of poor but 'respectable' housing—is still continuing and the position reached is that by 1960 Manchester corporation will have used virtually all the land available for building within its bounds: already the city is building houses outside them. According to the slum clearance returns of 1955, 68,000 of Manchester's 208,000 houses were unfit for habitation[10] and at the moment of writing efforts are being made to discover more and more 'overspill' sites. Although the city's population declined by 8 per cent from 1931 to 1951, the number of dwellings increased by 13 per cent. Households now consist of fewer persons (average 3·7 in 1931 and 3·2 in 1951), with the result that even a declining population will require more homes: inspection of the 1951 Housing volume of the Census[11] will show that practically every authority in the land had an increased number of dwellings. Greater London and the five provincial conurbations had 3,509,000 dwellings in 1931 but 4,606,000 in 1951,

FIG. 1. This map and Fig. 2 give a rough estimate of the areas where housing is poorest but not an infallible guide as three rooms may provide adequate accommodation for one or two people. Nevertheless, the administrative areas with the highest proportion of households in three rooms or less are also those where, according to the Housing volume of the Census, amenities such as fixed baths are least general. On Tyneside the standard of housing is lower than in other conurbations: the proportion of households in three rooms or less is 45·7 per cent on Tyneside, 22·7 per cent on Merseyside and 21·5 per cent in the West Midlands conurbation.

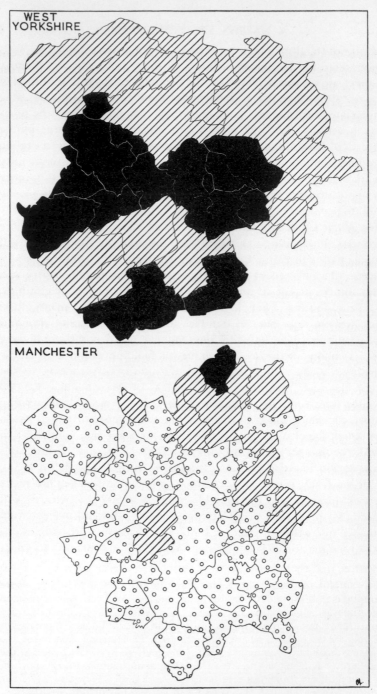

FIG. 2. LIVING ACCOMMODATION, WEST YORKSHIRE AND MAN-
CHESTER CONURBATIONS
Key as for Fig 1

that is over a million more, + 31 per cent. But these six conurbations had an aggregate population increase of only + 3 per cent, from 16,405,000 to 16,914,000, and the vast new suburbs of local authority or private enterprise homes have met a need better expressed by the statistics of households than of total population. The increase in the number of structurally-separate dwellings from 1931–1951 in the major conurbations was as follows: Greater London, + 38 per cent; Manchester (Southeast Lancashire), + 22 per cent; West Midlands, + 35 per cent; West Yorkshire, + 18 per cent; Merseyside, + 24 per cent; Tyneside, + 32 per cent.

The Major Conurbations

London, long recognized as what is now called a conurbation, was defined by Fawcett as having 8,203,000 people in 1931, using as a basis the city of London and the Metropolitan Police District (see Fig. 16). This area of 722 square miles had an increase of + 9·7 per cent from 1921 to 1931, but only + 1·6 per cent from 1931 to 1951 owing to the phenomenal decrease of 24 per cent within the inner area of 117 square miles that forms the county of London. Undoubtedly the effect of the 1939–1945 war was to accelerate the outward movement, and suburbs showing marked increase forty to fifty years ago are now declining in population. The expanding belt has moved outward so that between 1931 and 1951 considerable increases occurred within a radial zone some 40–50 miles from Charing Cross. C. B. Fawcett recognized this in his statement that areas of contiguous town had in all 9,150,000 people and that if neighbouring, though non-contiguous, urban areas economically part of the metropolis were also included, the population would number 10,000,000.[12] London experienced in 1888 the first—indeed the only—effort to define a conurbation as an administrative unit when the L.C.C. was formed, but much of the initial energy was given to efforts to incorporate the city of London and meanwhile, as W. A. Robson[13] pointed out, there grew up outer suburbs over which the L.C.C. had no control; Robson expresses the opinion that the L.C.C. could

---

FIG. 2. The position in the Manchester conurbation is better than in West Yorkshire, which has a belt of towns extending from Morley and Ossett in the east to Huddersfield and Halifax and their neighbouring urban districts, having very small houses, generally stone-built but far below modern standards. Statistically, the West Yorkshire conurbation is comparable with Tyneside, as 37·3 per cent of its households are of three rooms or less compared with 17·8 per cent in the Manchester conurbation.

more profitably have tried to control this development rather than waste energy on trying to absorb a city of impregnable resistance.

Definition of the other conurbations offers difficulties no less acute, but two main points appear to be significant. First, Patrick Geddes clearly had his eye on possible growth, C. B. Fawcett on actual land use at the time of definition: certainly not all the economic growth expected by Geddes has been seen,[14] for example in Lancashire and Yorkshire, but he wrote in days long before the world crisis of the thirties. The areas defined in the 1951 Census are closely similar to those of Fawcett, but with some interesting deviations that will be discussed later (see pp. 155, 177). A second point is that for statistical purposes a conurbation must be defined in terms of existing administrative areas. There has been little consideration of local administrative areas by geographical writers[15] though they have been very widely used for distributional mapping. These units differ enormously from one case to another: within the conurbations, some consist entirely of built-up land and others include within their bounds considerable areas of agricultural land which may perhaps be regarded as the town's 'lebensraum'. The largest of the county boroughs in size is Birmingham,[a] which has 80 square miles, the next largest Sheffield, 62 square miles, Glasgow, 60 square miles—Liverpool and Manchester each consist of c. 43 square miles. In other words, Birmingham has been more successful in adding unto itself neighbouring territory than certain other major cities, conspicuously Manchester, which is hemmed in by boroughs and urban districts on all sides except the extreme south. No single cause is operable, because the administrative districts owe their present form to a mass of local historical, economic and political factors. Each conurbation is a law to itself; and in many ways London is the simplest of all, as it is the nearest approach to a circle, though lacking the concentric inner green belt that could have been made had action been taken in time.

The West Midlands conurbation is readily divisible into three parts, first Birmingham with half its population; second, two large suburban areas, Solihull and Sutton Coldfield which together house 116,000 inhabitants (1951); and third, the Black Country which has twenty-one separate administrative boroughs and urban districts occupied by a million people. Though perhaps the most prosperous

[a] Oddly enough the largest urban administrative units, apart from Birmingham, are Thurrock M.B., Essex, 63 square miles, population 81,634 in 1951 and the Lakes U.D., Westmorland, 76 square miles, population 6,094 in 1951.

industrial area in Britain, this conurbation has vast areas of derelict land due to former mines and ironworks, many of which areas are now being used for housing and social amenities such as playing fields. Merseyside is sharply divided into two by the river, though recent industrial developments at Port Sunlight and at Ellesmere Port (some of them associated with the Ship Canal) have proved to be one of the many factors encouraging residential development in the Wirral. The Manchester conurbation is divided into fifty-two separate units, largely owing to the existence of distinct industrial towns showing enough obstinacy to avoid absorption by larger neighbours: for the past hundred years there has been a steady encroachment southwards into Cheshire. West Yorkshire, having thirty-three administrative divisions, has a far larger number of places recognized locally as separate small towns and villages: away from the major towns there is an intermingling of agricultural countryside and stone-built industrial villages. The towns are connected and interlocking, it is true, but the rural environment is seen to a greater extent than in any other conurbation. Tyneside is reasonably compact as an entity on the ground, but its thirteen administrative districts zealously guard their local rights. Here in 1937 a Government Commission recommended the replacement of existing local authorities by a new borough of Newcastle but this proposal was not accepted by the government of the day nor by the post-war Boundary Commission. Scottish conurbations have a range of problems somewhat different from those farther south, not least in their characteristic tenement housing. Clydeside is divided into three major parts, Glasgow itself with over half the population, the Renfrewshire and Dunbartonshire industrial towns to the west and the North Lanarkshire coalfield. It includes twenty administrative units: the County of the City of Glasgow, seven large and five small burghs, and seven county districts.

The Minor Conurbations

The minor conurbations of England and Wales are considered in three chapters (8–10) and those of Scotland at the end of Chapter 11. None of them are officially recognized as conurbations in the 1951 Census yet they are considered here because they include three-tenths of the population of England and Wales. Neither Geddes nor Fawcett apparently intended that the term 'conurbation' should be restricted to a few major examples, for both were concerned with the problems of the urban life of Great Britain. To the present author it appears illogical to exclude the South Wales coalfield or the ports and industrial centres on its margins, or to exclude Sheffield and district, Teesmouth, the Lancashire manufacturing towns or the Potteries merely because the 1951 Census fails to give them its imprimatur as conurbations. It would be possible to set a lower limit for conurbations at 250,000, 100,000, 75,000 or at any other figure but here 50,000 has been chosen in order that various industrial, commercial and residential-holiday towns may receive mention. If in some cases this has involved consideration of towns that can hardly rank as conurbations, it has also made possible the inclusion of many places greatly influenced by the conurbations near them. In the northwest, for example, Warrington, Widnes-Runcorn and the coalfield towns around Wigan and St. Helens all came within Geddes' 'Lancaston', and on the coast Southport and Formby, or Blackpool and its neighbours, have all grown in association with the industrial North.

The Subdivisions of the Conurbations (Fig. 3)

Efforts to subdivide each major conurbation on a basis of town land use have been made for 1951 in the Census volumes: for each of these areas separate figures are made available.[16] Inevitably there is a difference of definition from one conurbation to another and the efforts to establish some kind of uniformity have not been successful, especially as the boundaries of each subdivision must coincide with those of towns or their wards. The crucial factor is that those who

---

FIG. 3. In the West Midlands, the 'main industrial and commercial centres; older residential districts' cover the older parts of Birmingham and the Black Country, and the 'new residential fringe' bears a suspiciously exact relation to certain administrative boundaries. The 'transitional' area appears to be what is left. Merseyside's dockside and commercial centres come out clearly, and so too do the pre-1914 residential areas, with a limited and inevitable amount of generalization. It is unfortunate that the entire area of Ellesmere Port M.B. should be called 'dockside and commercial', which on the ground it is not. The Tyneside divisions include the Newcastle nucleus and the older residential areas, but this, the smallest of the conurbations, is perhaps easier to divide than the others. Critical one may be, but the compilers of these maps have had to do their work on inadequate data as few detailed maps of land use are readily available. They have also been obliged to keep to administrative boundaries in order to provide statistical material. Most of the divisions are subdivided further in the volume from which these maps are taken—Census of England and Wales 1951, *Report on Greater London and five other conurbations.*

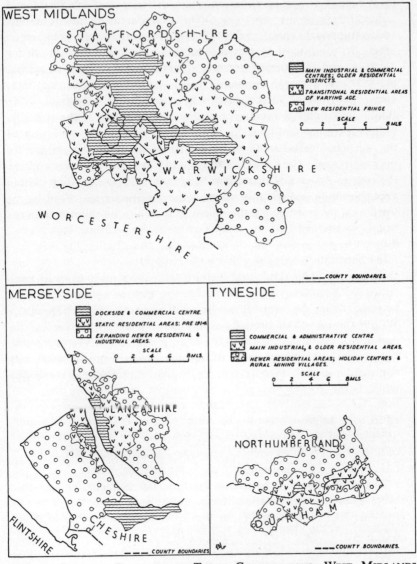

FIG. 3. OFFICIAL DIVISIONS OF THREE CONURBATIONS, WEST MIDLANDS,
MERSEYSIDE, TYNESIDE

made these subdivisions had little material on which to work—had
there been, for each conurbation, maps of town land use available,
it would have been easier to distinguish such areas as the 'dockside
and commercial centre', the 'static residential areas, pre-1914', and
others. In the case of Merseyside, there is a threefold division, first,
dockside and commercial centres, second, 'static residential areas,
pre-1914', and third, expanding newer residential and industrial
areas. The first of these includes a large part of Liverpool with
Bootle and a considerable area on the Cheshire side of the river as
well as the municipal borough of Ellesmere Port: the second covers
the older residential areas on both sides of the river and the third,
the newer areas. The use of the word 'static' is unfortunate for within
the area so designated there have been many changes by slum clearance, bombing and the general rebuilding characteristic of all large
towns: on the other hand, the maritime influence on industrial location is so marked that the main factory and warehouse belt is not
difficult to distinguish. The West Midlands conurbation has a threefold classification based largely on the residential aspects: at one end
there are the older residential districts with the main industrial and
commercial centres and at the other the new residential fringe—
between them the 'transitional residential areas of varying age'.
Within the inevitable limitations imposed by administrative boundaries, this classification works reasonably well but fails to bring out
the central commercial areas of various towns. For Tyneside, by
contrast, a special category is given to the small area of Newcastle
which is the 'commercial and administrative centre' of the conurbation: this is certainly in accordance with the facts, but there is no
effort to distinguish other town centres such as Tynemouth or South
Shields; and the remaining classifications consist of first, the main
industrial and older residential areas, and second, the newer residential areas with holiday centres and 'rural mining areas'.

The problems of subdividing London, the Manchester and the
West Yorkshire conurbations have proved even more complicated.
But this leads only to the point that each conurbation has evolved
differently from others, having particular qualities of physical
features and economic geography, not to mention the chance factors
that are sometimes grouped as 'historical circumstance'. And the
same could be said of the numerous smaller 'conurbations' or groups
of towns discussed briefly in Chapters 8–10. Everywhere too the
administrative boundaries seem to be an unsatisfactory or only partially satisfactory compromise. A modern novelist has written:[17]

They were all one, Manchester and Salford . . . but where one town ended and the other began who knew? Certainly not he. There wasn't a no-man's land, an interregnum; there were just streets and streets and streets reaching from the Cheshire plain in the south to the Lancashire hills in the north, and it was all one block of Manchester-Salford.

Or so the novelist's hero thought: in fact it was fifty-three separate administrative areas in the 1951 Census, reduced to fifty-two shortly afterwards.

CHAPTER 2

THE GREATER LONDON CONURBATION

WHAT is London? A vast, spreading town consuming villages by making them suburbs, a sprawling metropolitan area pushing outwards more and more, the greatest 'million-city' in the world and the worst defined; there are many answers. Unfortunately the Census authorities in 1951 did not seize the opportunity of making a new assessment of the Greater London area, but merely followed the Police Act of 1946 which used in a slightly modified form a definition of 1829.[1] This, the Metropolitan Police District, included all the parishes of which any part was within 12 miles of Charing Cross, or of which the whole was within 15 miles of Charing Cross, together with nine parishes partly outside the 15-mile radius.[2] Fig. 18 shows the effect of this definition, slightly modified in 1946 to coincide with the boundaries of existing boroughs and urban districts.

Attempts were made to define the metropolitan area from its inner core, from the end of the sixteenth century.[3] About 1592–1593, the registration of deaths began under the Bills of Mortality and the first records in 1603 covered an area of almost 3 square miles, including most of the city, both within and outside the walls, as well as parts of Holborn and Finsbury, and the parishes of Bermondsey and Southwark close to the river on the south side (Fig. 4). In 1604, another 6 square miles was added, including the greater part of Westminster, the remainder of Holborn and Finsbury, further slices of Stepney and Bermondsey and the whole of Shoreditch. In 1626, more of Westminster was added, and ten years later, there was a vast extension both in the east, covering all the rest of Stepney (except the Tower of London district, not specified in the Bills of Mortality), All Saints' parish in Poplar, Bethnal Green, Hackney, and Islington and also in the south, covering Rotherhithe and Newington, with the whole of Lambeth. The area included in the old Bills of Mortality by 1636 extended over nearly 34 square miles, of which a considerable proportion was rural as late as the eighteenth century, but by 1801 the metropolitan area had so extended that five additional parishes were included, Chelsea, Kensington, Paddington, St. Marylebone and St. Pancras, then growing suburbs: this gave London an area of nearly 47 square miles. This was less than half the

16

administrative county of 117 square miles, which was developed
from the 'metropolis' as defined in 1855, under the new Tables of
Mortality. But this area was effectively foreshadowed a few years
earlier: in 1839, the Registrar's annual abstracts included the 47
square miles noted above, together with Fulham, Hammersmith,
Stoke Newington, Camberwell, the remainder of Poplar (Bow and
Bromley), Deptford, and also parts of Greenwich and Woolwich: in

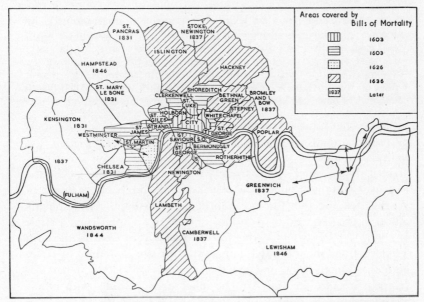

FIG. 4. AREAS COVERED BY THE BILLS OF MORTALITY 1603–1846

This is the area that was included under the Metropolis Management
Act of 1855 and, with little change, in the county of London from 1888.
The map is taken from the Census of 1851, Population Tables I, vol. 1,
Division 1, 38–45, section on 'London within the Bills of Mortality'.

1844 Battersea and Wandsworth were added, and in 1846, Hampstead, the remaining parts of Greenwich and Woolwich with the
large parish of Lewisham.

All this area, defined as 'metropolitan' under the Metropolis
Management Act of 1855, and administered for certain purposes by
the Board of Works, has been described by Mrs. Cole as

not chosen on any principle connected with local government . . . it
excluded West Ham, which was already largely built over and forms

a natural extension of the East End, with a continuous line of buildings; and it included Woolwich . . . at that period an independent and even isolated community, several miles further distant from the city of London than other places left outside. . . .' [4]

Mrs. Cole states bluntly that 'to delimit a capital city by Act of Parliament on a basis of death registers and main drainage is surely one of the oddest that can ever have been evolved'.[5] The result is that half of 'Stratford-atte-Bowe is in London and half in West Ham' and

in the north-west, 'London' is apparently unable to cross the Edgware Road . . . having left outside itself half the old built-up area in the north and east, on the south the county boundary sweeps into . . . the parklands of Putney, Sydenham and Eltham . . . on the south bank of the Thames, 'London' stretches a full three miles further to the east than it does on the north bank, save for a ridiculous little enclave called North Woolwich, clustered at the north end of the Free Ferry.[6]

In short, what became London county was an area used for statistical purposes by the Registrar General (see pp. 16–17 and Fig. 4). From the same source came the term 'Greater London', now commonly divided into 'Inner'—the County—and 'Outer'. In 1875, the Registrar said that London had overflowed the limits of the Board of Works area and that the merchant and professional classes having offices in the City and in Westminster lived in an outer ring, a circle of about 15 miles from Charing Cross.[7] At the 1881 Census, the term 'Greater London' was used, apparently for the first time to cover both the 'Outer Ring' and the Registration District as it had developed to 1846 (see Fig. 4). The inner area became, with minor modifications, the county of London in 1888 and the Outer Ring became the frontier zone of a London steadily encroaching on the countryside. In the 1921 Census, the Outer Ring was divided into two parts: first, places outside the L.C.C. area but wholly or partly within a radius of 10 miles from Charing Cross and second, the remainder.[8] But by 1951, this distinction had little meaning owing to the countryward advance of suburban housing; ironically enough the 1829 Metropolitan Police District was until recently an admirable unit for the study of a growing London but the 1888 definition of the county of London was at all times little more than an administrative curiosity.

The idea that London is far too large has been held for generations. The plain fact is that London, however defined, is itself the expression of a way of life characteristically English, marked by lateral rather than vertical growth,[9] in which most people desire immediate access to open ground in their own gardens, public parks and playing fields or—for the fortunate—open countryside. The drift of population from the inner boroughs has gone on for more than a century (see Fig. 6), and data in successive censuses has shown that decline of population has continued outwards so that by 1931–1951, every borough of the L.C.C. had a decline, except for Hampstead, Lewisham and Woolwich; and boroughs in the outer ring, such as Wimbledon and Tottenham, were already showing decreases. At the end of the nineteenth century, East Ham and West Ham were growing rapidly: in 1931–1951, they had declines of − 15 and − 42 per cent respectively.[10] The heavy decreases of inner boroughs were offset by the marked increases of Outer London, so that the whole conurbation had an increase of + 1·6 per cent from 1931 to 1951 but—far more significant—an increase of 36 per cent in the number of houses and flats, from 1,589,000 to 2,180,000.

The very extent of London is an intriguing fact. Mackinder, in 1931, said that Greater London was 'not a town but a region',[11] and Unstead in 1933 spoke of the London Basin as a 'tract' in which there are a number of 'stows', one of them London itself, 'a human settlement of wide extent, which should not be divided among other areas'.[12] Whatever system of regionalization one adopts, so large a conurbation must be regarded as some kind of unit. And this very fact makes the physical features of the London area of particular interest: its immediate neighbourhood, a basin floored primarily by London clay capped by various later deposits, is clearly defined by its limiting uplands, the chalk of the North Downs and the Chilterns. Many other cities have similar locations on navigable rivers at the first crossing place but the dominance of London in England and its claim to be the greatest city in the world, make it unique. In its beginning, a site of abiding value was chosen.

Physical Features

London's initial advantages of site are similar to those of many other towns—here was the first convenient crossing-place of a tidal river, in this case the natural line of entry from the continent facing the Rhine, the Scheldt and other rivers which flow into the North Sea. The Romans saw the advantages of a site that had gravel terraces on either side of a river, of which those on the north side were well-drained and of considerable extent:[13] the Roman town, which covered 330 acres, lay on the north side between the River Fleet on the west and the Tower on the east.[14] But since Roman times, the level of the land has apparently sunk some 15 ft. with the result that the tidal limit has advanced upstream and areas now threatened by tidal flood were much drier: it is probable that the tides did not go far beyond London Bridge in Roman times.[15] The evidence of the Roman crossing places is far from clear but a point of some significance is that from the beginning the heart of the town was on the north side of the river in the City and in Westminster. In all phases of history, the river has been the most significant physical feature of London. As Spate has shown, it was adequate for shipping as late as the early eighteenth century, when few ships drew more than 13 ft. of water and they came up with the flood-tide and went down with the ebb.[16] Nor was the advantage of a tidal river lost later, for docks were built in the East End using the flood-plains between the river's sweeping meanders, and wharves were made on the Barking creek and at Tilbury: London still remains the greatest port of Britain.

From the foundation of London the main course of the Thames has altered very little but peaty ground intersected by numerous small creeks, such as those in the lower part of the estuary, has been made into firm ground and the river has been gradually confined to its present channel by encroachment.[17] Alluvial marshes have been drained and covered by the debris of settlement, or 'made ground', of which there is estimated to be some 10 ft. on most of the level land of London. Mrs. Ormsby has given a vivid picture of early London.[18]

> At low tide, the Thames flowed between great expanses of clean gravel and sand, with here and there broad banks of fine silt. . . . On the south side of the river bank the tidal marshes lay green with rank grass and osiers, among which the tidal waters crept at flood-time in labyrinthine creeks. Here and there an eyot, as at Battersea or Chelsea, rising above the water-logged plain, would attract the eye by its group of trees. . . . North of the river the scrub-covered banks rose steeply between the marshy flats of Westminster and of the Lea and the view was shut in by the wooded heights of Highgate and Hampstead, beyond which lay the great forest of Middlesex.

The river was the main artery through the London basin, normally defined by its outer limits, the Chilterns on the north and the North Downs on the south: in the heart of this basin there is considerable topographical diversity.

Riverside alluvium is now seen mainly on the east side of London and in the Lea valley on the north side: elsewhere it has been so covered with 'made ground' that its original extent is far from obvious. The Thames-side gravel tract forms a wide plain to the west of London, which is continued eastwards as a lower terrace at 40–80 ft. above the river, and provides a high north bank to the river in central London. On the northwest, the Middlesex Clay Plain is a gently undulating tract rising from 100 to 200 ft. studded with residual heights such as the Harrow-Sudbury mass and minor eminences such as Kingsbury and Horsenden Hill.[19] But the most distinctive features of north and east London are the 'Northern Heights' at c. 400 ft. and the South Essex uplands, separated from one another by the lower Lea valley.[20] Much of the higher ground is covered with gravel overlying the 'London clay'; the term the 'Northern Heights' is applied by S. W. Wooldridge to 'the high ground at Totteridge, Mill Hill, Finchley and Muswell Hill and Highgate'.[21] Epping Forest, best seen as an 'upland' feature from the Lea valley, is partly covered by gravel: southwards, in the Wanstead flats, there is a vast spread of alluvium. Besides the Thames, the one-time tidal marshes of the flood-plain at Barking and Dagenham have been partially used for residential and industrial purposes. The attraction of residential areas in the north lies largely in their elevation; the 400-ft. level dominates the area and provides it with a topographical variety inadequately appreciated by the writers of the London Plan: '. . . the London Region . . . cannot be said to be very remarkable for the possession of dramatic, romantic or noble landscape features'.[22] True, there is nothing comparable to Arthur's Seat or the Castle Rock of Edinburgh, which would perhaps qualify for the somewhat lurid adjectives employed. But appreciation of the interesting topographical features is essential to wise planning and London's 'heights' are at least comparable with those of Montmartre and Montparnasse in Paris: they are scenically much more impressive than the sandstone ridges of Liverpool (see p. 98).

South of the river, many of the features described for the north are reproduced but the most striking feature is the dip-slope of the chalk. A narrow depression through Surbiton, Merton, Thornton Heath, Croydon and South Norwood, formed of clay but at least partially covered by valley gravels, separates the spurs of the North Downs from the numerous low hills seen throughout south London.[23] It is perhaps possible to recognize a southwestern and southeastern plateau, but various rivers, with their tributaries notably from west to east, the Beverley brook, the Wandle and the Ravensbourne, break up the plateaux into a number of separate units. Richmond

c

Park, Wimbledon Common, Clapham Common and others are formed of glacial gravels; the Norwood–Forest Hill ridge and its spurs form the core of a London clay tract extending from Streatham in the west to the Ravensbourne valley, and in the southeast, the Blackheath plateau is formed of pebbly Blackheath beds, dissected and partly covered by London clay. These Blackheath beds appear to the east of Croydon and are limited by a true Tertiary escarpment traceable to Erith. Only locally, for example at Shooter's Hill and in the Norwood hills, are the various plateaux above the general level of 200–250 ft., but they nevertheless give to south London a topographical diversity at least comparable with that on the north side. Apart from the clear value of the open spaces, the prospect from one patch of plateau to another, or to the Downs, is of interest. The winding hilly roads of Wimbledon, and the prospect of the Downs half-a-dozen miles away, are not unattractive features of a town landscape to some: many examples of a similar kind could be given from other parts of south London.

The Expansion of London

London has maintained its supremacy among British cities for almost two thousand years and it is therefore in no way remarkable that one current problem should be the control of its apparently limitless power of expansion. Like other great cities it has been partially rebuilt over and over again but for nineteen hundred years the city of London has remained its commercial heart. Here two hills, one later crowned by St. Paul's and the other by Leadenhall Market, were chosen as a settlement site by the Romans; here alone, between Purfleet and Hampton, the 50-ft. contour line closely approaches the Thames. Possibly the river was crossed by a ford at Westminster and by a bridge near the city. Roman London had more buildings of stone and brick than until after the Great Fire and more adequate and attractive facilities for bathing than until the latter part of the nineteenth century.[24] From the beginning, London was a port, having wharves along the river and havens in the Fleet and the Walbrook as well as small basins at Queenhithe and Billingsgate. And the road system of Roman times bears a close resemblance to the main line railways laid down eighteen centuries later.[25]

'Among the noble cities of the world that are celebrated by Fame, the City of London, seat of the Monarchy of England, is the one that spreads its fame wider, sends its wealth and wares further, and lifts its head higher than all others.' The famous description of the city by William Fitzstephen, written some time before 1183, shows that in the Norman period London was by far the greatest town of England.[26] It had more than a hundred parish churches and its citizens were renowned for 'their fine manners, raiment and table'. At once there was wealth and work; for 'those that ply their several trades, the vendors of each separate thing, the hirers out of their several sorts of labour are found each in their separate quarters and each engaged upon his own peculiar task'. And 'to this city, from every nation that is under heaven, merchants rejoice to bring their trade in ships'. Outside the city, agriculture was prosperous, both on the pasture lands and meadows, and in the corn-fields, 'not of barren gravel, but rich Asian plains such as make glad the crops and fill the barns of the farmers with sheaves of Ceres stalk'. It is generally agreed that London had maintained its strength through Anglo-Saxon and Danish times: but the widening maritime trade of the mediaeval period, especially between parts of the North Sea, and the Straits of Dover, inevitably helped London, which from its beginnings was a port. R. A. Pelham[27] has shown that in the mediaeval period, most east coast ports traded only with the Baltic and the Low Countries, and left the trade of southwest Europe to the Channel ports and Bristol: but London's trade was with *all* parts of the continent. And the city's merchants dealt in every branch of English trade and industry, even in tin and lead, both of which were drawn to the city's pewter workshops.

Geographical advantage was undoubtedly one factor in the abiding supremacy of London but it is a simplification to say that it was the only factor. London had acquired in England a unique position as a distribution centre, for raw materials came to the city to be manufactured, and from the city the finished products were sent to home and foreign markets. And even though mediaeval or Tudor London was small, it was by far the largest town of the land, and the main trading centre. Much of the wealth was drawn to London, not least because the Court was there; and as time went on it became the one great administrative centre. Everything combined to provide the favourable circumstances for its growth as the capital city of a nation always interested in marine trade and overseas expansion. Rodwell Jones has shown that to the end of the eighteenth century, 'the centre of gravity of our population was in the Southeast', the area best suited to agriculture, transport and continental connexions.[28] Within this area possible shipping sites of convenient depth, access and capacity were few—they included the Humber, the Wash,

Harwich, the Thames and Southampton water, with the Cinque ports, which needed great improvements to be useful. Of these, the only port able to rival London was Southampton but it was backed by an area of 'low cultivation and population' and 'lacked that quality of internal access which belonged to the Thames estuary'.

Camden in the sixteenth century was impressed by the growth of London, and loved it much as Defoe did nearly two hundred years later.[29] It seemed an expression of human enterprise and perspicacity, 'the epitome of all Britain, the seat of the British Empire'; London had grown and was still growing 'while the rest of the cities in England are rather decaying'. The city and Westminster were connected by splendid buildings and stately homes, and Holborn also had fine buildings, including 'some inns for the study of the common law'. Further, 'the suburbs have grown likewise on the north side . . . where is now a stately circuit of houses'. On the south bank there was a continuous line of buildings and the borough of Southwark was growing. Not all observers were equally enthusiastic and some thought the dominance of London a menace to the welfare of other places. Thomas Miles, Customer for Sandwich, wrote in 1604:

> All our creeks seek to one river, all our Rivers run to one Port, all our Ports join to one Town, all our Towns make but one City, and all our Cities and Suburbs to one vast unwieldy and disorderly Babel of buildings, which the world calls London.

At the end of the sixteenth century, Norden showed that the rural population near London derived 'great gayne' from their farming.[30]

> Such as live . . . in the body or hart of the Shire, as also in the borders of the same, for the most part are men of husbandrye, and they wholly dedicate themselves to the manuringe of their lande. And theis comonlye are so furnished with Kyne that the wyfe or twice or thrice a weeke conveyethe to London myllke, butter, cheese, apples, peares, frumentye, hens, chickens, eggs, baken and a thousand other country drugges which good huswifes can frame and find to get a pennye. And this yieldeth them a large comfort and reliefe. . . .

Through the seventeenth century the growth of London continued. Various estimates of the city's population made in the last quarter of the century ranged from 384,000 (Graunt, 1676) to $c.$ 700,000 (Petty, 1682 and Gibson, 1695), but even if the population was only $c.$ 500,000 by 1700, it is probable that the number had doubled within the century.[31] Restriction on building made London a mass of warren-like tenements and cellars in the buildings and

gardens of old mansions and monasteries: Defoe maintained that
after the fire of 1666, although the streets were built wider than
before to lessen the risk of fire, many more houses were built,
partly because the nobility and gentry were moving westwards and
northwards into new and more spacious quarters than those of the
City.[32]

> So many great Houses were converted into Streets and Courts, Alleys
> and Buildings, that there are, by Estimation, almost 4000 Houses now
> standing on the Ground which the Fire left desolate, more than stood
> on the same Ground before.
> Another Increase of Buildings in the City, is to be taken from the
> Inhabitants in the unburnt Parts following the same Example, of pulling
> down great old Buildings, which took up large Tracks of Ground in
> some of the well inhabited Places, and building on the same Ground,
> not only several Houses, but even whole Streets of Houses, which are
> since fully inhabited.

Defoe gives a large number of examples, such as 'Devonshire-Square
and Street, with several back Streets and Passages into Petticoat
lane one way and Houndsditch another Way; all built on the
Ground where the old Earl of Devonshire had a House and Garden,
and all are fully inhabited'. All this led to the extreme congestion
seen in the central parts of London at the beginning of the nineteenth
century.

Defoe regarded the 'prodigious Enlargements' around the city as
of even greater importance. 'What a Monster must London be,
extending from Chelsea, West, to Deptford-Bridge East':[33] his
famous 'circumference' of London was a route of over 36 miles, even
though areas almost joined to Westminster, such as Chelsea and
Knightsbridge, were omitted.[34] 'New Squares, and new Streets rising
up every Day to such a Prodigy of Buildings, that nothing in the
World does, or ever did, equal it, except old Rome.'[35] Defoe
wondered if the commerce of London could remain powerful and
feared that too much faith rested in speculation, but even if 'the City'
might have its difficulties, the parliament and government offices,
the great markets and the thriving port all contributed to the general
prosperity.[36] Large quantities of coal were brought from Newcastle:[37]
the whole river from London bridge to Black Wall was 'one vast
arsenal' of ships; and water was drawn from the Thames and from
the 'New river' which tapped the Lea at Ware.[38]

Numerous outlying towns and villages were affected by the
growth of London, partly because some of the wealthier inhabitants

had a country house which they occupied during part, at least, of the summer. And the outlying villages had their attractions.[39]

> The increase of the Inhabitants . . . in the Counties of Middlesex, Surrey etc. . . . causes those Villages to be much pleasanter and more sociable than formerly, for now People go to them, not for retirement into the Country, but for good Company . . . there are in these Villages, nay, in All, three or four excepted, excellent Conversation, and a great deal of it, and that without the Mixture of Assemblies, Gaming Houses and Publick Foundations of Vice and Debauchery.

Among the Essex villages favoured were Leyton, Leytonstone, Walthamstow, Woodford and Wanstead, as well as others from West Ham to Ilford: nearness to Epping Forest was esteemed.[40] Similarly Greenwich had its population of retired mariners[41] and Woolwich was a naval centre.[42] Blackheath was admired for its wonderful air and had an institution for decayed merchants who were to be made 'as comfortable as possible . . . as they had liv'd like Gentlemen, they might dye so'.[43] Croydon was a market town, with a thriving trade in corn for London. Carshalton, close to the Downs, 'the most agreeable spot on all this side of London' had a number of houses so large that they looked like seats of the gentry. Banstead had an even more attractive situation on the Downs and at Epsom 'four miles away over those delicious Downs', people came to drink the waters[44] and enjoy a variety of pleasures. Defoe noted that 'the Nobility and Gentry' drank the waters at Tunbridge, the 'Merchants and Rich Citizens' at Epsom, and the 'Common People' at Dulwich and Streatham.[45] On the west, Richmond was dignified by the residence in summer of the Prince of Wales, and attracted 'the First and Second rate Gentry', with a great deal of the best company in England: even in the winter 'many gentlemen live constantly there'.[46]

Gentry and rich merchants were able to indulge, for at least part of the summer, the English passion for living in rural surroundings, yet close to the large city which they visited for business, professional and social purposes. But areas closer to the city than those so far mentioned also had their attractions: of these, one of the chief was the pleasure of living on the high ground which is characteristic of the London area. From such a site[47]

> nothing can be more Beautiful; here is a plain and pleasant Country, a rich and fertile soil, cultivated and enclosed to the utmost perfection of Husbandry, then bespangled with villages . . . suppose you take your view from the little rising Hills about Clapham, if you look to the East, there you see the pleasant Villages of Peckham and Camberwell, with some of the finest Dwellings about London.

Similarly on the north side Hampstead and Highgate had delightful views 'over the whole Vale, to the City'.[48] At Hampstead the original attraction was a spa, but much of the hill-top had been settled, partly by wealthy Jews who 'live there in good Figure and have several Trades particularly depending upon them, and especially Butchers of their own to supply them with Provisions kill'd their own way'. At Islington it was also possible to take the waters and close by, Hackney was 'so remarkable for the retreat of Wealthy Citizens' that one author had said it had 'more coaches than Kristians'.[49] And along the northward road through Stoke Newington, Tottenham, Edmonton and Enfield, there were new houses.

The shape of things to come was apparent at the beginning of the eighteenth century but it was not until the nineteenth century that the outer areas expanded markedly in population. Some of the interesting squares of central London were laid out from the seventeenth century for there was no natural obstacle to building on the great Taplow terrace: the Covent Garden Piazza was laid out in 1631, Leicester square in 1635, Bloomsbury square in 1665, and both Lincoln's Inn Fields and Red Lion square in 1685. After the Great Fire there was more building in the West End: Soho square was laid out in 1681, St. James's square in 1684, Grosvenor square in 1695 and Berkeley square in 1698.[50] Meanwhile, by the end of the seventeenth century, there were houses to the east of the city in Whitechapel, Bethnal Green and Shoreditch, but the main spread was along the river, on both banks (Fig. 5). On the north, however, the expansion away from the river was more marked than on the south because many of the new houses for all classes of the population were placed as near as possible to the city or to Westminster.

During the eighteenth century, the City became an even greater commercial centre than before, having numerous tradesmen with their warehouses, banks, markets and exchange, and a great many offices or companies.[51] At this time the central square mile became steadily more congested: beyond it, industrial quarters developed and so the East End expanded as Clerkenwell, Shoreditch and Bishopsgate were filled up with workers' cottages, inhabited by people making various commodities, notably clocks and jewellery. Along the waterfront there were many trades linked with shipping, including rope walks, coopers' and boatbuilders' yards, as well as small foundries and forges, sugar boileries, oil, colour and soap works. Small docks were built also, and the industrial matrix had many thousands of workers' homes. Similar conditions prevailed

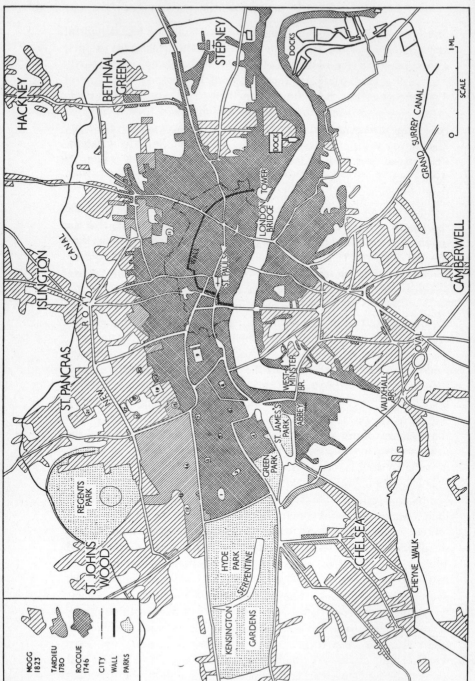

FIG. 5. LONDON IN 1746, 1780 AND 1823

FIG. 5. Based on the three maps listed below, this map shows that expansion on the north was more marked than on the south. For a time the 'New Road' was what in modern terms would be called an 'outer ring road', but by the early nineteenth century London spread well beyond it. Central London acquired numerous squares in the seventeenth and early eighteenth century and the Bloomsbury squares added distinction to Georgian London. By 1823, there was considerable building in the neighbourhood of Regents Park, including St. John's Wood, in Islington and on the south side of the river. But Pimlico was still a marsh between Westminster and Chelsea. Based on:

(a) Rocque's *Plan of London*, 1746
(b) Tardieu, *Londres avec le bourg de Southwark*, 1780
(c) Mogg, E., *London in miniature with the surrounding villages*, 1823.

These three maps are in the Mills collection, housed in the library of Manchester University (numbers C.399, C.400, C.405), and in the British Museum.

The following is a list of squares in London:

1. Grosvenor square
2. Berkeley square
3. Hanover square
4. St. James's square
5. Golden square
6. Leicester square
7. Soho square
8. Covent garden
9. Lincoln's Inn Fields
10. Queen square
11. Finsbury square
12. Portman square
13. Manchester square
14. Cavendish square
15. Bedford square
16. Carmarthen square
17. Euston square
18. Tavistock square
19. Russell square
20. Brunswick square
21. Clarendon square

on the Surrey riverside, and beyond it, at Southwark, leather trades were prominent. To the northeast, Spitalfields was populated largely by weavers, and on the north, between Moorfields and Lincoln's Inn, there were closely-packed areas in which metal trades were prominent. On all sides except the west, the city was ringed round by artisans' houses mixed with factories and workshops, and the congestion statistically so marked in 1801 was also a feature during the preceding century. At this time, one may note, London was as much as 2 miles deep from the river on the north side but on the south little more than half a mile wide except in the central part of Southwark (Fig. 5).

On the west side of the city, the legal quarter extended from the north of Lincoln's Inn to the river, beside the Temple: westwards again, along the Strand, were the theatres, coffee houses and much else besides: here too was the Covent Garden market. To the north of Covent Garden, there was an artisan quarter which in time became the notorious Seven Dials district, but to the west, as far as Hyde Park, the wealthy residential area had developed by the middle of the eighteenth century and Whitehall had a number of government offices, though there was another cottage area around the Abbey. The form of London was an oblong from east to west, having as its main centres the City and Westminster, the first becoming more and more congested and the latter acquiring, in parts, the spaciousness that it still possesses. From London bridge to the sea, some 42 square miles of alluvium had been reclaimed, probably from Saxon times onwards.[52] In 1767, by arrangement with the Middle and Inner Temple, the whole frontage 'to and including the Temple Gardens' was embanked: the next considerable enterprise was the embanking of Durham yard, now the site of the Adelphi terrace, at the end of the eighteenth century.[53] In 1761, the houses were removed from London Bridge.

Meanwhile expansion northwards continued, not least by the building of the Bloomsbury squares. Bedford square, for example, was laid out from 1775 to 1780 and, to quote the Danish writer, Rasmussen:[54]

> The green squares were quiet and calm, away from the traffic of the main streets. The approaches from the great arteries like Euston road and Oxford street were closed by gates, and people who had no business in Bloomsbury were not admitted to the quarter[a]. . . . These quarters are London's contribution to town-planning in the eighteenth century.

[a] This arrangement lasted until 1893 when gate-closing was stopped by legislation.

In the Bedford estate, 20 acres of gardens were laid out for the use of lessees of plots, and all buildings were to be grouped around greens scattered over a wide area.[55] And an equally effective contribution to the planning of London was the 'New Road', 1756–1757, which is now familiar as Marylebone, Euston and Pentonville Roads and connects Paddington with Islington. Shortly afterwards, in 1760, this north circular route was continued from the Angel as City road to link up with Moorgate. Inevitably building followed ... so that by 1760, Marylebone was said to be 'an integral part of the Metropolis'.[56] Hardly less important was the opening of Westminster bridge in 1750, Blackfriars bridge in 1769, and Battersea bridge in 1772, and the building of approaches to them, all of which stimulated development south of the river.[57] And throughout this period, the artisan suburbs spread, for example in Pentonville, Spitalfields, Bethnal Green and Whitechapel: in 1803 the Commercial road was built, to become a major route through the East End.[58] During the eighteenth century London had been growing in area, but the 1801 Census showed that there was extreme congestion in many of its quarters. At the first census in 1801, the population of the 'London' which became, with minor alterations, the Administrative county, was 959,300: as in previous centuries, it still towered above all other towns both in its population and extent.

NINETEENTH-CENTURY LONDON

The early nineteenth-century conception of London held by the Census authorities was of an area far larger than that actually covered by buildings, and the use of the parish as a defining unit gave wider boundaries than might otherwise have been drawn. Many of these parishes, with minor modification, emerged as boroughs in the London of 1888. Inspection of Fig. 6 shows that the outer areas of the Census London were growing rapidly in population during the first half of the nineteenth century but that the inner areas had stationary or declining populations: one must hastily add that an area regarded as 'outer' in this period would later be 'inner', for example Hackney and Clerkenwell as well as Westminster and Chelsea were outer areas, and so were all the parishes of the East End, as well as all areas south of the river except for the older part of Southwark. But of the thirty-six districts distinguished for Census purposes from 1801 to 1851 only thirteen, St. George's, Hanover square, St. Martin-in-the-Fields, St. James, Westminster, St. Giles,

Strand, Holborn, East London, West London, London city, Whitechapel and, on the south side, St. Saviour and St. Olave, (both in Southwark) and Rotherhithe, failed to double their population. Only two, St. Martin's and London city, had actual decreases, though in the district between them, West London, the increase was slight. The population changes during this fifty years showed that in the central areas land was needed for purposes other than housing to an extent sufficient to reduce the number of residents and that suburban growth was advancing rapidly. But it would be wrong to assume that any of the declines showed any substantial relief of congestion for there is considerable evidence to the contrary: in some parts of central London, the problem of overcrowding generally became more marked. Painfully London grew and the 1851 Census Commissioners, having reviewed the other towns of Britain, clearly recognized its unique position in the country.

London—the Metropolis—besides the churches and chapels of the villages, the markets of the towns, the courts of justice of the county-towns, comprises the commerce of a great seaport—the palace of the sovereign—the seat of the government, of the legislature, of the central courts, of the heads of commerce, of the learned professions, of literature, and of science.

London's extent, in all some 122 square miles in Kent, Surrey and Middlesex—hardly yet in Essex—and its population of 2,362,000, was regarded as phenomenal.[59]

Declines of population in the centres of several large towns were noted during the decade 1841–1851 (pp. 5, 7), but in parts of central London they were seen much earlier.[60] London city (boundaries on Fig. 7) had 64,615 inhabitants in 1801 and 57,101 in 1811, after which the population declined only slightly to 1851. In some of its numerous parishes, the explanations given for decline included the conversion of houses into warehouses (as in St. Mary Aldermany, 4·5 acres, with 822 people in 1801 and 687 in 1851), or the removal of all the houses in the Liberty of St. Martin-le-Grand to provide the Post Office site between 1811 and 1821. Even churches were demolished, for example (1831–1841) St. Benet Fink and St. Bartholomew-by-the-Royal Exchange, with several houses in both parishes for 'improvements near the Bank and the Royal Exchange'. Other houses were pulled down between 1811 and 1821 to give access to the new southward bridge (Blackfriars): and in 1831–1841 various houses were removed in the parish of St. Stephen, Coleman street, to make Moorgate street. Numerous other examples could

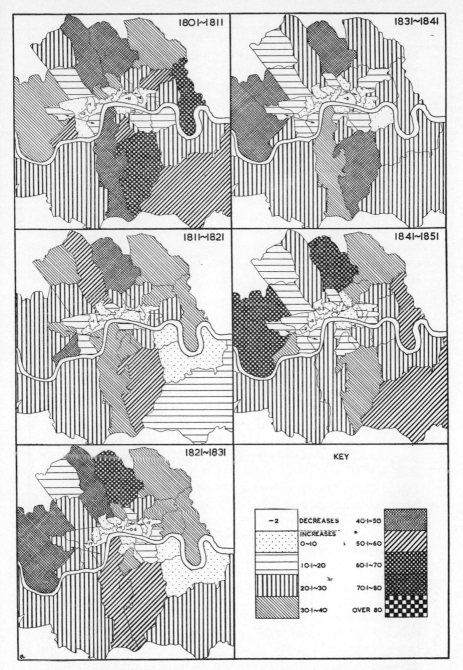

FIG. 6. LONDON, INCREASES AND DECREASES PER CENT, 1801–1851

The increases and decreases have been worked out for the divisions shown in Fig. 4. There were signs that central London reached its peak population early in the century, and some houses were pulled down for street improvements, new public buildings and, from the eighteen-forties, railways, their stations and goods yards.

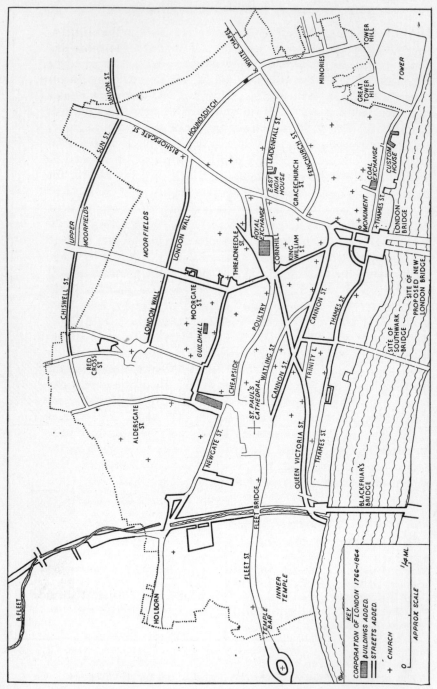

FIG. 7. SOME NEW STREETS IN THE CITY OF LONDON, 1766–1864

be given: for example, Farringdon market was built in the eighteen-twenties on the site of houses and westward, in the St. Martin-in-the-Fields district, houses were demolished for the reconstruction of the Haymarket area between 1811 and 1821 and for Strand improvements from 1821 to 1831. Similarly, in 1821, it was said that many houses had been pulled down 'to make room for the new street towards Marylebone' (that is, Regent street, Fig. 8). In some parts voluntary outward movement of the wealthier classes led only to further congestion: for example St. Anne's parish in Soho, which covered 53 acres, had 11,637 people in 1801 and 17,335 in 1851 due to 'the removal to western London of the higher classes, who are replaced by more numerous room-renters'—at a density of 327 to the acre. An even more sinister note comes from Christchurch parish, Southwark, 1841–1851, where families had moved to the suburbs through the fear of cholera and 'private houses formerly occupied by single families are in many instances let out in rooms to the poorer classes'. [61]

On the fringes of central London many of the good traditions of the eighteenth century continued into the nineteenth century: John Nash (1752–1835) laid out Regent's Park, including the neighbouring terraces and the two Park 'villages'. [62] The Marylebone estate around Regent's Park was planned for all classes of the population and for a wide range of economic activities. The large terrace houses had the advantages of a fine situation, and behind them small houses provided homes for workers, some of whom originally came from the slums pulled down when Regent street was built, 1813–1823. Large squares in the poorer quarters were intended for market places but later made into open spaces: the canal, planned to give easy transport from the docks and the East End, has remained a scenic attraction. The permanent recreational value of the park is clear, and Nash's idea

---

FIG. 7. Two maps have been used here:

(a) B.M. 3480(139), *Plan of London in the year 1766 showing Public Works erected, buildings erected and street improvements effected out of funds aided by coal duties received by the Corporation of London as trustees or otherwise up to and including the year 1852.*

(b) B.M.3480(189), *City of London 1864*, published by Charles Boyce at 44 Francis street, Newington Butts, Day and Son (Lithographers to the Queen).

Most of the improvements were made by 1852 but at this date only a short stretch of Queen Victoria street, to the south of Cannon street as far as Trinity lane, has been made. By 1864 the whole street had been laid out to give a direct route from Blackfriars bridge to the Royal Exchange.

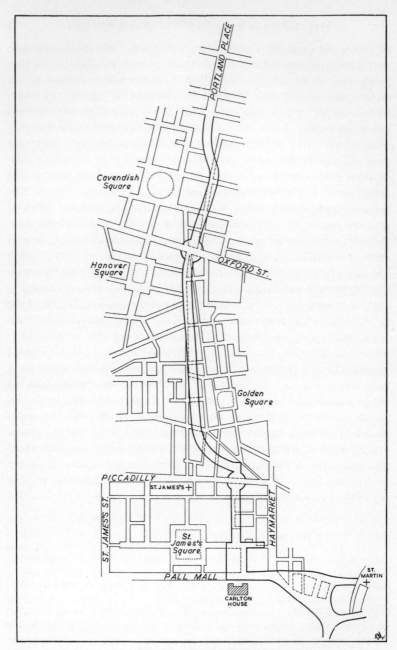

FIG. 8. REGENT STREET

of providing a complete suburb for all classes, with shops, markets and industrial possibilities is still relevant today. Nash left further memorials of his work in Trafalgar square, Carlton House terrace and Gardens, and Pall Mall East.[63] Thomas Cubitt (1788-1855) added several streets and places in Bloomsbury on the Bedford estate, including much of Gordon square in the eighteen-twenties. Moving west, he designed other residential areas on 140 acres leased in 1824, such as Belgrave square, Eaton place and Eaton square. His work included many solid middle-class houses in Highbury and Islington on the north, Pimlico and Clapham: the conception was broad streets, spacious squares and formal design. Most of these schemes were on the fringes of the areas then built-up but New Oxford street, cut through St. Giles under an improvement Act of 1839, involved some demolition of property.

Meanwhile industrial populations were crowding into the East End.[64] In Bethnal Green, the population increased from 22,000 in 1801 to 90,000 in 1851, and in the Census the increase was ascribed to the influx of Irish and other labourers working on the St. Katherine's docks, and also to improvements in the City, which had driven an 'immense number of poor into this and other adjacent Parishes'. Shoreditch and Whitechapel also showed substantial increases in population over the fifty years, but a decrease in Whitechapel from 1821 to 1831 was due to the demolition of houses on the site of St. Katherine's docks. Farther east, Stepney showed a threefold increase, from 35,000 in 1801 to 111,000 in 1851, but there also numerous houses were removed for dock-building in Wapping and Shadwell: in Limehouse (part of Stepney), the constant increase of population was due to the incoming of dock labourers. Poplar,

---

FIG. 8. This was one of the many improvements made in central London during the early nineteenth century: the aim was to make a processional way from Carlton House (pulled down in 1829) to Regent's Park. The new street, begun in 1817, was driven through a warren of narrow streets and the improvements made near Charing Cross, in the eighteen-twenties, were not exactly as shown on this plan. One result was that St. Martin's Church, originally in a narrow lane, acquired its fine position in Trafalgar square. The map is reproduced from B.M. 3535(8), *Plan of the proposed new street from Charing Cross to Portland Place, reduced from the Large Plan in the House of Commons,* published 7 June 1813 by E. Mogg, 51 Charing Cross: some interesting general information is given in Pevsner, N., *The buildings of England: London except the cities of London and Westminster,* 1952, 31, 341-2, 346-8; and *London, the cities of London and Westminster,* 1957, 90, 325-6, 559-61.

D

still an outer area, had 8,300 people in 1801 and 47,200 in 1851, of whom a considerable proportion were dock workers. On the south side, there were constant increases of population, for example in Bermondsey from 17,200 in 1801 to 48,100 in 1851, and in Lambeth from 28,000 to 139,000.

Extreme congestion marked much of the inner part of London early in the nineteenth century. Holborn covered 405 acres and had 95,676 inhabitants, 236 to the acre; and in Finsbury's 587 acres there were 125,418 people, 213 to the acre.[65] But the outward movement had begun and continued so effectively that at every Census more boroughs were found to have a declining population. Spectacular clearances of the nineteenth century made possible the building of a number of famous streets and of the Embankment, the latter connected partly with the removal of the shipping trade to the increasingly numerous docks of the East End.[66] At the opening of the nineteenth century, there were no large docks except at Blackwall (Perry's dock) and on the Surrey side of Limehouse reach (the Howland wet dock dating from the seventeenth century). Ships were still brought mainly to the Legal Quays, which extended from London bridge to the Tower, or the associated Sufferance Quays. But the West India dock was completed in 1802, the London docks in 1805, the East India dock in 1821 and the St. Katherine dock, Blackwall in 1829. This last, which has fine warehouses, still remains substantially unchanged. In 1855 the Victoria dock was opened, in 1868 the Millwall dock, in 1870 the South-West India dock, and finally the Royal Albert dock in 1880. On the Surrey side there was a jumble of timber ponds and connecting channels: the timber ponds were partly replaced by storage sheds and some big new docks were made, the Canada, 1876, Greenland dock (reconstructed), 1904, and the Quebec dock, 1926.[67]

Four new bridges were added early in the nineteenth century—the Vauxhall in 1816, Waterloo in 1817, Southwark in 1819 and the Hammersmith suspension in 1827.[68] From 1840 to 1860, the new houses of parliament were erected on reclaimed land, protected by an embankment which advanced the river-bank some 100 ft.[69] Meanwhile, when New Oxford street was laid out in 1847, over 5,000 people were displaced by the clearance of the 'Rookery' which was considered to be one of the worst in London, both for its hovels and for the character of its inhabitants.[70] In 1851, Victoria street, from Westminster Abbey to Buckingham Palace road, opened up a wide and useful route through a densely populated area, and from 1867 the

then notorious Seven Dials district was opened up by the building of
Shaftesbury avenue and Charing Cross road. The Strand widening
was made possible by the clearance necessary for the building of the
Law Courts in 1874–1882; in 1869–1870 the Albert and Victoria
embankments were added and the Chelsea embankment in 1874.[71]
These works were required partly to aid navigation in the river by
preventing shoals and also provided a wide road for east–west traffic,
as well as an amenity of London. Unfortunately it has proved far
more difficult to remove much of the unpleasant property on the
south bank of the river. It has been said that the nineteenth century
was the great age of arterial road building in London and that except
for Kingsway and Aldwych (1900–1905), the record of the twentieth
century is far less distinguished.[72] These highways, like the railways,
could only be made by removing slums, but the conversion or
demolition of houses for shops and offices, or warehouses and
factories was far more significant: seen first in central London, this
transformation was later seen in one inner suburb after another. The
writers of a survey of London in 1932 show that this process was
going on throughout London.[73] In other words, what happened
in the city in the early nineteenth century happened in Wimbledon
a century later.

Continental writers on London are prone to comment on the
vast numbers of small houses and contrast this feature with the
blocks of flats characteristic of their own cities.[74] The 1934 Survey
gave a series of examples, covering the housing developments of
the nineteenth century.[75] The oldest type is the two-room cottage,
built c. 1840, in some cases back-to-back with similar cottages,
and at a density, in a typical example, of over 80 to the acre. The
second type was the early nineteenth-century middle-class house,
on three floors, having basement kitchen premises, and three rooms
on the ground and first floors: unfortunately many of these are now
occupied by several families. The third type 'prominent in Outer
and External boroughs, and scattered in stark little rows through the
townships and villages of Greater London', is narrow-fronted, with
a parlour, a 'middle room', a kitchen and a scullery, and three
bedrooms but no bathroom. This 'back-addition' type developed
about 1840. All the above are familiar to students of provincial towns
but the 'cottage flat' type, found in such boroughs as Leyton,
Deptford and Walthamstow, is less widespread outside London:
each floor has a parlour, bedroom, kitchen and scullery, in most
cases with half the garden space, and the upper floor has a balcony

over the back room of the lower flat. In later variants there are two front doors. The fifth type, the model dwelling of several storeys, usually in flats of three rooms, has gradually become a familiar feature of the landscape of the inner district from c. 1880.

Flats were erected for the working classes, especially in the areas nearest to the city and to Westminster. In Stepney, for example, a few terrace houses were built between 1870 and 1914 but the main housing need was met by building blocks of flats, of which there were 8,800 by 1921.[76] The blocks regarded as the best were those put up by philanthropic institutions, such as the non-profit making Peabody Trust, or semi-philanthropic concerns such as the Improved Industrial Dwellings, which paid a dividend. Others were erected by private owners or by employers for their workpeople: in the Booth Survey of 1892, they were classified from 'very good', which had open spaces equal to the height of the building at both front and back, to 'very bad', small and badly lighted.[77] As early as 1885, Dr. G. B. Longstaff criticized the policy of building flats at all.[78]

> Everyone must have observed the tendency to erect all new buildings of a much greater height than those that preceded them, and it was to be hoped that the recommendations of the Royal Commission which had recently reported, would lead to some useful legislation against these high dwellings, otherwise ultimately the result would be a condition somewhat approaching that of Paris, where the density was very much greater than in London. The Waterloo Road district . . . was an example of this. There they found, owing to the demolition made by railway companies, the population had diminished, but the density had afterwards increased again, principally owing to the operation of the Peabody Trust, which succeeded in putting more people upon an acre than anybody else.

Many of the blocks of flats now seem stark and grim but they made it possible for many thousands of workers to live close to their jobs and have been copied widely in an improved form in all the larger British cities.

Railway building made possible the outward movement of the London population. First came the trunk and suburban lines, next the Metropolitan railway, and then later on the 'tubes' from c. 1890. The first lines, opened in 1836, were short railways from the Minories (later Fenchurch street) to Bermondsey, Blackwall pier and the Indian docks, and secondly to Deptford and Greenwich.[79] Next year, the London and Birmingham line was opened from Euston, but there was at first no suburban station nearer than Harrow, though in time there were developments at Willesden, Wembley and Hendon. In 1838 the line from Paddington was opened, and stations were opened at Ealing, Hanwell and Southall.[80] Lines were built through Shoreditch, Mile End, Stratford, Tottenham and Edmonton, which led on to the towns of East Anglia; in the south the London and Croydon railway was opened in 1839.[81] The Metropolitan railway was built from 1863, but the famous circle was not completed until 1884, although branches had been built to Hammersmith in 1874 and to Richmond in 1877.[82] The first 'tube' was the City and South London 1890, under the Thames from the city to Stockwell, 3 miles away: in 1900 there were extensions to Moorgate, and to Clapham, and in 1901 to the Angel at Islington. Meanwhile, in 1898, the Waterloo and City line was opened, and two years later the Central London line, the two-penny tube, was opened from the Royal Exchange to Shepherd's Bush.[83] Shortly afterwards the Metropolitan and the District lines were electrified. The first horse tramway was opened in 1861 for 1 mile from the Marble Arch along Bayswater road, but closed after a few months:[84] several others were added from 1870, and electrified from 1901. Omnibuses, also drawn by horses first appeared in 1829 and ran on all the main roads within a few years: in 1899 the first motor-bus appeared, but horse traffic was not finally ousted until 1906–1911.[85]

TWENTIETH-CENTURY LONDON

Each type of transport affected the growth of London. Horse buses and trams ran on main roads some 4 miles from the central area, but electric trams opened districts beyond this limit. Cheap workmen's fares led to the growth of densely settled artisan colonies, such as Tottenham and Walthamstow, and railways carried passengers to suburbs as much as 12 miles out by slow trains, and as much as 50 miles by expresses to such places as Southend or Brighton, which had a one-hour journey from 1933 when the line was electrified.[86] Brighton and Hove had, in 1951, 3,800 season-ticket holders to London[87] and 5,073 residents recorded as working somewhere within the county of London.[88] And the electric railways made possible the outward spread of population: on the northwest, for example, the tube was extended to Golders Green in 1907 and to Edgware in 1924, and almost at once vast new suburbs developed.[89] When Morden station was opened growth was marked as much as 3 miles away, for buses and private cars fed passengers into the tubes.[90]

To weld all the services together the London Passenger Transport Board was established in 1933, to serve an area of 2,000 square miles, of which 1,551 square miles was its own exclusive territory.[91]

Modern Industrial Development

In 1938, there were nearly 750,000 workers in 'productive industry' in the county of London: of these 234,000 were engaged in clothing, 90,000 in food, drink and tobacco, 67,000 in printing and paper, 69,000 in furniture and 43,000 in chemicals.[92] Heavy engineering, such as the manufacture of cranes, hydraulic apparatus and boilers, is located mainly in riverside boroughs, Woolwich, Greenwich, Deptford, Poplar and Battersea, but lighter forms of engineering, such as electrical and scientific supplies, are found in various boroughs, such as St. Pancras, Finsbury, Stepney and Islington, Fulham and Hammersmith in the west, and the southern boroughs of Camberwell, Lambeth, Southwark and Wandsworth. Clothing, mainly in small workshops, is found both in the West End and the East End and the fur trade is concentrated in Stepney, Bethnal Green and Hackney. Printing and paper trades flourish on the commercial needs of London and are found primarily in the boroughs close to the centre. Food trades are widespread but most of the large factories are close to the river, for example, bacon, butter, sugar, tea and coffee, and there are breweries in Stepney, Finsbury, Westminster and Southwark. Furniture trades have a long association with the East End, conspicuously Shoreditch, Hackney and Bethnal Green, but there has been an outward spread to Islington, St. Pancras and Finsbury—and farther afield to the Lea valley. Chemical industries are in large factories near the river, for oil, paints, soap and oil cake, and smaller factories away from the river.[93]

From 1932–1938, 3,635 factories were opened in Great Britain and 2,994 closed: in Greater London, 1,573 were opened and 1,055 closed. A count for 1934–1938 showed that in these years, 463 factories were opened in the County of London and 654 closed, but in Outer London (excluding the County), 629 were opened and 200 closed.[94] In Outer London, the new arterial roads built primarily to remove traffic from densely-settled areas were themselves quickly surrounded by residential and industrial areas. For many industries, a location beside a good road was as advantageous as railway sidings or canal transport had been in earlier industrial phases. Other advantages included lower rents and rates than those usual in large towns, and space for expansion. This last factor led to a considerable outward movement from London and even to the removal in 1931 of the Ford works from Trafford Park in Manchester to Dagenham where, on a

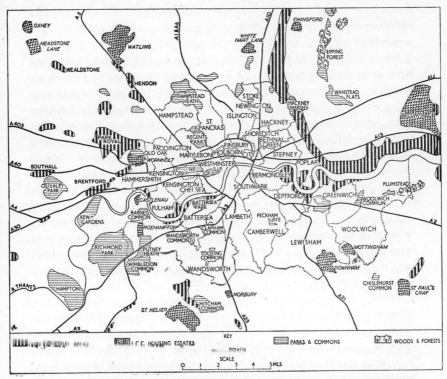

FIG. 9. METROPOLITAN BOROUGHS, INDUSTRIAL AREAS AND HOUSING ESTATES

Compiled from a variety of sources, but especially those mentioned under notes 92–103 on p. 361, this map gives the boundaries of the twenty-eight metropolitan boroughs, the main industrial areas and housing estates in outer London established by the L.C.C. Many factories and workshops are located in the artisan quarters of London, as in other cities.

HP, Hyde park; GP, Green park; S.J.P., St. James's park.

site beside a dock, the firm was able to build its own blast furnace and coke ovens.[95]

There are seven major industrial areas in greater London (see Fig. 9).[96] First, the Lea valley, from Waltham Abbey to the East End. This area has a number of factories which had been moved from the

East End in such trades as clothing, furniture and metal working, and since 1918 various medium-sized factories, such as electrical engineering and consumer goods, have been established, some of them along the new Cambridge arterial road. The valley, long free from houses but having good soil and abundant water, also has numerous glasshouses for tomatoes, cucumbers and other market produce.[97]

Second, lower Thames-side. During the last fifty years, there has been a marked development of heavy industries from Woolwich to Shellhaven, well outside Greater London.[98] Beckton gas works and the generating station at Barking, placed on either side of Barking creek, each consume 4,000-6,000 tons of fuel a day, which is imported from the Tyne: they also draw water from the Thames. Half the British supply of cement comes from Purfleet, where the chalk is quarried; and there are vast paper mills supplying London—the largest paper market in the world. Sugar refining, oil refining, timber storage and processing are all port industries, and there are many more such as flour milling and chemical trades, including the manufacture of margarine and soap. The great Bata shoemaking firm is established here; and Ford's, previously mentioned. This industrial area is spreading outer London far beyond its present defined limits: on this, see p. 267.

Third, the Cray valley.[99] Here paper-making is prominent, but there are also some small- to medium-sized engineering factories, especially on the Orpington and Sidcup by-pass road. At Crayford there is a large Vickers-Armstrong factory.

Fourth, the Wandle valley.[100] The flat land of this valley has been used for a wide range of industries from Wandsworth through Merton and Mitcham to Malden and the Croydon by-pass road. Some of the factories are modern, such as an aircraft works at Malden, but many are older: they include the manufacture of paint and varnish, electrical goods, cars, refrigerators and electric cables, but there are also food industries and the largest single factory is used for toy-making.

Fifth—on the Kingston by-pass,[101] near Raynes Park, manufactures include gramophone records, time-switches, banknotes and fish-paste. At Tolworth there is an engineering works.

Sixth, Southall and Hayes.[102] Industrial development began here over fifty years ago, but was most marked after 1918: there are factories with little break along the railway line from Southall to Slough. Most of the industries here fall into one of two classes, first, foods, such as jams, cocoa, tinned products, and groceries, and second, engineering, including cars, aeroplanes, bicycles and gramophones. Southall and Hayes were described in the Greater London Plan as a huge 12-to-the-acre housing area, mainly occupied by factory workers: '. . . crude and monotonous, deficient in local open spaces, unrelieved by anything beautiful'.

Seventh, Northwest London.[103] This is the largest and in many ways the most interesting of the newer industrial areas. On its present fringes, at Cricklewood and Willesden, especially where the Edgware road crosses the Brent valley, there are good road and rail facilities for all the main lines to the northwest cross this valley. The oldest factories are in Willesden: during the 1914–1918 war, the Royal Agricultural Society's permanent show ground, Park Royal, was used for the manufacture of munitions and later for other factories and after the 1924–1925 British Empire Exhibition, some of the buildings at Wembley were converted to industrial use. There is a westward extension of industries to Greenford and Perivale, and a northward extension along the Edgware road. Near the Hyde, there was a brewery and a mineral water factory before 1914, and the low-lying ground beside the reservoir gave excellent land for more factories: at Colindale, various works were established during the 1914–1918 war, and afterwards used mainly for the motor trades. On the west there are factories to the south of Acton along the Great West road. This factory area is hardly an industrial zone in the modern planning sense, though some of its factories are surrounded by gardens and 'clean' trades are general. There is an intermingling of houses and some of the land, chiefly on the margins of the area, is used for playing fields, some of which have been provided by the firms. The products are varied, but include especially those of the electrical and general engineering trades, foodstuffs and various (non-noxious) chemicals. It was natural that industry should be attracted here by excellent railway communications, good new roads, available sites including Park Royal and Wembley, and a clean atmosphere: no site would seem better to a manufacturer with a growing factory unable to expand in some congested area of central London. The essential problem is that this development expanded London more and more, with the result that suburbs in Middlesex grew to such an extent that almost the whole county was threatened. As more factories were provided here, those seeking the built-up edge went farther afield to Bushey, Oxhey, Watford (itself becoming increasingly industrial, see p. 266), St. Albans and towns beyond.

Fifty years ago, H. J. Mackinder divided England into two parts, industrial and metropolitan.[104] The first of these included the coalfields of the Midlands, of the North and of Wales and has the country's greatest industrial areas. The second, metropolitan England, merged into the first 'along a line drawn diagonally from the Severn to the Wash', though modified in Gloucestershire so that the area west of the Cotswolds, which includes Bristol, is allocated to industrial England. Metropolitan England, Mackinder continues, had then three main qualities: first, nearly all its main roads and railways led to London; second, its coastline, from Norfolk to Cornwall, looked across the Narrow Seas to Europe, and third, there were no considerable sources of motive power. And all this area was dominated by London: metropolitan England had the 'commercial as opposed to the industrial control' and 'the whole region is more or less of a residential character', having old and aristocratic elements in its life which contrasted with the 'new and democratic' qualities of industrial England. Time has changed this pattern in some degree but by no means completely. Electrification has made possible an expansion of industry in the London area (and beyond it) which has provoked comment—often angry comment;[105] as Mackinder justly said, London (fifty years ago) was the greatest industrial town of the country, drawing raw materials not only from Britain but from the world through its port—the first of the country, having in itself a vast market and the commercial entry to overseas markets through the mercantile offices of the City.[106] But once electricity turned the wheels, new industries were established in its suburbs to such an extent that its potential growth seemed limitless. And during the inter-War period, towns in some of the provincial industrial areas, such as Tyneside, Merseyside, Southeast Lancashire and South Wales, saw factories closed and mines exhausted at the very time when the new industries they needed were being established in and around a London apparently growing beyond all reasonable bounds.

Administrative Units and the Spread of London

At no time has the definition of London been considered effectively in relation to the distribution of population: even if it were so defined, the limits drawn would almost certainly be archaic in ten years. When C. B. Fawcett wrote of the London conurbation in 1932, he followed the practice of the Census reports which spoke of 'Greater London' as the rough equivalent of the Metropolitan

Police District: he added that there were many contiguous urban areas which brought the population 'up to 9,150,000' and also many near, though non-contiguous urban areas which are economically part of the metropolis', with which the population of the London area would be 10,000,000.[107] Unfortunately, no list of these towns was given but the vital argument was made clear—the London area had approximately one-quarter of the population of England. Further, more than half the total increase of the population in Great Britain, from 1921–1931, was 'concentrated in the metropolitan region, whose total population is now over 12,000,000 in the London conurbation and its satellite areas'. The article included two other arguments: one, that the area within a 50-mile radius of Manchester Town Hall, though still populated by 9,000,000 people, was hardly growing at all in numbers and second, that there was a 'southward drift of population', which was a major social phenomenon in British life.[108] In other words, since Mackinder wrote the whole balance of population had changed: metropolitan England was becoming industrialized to a greater extent than ever before, excessively so perhaps and the consequent problems included the provision of new homes for hundreds of thousands of people, of whom some were additions to the population and others migrants from the overcrowded slums inherited from the nineteenth century. The problem was not necessarily one of increasing population, but rather of its re-distribution. Between 1931 and 1951, the population of Greater London increased only by 1·6 per cent, but there was a decrease of over a million people in the County of London, and an increase of slightly more in the Outer Ring.[109] In fact, the Outer Ring is ceasing to be 'outer' and a wider definition of the metropolitan region is needed (pp. 65–70).

The L.C.C. Area

As Mrs. Cole has so justly remarked, the L.C.C. area was defined on a basis of death registers and main drainage by Act of Parliament.[110] In this, however, it was hardly unique for the driving force behind nineteenth-century administrative definition was public health and statistical registration. Fig. 4 shows the areas which were gathered under various bills of Mortality and served by the Metropolitan Board of Works and by the Commissioners of Sewers. Defined in the Metropolis Management Act of 1855, these areas, some 117 square miles (c. 74,029 acres) became a local government board in 1871, having powers which included slum clearance.[111]

The record of the Metropolitan Board of Works was not unimpressive: it built Victoria street, Queen Victoria street, Shaftesbury avenue, Clerkenwell road and Charing Cross road and also acquired thirty parks including Hampstead Heath, Clapham Common, Finsbury Park, Wormwood Scrubs and Southwark Park.[112]. After 1866 under the Metropolitan Commons Act the Board acquired all the commons and open spaces in the outer part of London, some of which were threatened by house building or by railway construction, already seen on Tooting and Wandsworth commons. Blackheath, of 270 acres, was transferred free, but for the 150 acres of Hackney Common, previously grazing land, £90,000 was paid.[113] As early as 1855, legislative provision was made for the use of London churchyards as recreational areas[114] and in 1884 it was laid down that there should be no new building in churchyards, except for church extensions. Through the work of the Metropolitan Gardens Association nearly one hundred churchyards, many of them in congested areas, have been transformed into gardens, in some cases with playgrounds, tennis courts and bowling greens.

The area covered by the Board in 1855 bore little relation to the limit of the built-up area either then or—still less—in 1888 when it became the L.C.C. area. Unfortunately one geographer has spoken of the L.C.C. as 'created out of the adjacent counties *to include substantially the urban area which then existed*' (author's italics). It was not so. As W. A. Robson[115] has rightly noted, 'the area of the L.C.C. was archaic from the first moment of its birth': the population of the 'outer ring', that is the part of the conurbation beyond the bounds of the L.C.C., increased from 155,000 in 1801 to 317,400 in 1851 and to 414,000 in 1861, after which each inter-censal period saw an increase of over 50 per cent so that by 1891 this same 'outer ring' had 1,405,000 inhabitants.[116] The 1888 definition might have defined successfully London before the railway age, even London of the eighteen-forties. The indivisibility of Greater London was abundantly demonstrated in the first few decades of the L.C.C.'s existence, for less than twenty years after its foundation the L.C.C.'s population began to decline, from a maximum of 4,536,000 in 1901 to 4,521,000 in 1911 and in the same ten years the Outer Ring

FIG. 10. For this period of ninety years, figures are available for the areas that became the Metropolitan boroughs in 1888. With each decade, the central boroughs show heavier declines and one by one the boroughs farther from the heart of London begin to lose population until, by 1931–1951, virtually the whole of the L.C.C. area shows decreases.

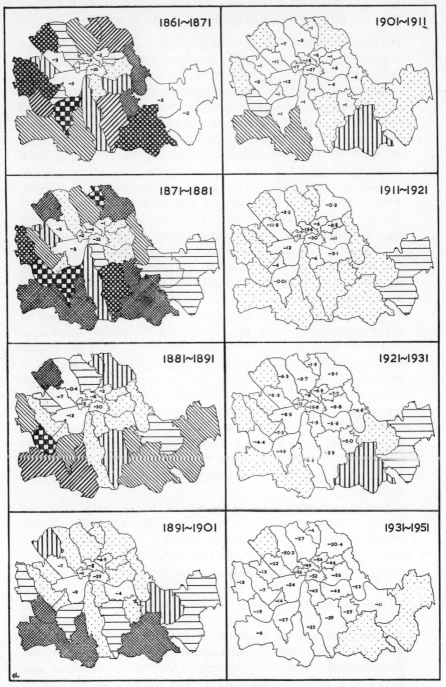

FIG. 10. LONDON, INCREASES AND DECREASES PER CENT, 1861–1951
Key as for Fig. 16. p. 33.

population increased from 2,045,000 to 2,730,000.[117] The consequences of the limited 1888 definition were numerous: in the first place it proved impossible to find within its own territory sufficient space for various institutions such as welfare homes, mental hospitals, parks and playing fields, so a form of arranged colonization of outer London was evolved by which various institutions were built by the L.C.C.; secondly, re-housing schemes were made possible only by finding sites outside the 117 square miles governed by the L.C.C. (v.i.).

Institutions belonging to the L.C.C. include sanatoria at Brentwood, Carshalton and Godalming, and mental hospitals at Friern Barnet, Hanwell, Ilford, Bexley, Coulsdon and Epsom. Various special schools, such as those for the deaf, or for delinquents, are located outside the L.C.C. area.[118] Of the open spaces provided by the L.C.C. the largest is Hainault Forest and golf course (1903, extended 1934), but others are Marble Hill at Twickenham, and Hampstead Heath. In 1894, the L.C.C. acquired Lincoln's Inn Fields for public use, and the general policy has been to acquire or extend open spaces as in the days of the Metropolitan Board of Works.[119] There is perhaps little objection to any of these arrangements: a mental hospital, or a residential school of a special type, is best placed some distance away from a vast town. Nor is it unreasonable that the L.C.C. should provide parks visited by its people outside the area under its control, especially as it has inside its domain the Royal parks. And the City corporation has from its vast wealth acquired Epping Forest (6,000 acres), Burnham Beeches (301 acres), a stretch of commons and downs at Coulsdon and Purley (300 acres) and several smaller parks and recreation grounds.[120].

Far more serious is the rehousing of people moved from the L.C.C. area on land controlled by other authorities. From 1889 to March 1938, the L.C.C. provided 86,700 new dwellings, of which 60,800 were cottages or cottage flats in buildings of two or three storeys, and 25,900 were flats in blocks.[121] Over half these new dwellings, some 47,000, were situated outside the county of London. Of the housing areas the largest is the Becontree estate, of 4 square miles, designed for a population of 115,000 in 25,000 houses, and built on good market gardening land under the control of three boroughs, Ilford, Barking and Dagenham.[122] The first site beyond the county at Tooting, was acquired in 1900 but in time other sites were used at Barnes, Bromley, Croydon, Carshalton, Hammersmith,

Hendon, Tottenham and Wood Green.[123] Within London, the
usual policy has been to replace slums by blocks of flats comparable
to those of the various housing trusts but better than the earlier
examples, so that large numbers of people can be settled on limited
areas, at a density of 200 per acre in central London, decreasing to
100 per acre away from the heart of the metropolis.[124] The vast war
devastation of the East End, combined with the need for slum clearance of much that survives, inspires the expectation that this type of
housing will become increasingly characteristic. It has two advantages. It makes it possible for hundreds of thousands of people
to live close to their work and it removes the fear that a large area
of the metropolis will become a residential desert.

Decline of population in London through the change of land use
from residential to commercial and industrial purposes had been
noted early in the nineteenth century. From 1921 to 1931, only eight
of the twenty-nine metropolitan boroughs had an increase of population, and only one, Lewisham, had a substantial increase, + 26
per cent, though Wandsworth showed a rise of + 7·6 per cent: both
these boroughs had substantial areas available for new housing.
There were small increases in Hammersmith, + 4 per cent, and
Hampstead, + 3 per cent, and Woolwich, Greenwich and Paddington each had practically stationary populations (+ 0·5 per cent),
but all the other London boroughs had decreases, of which the most
conspicuous (apart from the loss of 19·8 per cent from the city of
London) were those in the inner areas, Holborn, — 10 per cent,
Stepney, — 9·8 per cent, Westminster, — 8·5 per cent and Finsbury,
— 9·0 per cent.[125] Much of this population movement was in line
with earlier developments: for example, in 1922, it was said that
Finsbury was attracting more warehouses, offices and factories,
notably in the textile trades, and also had the premises of some
famous carriers, notably Pickford and Carter Paterson.[126] 'The city
has already invaded Finsbury by way of four main arteries, Farringdon road, St. John street, Aldersgate street and City road . . . large
areas in the southern part of the borough are indistinguishable
physically from the City . . . its destiny is to become within a comparatively short period wholly an important business area.'[127] Comparable developments were seen in Holborn, and Westminster was
'more and more an important business and trading centre, with a
larger and increasing day population'.[128] In Stepney the decline was
due largely to the relief of congestion: from all the East End boroughs
the more fortunate members of the community moved 'farther out'.

Mr. Lansbury, speaking on Poplar, explained that labourers only were left—most of these casual labourers—for the manufacturers had long since gone, followed by the technical and clerical employees and even by the shopkeepers.[129]

The loss of a million people from the L.C.C. area between 1931 and 1951, a decline of one-quarter, is itself a dramatic incident in the population history of Britain: in the years 1931–1938, there was an outward movement greater than that of the previous ten years, with the result that the population declined to 4,013,000; the destruction of houses in the years 1940–1944 and the evacuation reduced the population to 2,320,000 in 1941 and 2,462,000 in 1944, and the subsequent return of migrants was not sufficient to bring the number up to the pre-War level.[130] With 3,348,000 people in 1951, London had lost 1,049,000 inhabitants (− 23·9 per cent) and failed to absorb its natural increase (of + 3·9 per cent). Only two of its boroughs, both peripheral, Hampstead (+ 6·9 per cent) and Lewisham (+ 3·5 per cent) had increases of more than 1 per cent (Woolwich had + 0·6 per cent). The City almost ceased to be a residential area at all, as its population fell to 5,268[131] compared with 10,999 in 1931; and there were notably heavy declines in the East End boroughs such as Shoreditch, − 54 per cent, Bethnal Green, − 46 per cent, Stepney, − 56 per cent, and Poplar, − 53 per cent. And on the south side, almost equally sharp decreases were recorded, for example in Southwark, − 43 per cent and Bermondsey, − 46 per cent. The inner boroughs close to the central area also had marked declines such as − 24 per cent in Westminster, − 49 per cent in Finsbury, − 36 per cent in Holborn, − 30 per cent in St. Pancras, − 22 per cent in St. Marylebone. Many other boroughs of a varied residential character had almost equally significant declines: among these are Battersea, − 27 per cent, Camberwell, − 29 per cent,

---

FIG. 11. The main West End shopping district is included here, with the government quarter of Whitehall. Behind many shopping streets there are small factories or workshops but the most interesting recent trend has been the spread of offices through much of inner residential London, conspicuously Mayfair. Public buildings are of many types, including cinemas, theatres, clubs, churches, schools, of which all except the last are liberally represented in central London. In spite of the decline of population, there are still many thousands of people who from necessity or choice live close to the central areas.

Based on the *Land Use Survey of the Development Plan for the Administrative county of London*, 1951.

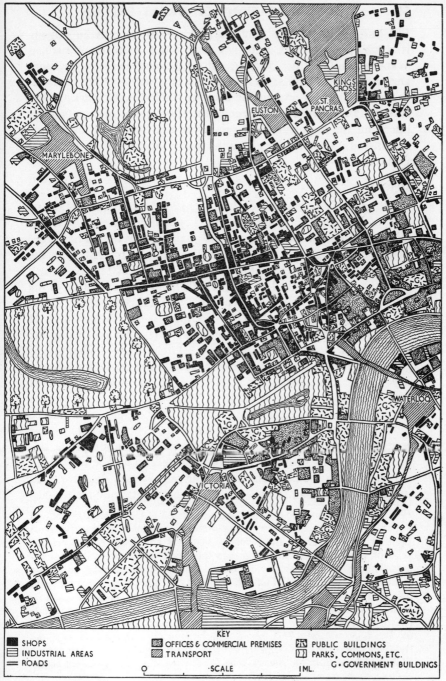

KEY

■ SHOPS   ▨ OFFICES & COMMERCIAL PREMISES   ▤ PUBLIC BUILDINGS
▤ INDUSTRIAL AREAS   ▨ TRANSPORT   ▥ PARKS, COMMONS, ETC.
═ ROADS   ⊦—————————————⊦ SCALE   G · GOVERNMENT BUILDINGS
0   1 ML.

FIG. 11. LAND USE IN PART OF CENTRAL LONDON, 1951

E

Lambeth, — 22 per cent, and Hackney, — 20 per cent. In general, it would perhaps be true to say that in the outer areas such as Wandsworth (— 7 per cent) and Stoke Newington (— 4 per cent), and in the West End areas such as Kensington (— 7 per cent) the decline was at least undramatic over the whole twenty years. Clearly so great an outward movement in the short space of twenty years opens up the opportunity of rebuilding and rehousing over large areas. And it demonstrates fully the futility of the 1888 definition of London.

Outer London

Although the population of the Outer ring doubled during the first half of the nineteenth century, its population did not pass the million mark until the eighteen-eighties, though by 1901 it had more than two millions and by 1951 almost five millions. In 1931–1951, the increase of 31 per cent meant the addition of 1,179,000 people, which more than balanced the loss of 1,049,000 from the population of the L.C.C. area, though the entire conurbation increased only by + 1·6 per cent to 8,346,000 in 1951.[132] Yet there is no real cessation of population increase in the London area, but rather an inadequate definition of the metropolitan 'region'. On p. 65, consideration is given to the very large increases of population in areas immediately beyond the conurbation and reference to the wider spread of of metropolitan workers is made on pp. 266–7, 273. To allege that the problem of defining the conurbation is easy of solution would be foolish. It would also be unjust to close this chapter without some consideration of the past attempts to establish appropriate administrative units within an area broadly defined as 'metropolitan'.

Fig. 12 shows the position early in the railway age. A central area was closely occupied, ribbons of settlement swept along main roads

FIG. 12. At this time the railways had penetrated to points similar, though not in every case identical with the present mainline stations, the West London railway ran to the Kensington canal and most of the present suburbs were growing villages, due to the desire to live in rural surroundings. The main roads have a clear resemblance to those of today and some of the docks were already built, though much of the Isle of Dogs was still marsh. The original map (B.M. 3479(48)) is described as *London and its environs, containing the boundaries of the Metropolitan boroughs, the different railroads and stations, the cemeteries, roads, docks, canals and all modern improvements. This map is chiefly from the Ordnance Survey: the railroads and other improvements are from the Official Copies, the borough of Marylebone from the Survey. The whole corrected from personal observation and measurement in 1847.*

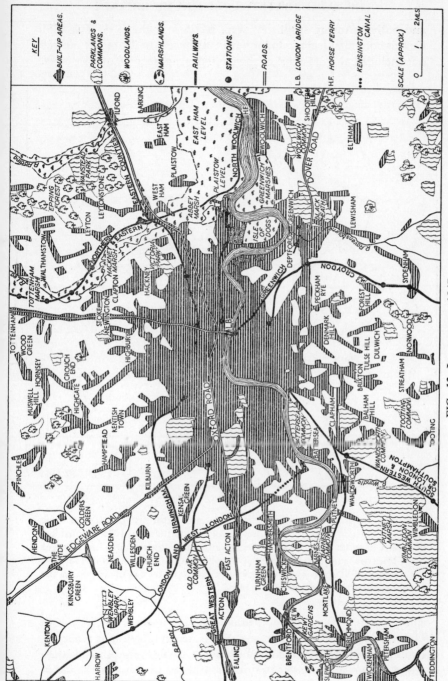

FIG. 12. LONDON IN 1847

and outlying towns or villages were incipient suburbs.[133] The 1851 Census commissioners found it hard everywhere to distinguish towns but included the old market towns and a number of other places.

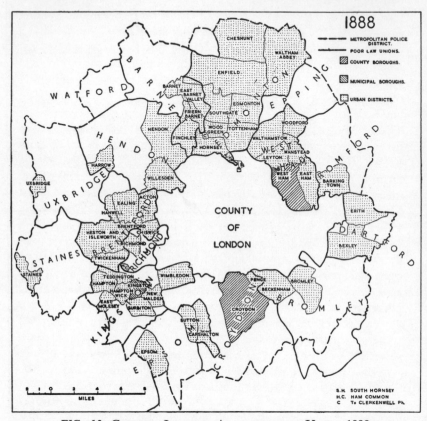

FIG. 13. GREATER LONDON, ADMINISTRATIVE UNITS, 1888

The poor law unions included both urban and rural districts and in some cases, such as Edmonton, extended into two counties. By 1888 a considerable part of outer London had been given urban government, but much of Middlesex was still rural except for the well-established towns of Harrow, Uxbridge and Staines. The Metropolitan Police district is shown on all the administrative maps (Figs 14–18).

They gave recognition to Brentford, Hounslow, Staines and Uxbridge in Middlesex; Barking, Stratford and Waltham Abbey in Essex; Kingston-upon-Thames borough, Croydon, Epsom and Richmond in Surrey. But as the population began to colonize the Outer

Ring, so one place after another acquired a measure of local self-government and became an urban district—sanitary districts before 1894 (see Fig. 13). In 1891, the Outer Ring had twenty-two boroughs or urban districts in Middlesex, eleven in Surrey, six in Essex and four in Kent. The rural portions of the Poor Law Unions became rural districts in 1894, with various modifications.

Chance definitions of areas as 'urban districts' were numerous. Esher and the Dittons, for example, became an urban district in 1895 but was described in 1922 as 'rural in character, containing a number of farms, fruit gardens, orchards and heathlands . . . formed by an amalgamation of four villages . . . Esher, Long Ditton, Claygate and Thames Ditton' which 'were thought to comprise a convenient group for local government purposes'.[134] The justification was not by faith but by works as all this area was drained to one common sewage farm. Later, in 1933, this urban district was expanded from 9 square miles to 23 square miles by the addition of the East and West Molesey U.D. and of two parishes from Epsom R.D.[135] Similarly, in 1922 a representative of East Barnet, which had a local board from 1874,[136] said: 'We are an urban district with rural characteristics . . . the District consists mainly of park-like land, meadow land, and open and sparsely built upon areas'.[137] In theory local control of an area only just becoming invaded by suburban expansion for planning purposes was excellent, but in practice it was 'impossible to obtain any general scheme for urban development from so many Authorities some of which are necessarily, by their small size, and want of staff, incapable of dealing with so large a question'.[138] And the proof? 'We have only to travel along the main traffic routes . . . to see . . . the invasion of London, and the disorderly manner in which development is taking place.'[139] Figs. 13–18 show the administrative changes that took place in outer London from 1888 onwards. Only 23 square miles of Middlesex was left as 'rural districts' by 1934 and under the County Review order of the following year the 14½ square miles of Hendon R.D. (Great and Little Stanmore, Harrow Weald and Pinner) was added to Harrow U.D. and the South Mimms R.D. became Potters Bar U.D.[140] The similar orders for Surrey in 1933, for Kent in 1934 and for Essex in 1933, enlarged the areas under town administration.[141] In Hertfordshire, the 1935 Review Order reduced the area of Barnet R.D. and Watford R.D. by additions to the urban districts of Bushey and Barnet: in 1941, the Barnet R.D. was renamed Elstree. This is now the only Rural District within the London conurbation area.

The general effect of these changes has been to strengthen local administrative powers, by making new boroughs and by enlarging the area of existing urban areas. So far, efforts to create some kind of

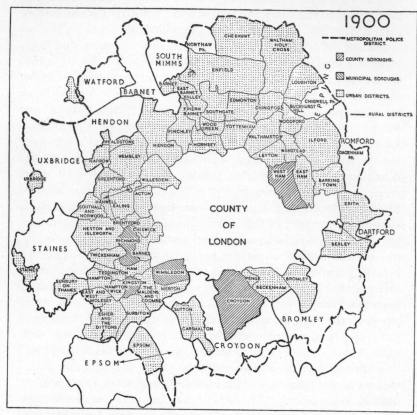

FIG. 14. GREATER LONDON, ADMINISTRATIVE UNITS, 1900

Much of outer London was still under rural administration, and the rural districts consist of the non-urban residue of the poor law unions. Several new urban districts have been added, notably in Essex, and on the west between Chiswick and Kingston. Northaw parish, though within the Metropolitan Police District, is not included in the modern conurbation.

supra-authority to deal with the entire conurbation have not succeeded, though in the evidence given to the 1922 Royal Commission such ideas were freely canvassed. Was Greater London one whole, or was it not? And for what social purposes? A witness from Finchley, asked if the inhabitants had any responsibility for helping the poorer districts, stated that 'We have tried to look at it from the scientific point of view and not from the empirical one and we have never considered the question of our duty to anyone else'.[142] But this was not the only view: a memorandum from Southall-Norwood suggested that there should be a central authority, probably the Metropolitan Police District, altered to include drainage basins for sewage and other purposes.[143] And other reasons were given. 'The suburbs of London being largely dependent upon London for their prosperity, and *vice versa*, the area should be treated as one community having common interests, responsibilities and liabilities. . . . Probably the majority of those workers who sleep within the District work in London. Others come to work from London. The factories are part of the London business system: the roads bear London traffic.'[144] And the memorandum also stated that 'town planning and large schemes of housing shall be the concern of a Greater London authority'.[145]

Possibly the different reactions of these two local authorities can be explained by the fact that each would gain by the arrangements they suggest. A compromise proposal considered in 1922—to make a number of strong county boroughs—met stern opposition from places likely to be absorbed.[146] Coulsdon and Purley, made into an urban district in 1915 spoke of their 'entire disagreement with the suggestion that the building development . . . is an overflow from Croydon. The rapid growth of population . . . has been occasioned by the district's suitability for residential purposes, and the provision of good travelling facilities', including 'eight railway stations' not provided by Coulsdon and Purley U.D. Mitcham also was opposed to amalgamation with anyone.[147] And on the north side of London, Willesden, in 1921 an urban district of 165,700 people, had suggested an amalgamation with Hendon, Kingsbury and Wembley, to give an area of *c.* 30 square miles of which about half was then agricultural land[148] but 'none of the adjoining districts expressed any present desire to amalgamate with Willesden'. Hornsey, in 1921 having 87,600 people in 4 square miles, argued that the neighbouring urban districts of Finchley, Friern Barnet, Southgate and Wood Green, should be united into a borough of 20 square miles with 241,600 people (322,900 in 1951) but the first two of these opposed the scheme vigorously, and Southgate gave it only qualified support though Wood Green was more favourable.[149] But perhaps the most interesting case was that of Ilford, whose individuality was stressed, partly by emphasizing that the Roding valley definitely separated it from East Ham.[150] Could it not therefore be fused with Barking, Chigwell parish in the Epping rural district and Dagenham parish in Romford rural district? This new, greater Ilford would cover 13 square miles, of which only one-quarter was then built-up, and

FIG. 15. GREATER LONDON, ADMINISTRATIVE UNITS, 1909

The most interesting change since 1900 is the creation of new urban districts on the southeast, between Bromley and Bexley and the marking out of new urban districts in Middlesex, Feltham, Hayes, Ruislip and Northwood.

would include the whole of the Becontree estate, then under construction. Barking was apparently in agreement[151] but Dagenham became an urban district in 1926 and a municipal borough in 1937.[152]

On the whole, outer suburbs showed every possible determination to preserve identity: Surbiton, for example, with nearly 20,000 people

in 1921 within its 4½ square miles, had possessed Improvement Commissioners since 1855: '. . . more than one attempt had been made
by the neighbouring Borough of Kingston to absorb Surbiton, but
each attempt had been successfully repulsed'.[153] Actually Surbiton
was enlarged in 1933 and became a borough in 1936.[154] And even the
tiny urban district of Hampton Wick with 3,265 people in its 3
square miles, reported that it only wanted to be left alone.[155] But
in 1934 it was absorbed into Twickenham, which also acquired
Teddington, an area of 2 square miles with 21,200 people in 1921,
when it was 'extremely antagonistic' to any such arrangement.[156]
These are only a few examples out of many but they help to explain
the difficulty of establishing any kind of Greater London authority:
one more example may be given. At the Commission, witnesses
speaking on behalf of six urban districts—Harrow, Kingsbury,
Ruislip-Northwood, Uxbridge, Wealdstone, and Wembley—and
also the rural districts of Hendon and Uxbridge, made three crucial
points.[157] First, their areas had no physical connexion with London
as such and therefore should not be governed differently from any
other part of the country: second, they did not share in any public
services provided by London except trams, and third, the average
population density was only 2·5 per acre and therefore it would be
fallacious to regard them as 'part of the built-up area'. But it was in
these very areas that the greatest problems were likely to arise as it
was there that industrialists and house builders would inevitably turn
for expansion.

   At no time have local government units borne a clear relationship
to population distribution, nor can they in an area where the
suburban development cannot be foretold. On the one hand, Esher
and the Dittons became an urban district as early as 1895 but the
Elstree area, though partly industrialized and partly residential, is
still a rural district. In most cases the area controlled was a civil
parish derived from an ecclesiastical parish, though as various
adjustments were made the boundaries generally became more
logical. During the last decade of the nineteenth century, a number
of new places acquired urban powers, in addition to those that
already had improvement commissioners, a board of health or a
sanitary authority and thereby automatically became urban districts
in 1894. In Middlesex, for example, Greenford U.D. was constituted
out of three civil parishes in 1894, but absorbed by Ealing in 1926:[158]
Sunbury-on-Thames, Wembley and Wealdstone were also constituted in 1894, but the last was divided between Harrow and Wembley

in 1934.[159] Feltham, Hayes and Ruislip-Northwood became urban districts in 1904 and Yiewsley in 1911.[160] Similar developments were seen in Surrey: Barnes became an urban district in 1893, East and West Molesey in 1895, Esher in 1895,[161] and Merton in 1907:[162] in Kent, Chislehurst was made an urban district in 1900 and Foots Cray (later Sidcup) in 1902 (these were united in 1934).[163] In Essex, Buckhurst Hill and Chingford became urban districts in 1894, and Loughton in 1900.[164] A few urban districts were added after 1914: these were, in Middlesex, Heston with Isleworth 1927,[165] Potters Bar 1934,[166] in Surrey, Beddington-Wallington, Coulsdon-Purley, and Mitcham in 1931 and Banstead in 1933:[167] in Kent, Crayford 1920, Erith and Orpington 1934:[168] in Essex, Dagenham 1926.[169] The creation of new urban districts and the enlargement at the expense of the rural districts of those already existing, brought town services to the new suburbia. The Uxbridge rural district was gradually carved up between the neighbours: in 1928, 3 square miles was given to Ealing and 100 acres to Harrow, and in 1929, 16 square miles was added to Uxbridge U.D.[170] And the Staines R.D. was carved up between new and older urban districts in 1930.[171] In 1931 the onslaught on Hendon R.D. began by the addition of 3 square miles to Hendon U.D.[172]

Piecemeal adjustments have made the existing administrative map (Fig. 18) a document with a complicated history. That it is not more complicated is due to the Review Orders of the nineteen-thirties: even so, the 5,000,000 people of the Outer Ring are governed by sixty-six authorities, of which three are county boroughs (Croydon, East Ham, West Ham), thirty-six are municipal boroughs, twenty-six urban districts and one (Elstree) a rural district. Over fifty of these areas are increasing in population, some markedly so. Harrow, for example, had 219,000 people in 1951, 127 per cent more than in 1931, yet it was still an urban district until it became a municipal borough in 1954.[173] It was felt to be unjust that Harrow should have less self-government than many places far less populous. This raises a further point of definition. In 1922, there was talk of making areas which would have half a million people, and in their 1947 Report, the Local Government Boundary Commission suggested that there should be two types of new counties with 200,000–1,000,000 or 200,000–500,000 people, county boroughs with population normally of 60,000–200,000, but including a special group of larger cities.[174] It is interesting to observe that both in 1922 and twenty-five years later, there was great faith in definition by the number of population but these may change swiftly: study of the 1951 Census—or even of Fig. 10—will show that the changes are almost dramatic within twenty years, even in ten years.

Many new boroughs were created in Outer London during the

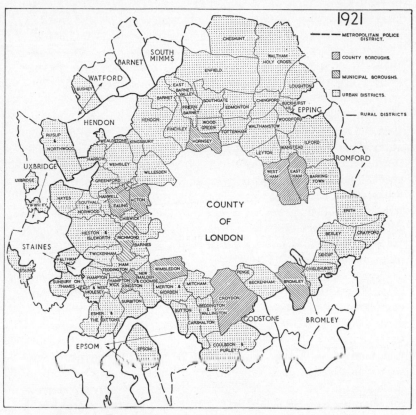

FIG. 16. GREATER LONDON, ADMINISTRATIVE UNITS, 1921

Several more urban districts have been created and a few more places have become municipal boroughs. But the inter-war spread of London was only just beginning.

inter-war period: two of the three county boroughs, Croydon and West Ham were constituted in 1888 though East Ham had to wait until 1915.[175] In Middlesex, Ealing became a municipal borough in 1901 and Hornsey in 1903[176] but no more were created until Acton was added in 1921, and Twickenham in 1926.[177] In 1932 three more were added—Brentford-Chiswick, Hendon, Heston-Isleworth (made an urban district only in 1927), and in 1933, Finchley, Southgate, Willesden and Wood Green with Tottenham in 1934: in 1936 Southall became a borough, Edmonton and Wembley in 1937 (and Harrow in 1954).[178] In Surrey six new boroughs were created in the

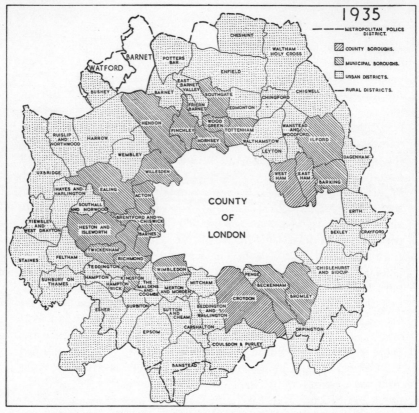

FIG. 17. GREATER LONDON, ADMINISTRATIVE UNITS, 1935

All Middlesex is now under urban government, and the substantial expansion of the area defined as urban elsewhere reflects the continued outward movement of the inter-war period. Several new boroughs have been created. In 1933, Chigwell U.D. was created.

thirties: Mitcham and Sutton-Cheam in 1934: Surbiton and Malden-Coombe in 1936: Beddington-Wallington and Epsom-Ewell in 1937.[179] In Kent, Bromley, having a charter of 1447, was made into a municipal borough in 1903:[180] Beckenham was given a charter in 1935, Bexley in 1937 and Erith in 1938.[181] Essex's seven municipal boroughs were all created during the inter-war period—Ilford and

Leyton in 1926, Walthamstow in 1929, Barking in 1931, Wanstead-Woodford, Chingford and Dagenham in 1937.[182] These arrangements did much to set the seal on the existing administrative organization for it rarely happens that a borough is absorbed (but see pp. 88, 250).

The Outward Movement Continues

Throughout this chapter the outward movement of population has been a leitmotif. Those who sought a calm environment in the new square of Bloomsbury from the end of the seventeenth century were the forerunners of those who now favour Purley, Potters Bar, or places remoter still. This outward movement is now affecting boroughs and urban districts beyond the boundaries of the L.C.C., notably from 1931 to 1951, twelve of its urban neighbours. Of these four are in Essex, marginal to the industrial northeast and east of London—West Ham (− 42 per cent), East Ham (− 15 per cent), Walthamstow (− 18 per cent) and Leyton (− 9 per cent); in Middlesex, Tottenham (− 19 per cent) and Wood Green (− 4 per cent) are also close to central London. Willesden (− 3 per cent), Acton (− 4 per cent), Brentford–Chiswick (− 6 per cent) carry the line of declining boroughs round to the Thames; and on the south side Barnes (− 4 per cent), Wimbledon (− 2 per cent) and Penge (− 10 per cent), have passed their peak population.[183] At each census these population declines are seen farther out: for example only four of the twelve urban areas noted above showed a decline between 1921 and 1931 (see Fig. 10). Much more interest lies in the areas of increase. Hendon had 57,600 within its (present) 16 square miles in 1921 but 115,600 in 1931 and 155,800 in 1951: here the greatest increase came after the opening of the tube railway to Edgware in 1924. Chislehurst and Sidcup, Kent, covering 14 square miles, had 22,400 inhabitants in 1921, 27,200 in 1931 but 83,800 in 1951—an example of recent growth on the outer fringe. In general, the remoter the area from central London, the greater the increase, up to a limiting zone in which this tendency becomes less marked. In fact it seems to occur only a short distance from the present limits of the conurbation, for from 1931 to 1951 places like Reigate (+ 22 per cent), Leatherhead (+ 23 per cent), Walton–Weybridge (+ 49 per cent) and Egham (+ 43 per cent), had increases less than those of their neighbours nearer to London, such as Chertsey (+ 83 per cent) or Carshalton (+ 120 per cent).

The Metropolitan Police District was a suitable basis for a

definition of Greater London in 1901 but it was not appropriate in 1951, for it was already inadequate. It is therefore unfortunate that the anonymous definers, able to give the first official recognition to a

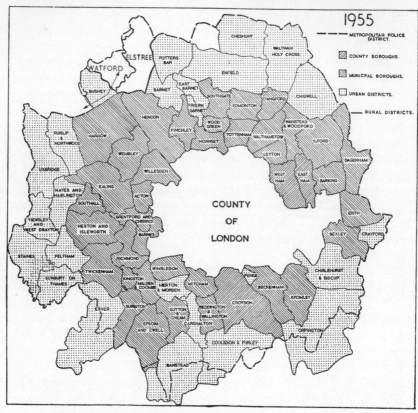

FIG. 18. GREATER LONDON, ADMINISTRATIVE UNITS, 1955

This shows the present position, in which the county of London is almost surrounded by boroughs. Twickenham absorbed three neighbours in 1937 and Harrow became a municipal borough in 1954. The conurbation includes all the boroughs and urban districts named and the rural district of Elstree.

conurbation that undoubtedly exists, did not make more of their opportunities. All definers of conurbations find that the real difficulty is to know when to stop but if one adopts a conservative technique, and includes only those areas which are physically joined to London, the additions would be as follows:

TABLE 1

RECENT INCREASES OF POPULATION IN TOWNS, MARGINAL TO THE
GREATER LONDON CONURBATION

	Area in acres	1931	1951	Increase, %
SURREY				
Caterham and Warlingham	8,233	21,744	31,290	44
Reigate M.B.	10,255	34,547	42,234	22
Leatherhead	11,187	16,483	21,203	23
Walton and Weybridge .	9,052	25,658	38,091	49
Chertsey	9,983	16,988	31,029	83
Egham	9,350	17,198	24,515	43
	58,060	133,618	194,362	46
KENT				
Dartford M.B. . . .	2,333	28,871	40,518	40
ESSEX				
Romford M.B. . . .	9,342	37,840	88,002	133
Hornchurch U.D.. . .	19,768	39,389	104,092	164
	29,110	77,229	192,094	149
HEREFORDSHIRE				
Watford M.B. . . .	5,296	58,523	73,130	25
Rickmansworth . . .	7,639	11,529	24,508	113
Watford rural parish . .	5,141	3,894	22,415	475
	18,076	73,956	120,053	63
Total	109,479	313,674	547,027	74
	(185 square miles)			

Note.—In compiling this table, it would have been possible, and no doubt justifiable, to include many more places; but a restricted area has been deliberately chosen. See also pp. 219, 266–8.

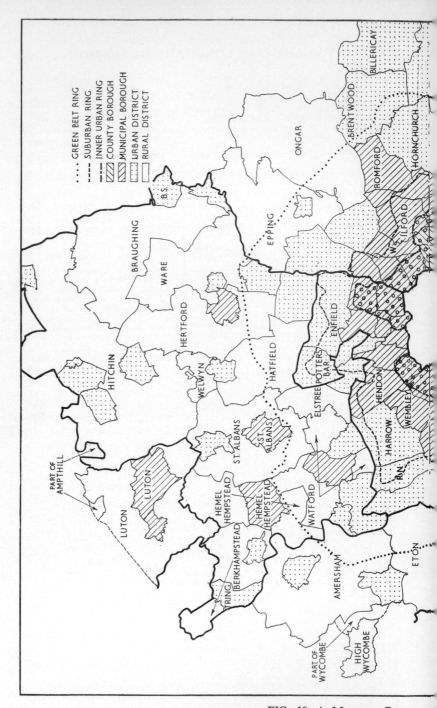

FIG. 19. A MODERN CONCEPTIO

The area shown here, covering 2,599 square miles was considered in t
named. See pp. 22, 23, 30. The area beyond the green belt was called t
population of the metropolis to be broadcast at random over its surfac

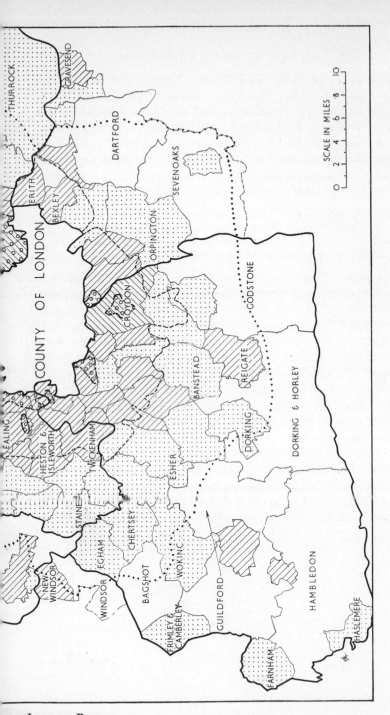

THE LONDON REGION

reater London Plan (by P. Abercrombie, 1945) under the headings
iter Country Ring': 'not by any means', it was said, 'is the surplus
26).

F

The essential problem of defining the London area remains unsolved: even if the above had been included in the 1951 definition, probably by 1961 the spread of housing would make the line drawn appear out of date. Recognizing such difficulties, one may perhaps understand why 'at no point in the modern history of London has the machinery of local government been adjusted so as to take the facts of population into account'.[184] This is apparent to students of housing, such as Quigley and Goldie who said that:[185]

> The administration of London is carried out by too great a multiplicity of authorities for any concerted action to be possible on an urgent and vital issue, and even when a definite policy is agreed, the division of responsibility for action causes delay and inefficiency. . . .

Over a hundred local authorities (now ninety-five) 'undertake a pressing problem with varying degrees of enthusiasm, intelligence and fortitude'.[186] In 1922, Herbert Morrison said that there was no valid reason for the continued existence of the present boundary of the administrative county of London which was described as 'a purely artificial line running through built-up populous areas for the most part'.[187] 'You cannot', he added, 'surround each Borough in London or Greater London with a municipal moat and drawbridge and let it live a life entirely apart from its neighbours.' But of these problems none is nearer solution: nor is there a definition of the conurbation on the lines suggested in 1922 by putting the boundary of the county of London farther out—where? On this Mr. Morrison's statement of 1922 says 'exactly where, they are not prepared to say, but . . . it should include the continuously built-up area with a margin sufficiently large to prevent, if necessary, the further growth of Greater London outwards, except on town planning lines'.[188]

CHAPTER 3

THE WEST MIDLANDS

SURROUNDED on the west, south and east by rural areas, this conurbation alone among the major conurbations of Britain has increased markedly in population since the beginning of the twentieth century; and there is every sign that population growth still continues. In 1921, it had 1¾ million people, in 1931 nearly 2 million and in 1951 2¼ million on 269 square miles, and the increase of + 9 per cent from 1921 to 1931 was followed by an increase of + 16 per cent in 1931 to 1951.[1] Within this same twenty years, the number of structurally separate dwellings increased by + 35 per cent, to 606,000, though there are over 32,000 occupied by more than one household. The post-war surveys of the West Midland group showed that one-tenth of the area was derelict land,[2] that many of the towns are extremely drab, and that at least one-third of the houses need to be replaced. Many of the factories are in old premises, some of them in groups of old houses or converted halls though there are fine new ones, conspicuously in the suburbs of Birmingham.[3] The 'industrial collar' round the city centre of Birmingham, now being demolished, has an even finer and larger museum of out-of-date factory buildings, mixed with houses, than the comparable area of Manchester. Birmingham differs from several other cities in the lack of need for any new industries, for it has attracted so wide a range of trades, and shown such ability to meet changing economic circumstances, that its people are now faced with the problem of preventing indefinite population growth.[4] It is therefore of some significance that outlying towns, such as Coventry and—in less degree—Rugby, have received some of the large concerns in new industries, such as cars, artificial silk, electrical equipment, which might have been attracted to Birmingham.

Many efforts have been made to account for the continued economic success of Birmingham and neighbouring towns: good communications, the existence of iron, coal and wood for charcoal, abundant water, centrality of position in England, an invigorating climate, citizens of business acumen and foresight, even a strong Nonconformist tradition have all been given as reasons for prosperity not easily shaken in periods of slump.[5] Economic historians have shown that as one industry decayed, another arose; and no area

71

has greater diversity of manufactures. As metal industries have been, and are likely to remain essential needs, the West Midland area must therefore remain economically strong, provided that its production is adapted to current demand. And this ability to serve the present age

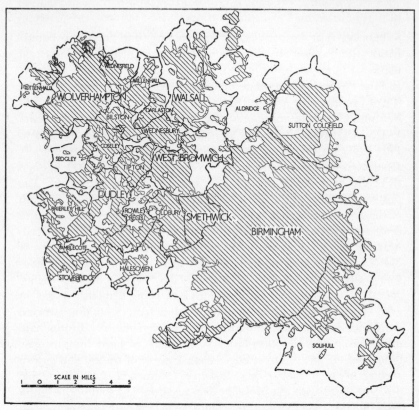

FIG. 20. BUILT-UP AREA OF THE WEST MIDLANDS CONURBATION *c.* 1950

Alone among the conurbations, the West Midlands has a large area of derelict land, now being used for housing and industrial purposes.

has always been conspicuous, never more so than now. Many areas such as Lancashire, depending historically largely on cotton, or Tyneside on mining and shipbuilding, will seem less fortunately placed, more liable to spells of unemployment, less able to absorb their natural growth of population than the West Midlands, and the industrial diversity of Birmingham, if not of the Black Country, has been both envied and emulated by industrial communities elsewhere.

This conurbation consists of Birmingham and the Black Country, the first famed mainly for a variety of small, intricate metal manufactures and the second for larger and heavier products or for wrought metals taken to Birmingham for finishing processes, though such a distinction is necessarily generalized. Over half the population of the conurbation live in Birmingham (1,112,000) and its two neighbours, Solihull and Sutton Coldfield (116,000); and another million people live in the twenty-one other towns of the conurbation. On the ground the Black Country appears as a group of separate towns fused into one another by housing estates with a sad legacy of past industrialization in its derelict land, described as 'spoiled by the past working of extractive industry, by old industrial waste or by abandoned buildings'.[6] Although many local government boundaries appear to be quite illogical, or at least unsuited to mid-twentieth-century conditions, the administrative position is less intricate than in other conurbations.

Birmingham dominates the conurbation as a trading and commercial centre but Wolverhampton (163,000), 14 miles away, is commercially strong with a retail trade valued at £27,300,000 in 1951, an average of £168 per head.[7] In a careful study, Brennan shows that many thousand shoppers are attracted to Wolverhampton, which is sufficiently far from the main city to develop its own trade and possess an individuality that is perhaps matched by that of Huddersfield in relation to Leeds.[8] But many of the towns lack well-equipped shopping centres and consist of groups of factories and houses separated from one another by railways, canals or patches of derelict land: in other words, thousands of people live under industrial conditions but lack many of the distinct advantages of town life close to their homes and—in part at least—the Black Country has the amorphous character of a landscape of industrial villages.[9]

Physical Features

The term the 'Birmingham plateau', commonly given to this area, emphasizes the general physical character of an area mainly 400–450 ft. above sea level having the Trent and its tributaries on the north and east and the Severn and its tributaries on the west and south. And river valleys break up the plateau surface: from Wolverhampton to Birmingham (at Aston) the Tame flows in a wide valley and the tributary Rea and Cole rivers flow through the city's southern suburbs, the first to join the Tame at Aston and the second some miles farther east deep in the countryside. The Sedgley-Northfield ridge, which rises to 866 ft. at Turner's Hill and divides the Black Country into two parts, forms the watershed between the Tame and the Stour and is so formidable a barrier to canals and railways that its canal tunnels are famous for their length. The ridge, of complex geological structure, includes Silurian limestones which form the three hills of Sedgley Beacon, Wren's Nest Hill and Dudley Castle Hill: the lower parts of the ridges are of Middle Coal Measures, and these Carboniferous beds also form the ridge farther south, though at Rowley Hill there is a much-quarried intrusion of dolerite.[10]

The middle Coal Measures include some thick and famous seams of coal and of ironstone which was the basis of the dominant industry, but where these strata pass beneath the unproductive Upper Coal Measures, the thickness and quality of the seams gradually decline. The first part of the coalfield to be worked actively lies to the north of the Sedgley–Northfield ridge, where large areas were underlain by coal and ironstone measures, including the famous Thick Coal seam, of 18–30 ft. at shallow depths.[11] As coal could be extracted by opencast working or by shallow shafts, a vast area, covering in all several thousands of acres, was made derelict, and the landscape marred by hundreds of separate patches or mounds, 'hills and hollows'—the latter due to subsidence. In 1843[12]

> The whole country might be compared to a vast rabbit warren. It is a matter of everyday occurrence for houses to fall down, or a row of buildings inhabited by numerous families to assume a very irregular outline . . . caused by the sinking of the ground into old workings.

To the south of the Sedgley-Northfield ridge, where the coal measures lie beneath the Etruria marls, mining was mainly by shafts, but there too derelict land is widespread.

On either side of the Coal Measures, the Triassic rocks that appear at the surface consist largely of sandstones and form low plateaux extending from Stourbridge to Wolverhampton, and from Northfield to Lichfield. To the south-east and east of Birmingham there is a lowland floored by Keuper marl over which Solihull, Sutton Coldfield and the city's eastern suburbs are now spreading. One factor in the choice of sites for settlement was the existence of a low but distinctive ridge of Lower Keuper sandstone, from Northfield in the south to Sutton Coldfield in the north, on which the villages of Edgbaston, Birmingham and Erdington first took shape.[13] The advantages of site included excellent building stone, a comparatively good water supply and a soil of sandy or gravelly drift which was of reasonable fertility. For most of historical time there was little agricultural attraction in the clay soils of what became the Black Country, but more on the margins. Heaths and commons on the Bunter pebble beds separated Birmingham from the early industrial villages of Wednesbury and Dudley, and even Birmingham Heath remained largely unenclosed until the nineteenth century.

Industrial Development

Birmingham was recorded as a manor in Domesday and some time between 1154 and 1166 its markets were mentioned as given to one Peter de Birmingham. In the twelfth and thirteenth centuries it was apparently a market town, growing steadily, and by 1327 it was the most populous place in Warwick county except for Coventry and Warwick. It was, says Gill,[14] 'a nodal point . . . a natural centre of exchange for all the district within a radius of two dozen miles'. And this market function has never been lost, but rather strengthened by the industrialization which was well established before the end of the sixteenth century. By 1600, the local advantages for industry were apparent, for coal, ironstone and wood were all available.[15] Charcoal iron-smelters used wood from the local forests and coal was mined at Brierley Hill, Dudley, Sedgley, Wednesbury and Bilston. At Birmingham and the surrounding villages various smallwares were made including bits, stirrups, horseshoes and nails, with swords, scythes and cutlery in the Elizabethan age. Already the industrial pattern was marked out for the iron made in the incipient Black Country was used for the manufactures of Birmingham and district, but the goods made were of comparatively high value in proportion to their bulk and therefore able to withstand transport costs. Even though the ironworks decayed for lack of wood towards the end of the seventeenth century the smiths remained and worked on iron imported from South Wales and from Sweden.[16] And at some time not known, but before the end of the seventeenth century, the manufacture of brass and copper, and gun-making were firmly established in Birmingham:[17] in the Black Country iron-smelting and the making of iron-goods, especially nails and locks,[18] continued on a larger scale—indeed the making of locks was recorded as early as the sixteenth century.[19] Other trades were introduced and by the eighteenth century buckles, buttons and trinkets of iron, steel and brass were made in Birmingham and glass at Stourbridge. From the seventeenth century, Birmingham had saddlery and harness manufactures.

Success did not reward all the industries, but there was a constant willingness to experiment. Gill, quoting William Hutton, the eighteenth-century historian, said that some 'spring up with the expedition of a blade of grass and, like that, wither in the summer'.[20] But the firmness with which metal trades were established during the seventeenth century gave the area its destiny. The advantages included the special facilities for metal manufactures, the presence of workers skilled in these trades, the growing demand for metal buttons, buckles and the like, and the connexions established with the London merchants.[21] So long as metals were needed in one form or another, the goods could be made in a city and district having such traditions, provided that the raw materials could be acquired in sufficient quantity. And here lay the problem during the eighteenth century: '. . . at no time during the eighteenth century was the region self-sufficient in pig-iron production . . . the available manuscript evidence strongly supports the view that normally more pig-iron was brought into the district than was smelted' locally.[22] One by one the charcoal furnaces were abandoned, and the last, at Aston, was closed in 1788. The need for imports was also due to the demand for the higher qualities of iron for making tools.[23] Supplies came from north Staffordshire and south Derbyshire, from the Welsh Border, from central Shropshire and the Forest of Dean, and the main primary manufacturing area was the Stour valley, probably because much of the pig-iron was brought by water along the Severn at about half the cost of land transport.

'Industrial momentum' is a phrase somewhat discredited though once frequently used. But there was every sign of it in Birmingham during the eighteenth century, as the town's wide range of manufactures involved the use of all the metals known to the industry of that time. Towards the end of the eighteenth century, brass was brought from Cheadle (Staffs.) and Keynsham (Bristol), but the price was rising so Birmingham manufacturers made their own.[24] And in 1790 the Birmingham Copper and Mining Company arranged for the supply of Cornish ore and set up smelting works in Cornwall and in South Wales. Birmingham merchants and manufacturers grasped the nettle and plucked forth a flower (as one of them said in less happy circumstances in 1938). The need for good communications was partly met from the latter half of the eighteenth century by canals, which supplemented road traffic rather than superseded it, for in 1785 there were reported to be more than eighty lines of carriers' vehicles and twenty-eight coach organizations and by 1812, there were many more.

Although this great industrial area has within it, in the ridge through Dudley, the major water-parting of England between the Severn and the Trent, neither the necessity of building long flights of locks, nor that of making tunnels and deep cuttings deterred the canal builders from making Birmingham the hub of the canal system of the country by the beginning of the railway age.[25] In 1777, the Trent-Mersey canal was completed and by 1790 a connexion was made to the Thames through Fazeley (near Tamworth) and the Coventry canal. These canals lay on the north and east sides of the Birmingham area, and in 1772 the Birmingham canal was joined to the Staffordshire–Worcestershire canal at Autherley near Wolverhampton. This canal, begun in 1766 and completed to Tipton by 1770 was used to carry coal to Birmingham. Similar advantages followed when the Stourbridge canal was constructed and shortly afterwards— in 1785—joined to the Dudley canal, both of them were on the west side of the ridge but connected in 1790 with the Birmingham canal through the famous Dudley tunnel, 1¾ miles long. Steadily more canals were built and the general effects were two, first to open up every part of the Black Country to industry, and second, to give the whole area wide contacts by water.[26] In some areas tramroads came down to wharves on the canals: risking the old trap of 'the chicken and the egg' argument, one might say that it was not the canals that made the area industrial but that their construction enabled enterprising men to develop the industries already there and to draw forth and circulate the minerals needed for still further expansion.

Gill has said that during the eighteenth century no town in England derived more benefit from the turnpike roads and the canals—and other advantages followed from the foundation of various local banks.[27] During this century, Birmingham grew from a manufacturing and marketing centre of some 12,000–15,000 to a great industrial town of 74,000 people, exceeded in population only by London, Liverpool and Manchester. In spite of times of depression (see p. 83), there has been a steady increase of population since the early nineteenth century: most of the industrial centres increased in population three or four times from 1801 to 1851.[28] Purely residential quarters were few, though at Edgbaston, the Gough family refused to allow workshops or warehouses to be built on the Calthorpe estate beside the canal.[29] Happily this area has changed less with the passing of more than a century than other late eighteenth and early nineteenth century inner suburbs,[30] which have been transformed into industrial quarters or swamped by artisan housing, as in other cities.

In New Hall for example, beyond Colmore row, the Colmore estate was sold for building in 1746 and planned on the rectangular lines which still remain in the street pattern, but the manufacturer of toys or buckles or guns 'used his house as a workshop, annexed another, and then built upon the garden or yard as his needs increased'.[31]

Unfortunately many factors favoured congestion both in Birmingham and in the Black Country, where proximity to a mine for coal or iron, or to a canal and a road, resulted in close industrial settlement. Numerous small workshops were established close to the centres of towns and larger works were built beside the canals and railways. One such, the famous Soho foundry, was set up in 1761 beside the Hockley Brook, a tributary of the Tame and ran on water power, though in 1767 an engine was installed.[32] In 1795 a new foundry was built beside the Birmingham and Wolverhampton canal in Smethwick, where steam engines were manufactured, and machines are still made. The older industrial districts (pre-1860) grew around central Birmingham as a kind of 'industrial collar' and along the road, canal and in time railway routes to the Black Country towns (Fig. 21). Within the Black Country the expansion of the first thiry years of the nineteenth century was remarkable: in 1796, there were only fourteen blast furnaces but by 1830 there were 123.[33] By the middle of the nineteenth century there were 180 blast furnaces but the maximum production of pig iron, c. 750,000 tons a year, was reached in the eighteen-fifties, as the local ironstones were almost exhausted.[34] Now, a century later, pig iron is produced only at Spring Vale, Bilston and a few smaller works that have managed to survive, but steel is made at several places, including Bilston, Wednesbury and Round Oak.

At the beginning of the nineteenth century Birmingham had four staple trades, brassfounding, jewellery (toys), gun and button manufacture,[35] and the Black Country was in the full tide of industrial

---

FIG. 21. The central area lies between the two railway stations and the 'industrial collar' is marked. Developed mainly before 1860, it is now in a process of transformation and the jewellery and gun areas are being altered. Inner Birmingham merging into Smethwick and the Black Country is also shown by the artisan houses with industry (taken from the Land Utilization Survey map) and both the inter-war housing spread have been noted from Ordnance Survey maps.

Based on data in Wise, M. J., and Thorpe, P. O'N., 'The growth of Birmingham 1800–1950', in B.A. Birmingham, 1950, esp. pp. 221, 223: also used were modern O.S. maps and the Birmingham sheet of the Land Utilization Survey, 1934.

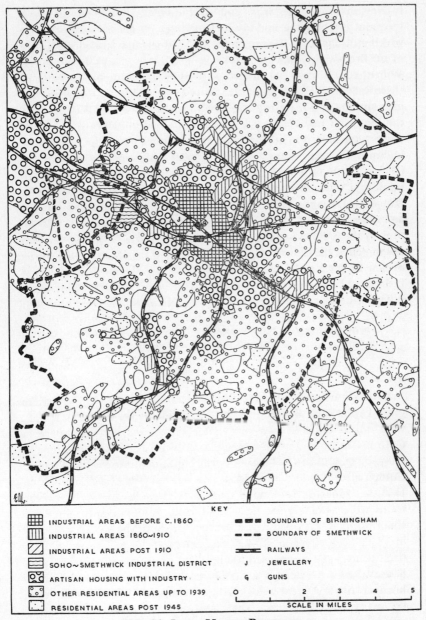

KEY

INDUSTRIAL AREAS BEFORE C.1860		BOUNDARY OF BIRMINGHAM
INDUSTRIAL AREAS 1860~1910		BOUNDARY OF SMETHWICK
INDUSTRIAL AREAS POST 1910		RAILWAYS
SOHO~SMETHWICK INDUSTRIAL DISTRICT	J	JEWELLERY
ARTISAN HOUSING WITH INDUSTRY	G	GUNS
OTHER RESIDENTIAL AREAS UP TO 1939		
RESIDENTIAL AREAS POST 1945		SCALE IN MILES

0 1 2 3 4 5

FIG. 21. LAND USE IN BIRMINGHAM

expansion as a coal, iron and steel district. Examples of local specializations by the middle of the nineteenth century included the making of chains at Tipton, tubes at Wednesbury, coiled springs at West Bromwich, nuts and bolts at Darlaston, locks and keys at Willenhall and cast-iron hollowware at Wolverhampton.[36] Some of these still survive—for example, thirty firms at West Bromwich provide springs and there are some two hundred firms at Willenhall in the lock and key industry, though cast-iron hollowware manufacturers have turned to other lines such as motor and electrical castings, and motor wheels.[37] But the metallurgical basis remains even though iron and steel have been imported in increasing quantities and coal-mining is now represented by only four pits, of which only one, Baggeridge, has more than 1,000 workers.[38] These mines now provide less than a million tons of coal annually, compared with 7,500,000 tons in the eighteen-sixties and 3,000,000 tons in 1913. But this has not impeded the growth of new industries and the careful substitution of new trades for old ones, some of which are affected by changes of fashion and demand. G. C. Allen[39] writing in 1929, before the modern policy of bringing industries to depressed areas was normal, said that

> It is obvious that an industrial area which is well supplied with capital equipment, enterprising manufacturers and skilled workers will have a better chance of securing a large share in any new industries that may arise than districts which are less well endowed.

Railways came early to the West Midlands, for by 1838 'the three great capitals of England, London, Birmingham and Liverpool', were linked by rail. Two years later a line was constructed from Cofton, 8 miles south of Birmingham, to Worcester, Cheltenham and Gloucester, and in 1842 this line was continued into Birmingham at Curzon street station: in 1844, it was built to Bristol. Meanwhile, in 1841, a connexion was made from Lawley street to Derby, where trains were available for Leeds and Hull. Within a short time the small original stations proved inadequate, and Snow Hill was built in 1852, New street in 1854.[40] The extensive tunnelling needed for these central stations caused the removal of some old and insanitary houses. Railway extensions, says Briggs, of the seventies and eighties, brought 'the first great work of slum-clearance'.[41] As the years went on, many more lines were added and stations became so numerous that local journeys are slow. At first the canals increased their trade—for example the Grand Junction canal carried 708,000 tons of cargo in 1833 but 1,145,000 tons in 1852, though there was a decline later.[42]

The railway network matched in intricacy that of the canal network made some seventy years earlier, because the West Midland area was economically sufficiently strong to attract any form of transport.

Population

By 1801, there were 192,000 people, 710 to the square mile within the area now covered by the West Midland conurbation. By 1831, the population had almost doubled, to 376,000, and twenty years later almost 650,000, of whom only 350,000 were within 'towns' as recognized by the Census authorities. These included Walsall (25,700), Wolverhampton[a] (50,000) and Birmingham (232,800), all of which were boroughs under the Municipal Corporations Act of 1838, the parliamentary borough of Dudley (38,000), and the towns which were neither municipal nor parliamentary boroughs, Wednesbury (11,900), Halesowen (4,400), Oldbury (5,100) and Stourbridge (7,800).[43] Here, as in other growing industrial areas many industrial villages were left outside the town definition, but the older towns have remained significant. In the case of Birmingham, the 1838 charter had extended municipal control to the limits of the parliamentary borough, to include Edgbaston, Deritend, Bordesley, Duddeston and Nechells as well as the parish of Birmingham itself.[44] In 1851 the addition of population at Birmingham was ascribed to the 'extent and variety of the manufacturers' and growth at Aston and Handsworth was due 'to proximity to Birmingham'.[45] The 'opening and extension of collieries and ironworks' accounted for marked increases at Wolverhampton, Walsall, Oldbury, Wednesbury, Dudley and Stourbridge. In the Wolverhampton area, it was observed, marriages were early among the miners.[46] At Bilston there was little recent building as much of the 'uncovered' land was insecure,[47] but elsewhere population increase was universal in the industrial areas. Two other contemporary notes are of interest— there were numerous camps of workers on the new railways, and in the extensive rural parish of Solihull many farm workers were seeking industrial employment.[48] But such comments are frequent in the 1841 and 1851 Census notes for industrial areas of Britain.

As early as 1797 one observer said that Birmingham was not 'a place where a gentleman would chuse [sic] to make a residence' and a few of the fortunate moved a mile or two away to Handsworth,

[a] The parliamentary borough had a population of 119,700 but included the townships of Wolverhampton, Wednesfield, Willenhall, Bilston and the parish of Sedgley.

Edgbaston or other villages in the vicinity.[49] But doctors and lawyers still lived close to the town centre until the eighteen-seventies and thriving tradespeople still lived over the shop.[50] The first signs of population decline in the city centre were noted at the 1851 Census, when St. Philip's ward had 11,087 inhabitants compared with 12,197 in 1841.[51] There were only 9,375 in 1861 and 7,779 in 1871, by which time the same phenomenon was noted in all the central wards (St. Peter, St. Philip, St. Paul, St. Mary), due to the demolition of houses to make room for improvements in the town and to the conversion of private dwellings into warehouses and—one must also infer—small factories and workshops.[52] All this is characteristic of the large and growing nineteenth-century industrial town: also characteristic is the existence of a severe housing problem due to the very rapidity of building induced by success. In Birmingham there was neither cellar dwellings nor old tenements but in 1830 there were over 2,000 courts, 'close, dark and filthy; the houses were badly constructed slums almost from the beginning, and many of them were built back to back'.[53] Even now, this problem of back to back houses remains. The town in 1860 was growing beyond the boundaries laid down in 1838 and then regarded as far-sighted. At Edgbaston (within the borough) the increase from 12,907 in 1861 to 17,442 in 1871 was due to the settlement of people from areas near the city centre, owing to the removal of buildings for railway accommodation, the widening of streets, and other improvements,[54] and similar increases were reported at King's Norton, Bordesley, Duddeston, Handsworth and Perry Barr—but partly through an extension of the industrial area[55] (p. 84). And remoter areas were now chosen for residential purposes: in the parish of Sutton Coldfield, which covered 20 square miles, the population increased from 4,662 to 5,936 in 1861–1871 due to 'the erection of houses of an attractive character',[56] and there were similar increases at Yardley and Solihull, which were described as 'favourite localities for the residence of persons engaged in business'[57] in Birmingham. Some people were clearly willing to face train journeys of some length but the main development of the outer suburbs came very much later.

Although the population of the conurbation area as a whole was more than doubled (from 650,000 to 1,479,000) during the latter half of the nineteenth century, some districts had only slight increases or even actual decreases of population at this time. In this phase a number of the mines were worked out, the area's supremacy in world markets for hardware was challenged and the readjustment to other trades was not achieved without stresses. Allen has called the years 1860–1886 'the end of the iron age . . . an era of readjustment and of only slow growth'.[58] After 1886, the motif of industry was the making of composite products and concentration on finishing processes, combined with the attraction of new trades and inventions. Allen lists nine townships or parishes (Bilston, Sedgley, Wednesbury, Darlaston, Willenhall, Kingswinford, Tipton, Dudley and Stourbridge) in which the population[59] increased only from 230,000 people in 1861 to 240,000 thirty years later—but in 1901, 267,000. At the 1871 Census it was noted that at Dudley there was 'depression of trade and consequent migration';[60] at Bilston there was a decrease due to 'the emigration of miners to other localities as many of the mines in the locality were exhausted'.[61] On the other hand, prosperity at Wolverhampton was ascribed to the plentiful employment at the carriage works of the Great Western Railway,[62] a new colliery had been opened at Aldridge[63] and at Rowley Regis there were new mines, with expansion in the iron works and stone quarries.[64] Other places were also reported to be prosperous: at West Bromwich the coal and iron trades were doing well,[65] and the iron trade was also increasing around Stourbridge.[66] At Oldbury, the chemical, soap, iron and other works were drawing so many workers from the surrounding district that the population had increased from 15,700 in 1861 to 21,500 in 1901.[67] Some suburban areas increased markedly in the second half of the nineteenth century, for example Tettenhall, near Wolverhampton (3,700 in 1861 and 8,800 in 1901), Rushall near Walsall (2,840 in 1861 and 7,000 in 1891), and Bloxwich (9,200 in 1861 and 15,300 in 1891), on the northern edge of the Black Country.[68]

Birmingham's growth continued steadily through the second half of the nineteenth century. Within the parish, of 4½ square miles, the population rose from 60,800 in 1801 to 174,000 in 1851, and reached its peak population of 246,400 in 1881. Inside the parliamentary and municipal borough of 1838, the population increased from 296,100 in 1861 to 448,300, but by the end of the century all the inner wards of the town were declining in population[69] and, as noted on p. 82, some had shown decreases before 1851. At the 1871 Census, an increase of population in the Ladywood and All Saints' areas (that is, eastwards towards Smethwick) was ascribed to the general increase of trade and the building of new factories; in Bordesley and Duddeston-cum-Nechells similar developments were seen.[70] What has now become the 'middle belt' was then being 'developed' to use the modern term.[71] Industrial areas were growing 2–3 miles from the centre of the town along the Birmingham Canal, beyond Ladywood, along the Warwick Canal and the railway line to Oxford—(for example the Small Arms factory at Small Heath in 1861), and to the northeast on the Fazeley and Aston sides. An interesting case of the remoter spread of industry is the Cadbury settlement[72] at Bourneville in 1879: the Cadbury family began shopkeeping in Birmingham in 1824 and ground cocoa with a pestle and mortar for sale in the shop but opened a factory in 1831 which, by 1880, tapped world markets. The fame of Bourneville rests partly on the spacious planning with only seven houses to the acre and, in 1911 only 4,400 people within 672 acres. Such standards of housing density are far higher than those of the modern housing estate and their early development here was in some degree the inspiration of various reformers.

During the second half of the nineteenth century, suburban growth steadily united one town to another. One by one the outer villages were absorbed. Small Heath was in fact a heath in the eighteen-sixties having cottages and farms, but in 1879 the B.S.A. factory was built here and rapidly residential development followed.[73] Places such as Moseley and Erdington were absorbed by housing, and at Handsworth, originally a suburb of large houses, the population increased from 11,000 in 1861 to 70,000 in 1911. Briggs has spoken of the outward movement as 'ripples of expansion, farther and farther from the city core', but though this analogy is true enough, it is incomplete.[74] A second analogy, also based on stone-throwing, is also helpful. If a stone is thrown on water with a certain motion, it hits the surface several times ('ducks and drakes'), causing ripples at each impact. As nearer suburbs such as Handsworth changed in character, so the wealthy moved out some distance, to Solihull or even beyond it, and small houses were added around Olton which before the early years of the twentieth century was a comfortable residential area with semi-detached villas. At the same time houses were built along the main roads and terraces added in a rectangular street pattern all round Birmingham from Perry Barr[75] and Astley in the north through Saltley and Small Heath in the east to Sparkhill and Selly Oak. Elsewhere terraces were built, for example at Erdington, Yardley and Harborne. Such housing is found widely in all English conurbations and forms as characteristic a memorial of the period from 1860 to 1910 as the housing estates of the inter-war period and the mid-nineteenth century leave for posterity.

Meanwhile in central Birmingham houses were pulled down and

from 1861 to 1871 the population of the three central wards, St. Philip, St. Paul and St. Mary, declined from 36,300 to 31,100 but in the same ten years there was an increase in All Saints' ward (Soho) from 19,800 to 29,700.[76] From the eighteen-seventies, the shops aspired to attract customers from all the midland counties and in 1875, J. H. Chamberlain said that the town could become 'the retail shopping centre of the whole of the midland counties of England'.[77] In the following year the Council acquired part of the land on which Corporation street was built and by 1882 over 600 houses, two chapels, two hotels and many factories and warehouses had been pulled down so that new streets and buildings could be erected.[78] The Birmingham city fathers, increasingly aware of the city's destiny as a regional capital, bought the market rights in 1851, and the retail and wholesale markets were gradually extended from 1869–1903.[79]

Unfortunately the city fathers of the nineteenth century left a sad legacy in housing for the twentieth-century reformers. When the Artisans' Dwelling Act was passed in 1875 by which local authorities could remove insanitary buildings and arrange for new houses to replace them, the deathrate in St. Mary's ward was twice that in Edgbaston.[80] Some houses were repaired or demolished as part of the Corporation street scheme, and in 1890 the first flats, of two storeys, were built.[81] Even so, in 1913 there were 200,000 people in 43,366 back-to-back houses compared with 2,881 such houses in Liverpool and none in Manchester.[82] And in 1946, there were still 29,000 such houses, almost one-tenth of all the houses in Birmingham.[83]

Birmingham's problems are severe. In the city there are 311,000 houses, of which, 50,250, one in every six, are regarded as unfit for human habitation. Some 105,000 houses were built from 1919 to 1939: of these almost half were built by the Corporation and here, as in other cities, the re-building epoch divides itself into two parts: from 1924 to 1931, 32,829 municipal and 14,869 private enterprise houses were built, and from 1932 to 1938, 38,070 private enterprise and 13,485 municipal houses were erected.[84] The effect was that familiar to all students of industrial cities—the addition of vast new suburbs, and the increase—almost to double the size—of the built-up area. Meanwhile the wealthier residents went further afield, not only to Solihull and Sutton Coldfield or to Bromsgrove, but even to Stratford and Malvern or to rural areas around the conurbation. Since the War, between April 1945 and October 1957, the Corporation has provided 34,740 dwellings. The effect on the ground is that a large central area of the city is being rebuilt, so markedly in fact

G

that there is a partial transformation from a nineteenth-century to a twentieth-century industrial city. Nor will the problem end when this reconstruction is finished; for the 'middle ring', with two-sevenths of all the houses, is a densely packed area ripe for replanning.[85]

Rebuilding of industrial and mixed areas has long been desired by planners and the Birmingham Corporation's efforts are therefore of special interest. In 1946 the city acquired five central areas for development, covering in all over 1,400 acres, including 311 acres of industrial premises. All of this area was within the seven central wards of the 1801 town and within it there were 27,861 houses (18,000 of the back-to-back type), 2,120 shops and dwellings and 145 business premises and dwellings. Much trouble was caused by the disturbance of factories and workshops but new premises, including some flatted factories, are provided. The most striking addition to housing is the twelve-storey flats of Duddeston and Nechells, which provide 48 dwellings and 142 rooms to the acre but at very heavy cost with consequent high rents. According to A. G. Sheppard Fidler, the area cleared for the building of these flats had only 30 dwellings with 94 rooms to the acre, covering 30 per cent of the space in congested conditions.[86] Even three-storey or four-storey flats may provide some 25–30 dwellings to the acre. In theory, therefore, it should be possible to rehouse everyone, or at any rate a substantial proportion of the residents, in the same central areas: in fact it is not so. Many districts have such high housing densities that even with twelve-storey flats it is only possible to replace rather less than one-half of the dwellings cleared. In 1956, it was reported to the City Council that

> Virgin housing land in the City is being rapidly absorbed and it is feared that the slum clearance programme and the redevelopment of the central areas may come to a standstill by 1961 unless more land can be found.[87]

The problem of re-housing is serious everywhere, conspicuously in Dudley, Bilston, Coseley and Darlaston, all of which in 1946 had at least one-quarter of their houses in the poorest and oldest known type distinguished by the West Midlands group.[88] On the other hand, the problem of finding space for new houses was in 1945 less serious in this conurbation than in others (cf. pp. 140–3) because approximately half the area was technically 'undeveloped' at the end of the 1939–1945 war. In Bilston, for example, 539 acres was scheduled as derelict in 1945, but since then 383 acres have been reclaimed, leaving 156 acres mainly in small patches. There are some large projects in hand such as the building of schools or the making of public parks, so very little land remains for housing. Bilston corporation has built 2,300 houses since 1945 and now faces the problem of building multi-storey flats or of arranging for its people to move elsewhere.[89] In the whole of the Black Country, which had 9,300 acres of derelict land in 1945, some 3,500 acres had been reclaimed by 1955 for housing and open spaces; and the process continues. An architectural writer[90] has complained that a splendid opportunity of changing the Black Country has been missed, for no general plan was followed and each local authority used its reclaimed land without reference to the neighbours, one for houses, another for parks and open spaces.[91]

Some expansion is likely on the residential fringes such as Sutton Coldfield, Solihull and Tettenhall and the Meriden R.D.C. has agreed to allow Birmingham 'overspill' housing in its area.[92] There are proposals to take over areas in the rural districts of Atherstone and Tamworth and to settle some 72,000 people in other Midland towns, of which three, Tamworth, Redditch and Bromsgrove, are only 13 miles from the city centre and the first two only 5 miles from the outskirts of the conurbation. And Cannock, though 17 miles away, is linked with Birmingham by continuous building. Lichfield, 16 miles from the centre but only 4 from the outskirts, could perhaps double its present population of 11,000 by city migrants without loss of character and Rugeley might welcome its proposed 5,000 immigrants. The most distant of the reception towns, Malvern, 35 miles away, has an obvious interest in the preservation of its amenities. Other authorities within the Conurbation are facing housing problems:[93] Wolverhampton, for example, has arranged that some of its people shall settle in Wednesfield U.D. and in Seisdon R.D., and Walsall has made similar arrangements with Aldridge and Brownhills. The very prosperity of the area makes the problem of expansion so acute that some observers regard the building of new towns in the Midlands as essential.

Administrative Divisions (Figs. 22, 23)

Half the population of this conurbation live in Birmingham, on less than one-third of the area. Steadily the city has absorbed adjacent urban and rural districts and even a municipal borough to bring its area to 80 square miles. Far more successful in its expansion than Manchester or Liverpool, the city made its policy clear by the 1887 statement that it proposed to absorb within the bounds 'all persons who might reasonably be supposed to be connected in any way with

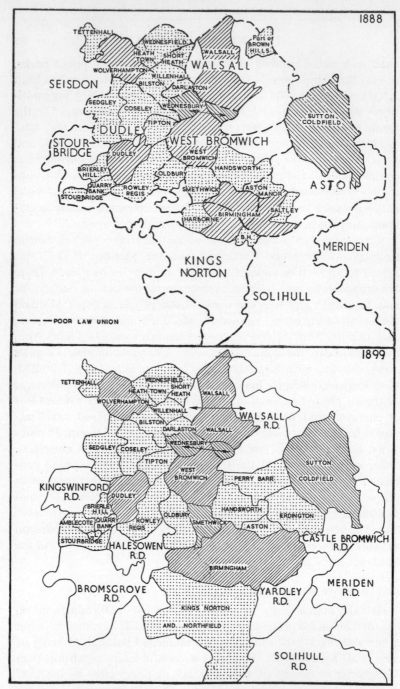

FIG. 22. WEST MIDLANDS, ADMINISTRATIVE AREAS, 1888 AND 1899

This conurbation never had a multiplicity of very small urban districts like those of Yorkshire or Lancashire, though both these maps show that there were a number and that several rural districts existed. These maps show the administrative expansion of Birmingham.

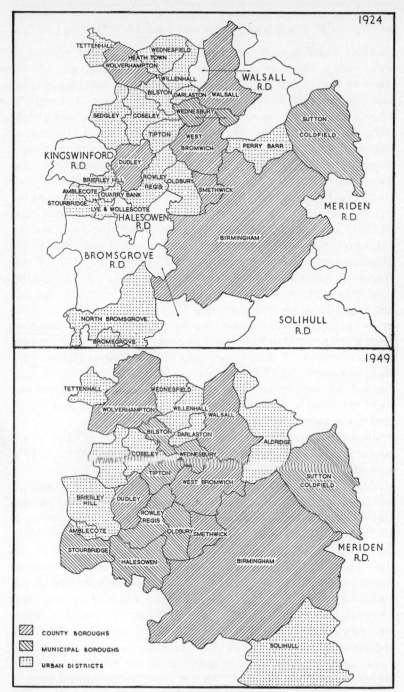

FIG. 23. WEST MIDLANDS, ADMINISTRATIVE AREAS, 1924 AND 1949

In the nineteen-thirties the whole pattern was modified so that all the last relics of rural districts were drawn within some urban net, various small urban districts were united and Birmingham reached what is apparently its maximum expansion.

the trade and manufactures of the town, and who were residing in areas outside the borough, but yet within a distance not too far removed from it for the purposes of efficient and economical municipal government'.[94] In 1838 municipal government covered the 4·5 square miles of the original parish of Birmingham and almost twice this area in Edgbaston, Deritend, Bordesley and Duddeston-Nechells (8,433 acres). Birmingham having become a county borough in 1888, and a city in 1896, spread its bounds wider and wider. In 1891, it absorbed three urban districts, Saltley, Balsall Heath and Harborne with the hamlet of Little Bromwich, to give the city 20 square miles[95] and a population of 478,100 in 1891 and 522,200 in 1901. The great expansion of 1911 increased the city's area to 67½ square miles by absorbing the borough of Aston Manor, the urban districts of Erdington and Handsworth, part of the Kings Norton–Northfield urban district and the whole of the Yardley rural district. Two years earlier in 1909 the civil parish of Quinton had been added, due to a resolution of its parish council.[96] The 1911 extension gave Birmingham an area three times as large as Glasgow, twice as large as Manchester or Liverpool and recognized the continuity of a town 13 miles across.[97] At least these arrangements were realistic though the 1887 principle gradually had less relevance as journeys to work became longer and people colonized villages and small towns ten or more miles away from their factories and offices. And the outwards movement continues.

Absorption of a borough was rare even in a period of great administrative change: Aston Manor had achieved this status in 1903 and had its own tramway system, libraries, fire station and other services.[98] Built mainly between 1851 and 1881, it had 53,800 inhabitants in 1881 and 75,000 in 1911. Handsworth was an urban district covering almost 6 square miles, having 68,600 inhabitants in 1911 compared with 10,400 in 1861, and Erdington was also an urban district of 7 square miles, and a population of 32,000 in 1911. All these places had gas and water from Birmingham and at Erdington fire-brigade services and electricity were provided by the Aston authorities. King's Norton and Northfield urban district covered 35 square miles with a population of 79,200 in 1911, most of whom were city workers, and depended on Birmingham for services, including electricty and sewage disposal. The other places mentioned had some claim to be regarded as independent but King's Norton was merely a suburban overflow. And in the Yardley rural district in 1911, where 59,200 people lived in an area of 12 square miles, compared with less than 10,000 thirty years earlier, the need for city services was considerable for there was no electricity and both gas and water were acquired from Birmingham. Here too the trams came from the city.

The considerable expansion of 1911–1912 added 314,400 people to the city's 525,800, making 840,200. Two later extensions brought the city to its present limits: in 1928 most of the urban district of Perry Barr was added to Birmingham but the part within Staffordshire was divided between Sutton Coldfield and West Bromwich.[99] At the time of its extinction, Perry Barr had a population only of 2,700 in an area of $6\frac{1}{2}$ square miles and was ripe for the suburban expansion that is now virtually complete. The last extension, which brought the city's area to 80 square miles, the addition of 7 square miles inhabited by only 1,574 people from the Meriden rural district in 1931, anticipated the city's need for more houses and industrial premises.[100] Here, conspicuously at Castle Bromwich, some remarkable industrial expansion has been seen. In 1933, the Birmingham city council stated that no more territory was wanted.[101] so the principle stated in 1887 (pp. 87, 90) was in fact retracted.

Administrative changes elsewhere have been considerable but not revolutionary. If towns are definable from their centres rather than from the margins, the older-established places, conspicuously Wolverhampton, Walsall, Wednesbury and Dudley, have the best shopping and administrative centres.[102] But the same cannot be said of all the places in the Black Country; Tipton, a municipal borough, has been described as a number of scattered small towns and villages, collected into one borough, separated from one another by barriers such as canals, railways and derelict land,[103] the last now being reduced in area. Figs. 22 and 23 show that many administrative units have been little changed for more than sixty years, though the rural districts of Walsall and Kingswinford disappeared by 1934, and other rural districts on the margins of the conurbation, such as Meriden on the east and Seisdon on the west have been reduced in area. Except near Birmingham only a few places have failed to keep their name on the administrative map, notably Wednesfield Heath (or Heathtown) which was united to Wolverhampton in 1927 and had a population of 13,000 in its 885 acres (1921).[104] Similarly Short Heath U.D., Staffs., united to Willenhall in 1934, had 5,000 inhabitants and an area of 1,055 acres.[105] On the southwest side of the conurbation, Lye and Wollescote U.D. (12,200, area 1,028 acres) was added to Stourbridge M.B. in 1933;[106] Brierley Hill in 1934 acquired Quarry

Bank (8,100, 666 acres), and 7 square miles from Kingswinford R.D., with 22,200 people in 1931[107] to cover 9 square miles having a population (1931) of 44,700 and 49,000 in 1951. This development is familiar—a couple of industrial centres and a few square miles of countryside where houses have been built in considerable numbers are united into a borough.

Suburban growths have had varied fortunes as administrative areas and the main areas unabsorbed by Birmingham, Solihull and Sutton Coldfield, now cover 22·5 and 31·6 square miles respectively (Fig. 23). In a similar area, Aldridge, some 14·5 square miles between Sutton Coldfield on the east, Walsall on the west and Birmingham on the south, the population increased from 14,400 in 1931 to 29,000 in 1951 and clearly further large increases may be expected. Aldridge was constituted an urban district in 1934, when the Walsall R.D. was abolished:[108] a few hundred acres were added to Walsall in 1931 (986 acres), to Darlaston in 1934 (617 acres), and to Willenhall in 1934 (503 acres) and the residue became Aldridge. On the 1947 O.S. map, 1 in. to 1 mile, housing on the north side of Birmingham extends to the Aldridge boundary and not beyond it, giving a frontier of suburban settlement. Sutton Coldfield became a municipal borough in 1885, when the parish covered 20 square miles with a population of 7,800 (in 1881): enlarged in 1928 by the addition of part of the disbanded Perry Barr U.D. and by parts of the adjacent rural districts in 1932,[109] it covered 22 square miles and had 47,600 inhabitants in 1951. Solihull, which became an urban district in 1932 and a borough in 1954, increased in population from 16,100 in 1921 to 68,000 in 1951 and there is still room for further expansion.

Most of the remaining towns have changed little in area since 1900, though there have been numerous minor adjustments of boundaries. Amblecote, made an urban district in 1898, has still the same area of 665 acres, Wednesbury, a borough since 1886 has changed its boundary only by an exchange of almost equal areas with West Bromwich, Wednesfield U.D. lost a few acres to Wolverhampton and Coseley lost 448 acres to Dudley in 1929. Sedgley, covering 6 square miles, was unchanged in area from 1901, when its population was 16,000 to 1951, when its population was 23,100. In short most of the towns in the heart of the Black Country have had no chance of territorial expansion, except for those such as Walsall and Darlaston which have been able to absorb parts of rural districts. But West Bromwich, incorporated as a municipal borough in 1882 and a county borough in 1890, now covers 11 square miles compared with 9 square miles in 1890: in 1928 it absorbed one square mile from **Perry Barr** and in 1931 the parish of Great Barr (727 acres) from Walsall R.D.,[110] consequently it has land available for housing schemes. Smethwick, made a municipal borough in 1899 and a county borough in 1906, absorbed 567 acres from Oldbury in 1928[111] but consists of less than 4 square miles with a population of 76,400 in 1951, compared with 84,400 in 1931. This decline—the only one recorded for any area in the conurbation—is due not to any decline of employment but to rehousing outside the borough bounds, partly in Oldbury.[112]

Wolverhampton more than doubled its area in 1927 by the addition of 5½ square miles, including Heathtown U.D. and parts of the rural districts of Cannock and Seisdon. Six years later other parts of these rural districts were added to give the borough an extent of more than 14 square miles,[113] and meanwhile the population increased from 124,400 in 1921 to 162,700 in 1951. Immediately to the west of the town, Tettenhall, an urban district since 1883, added part of Seisdon R.D. in 1934,[114] and increased its population from 6,000 in 1931 to 7,700 in 1951. Similarly Wednesfield, on the east side of Wolverhampton, almost doubled its population between 1931 and 1951, from 9,100 to 17,400.

Various suggestions have been made for the rationalization of administrative boundaries. After the 1939–1945 war the Local Government Boundary Commission put forward a proposal for the creation of four enlarged county boroughs based on the four major centres, Wolverhampton, Walsall, Dudley and Smethwick-West Bromwich.[115] The remainder was to be a new county of South Staffordshire. The statistical uniformity achieved by these proposals is perhaps their only merit—and even that a dubious one—and the proposal to create the new county met with the strong disapproval of the county borough authorities. And the main feature of the area is that the problems of all the Black Country towns are interlocking problems, for re-housing of the many thousands in sub-standard homes can be achieved only by the reclamation of areas now derelict: and some authorities do not possess the land necessary for essential re-housing.

Current Problems

Fundamentally the problem of land use in the conurbation is so clearly a population problem that the view has been expressed that no increase in numbers is to be desired, and that emigration from and immigration to the area should be equal.[116] Nevertheless, movement into the area still exceeds that from it, though it appears from past experience that there may be a fairly quick reaction to economic circumstances. G. Walker,[117] in a careful analysis of the annual official figures, shows that after the 1919–1921 boom, men left the conurbation area in considerable numbers, culminating in a marked outward movement in 1926, the year of the General Strike and the great coal lock-out.[118] Trade revival in 1928 and 1929 reversed the movement but when the full impact of the depression came in 1932, outward movement began again and it was not until the late thirties that Birmingham and the Black Country began on balance to attract immigrants.

TABLE 2

RECENT POPULATION HISTORY IN BIRMINGHAM AND DISTRICT

	Increase	Natural increase (excess of births over deaths)	Net immigration (+) or emigration (−)
1921–1931	+ 141,029	+ 154,605	− 13,576
1931–1934	+ 22,681	+ 30,214	− 7,533
1935–1939	+ 120,657	+ 60,901	+ 59,756

Note:—This table covers an area slightly greater than the Conurbation, that is also including Meriden R.D., Bromsgrove U.D. and R.D., and Seisdon R.D., having in 1951 a population of 2,353,000 (conurbation 2,237,000). The West Midlands, alone of the conurbations, has had a marked increase of population during the past fifty years. Study of this table shows that in the depression period of the early thirties, there was considerable outward movement of population, and that before 1931 the area failed to absorb its natural increase. From 1935, however, the inward movement has been considerable. From Walker, *op. cit.* in note 117

Much of the increasing economic strength of the conurbation area lies in its variety of trades, in its long-standing adaptability and in the resilience of the newer trades, conspicuously those associated with electrical engineering and forms of metal working. Traditional trades such as jewellery and the making of sporting guns have declined, but industries such as bicycles, motor-cycles, cars and aeroplanes as well as armaments have remained prosperous[119]. In 1951, 243,700 of the 736,700 occupied males of the conurbation were 'workers in metal manufacture, engineering and allied trades'.[120] When blast furnaces were closed in the Black Country, manufacturers turned to the development of foundries, press and machine shops for which much semi-finished steel was imported.[121] At Small Heath, metal trades remained basic, conspicuously in the famous B.S.A. and Singer works, but non-ferrous castings, steel tubes, varnishes and paints were also made.[122] And in the Tame valley, from Perry Barr in the west to Bromford and Castle Bromwich in the east, the wide flood-plain of the Tame was drained and used for building a vast aeroplane factory and smaller works producing electrical and motor accessories, drawing employees living on the new and neighbouring estate at Erdington.[123] All this continues the long historical tradition of adaptability but it is fortunate that the conurbation possesses some trades which are expanding.

CHAPTER 4

MERSEYSIDE

MERSEYSIDE includes Liverpool, the towns immediately adjacent, and the whole of the Wirral peninsula across the river. To some, the official definition of this conurbation on the Lancashire side will seem restricted, for there is little break between Speke and Widnes, or between Huyton and Prescot. Here the essential difficulty of defining a conurbation is seen, but the present definition follows closely the practice of C. B. Fawcett who regarded the essential feature as continuous town,[1] though he did not include Ellesmere Port, marginally placed at the eastern fringe of the Wirral and the scene of a remarkable and recent industrial expansion. This town, recently elevated to borough status, contests its inclusion within the conurbation and is clearly determined to preserve and develop its individuality. The official conurbation[2] had 627,000 workers, of whom only 27,000 (4 per cent) came from outside areas, including Southport, though over 33,000 left for jobs beyond its bounds, many thousands to the Kirkby industrial estate. Although there are fears that eventually continuous town will link Merseyside and Manchester, Liverpool and its neighbours are still largely surrounded by a farmed countryside. Between Crosby and Formby, the sand-dune coast and a lowland composed largely of moss-lands, now richly cultivated, are regarded as unsuited to residential development. On the east side of the city, where there is no such natural barrier to expansion, the newer houses and factories, especially of the inter-war period, have been built in Huyton with Roby, West Derby, Fazakerley and Aintree. And on the southeast side, beyond the comfortable and somewhat Victorian suburbs of Mossley Hill, Allerton and Woolton, the new housing estate of Speke has spread the city to a point within sight of Widnes and Runcorn.

In spite of the extension inland towards Prescot, Liverpool remains typically maritime in appearance. Before the great inter-war spread of housing, there was a continuous line of town for 13 miles from Blundellsands to Garston but only at West Derby was the city even 4 miles deep from the riverfront. The traditional form of the city and suburbs reflects its dependence on the 7 miles of docks along the waterfront. The small creeks that formed the original haven of Liver-

pool have long since been covered in, but across the river the Great
Float penetrates for more than 2 miles inland and forms the industrial heart of the Cheshire suburbs. All of the Wirral is under some
form of town administration: happily not all of it is town yet. But
the ferries across the Mersey, the under-river railway tunnels, the
road tunnel, have all opened this area to the expansion from Liverpool, and industry has settled at various points, initially at Birkenhead and later at Bromborough (especially Port Sunlight) and at
Ellesmere Port beside the Shropshire Union canal and the greater
Manchester Ship canal. Here on the fringe of the conurbation there
is now, at Stanlow, a vast oil port and refinery with its own deep
water docks and an extensive plant on reclaimed marsh.[3] Indeed, the
area is now so conspicuously prosperous that it draws its workers
from a wide area in and beyond the Conurbation.

Physical Features

Like most of the world's major ports, Liverpool now depends on
the maintenance of an artificial channel for access at all states of the
tide. For 4 miles upstream from the entrance at New Brighton the
river is everywhere less than 1 mile wide, narrowing at the landing
stage to 1,000 yards.[4] The inner estuary is markedly different: between Dingle and New Ferry the river widens to 3 miles at Ellesmere
Port, narrowing again near Runcorn. In this river estuary a large
amount of water accumulates during the flow of the tide, producing
a rapid flow at the ebb, which scours the channel, especially opposite
Liverpool, where the depth is *c.* 65 ft. at low water spring tides.[5] The
outward tidal current flows at four to five knots opposite New
Brighton. The approach to the port has a depth of at least 30 ft. at
low water spring tides in the Crosby Channel, which is defined by
revetments: the most recent of many improvements was the
extension seawards of the outer or Queen's channel between 1933 and
1946.

Owing to the tidal range of as much as 30 ft. on both sides of the
estuary, it is not possible for ocean liners to be moored at fixed open
quays and a vast system of docks with a floating landing stage has
been built. Until the early part of the eighteenth century, ships used
the Pool beside the mediaeval town, and the creeks at Wallasey,
Tranmere and Bromborough.[6] Chester had been a port from Roman
times, when the Dee estuary was a wide arm of the sea but by the
middle of the fifteenth century, its gradual decay through silting
became certain.[7] No merchant ship could come within 12 miles of

the city, and the efforts of the townsmen to make outports beside the
Dee were only temporary irritants to Liverpool. In 1715, when the
first dock was opened, the Mersey was 'transformed overnight from
a dangerous harbour where vessels lay at the mercy of fast-running
tides into a port where they could berth in comparative safety when
loading and discharging their cargo'.[8] To summarize, natural scouring of the channel has been a permanently favourable factor, but the
swift-running tide was a natural hazard for ships obliged to moor in
creeks before docks were built.

On either side of the estuary the lowland is generally flat or gently
undulating but varied by a number of sandstone hills, Triassic in age,
at an altitude of c. 200 ft. O.D. Boulder clays and occasional patches
of the Shirdley Hill sands form the lower ground, and the glacial dis-
organization of drainage has permitted the growth of fen peats, now
transformed by reclamation into fine arable country, generally open
and hedgeless where no stock are kept. For 16 miles north from Seaforth to Southport there is a belt of sand dunes, subject to occasional
heavy erosion in the Blundellsands area.[9] The sandstone hills prominent in Liverpool are at Everton (225 ft.), Wavertree (200 ft.) and
Woolton (200 ft. with a rise to 275 ft.). Comparable features across
the river include the hill at New Brighton (188 ft.), Bidston Hill near
Birkenhead (231 ft.) and, on the west side of the peninsula, Caldy,
near West Kirby, and the line of hills that stretches from Thurstaston
and Heswall for some 3 miles (Heswall hill, 359 ft.). The north coast
of the Wirral consists partly of sand dunes which extend round
Hilbre point to West Kirby (and have provided sites for some famous
golf courses), but at Leasowe an embankment guards the low-lying
area of peat and alluvium that extends inland to Wallasey Pool. The
Leasowe embankment was made in 1829, extended westwards in
1850 and further extended later, and Wallasey Pool was enclosed in
the middle of the nineteenth century.[10] The west side of the Wirral
has a coast of low boulder clay cliffs, flanked from Parkgate southwards by salt marshes.

Merseyside residents are prone to draw attention to the open
character of the area, swept by sea breezes and having close at hand
a rural scene, varied from sand dunes and reclaimed peat mosses to
the rolling drift countryside so bountifully productive of crops. In
the Wirral, it has been said, one may have a home located in surroundings essentially rural, yet be within easy reach of Liverpool:
there lies the problem for the future. Even if there is no considerable
increase in population, replacement of sub-standard houses must

result in a spread of housing comparable with that of the inter-war period. On the land classification map, the immediate hinterland of Liverpool is shown as first-class arable land, comparable in its present state with the equally-famed countrysides of the Fens, the warplands of the Trent and Humber, the heart of the Vale of Evesham and a few other areas.[11] The Wirral peninsula is shown as good grassland.

Historical Aspects

Liverpool became a borough in 1207, when its burgesses were given 'all the liberties and free customs enjoyed by any borough on the seacoast'.[12] From Liverpool's haven, men and supplies could be sent over to Ireland, but the town remained small, even though it acquired so much of Chester's trade by 1445 that the mayor and burgesses supplicated for a reduction of their dues to half.[13] When Camden visited Liverpool c. 1600, he spoke of the town as 'the most convenient and usual place for setting sail unto Ireland, but not so eminent for antiquity as for neatness and populousness'.[14] Nevertheless it remained a small borough of a few streets close to the river and having St. Nicholas' as its church: only in 1699 was the parish made independent of Walton.[15] By the end of the seventeenth century, Celia Fiennes (1698) found Liverpool 'a very rich trading town . . . London in miniature'. Gibson (editor of Camden, 1695) noted the passenger trade with Ireland, the West Indian trade and the manufactures, all of which were responsible for 'the vast growth of this town of late years . . . Its buildings and people are more than doubly augmented and the customs eight or ten-fold increased within these 28 years past'.[16]

Seven streets had formed the town in 1668[17] (Fig. 25), but by 1725 there were thirty-seven streets, according to the famous Chadwick map. Several of these, including Whitechapel and Paradise street, were on the site of the former Pool, which was filled in between 1709 and 1715.[18] The opening of what later became known as the 'Old Dock', also in 1715, was a landmark in the town's industrial expansion.[a] Between Celia Fiennes' visit in 1698 and 1725, the built-up area and the population had doubled so that Defoe[19] found it 'not rivalling Bristol in the trade to Virginia and the English Island Colonies in America only, but in a fair way to eclipse it, by increasing every way in wealth and shipping'. He also speaks of the trade with

[a] This dock was condemned in 1811 and filled up in 1826: it occupied the site of the Custom House, Canning Place. Allison, *op. cit.*, 28.

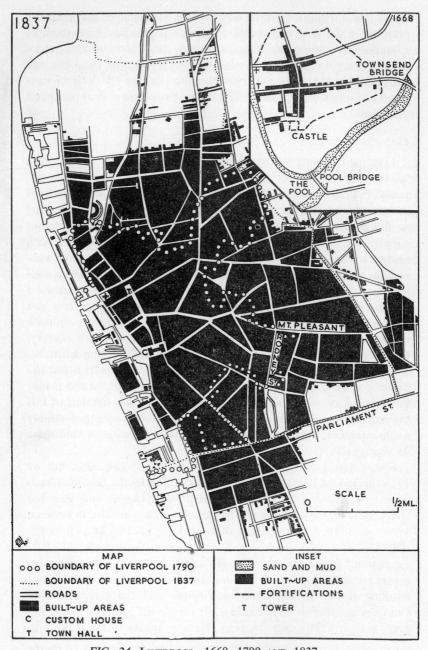

FIG. 24. LIVERPOOL, 1668, 1790 AND 1837

Norwegian and Baltic ports as well as with Hamburg and the ports of the Low countries. The foreland was the ocean ways of the world, the hinterland the growing industrial areas of the north, not least the Cheshire salt fields, the textile areas of the Pennines and their fringes and the metallurgical areas of the Midlands. During the eighteenth century, Liverpool became a greater port than Bristol and by 1801 its population was 78,000 compared with 64,000 at Bristol. Liverpool's rise was indicative of the changes in population distribution of the time and it grew more and more as industry, based partly on imported products, developed beside the port.

During the eighteenth century, Liverpool was a compact town, focused on the commercial quarter that occupied the original area (and still does) and the new shopping-with-residential area 'over the Pool'.[20] By the end of the century docks extended from the parish church of St. Nicholas to the town boundary at Parliament street, but though there were ferries across the river to the Wirral, and apparently had been for centuries, the main development on the Cheshire side came in the nineteenth century and not in the eighteenth. Within the town there were houses as far inland as Mount Pleasant,[21] and in part of Rodney street (built from 1782), on the sandstone hill now crowned by the Anglican cathedral, and on the hill at Everton, which also became a residential area for the wealthy.[22] As early as the eighteenth century there were signs of the flight from the town by merchants no longer content to live beside the shop or the warehouse.[23] And this inevitably meant that from the first effective beginnings, in some parts of the town, one type of land use succeeded another: Renshaw street, for example, was originally residential and ultimately became commercial, but in some parts of central Liverpool, conspicuously around the Town Hall[b] it is not hard to

[b] Originally built in 1754: burnt in 1795 and rebuilt as it is now.

FIG. 24. The inset map is redrawn from a plan in Irvine, W. F., *Liverpool in King Charles the Second's time*, 1899, in *B.A. Merseyside*, 190. It shows the town on the peninsula between the open river and the inlet of the Pool, and it will be noted that St. Nicholas Chapel, now Liverpool Parish Church, was on the shore. The main map is from Part 2 of the *Report of the Commissioners appointed to report and advise upon the boundaries of certain boroughs and corporate towns*, 1837, with the extent of the much smaller city in 1790, taken from *A plan of the town of Liverpool with all the late improvements from an actual survey made in the year 1790*, published August 12, 1790 by John Gore, Liverpool, engraved by Thos. Conder (B.M. 3200(3)).

H

realize the dignity of the main parts of the eighteenth-century town. But behind the main streets there were execrable houses with the inhabited cellars that were a curse here as in Manchester. Of all the eighteenth-century developments, the most crucial was the improvement in communications by land, without which the town and the conurbation that grew from it could not have developed.

Communications

In spite of Chester's loss of trade in the fifteenth century, Liverpool long remained a small market town and port with trade drawn mainly from the immediate neighbourhood. Even the Mersey was an obstacle though Defoe,[24] on his third visit, probably in 1727, crossed by ferry from the Wirral.

> We land on the flat Shore on the other side, and are contented to ride through the Water for some Length, not on Horseback but on the Shoulders of some honest *Lancashire* Clown, who comes knee deep to the Boat side, to truss you up, and then runs away with you, as nimbly as you desire to ride . . . I was shaken . . . more than I car'd for, and much worse than a hard trotting horse would have shaken me.

Defoe notes that Liverpool was well placed to acquire the trade of North Wales and of the northern counties of Ireland and that the port could serve all the 'northern inland counties' of England as well as Cheshire and Staffordshire by improvement of the Mersey, the Weaver and the Dane rivers. Defoe[25] commented that use of the Weaver and the Dane would open a way to Hull through Burton-on-Trent. With such possibilities, and with the visible evidence of new building and commercial expansion in the existing town 'What it may grow to in time, I know not'.

The Weaver was deepened by the middle of the eighteenth century and the Sankey canal was cut from St. Helens to the Mersey and opened for trade in 1757. The Mersey and Irwell navigation was made from 1720, but before 1700 the river had been made navigable to a quay in Warrington. The Bridgewater canal from Manchester to Runcorn was opened in 1773, the Trent and Mersey (Grand Trunk) Canal in 1777; and the Leeds and Liverpool canal was opened to Wigan in 1774 but not fully completed until 1816.[26] Gradually through the latter half of the eighteenth century the position of Liverpool was strengthened by the development of water travel but movement by road was still difficult as Arthur Young constantly pointed out. In 1765 a stage-coach from London reached Liverpool for the first time and gradually inland communications were improved by the making of turnpike roads. At the end of the eighteenth century, Liverpool drew food supplies from the rich lowland that surrounds it, and by ferry from the well-farmed Wirral; coal was brought from St. Helens and Wigan by canal and river, and salt from Cheshire.[27] And all this time, as the overseas trade developed, new docks were built along the waterfront. Further, coal and salt were valuable raw materials of industry, which developed largely in association with the port not only in Liverpool but in time on the other side of the river.

Steamships and—at a later stage—railways brought further advantages to Merseyside, and made possible the industrial and residential growth in the Wirral which still continues, and is regarded by some people as a major social problem. The first steamboat on the Mersey,[28] the *Elizabeth*, arrived from the Clyde in 1815 and was used on the river from Liverpool to Runcorn and in 1816, another steamboat, the *Princess Charlotte*, was first used on the Eastham service. The Tranmere Ferry was opened in 1817, the Birkenhead ferry in 1820, the Egremont ferry and the New Brighton ferry in the eighteen-thirties.[29] Others opened by 1840 were at Seacombe, Woodside, Monks ferry (closed 1878), Rock Ferry and New Ferry. The construction of the Chester road to Woodside in 1835, and of the Chester railway to Birkenhead near Monks ferry in 1840, opened up the Wirral still more and along the shore from Rock Ferry to New Ferry the line of fine houses facing the river and known as Rock Park,[30] was built in 1836. Birkenhead developed in the early ferry days as a centre for short pleasure trips with tea-gardens and an hotel, and as early as the eighteen-thirties Oxton and some higher areas were favoured by 'carriage folk' for residential purposes. In spite of the addition of road and rail tunnels nowhere else in Britain are so many passengers carried by water, even though only the Seacombe and Woodside ferries now have full-time services, with a summer service to New Brighton.

Railways added further to the commercial strength of Liverpool. The line to Manchester was opened in 1830, at first from Edge Hill though the Lime street terminus was built in 1836 and the line was thrust through a series of tunnels and cuttings: other lines were built through tunnels for goods traffic to Wapping dock and to Waterloo dock (Fig. 25).[31] The Liverpool and Bury railway, formed in 1845 and ultimately united with others into the Lancashire and Yorkshire, has its terminus at Exchange station and the line leaves Liverpool for Wigan by a northerly route close to the Leeds-Liverpool canal for a couple of miles, and then cuts into the Walton sandstone hill.[32] The line to Southport, constructed in 1848 (and electrified in 1904), launched the town as a residential centre. Nearer to Liverpool, Waterloo and Crosby became favoured suburbs, but the development of a continuous line of suburb was happily prevented by the existence of peat mosses behind the sand dune belt. The last major railway[33] to be built was the Cheshire Lines from Central Station, in 1874, which runs partly through tunnels close to the waterfront for several miles. Although none of the railway passenger terminals are beside the docks, inspection of Fig. 25 will show that there is a series of goods stations connected with the trunk lines. The Overhead railway, opened in 1893, connected the whole line of docks as a passenger route until 1956, and beneath it there were goods lines with branches to various quays. Warehouses, docks and railway lines as well as the famous Landing Stage form the waterfront and there is easy access for the public to the river only at the Pier Head. Here, close to the old but now reconstructed Parish Church, all the tram services of the city met until they ceased to run in 1957.

Over the river, the line from Chester to Birkenhead was opened in 1840 to a station near Monks Ferry (Fig. 25). The line from Hooton to Frodsham, through Ellesmere Port, was opened in 1863, and the line from Hooton to Parkgate was added by 1866, and extended to Hoylake twenty years later.[34] The first railway to Hoylake was a narrow-gauge line from a station called 'Docks' near Wallasey Pool, with a horse tram to Birkenhead but in 1884 it was reconstructed on the standard gauge, extended to West Kirby and to a station close to the Seacombe ferry. Four years later a connexion was made to Birkenhead Park station, and so to the line through the Mersey tunnel, which was opened in 1885, and electrified in 1903. A line from Docks station to New Brighton was opened in 1886, and in 1884 the line to Connah's Quay and Hawarden and Wrexham was begun: Mr. Gladstone[35] foresaw that this line would not only save 20 miles of travel, but also ease the transport of agricultural produce to the markets of Merseyside, as well as of heavy mineral products such as stone setts, road metal, slates, coal, bricks and clay. In the Wirral, apart from the main line through Chester built by 1840, the main period of railway building was the eighteen-eighties. The ferries had opened a limited area of the Wirral to commercial expansion and residential settlement, but from 1880 to 1890 railways gave easy access to a wider area.[36] Nevertheless, apart from the suburban spread to West Kirby and to Port Sunlight, in effect the area served by the Mersey railway, most of the Wirral remained untouched until the inter-war period, when the use of private cars and motor-bus services enabled people to look farther afield for building sites.

Roads were improved during the latter half of the eighteenth century and the early part of the nineteenth when the main need appeared to be to improve transport between Manchester and Liverpool. From c. 1750 to 1830 the port development depended largely on roads and canals and with one exception the modern road system grew out of the network of country lanes, widened and straightened through the years.[37] The East Lancashire road, built during the nineteen-thirties, gave a modern trunk road from Liverpool to Manchester: smoothly graded, with cuttings and embankments, it incorporated few existing roads and runs from the northern and newer dock area of Liverpool to the north side of Manchester, passing north of St. Helens and striking through the coalfield area halfway between Wigan and Warrington. Far better suited to modern fast lorry and car traffic than the older roads, this route has now many new factories located beside it in the neighbourhood of Liverpool. Within the city, the Queen's Drive provides an excellent route through the suburbs and as Fig. 26 shows, it marks the virtual limit of the city before major housing estates of the inter-war period were built.

In Wirral, the most important route is the 'new' Chester road still attractive to residential settlement, opened in 1835 to replace an older turnpike road which as early as 1762 was reported to have three coaches daily in each direction.[38] The major curiosity of the road system is the lack of effective road or rail passenger transport across the Pool from Birkenhead to Wallasey, as the road system of northeast Wirral is focused on the Seacombe ferry. The most spectacular recent addition to the road system is the Mersey tunnel, opened in 1934, and fully used both for car and lorry traffic from Birkenhead to Liverpool, who financed its building with a government grant as agreement with Wallasey and Bootle could not be reached.[39] This tunnel, the railway tunnels and the ferries have opened up the Wirral to an expansion which threatens the countryside more and more and the new road built during the nineteen-thirties across the Gowy marshes has helped to open up the area now used for the vast Stanlow oil refinery.

Docks have been added steadily from the early part of the eighteenth century, so that there is now a line 7 miles long, broken only at the Pier Head.[40] The Salthouse dock was built from 1734 to 1753; then followed George's dock (1771), now filled in, Kings' (1781) and

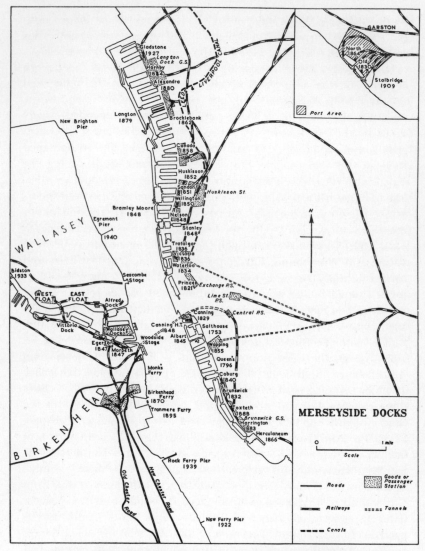

FIG. 25. THE MERSEY ESTUARY AND ITS DOCKS

The dock system has been steadily developed from the eighteenth century and until recently was served by the overhead railway: on this map the main goods service lines to the docks are shown. On the Cheshire side, the growth came with the railway, shown here: the dates of the closing of ferries are shown. See Allison, J. E., *The Mersey estuary*, 1949.

Queen's dock (1796) to the south of Salthouse dock. Prince's dock (1821) was the first addition north of the pier head: all this series was built by the corporation of Liverpool. In 1825 a new Dock Committee was formed, and many more docks were built both to the north and the south: in 1857, the Mersey Docks and Harbours Board was set up and the system was extended to Herculaneum dock (1864), cut in solid rock at Dingle point on the south, and Gladstone dock (1927) on the north, which has an entrance lock larger and wider than the biggest vessel ever built. Across the river, Morpeth dock and Egerton dock were opened in 1847 and the other docks were all added by 1870, except for Bidston dock (1933) on the extreme inner side of the Pool. The steady expansion of the main port stimulated industrial growth in the dockside area and along the Leeds–Liverpool canal (see Fig. 25). Other places on the Mersey, including Runcorn, Widnes and Warrington, acquired industries based partly on the processing of raw materials brought from Liverpool by river, canal and railway during the nineteenth century. Garston and Ellesmere Port, now within the conurbation, grew around small ports.[41] At Garston, the first dock was constructed in 1830 by the St. Helens and Runcorn Gap railway company, the North dock was added in 1869 and Stalbridge dock in 1909. Coal, coke and patent fuel are sent out to Ireland, the Isle of Man and various southwestern ports: Garston is the main coal port of the northwest. Imports include pit-props from Norway, Sweden, Finland and Russia, ores from Spain, tropical fruit—conspicuously bananas. From 1869 a number of industries developed at Garston, which now has some 2,650 workers in eleven factories, which include sawmilling, a large match works, a tannery, a bottle works, and constructional engineering in which a variety of imported ores are used. From the beginning the Garston docks have been owned and developed by the railways.

Ellesmere Port[42] arose—first as Whitby—when the Dee–Mersey (later Shropshire Union) canal was opened in 1795: in 1816 steam packet services began as part of a route from Liverpool to Chester. In the eighteen-forties iron ore was brought from Whitehaven and Ulverston to Ellesmere Port for transshipment to the Midlands, and Welsh slates, grain and china clay for the Potteries were also handled. The opening of the Hooton railway in 1863 gave a further stimulus and the 1871 Census mentions 'briskness of trade . . . in transferring cargoes from boats on the canal to vessels in the Mersey'. The first works built at the crossing of the canal by the railway was a mill where iron products manufactured in Wolverhampton were galvanized by a firm from Liverpool wanting to expand and also anxious to avoid dock charges. Three flour mills were established, into which the grain was loaded directly from lighters filled either in Liverpool docks or in the river. Later steel re-rolling was added to galvanizing, and a German firm began the manufacture of dye-stuffs, especially synthetic indigo. In the early thirties, a famous paper firm began the manufacture of newsprint here and later added the making of sacks for the sugar and flour industries of Merseyside. Other industries include the making of metal containers, chemical by-products such as road dressing, and of electrical accessories for radios and motor cars. The junction of the Shropshire Union and the Manchester Ship canals has proved an advantageous site for industrial growth, especially at Stanlow where some thousands of men are working at the oil refinery. In the later phases of the 1914–1918 war, the Gowy marshes were drained, partly by German prisoners, and in 1922 a deepwater port was built by the Ship Canal Company and the railway company so that ships of 16,000 tons could be brought in to the Stanlow docks constructed in a small hill of sandstone. At present a new dock is being made at the entrance to the Ship Canal, from which oil will be pumped directly to the Stan-low refinery. Here on the fringe of the Merseyside conurbation there is an area of marked industrial expansion, outwardly seen as a land-scape of fantastic character. It is ironic that the Manchester Ship Canal has provided the opportunity for this vast development of industry on the fringe of the Merseyside conurbation, as its construc-tion was planned partly to convey cotton cheaply to Manchester by avoiding shipment at Liverpool, an enterprise strongly opposed by the merchants of Liverpool. In fact, the canal has proved to be a stimulus to port industries rather than a lane for cotton-carrying boats to Manchester.

Population

Merseyside differs from the other provincial conurbations in one major respect—much of its growth is due to the expansion of its one large town. In the case of the West Midlands, West Yorkshire and the Manchester conurbations, there were several towns well estab-lished before the railway age, but on Merseyside, Birkenhead was insignificant before the eighteen-forties, Bootle was an industrial offshoot of Liverpool at all times indistinguishable from it to the ordinary traveller, and such places as Crosby, Huyton-Roby, Wallasey, Hoylake, and West Kirby became 'towns' in an administrative sense only through the movement to outer suburbs. The growth of outer industrial areas, conspicuously Port Sunlight, was due partly to new settlement and to the recent develpoments close to the Manchester Ship Canal. And a further recent feature is the building of new industrial estates, especially at Speke, Kirkby and Aintree.

In 1801, the population of the conurbation area was 99,000 of whom only 9,400 were living in the Wirral peninsula;[43] by 1851, the population was 469,000, of whom 57,000 were on the Cheshire side and in 1901, the population was 1,022,000, of whom 209,000 were across the river. There was a further rise to 1,347,000 in 1931, with 342,000 in the Wirral, but the increase in the next twenty years was only + 2·6 per cent, to 1,382,000, of whom a million were on the Lancashire side. The statistical story is simply told—the population multiplied fourfold within the first fifty years of the nineteenth century, then more than doubled to 1901, and increased by one-third to 1931, after which there was little change but not, it may be noted, a decrease as in the case of Tyneside or the Manchester conurbation. Although Liverpool is virtually surrounded by open country, the most remarkable feature has been the increase of population in the Wirral, from 209,000 in 1901 to 382,000 in 1951. The part of the conurbation in Lancashire, though stable in population, has lost by the decline of population in the central city wards and gained by the increases in the new housing areas and in outer suburbs. And a similar though less intense decrease is recorded in the central wards of Birkenhead and Wallasey.

Central Liverpool, which consisted of almost 3 square miles made into a registration sub-district, increased in population more than three times from 1801 to 1861 and then declined almost by half within the last forty years of the century. In 1801, the population was 77,653, in 1861, 269,742 and in 1901, 147,405: but signs of change were noted as early as 1841–1851 in the Dale street ward (from 35,861 to 31,763) through the 'removal of houses and appropriation of the sites occupied by them to railway purposes'.[44] Every ward of central Liverpool was decreasing in population by 1871 and the Census included the comment that the 'great decrease of population . . . is attributed to the demolition of old and overcrowded dwelling-houses, for effecting sanitary improvements, for the erection of offices, shops, warehouses, for the construction of a central railway station and for the formation of docks'.[45] In Liverpool, as in similar great cities, the outward movement of population began as a natural consequence of the growth of commerce, seen in the demolition of houses for shops, warehouses, railways, docks and public buildings. Nevertheless Liverpool had throughout the nineteenth century, and still has, a considerable part of its population settled close to the docks and to the city centre.

The plain fact was that central Liverpool reached saturation point in housing by 1861.[46] Meanwhile the surrounding area of the West Derby union received the overflow and increased its population from 12,000 in 1801 to 153,300 in 1851 and 666,000 in 1901. By 1871, it was noted that 'proximity to Liverpool and convenience of access thereto has led to the erection of a number of houses, especially in Toxteth Park, Everton, Walton on the Hill, Bootle cum Linacre, Great Crosby, Litherland, West Derby and Wavertree'.[47] Woolton, on its ridge grew as an outer suburb by 1841, and had 5,800 people by 1871 after which there was little change in population until the inter-war period: Woolton was one of a number of suburbs, such as Mossley Hill and Sefton Park where houses of considerable size were built. Poor, narrow streets, including some back-to-back property, gradually spread behind the dock area, though such older districts as Rodney street, Abercromby square and other Georgian or neo-Georgian areas maintained their characteristic dignity even when surrounded by poor housing. The form of Liverpool was already clear:[48] inland, to a depth of 2–3 miles, there was a vast expanse of dull streets in Kirkdale, Everton, Edge Hill and Toxteth except on the Great Heath (Abercromby square and neighbourhood) but the line of parks marked the boundary between the unrelieved sea of streets and the patchwork of house and gardens in suburbs and housing estates.

Birkenhead was in 1801 a township having 110 inhabitants within its 2 square miles: in 1821, it had only 200 people, but 2,600 in 1831 and over 8,000 in 1841. The impetus came from the activities of Mr. Laird of Greenock,[49] who founded a boiler-making and ship-building yard near Wallasey Pool in 1824. The first Birkenhead docks were the Egerton and Morpeth opened in 1847, followed by the Great Float and the Alfred dock in 1851 and the Wallasey dock in 1877. Shipbuilding and repairing remained successful, many warehouses were built and several industries attracted. The Laird shipbuilding yard spread until it occupied the whole river frontage from Woodside to Tranmere. In came the labourers, especially from Ireland, and by 1851 the population of Birkenhead was 24,300 . . . the report of the Census speaks of 'extensive improvements and

building speculations, which, combined with the facilities of communication on the Mersey, have caused it to become the residence
of a portion of the mercantile community of Liverpool'.[50] In 1847, a
park was opened covering 190 acres and designed by Joseph Paxton.[e] This park, originally marshy ground, in time marked the frontier between the artisan and residential parts of the town—for many
of the original squares and streets failed to keep their original standard. They were planned largely on a Scottish model, still perceptible
in the four-storey edifices of Hamilton square and its neighbouring
streets, which were built from 1835 to 1846.[51]

By 1871, when Birkenhead had 43,000 people, Tranmere township, immediately to the south, had 16,000, compared with 10,000 in
1861 and less than 3,000 ten years earlier. Here a similar story was
told: '. . . the increase (is) . . . attributed to the operations of land
and building societies which have been established within the last
ten years, mainly in consequence of its proximity to, and facility of
communication with Liverpool and Birkenhead'.[52] In Liscard and
Seacombe there were 7,000 in 1851 and 13,000 in 1871, compared
with less than 400 in 1801, but in the Wallasey township—that is in
much of North Wirral away from the river—growth was much
slower. The new settlement was due to 'the introduction of gas and
water works, an improved service of ferry steamers, the establishment (at Seacombe) of an iron shipbuilding yard and patent guano
works and the increase of commerce at Birkenhead docks'.[53] By
1890, there was an extensive engineering works at Birkenhead docks,
and on the Seacombe side of the Pool a fertilizer works, a sugar
refinery, oil and cake mills and oil storage tanks, with a cement
works. A sign of the quest for outer suburbs was the building of new
houses at Claughton-cum-Grange and Noctorum, west of Birkenhead, for Liverpool merchants, and even farther afield, at Meols in
the north, West Kirby, Heswall and Neston beside the Dee, and at
Great Sutton, Childer Thornton and Eastham along the Chester
road.[54] Hoylake developed first as a seabathing place[55] and the Royal
Hotel was built in 1792. New houses were built from 1835, and the
road to Birkenhead was turnpiked in 1841. By the middle of the
century some of the steam packets from Liverpool to North Wales,
especially those to Bagilt, called at Hoylake and in 1869 the Royal
Liverpool golf course was laid out on the sand dunes, but the
main development followed the building of the Mersey railway.

[e] Paxton designed the Chatsworth gardens but is most famed for the Crystal
Palace at the 1851 Exhibition.

Nevertheless the suburban destiny of the Wirral was already clear by 1871.

During the period from 1870 to the present time the development of Merseyside appeared to be revolutionary but in fact it followed trends already marked out. These included first, the outward spread of housing and industry on the Lancashire side; second, the intensification of the movement to the Wirral, which was in time stimulated by the industrial developments at Port Sunlight and Ellesmere Port; and third, the development of central Liverpool as a regional capital, having city quarters for finance, retail shopping, entertainment, administration, transport, medicine, higher education and now two great cathedrals in course of construction. The outward movement of population from the Dale street ward was noted as early as 1841–1851 (p. 109): this ward had only 12,931 people in 1891 and 9,381 by 1901. Similar decreases were recorded from all the remaining wards from 1861 in the old township[56] of Liverpool,[d] an area of c. 3 square miles, with the result that the nuclear area had 269,742 people in 1861, 238,411 in 1871, 210,164 in 1881, 156,981 in 1901 and 147,405 in 1901. Within forty years, the population had declined almost to half. Even though this process has continued with such strength that from 1931 to 1951 the population of the whole of Liverpool declined by 7·8 per cent, from 856,100 to 789,500 with decreases of as much as 50 per cent in some central wards, visitors to the city are still impressed by the amount of housing close to Lime street station or any other central point. This is partly due to a negative factor—that warehouses and factories are located primarily beside the docks rather than beside the city centre as in Manchester (p. 135) or Birmingham (p. 78). Equally important is the city's policy[57] of allowing 'municipal rehousing on an extensive scale in the central areas of the city . . .' In a description of a block of 200 five-storey flats, it has been said that 'being in close proximity to the dockyard area and large industrial concerns, the accommodation in these flats is very keenly sought'. Nevertheless, the main development since 1914 has been the building of housing estates on the margins of the city, and even beyond it in a number of large estates, conspicuously Speke. At this point it is necessary to turn to the administrative changes that have brought the whole of Merseyside under some form of town government, though as the authors of the Merseyside Survey

[d] This area, recorded as 2,200 acres to 1851 and as 2,471 acres in 1871 and 1891 (but 1,871 acres excluding tidal water and foreshore) became the Registrar's subdistrict of Liverpool.

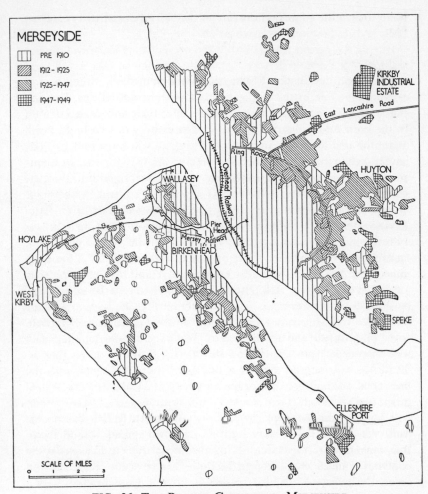

MERSEYSIDE

☐ PRE 1910
▨ 1912–1925
▨ 1925–1947
▨ 1947–1949

KIRKBY
INDUSTRIAL
ESTATE

East Lancashire Road

Ring Road

Overhead Railway

WALLASEY

HUYTON

Pier
Head

Mersey Railway

HOYLAKE

BIRKENHEAD

WEST
KIRBY

SPEKE

ELLESMERE
PORT

SCALE OF MILES
0   1   2   3

FIG. 26. THE RECENT GROWTH OF MERSEYSIDE

In spite of virtual stability of population, the territorial expansion of
Liverpool has been considerable, even though the policy is to build large
areas of flats for the many thousand workers who wish to live near the
docks. The Queen's Drive at first formed a virtual limit to the city but large
areas beyond it have been covered with houses. The Wirral peninsula has
a line of towns from Birkenhead along the Chester road, and from Birkenhead to West Kirby: elsewhere there are suburbanized villages. Ellesmere
Port claims to be an entity separate from the conurbation.

point out with regret 'there is no single authority to represent "Merseyside opinion" as a whole'.[58]

Administrative Divisions

Liverpool dominates Merseyside in commercial strength and population to an extent not general in other conurbations. Leaving the original parish, Liverpool residents built their houses in Toxteth, in the West Derby district, and along the estuary to Crosby through Waterloo and Seaforth. Inspection of Fig. 27 will show that by 1888 several urban districts had been created on the Garston side of Liverpool, but by a series of acts all these were incorporated into the city, except for Huyton-with-Roby. At the northern end, Litherland, Bootle and the area that is now Crosby M.B. remained apart from Liverpool in administration: a bill to unite Bootle with the city was rejected by the House of Lords in 1903.[59] In the Wirral peninsula, urban units were formed as various areas were settled from the early nineteenth century; of these Birkenhead C.B. and the urban districts of Wallasey, Higher Bebington, Lower Bebington, Bromborough and Neston-with-Parkgate had appeared by 1888. It was perhaps fortunate that Egremont, Seacombe, Liscard and New Brighton, were all grouped under the wing of Wallasey, an old parish which became the 'urban district' and in time the borough. Even Birkenhead was not incorporated as a borough[60] until 1877 and until the last great administrative reorganization of 1933 most of the Wirral peninsula remained 'rural' in its administration.

Liverpool was an overcrowded town in the early nineteenth century, for as new docks were built so the town spread behind them, but convenient ferry services induced some citizens to live across the water. The initial expansion to Toxteth Park, Everton, Kirkdale and West Derby gave Liverpool in 1888 an area of 8 square miles with a population that declined from 552,500 in 1881 to 518,000 in 1891.[61] Four years later four of the neighbouring urban districts, Toxteth Park, Walton-on-the-Hill, Wavertree and West Derby, were added to the city: these newly added areas had 113,400 people in 1891 compared with 73,600 ten years previously.[62] The loss from the old Liverpool was balanced by the gain in the developing suburbs, and the city as defined in 1895 covered some 21 square miles.[63] Seven years later, Garston was added (population in 1901, 17,300) and in 1905 the first rural expansion took place when Fazakerley civil parish was added.[64] The next addition, in 1913, was four urban districts in the southeast, Allerton, Childwall, Little Woolton and Much Woolton,

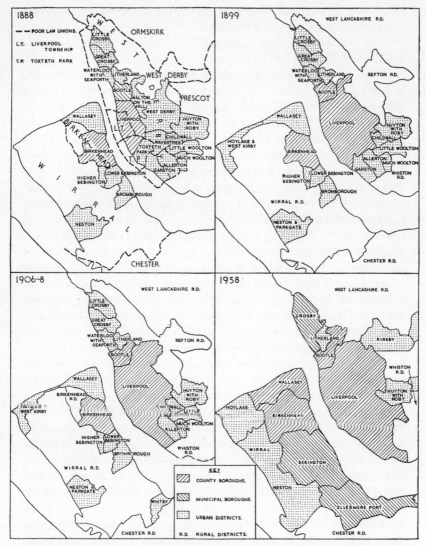

FIG. 27. Merseyside, Administrative Areas, 1888 to Present Day

Many small urban districts were added to Liverpool, but Litherland and Bootle were never absorbed. On the Cheshire side the main development gives the steady expansion of urban districts until by the middle thirties no part of the peninsula remain 'rural'. When Kirkby U.D. was instituted in 1958, its population was *c.* 30,000.

which had shown little increase in population for several decades and in 1913 had less than 8,000 people in 7 square miles, with only 144 persons in Childwall U.D.:[65] part of this area has now been used for housing but it still preserves some of the parklands and, with Mossley Hill, remains one of the pleasanter areas close to the city. In 1928, 5 square miles of territory was added in Croxteth Park and West Derby rural parish,[66] and in 1931 Speke parish, beside the river east of Garston, was added and Liverpool attained its present area of 42·7 square miles.[67]

Unfortunately, Huyton-with-Roby remained outside the city, even though over 3,000 of its houses were built by Liverpool. In 1931, there were only 5,200 people here but in 1951, there were 55,800, an increase of 973 per cent. The suggestion that the boundaries of Liverpool should be extended was opposed both by the county council and by the urban district council, and it is rumoured that a municipal borough may be created here in time.[68] Elsewhere too Liverpool is expanding beyond its present boundaries. The Kirkby estate, of 2,800 acres, which lies entirely beyond the city, with the old village as the civic centre, is planned as an industrial and housing site with 11,287 houses, of which 10,000 will be built by Liverpool and the remainder by private enterprise.[69] And some 352 acres of the Speke estate are outside the boundary, but owned by the corporation.[70] In both these areas one may see two main features: first, the attempt to make a complete unit of houses and industries (which at Speke include a large aircraft factory brought here instead of Maidenhead before the war, and numerous others), and second, the practical negation of what has been called the 'Birmingham principle' on page 87, that is, where people belong to the city they should live within its bounds. The whole of Kirkby exists as an offshoot of the city and it would seem reasonable that it should be part of it, and one could also argue that Huyton-with-Roby could well be united to Liverpool.

Bootle had an area of $2\frac{1}{2}$ square miles in 1901, and by extensions at the expense of rural areas in 1905, 1940 and 1951 it almost doubled its area.[71] Litherland's simpler story is that it consisted of 857 acres in 1901, and lost 39 acres to Bootle in 1940 so that it now has 818 acres. Each of these seems indistinguishable from Liverpool, though Litherland is on the margins and grew up partly through the industrial development beside the Leeds–Liverpool canal. Beyond them, the borough of Crosby was made in 1937 by the union of Great Crosby and Waterloo-with-Seaforth,[72] the residential area that for over eighty years has slowly expanded beside the Mersey approach, beyond the limit of the dock belt. As now constituted, it is an area of some 7 square miles inhabited by more than 50,000 people sufficiently far from the city to have a strong shopping trade of its own, the convenience of electric trains to Liverpool, and a degree of amenity that increases progressively away from the city.

In the Wirral, Birkenhead was the longest established town but by 1888 Wallasey, Bromborough, Higher Bebington, Lower Bebington, Neston and Parkgate were all recognized as urban districts. The remainder was agricultural land farmed by people living mainly on small and usually elevated driftfree sites, but there was every sign of the shape of things to come in the building of houses at various places in the peninsula, such as Eastham, Heswall, Childer Thornton and others. At Neston a colliery[73] was worked from the middle of the eighteenth century until 1927, but here too the main development was of a residential character. Industrial enterprise was most marked at Birkenhead, around the Great Float and to the south, where there were shipbuilding and repairing yards. But the most striking industrial developments[74] came first at Bromborough in 1852 and at Port Sunlight in 1887–1888. Close to Bromborough Pool, Price's Candle Company was established in 1852: the attractions included cheap land, good transport, and palm oil from Liverpool. The factory covered 10 acres, and 60 acres of housing were laid out: 'a well-built colony with allotment gardens, reading rooms, schools and recreation grounds'. The Lever family built Port Sunlight (from 1888), an area of housing similar to Bourneville. Gradually the works have been expanded until now some 8,000 people are employed here. the Bromborough docks are still used and raw materials are brought up direct to the works. The developments at Ellesmere Port are discussed below.

Developments after 1888 gradually brought all the remainder of the Wirral under town administration (Fig. 27). Hoylake and West Kirby[75] became an urban district in 1891 and was enlarged by the addition of part of Wirral R.D. in 1933; its population was 10,911 in 1901 and 30,920 in 1951. This urban district was created as West Kirby and Hoylake but the name was reversed in 1897 and in 1933 it became Hoylake U.D. Ellesmere Port[76] became an urban district (Ellesmere Port and Whitby) in 1902 and was enlarged in 1910 and 1933 by the addition of parishes from the Wirral and Chester rural districts so that it now covers 14 square miles, and has a population of 32,600 with a growing industry. The continued success of industry

I

here presages further growth, probably to 60,000 or more, and the town was raised to borough status in 1955. Both Higher and Lower Bebington were originally separate urban districts, but they were joined by houses both to each other and to Bromborough, and in 1922, all three were made into the Bebington and Bromborough urban district, which, on further extensions in 1933, covered an area of 19 square miles and was called Bebington U.D.[77] It became a borough in 1937. Birkenhead was enlarged twice, in 1928 and in 1933, and Wallasey, which became a municipal borough in 1910 and a county borough in 1913, was extended in the same years.[78] Neston and Parkgate also had their share of the Wirral R.D. in 1933, and the residue, some 9 square miles, became the urban district of Wirral.[79] In this area there was an increase of population from 5,900 in 1921 to 17,400 in 1951. Writing in 1927, Rideout[80] refers to 'those nebulous, semi-suburban, semi-rural wastes which occupy so much of Wirral . . .' He adds: 'It cannot be long before the extensions from Liverpool and its satellites in the north, Ellesmere Port in the east, and Chester on the south, spread over what remain the most delightful rural townships in all Wirral.' From 1931 to 1951, the number of structurally separate dwellings within the conurbation increased by 24 per cent[81] and it is estimated that some 20 square miles will be required for new urban development on modern standards.[82] 190,500 people in Lancashire, of whom 147,000 are in Liverpool and 35,000 in Bootle, need new homes and 67,550 on the Cheshire side, including 38,000 in Birkenhead and 27,300 in Wallasey, have similar social claims. Allowing for industries, for an increase in the number of families and for some suburban development of a more open character than in housing estates, the requirement of land is 12 square miles of Lancashire and 8 square miles of Cheshire. These provisions are based on the assumption that no considerable increase of population is likely in the near future. Elevated sites in the Wirral have long been favoured for residential purposes. Over a century ago Oxton and other pleasant places had the homes of men who were taken to the ferry or the railway station by carriage day by day, and at Heswall, prosperous business men built large houses in extensive grounds, rejoicing in a good drift-free and well-drained site with a view of the North Wales hills. In some Wirral villages the suburbanization is recent and due to the 'opening up' provided by bus services. Wirral U.D., for example, includes the old centre of Heswall, and three other villages that have grown only recently, Barnston, Pensby and Irby. Hoylake U.D. has its two well-established centres, but inter-war houses have been added around the villages of Frankby and Greasby. It is unlikely that the whole of the Wirral peninsula will be engulfed by housing but there are obvious dangers in haphazard suburban growth.

The 1950 Census of retail trade shows that the Merseyside conurbation had average sales of £111 per head, less than the average for the country (£124) or for the other conurbations.[83] Of the total amount received by shops and certain service establishments, £118,370,000 is taken on the Lancashire side and £35,912,000 in the Wirral. Liverpool's retail trade was valued at £98,650,000, an average of £122 which is comparatively low for a regional capital but the city lost heavily through war damage in its shopping quarters. Crosby borough, with retail sales of £11,103,000 had average sales per head of £186, but a strongly developed retail trade is found elsewhere in places on the edge of a conurbation (cf. pp. 73,144). Litherland and Bootle, both in effect parts of industrial Liverpool, have retail sales averaging only c. £70 a head, and Huyton-with-Roby has only £38 as its shops consist of little more than groups in housing estates supplying daily needs.

On the Cheshire side many features comparable to those already noted are seen. Only two places, Birkenhead (£113) and Hoylake (£116) have an expenditure per head similar to the national average: Birkenhead is the oldest-established of the towns here and Hoylake U.D. which includes West Kirby, has the advantage of relative remoteness from Liverpool, and a comparatively wealthy population. Wallasey's shopping quarters have been described as 'groups of shops in the old village centres such as Wallasey, Seacombe, Liscard and New Brighton':[84] the sales per head average £81. And the figures for the remaining administrative units are similar— Bebington M.B., £66, Ellesmere Port U.D., £86, Neston U.D., £71, and Wirral U.D., £77. But it is not only Liverpool that attracts purchasers from the suburban areas of the Wirral for in Chester the 1950–1951 takings were £15,383,000, an average of £317 for each inhabitant.[e] Clearly much of this trade comes in from areas outside the town including the rural areas and the industrial areas of Flintshire: but some of the trade of this unusually attractive town, so fortunate in its shopkeepers, is also drawn from the Wirral, especially

[e] In 1953, Chester was united to Hoole, population, 9,113, retail sales, £452,000, an average of £48 a head. The combined figure for the enlarged Chester is: population, 57,793, sales, £15,835,000: average per head, £285. And an apt comparison is perhaps seen in Birkenhead, population, 143,150, sales, £16,167,000, average £113.

as bus services are frequent and from many places the journey to Chester is easier than that to Liverpool.[f]

Land Use

Liverpool main centre, within a short distance of the pier head, is extremely well-defined, for the area of the mediaeval town is now covered with offices, some of which have several storeys, where merchants, shipowners, solicitors, accountants and many more have premises close to those of banks and insurance firms.[85] The only shops in this business core are stationers, office furnishers or those in men's trades such as tobacconists, hairdressers, tailors and out-fitters. There is good transport to the Wirral peninsula by the underground railway, and to Southport or intermediate places from Exchange station. Such a business core is characteristic of other large cities but rarely so well marked, possibly because much of its life is associated with the river and port. Indeed, the Liver Building, located so prominently beside the river, seems to visitors the symbol of the city. Immediately beyond the business core, the main shopping area of the city covers a number of streets 'over the Pool' in streets first laid out in the eighteenth century, with an outlying shopping area in London road, that is along the road to Prescot where the city has had its greatest inland extension.

Although the commercial and the shopping quarters are well-defined, the administrative area has no such clear definition. St. George's Hall, the Walker Art Gallery and the Picton Library form a dignified group of buildings but the Town Hall and the general post office are in the business quarter and many major offices are scattered through the city centre. As in most towns, the expansion of national and local administration has made problems of lebensraum. The entertainment area is well defined for since the eighteenth century theatres have existed close to the major shops and the large cinemas are here too. Marginal to all these central areas there are the three great railway stations, Lime Street, Central and Exchange, with the chief hotels close by. As a whole the central area of Liverpool has become a reasonably compact and integrated unit, less marred by the immediate presence of industry than similar areas in other towns, but this has been achieved only by radical changes in land use, con-

---

[f] Southport is also a competitor with Liverpool for occasional shoppers: its population is 85,500, retail trade, £14,149,000, average, £166. Holiday towns normally have a stronger retail trade than others but Southport draws a certain amount of trade from the industrial areas of central Lancashire.

spicuously the withdrawal of people from the city centre and the building of offices, shops and other premises on the sites of abandoned houses.

In the stately late eighteenth and early nineteenth century 'Blooms-bury' of Liverpool, the university, hospitals, the new cathedrals and numerous institutions, have gradually acquired land used for housing or in some cases occupied existing houses that passed through an intermediate state of sub-letting in flats. Parts of this area have sunk to the tenement status but the eventual destiny of the area appears clearly to be a kind of ecclesiastical, intellectual and medical enclave in the city. The rapid population growth of the nineteenth century was marked by the addition of houses in endless dreary streets, and the erection of larger homes for the well-to-do at Mossley Hill, Woolton, the fringes of the parks and other relatively distant places. Fig. 26 shows that before the 1914–1918 war, Liverpool was a compact town, almost entirely within the line of the Inner Ring road and of the parks 2–3 miles from the Pier Head, except for extensions along the railway line towards Aintree but the built-up area is now almost twice as large. In the outer area the population doubled from 1911 to 1931, and again in the following twenty years.

Factories and warehouses are grouped into a number of fairly coherent zones.[86] Along the waterfront, many of the factories deal with imported commodities in sugar-refining, oil-seed crushing, newsprint manufacture and oil-refining, and the warehouses are intended primarily for the bulk storage of commodities. Flour milling, once prominent in Liverpool, is now concentrated on the Cheshire side. Other industries such as leather tanning and cattle food manufacture, are still located advantageously in the dockside belt, but others have been moved to new premises away from the river. There is a line of nineteenth-century industries along the Leeds and Liverpool canal, but this belongs essentially to the dockside belt. Garston also has port industries, though separated by some 4 miles from the main dock system. The second major industrial areas are around Edge Hill and Old Swan, and Fazakerly and Aintree, where a complex of railway lines and marshalling yards gives excellent communications including in some cases tracks run straight into the factory premises. The industries here are varied and include those connected with food, such as biscuits, sweets and jam, or with metals, such as tin boxes, metal toys and telephones and others such as rayon, rubber, soap and polishes. The third major industrial areas are the new trading estates at Speke and Kirkby, where the diverse products include manufactured rubber goods, metal safes and non-ferrous metals, parts of vehicles and vehicle assembly, industrial chemicals, medical preparations, fine chemicals, paints and furniture, cardboard boxes and paper bags.[87] The Speke industrial estate (1955), though not complete, had thirty-seven firms with 13,000 workers, including 5,500 women and girls.[88] 57 per cent of the workers were in miscellaneous industries, mostly small but including one rubber factory with 6,000 employees, 18 per cent in light engineering, with one firm having 1,200 workers making hydraulic brakes and aircraft components, 16 per cent in chemicals notably penicillin and other medical supplies, 7 per cent in printing and allied trades, and the rest mainly in electrical trades. Some of the firms in these estates have migrated from central Liverpool in order to expand, but others are new concerns. And the locational advantage now lies in good road rather than rail communications. Lastly, there are still some work-shops close to the city centre, housed in back streets close to the main central shopping quarter and also near to London road, which include premises for tailoring and making-up trades, and those of furniture makers and upholsterers.[89]

Merseyside in Cheshire has a pattern of land use not unlike that described above, but with certain differences. There are three main industrial areas, all of them associated originally with access by water. The first of these, Wallasey Pool, has still a maritime character in its industrial life with such industries as ship repairing and flour milling; the second, Bromborough Pool, was chosen as the site of a candle factory in 1852 because supplies of raw material could easily be brought from Liverpool; the third, at Ellesmere Port, now depends largely on the import of raw materials along the canal, and here the expansion of the new Stanlow oil refinery as well as of other in-dustries presages further growth of population. Port Sunlight began when Mr. Lever came from Warrington in 1887–1888 in search of cheap land and began to develop what has now become a wide range of industries but still includes soap and seed-crushing: some of the raw materials are brought to the private docks at Bromborough.[90]

As a residential area, Wirral consisted in 1914 chiefly of Birken-head, which was also partly industrial, of the various places which had merged to form Wallasey, of the Bebington suburbs, and of the places on or near the Dee shore, Hoylake, West Kirby, Heswall, Parkgate and Neston. By 1951, some of the inner areas of Birkenhead and Wallasey were already declining in population and in need of new houses for those in sub-standard houses. Fig. 26 shows clearly that though the post-1918 expansion of housing was considerable, so substantial a rural residue remains that purists might even wonder whether the 1951 definition of the Conurbation was not too wide (on the Fawcett scheme). The real problem is to prevent in the future the type of development so prevalent during the inter-war period, in which a couple of suburban roads were run off here and there into an essentially agricultural landscape.

Conclusion

Through most of the literature on Merseyside, there runs the assumption that although new industries are needed in Liverpool with its bleak record of unemployment in the nineteen-thirties and danger signs in the post-war period[g], the industries on the Cheshire side may expand all too quickly. On the other hand, no great increase of population is to be expected though more homes will be needed both as flats in the city and houses on the outskirts. Inevitably the onslaught on the farmlands continues; through Huyton, there is now continuous building to Prescot (and thence to St. Helens), and when Speke is complete there will be little break between the houses there and those at Widnes. On the Cheshire side there are fears that Ellesmere Port may link up with the expanding and prosperous town of Chester, and that housing may spread along the whole length of road from Birkenhead. In Lancashire, it is perhaps fortunate that physical features prevent the growth of a continuous line of suburbs along the railway line to Southport.

[g] The spread of football pools has given employment to thousands of female workers in Liverpool.

CHAPTER 5

THE MANCHESTER CONURBATION

OFFICIALLY this conurbation is listed under the title Southeast Lancashire, but as it spreads deep into Cheshire this title seems unfortunate. All the other provincial conurbations spread into at least two counties, but in other cases it has been found possible to avoid the use of county names. As Manchester is the undoubted regional capital for the whole of the area now to be considered and also for a wider area beyond it, the choice of the present title seems reasonable. Hard to name, the conurbation is equally hard to define: C. B. Fawcett, in 1932, covered much the same area as that included in 1951 but with the addition of two urban districts in Yorkshire, Springhead and Saddleworth in the upper part of the Tame valley.[1] The various industrial villages of this valley are so close to the remainder of the conurbation that there appears to be almost uninterrupted building for several miles along the main railway line, but there are such extensive rural enclaves to the east of Oldham, Lees, Ashton and Stalybridge, that the landscape, though dotted with industrial villages, is hardly of the normal conurbation type. Similar difficulties arise on the north, between Bury and Ramsbottom, for houses are spread along the main roads as ribbon-like industrial villages. Both the Rossendale and Pennine valleys have numerous old factory villages. On the west side it seems to the present writer that Horwich and Westhoughton, both included, are not more closely linked to the conurbation by continuous building than Tyldesley and Atherton, which were not included but some form of compromise was inevitable. On the other hand, the steady expansion of housing estates around the various towns, even those now declining in population, is making the fusion of the built-up areas even more certain. Already there is little break in main-road settlement from Manchester to Wigan, from Wigan to St. Helens, and from St. Helens to Liverpool. Patrick Geddes' original definition of the whole of south Lancashire as one conurbation, Lancaston,[2] therefore seems an interesting but frightening probability in the course of time. But due west of Eccles, Chat Moss and Barton Moss limit the built-up area, and on the south side of the Ship canal, Carrington Moss is a similar area of reclaimed peatbog now richly farmed. On the south side there is a reasonably clear frontier between the built-up area and rural Cheshire.

Historically the Mersey is the boundary between Lancashire and Cheshire, but this was changed in 1901 and in 1913 when Stockport acquired areas north of the river, and in 1930 when four parishes covering nearly 9 square miles, were absorbed into Manchester as Wythenshawe.[3] Except at Stockport where mills cluster round the river and its tributary the Goyt, the wide flood-plain of the Mersey interposes a natural green belt still liable to occasional flooding in spite of constant attention by the river board. This green belt is used largely for pasture and golf courses, but to the east of Stockport there are some attractive stretches of river scenery, with the streams meandering through narrow floodplains and gorges. In this south-eastern part of the conurbation, industrial villages and hamlets have grown around mills using the water-power of swiftly-flowing streams in valleys separating Pennine ridges 700–1,000 ft. high. Ironically this southeastern area possesses the most interesting natural scenery of the conurbation yet it is hardly the most favoured residential district, largely because it is swept by the smoke of the industrial towns of the lowland to the west, though in Marple, Disley, Romiley, Bredbury and Woodley residential areas are overlaid on the old mill villages.

Manchester workers have settled deep in Cheshire during the past hundred years. As shown on pp. 136–8, the opening of railways led to the growth of a number of outlying towns and villages, such as Altrincham and Sale, Cheadle, Gatley, Cheadle Hulme and Bramhall, of which all except the first two are suburban also to Stockport. In the southeast there are suburban sprawls of a sadly unplanned type, characteristic of the inter-war years and earlier phases of building, having houses for people from numerous industrial towns. The southern limit of the conurbation is best marked at Bowdon and Hale but building continues at Wilmslow, Alderley Edge, Bramhall and Cheadle Hulme. Before 1914 there were ribbons of settlement along the railway lines to Altrincham and to Wilmslow, but the intervening wedge, due south of central Manchester, showed little suburban growth, except at Northenden. It was this wedge of agricultural country, therefore, that was acquired by Manchester for re-housing, and became Wythenshawe. The conurbation[4] now extends into Cheshire to a depth of 5 miles from the Mersey at Bowdon, Hale, and Wythenshawe, to a depth of 7 miles at Alderley Edge, and about 4 miles at Bramhall. The figures given in the 1951

Census show that of 777,000 occupied people in the conurbation, only 41,000 (3·3 per cent) live outside it and only 22,000 (1·8 per cent) go from areas within the conurbation to work elsewhere:[5] this suggests that in its present form the conurbation is reasonably well defined.

Site and Situation

Manchester and Salford developed as towns on either side of the Irwell, in the centre of the lowland bounded by the Rossendales to the north and the Pennines to the east. Both the Rossendales and the Pennines are made up of Carboniferous beds, among which Millstone grits form plateau-like summits, normally 1,300–1,500 ft. above sea level. Seen from a distance, the Rossendales appear as a range of smooth-topped hills, cut by a number of deep valleys thought to be partly moulded by glacifluvial waters, through which there are easy communications for road and rail. There are also some easy routes through the Pennines, including that from Rochdale to Todmorden used by road, railway and canal, and the much-used line to Leeds by the Tame valley. The main line to Sheffield by the Etherow valley to the Woodhead tunnel is now electrified to carry the heavy coal imports from Yorkshire. The Rossendales divide the coalfield of Lancashire into two parts, of which that to the south extends from Stalybridge to Prescot: coal seams have existed, or in places still exist beneath parts of the northern towns of the conurbation, including Rochdale, Bury and Bolton. The coal measures dip steeply southwards and westwards beneath newer rocks but the present trend is for the construction of deep and big mines of which one—at Bradford—is within the city of Manchester. In much of the area, past mining has left the scars of old spoilbanks and pitheads but the problem of derelict land is less severe here than in the Black Country. A much more serious menace is subsidence due to mining, conspicuously in Oldham and in Bolton, but many of the newer colliery workings are at such a depth that with modern methods of mining the subsidence will not have serious effects. On the south, the Triassic beds are largely covered with glacial sands, gravels and clays, which offer possible building sites except in certain valleys and on small areas of mossland.

As gathering grounds for water, both the Pennines and the Rossendales have been and are still of great significance. Ogden[6] showed in a classic paper that the location of the cotton industry in the east of Lancashire, and neighbouring areas of Cheshire, Derbyshire and Yorkshire, was due largely to the existence of plentiful supplies of soft water collected in reservoirs varying from mere ponds to the fleet of artificial lakes in the Woodhead valley built for Manchester. Chemical methods of water-softening now enable cotton to be finished elsewhere but as the industry has been contracting for thirty years, it still retains its original location with little change. For bleach and dye-works, as well as for cotton mills, a stream-side location has been favoured from the eighteenth century.

Streams break up the lowland into a number of interfluves which to the north are rolling and in places sufficiently irregular to provide difficult building sites. In the north various residential districts, such as Broughton and Cheetham Hill (once fashionable but now decayed) are on high ground above the Irwell and the remoter and more modern Prestwich is on a similar site. On the south side of the city centre the surface is virtually flat and in the absence of natural obstacles the street pattern was at first rectangular and then acquired the various curves that were regarded as desirable. And similarly in Stretford and Urmston, no natural features prevent the development of the town as on a draughtsman's board up to the limit of the Mersey floodplain. In Cheshire too the towns have developed mainly on low-lying sites, but in Altrincham, Bowdon and Hale, as H. B. Rodgers has shown,[7] a ridge of glacial sands at 150–200 ft. has the greater part of the substantial housing. Conditions are similar in Cheadle, Gatley and Bramhall, and in the southeast of the conurbation suburban housing is placed on the higher ground, for example at Gee Cross, a suburb of Hyde, and at Hurst, Ashton-under-Lyne.

Manchester's centrality in the conurbation is apparent from a glance at the map: a Roman road went through it and the main London–Carlisle road (A6) still passes through the very centre. Some have spoken of this centrality as due to the convergence of numerous streams from the hills to the north and east but roads avoid the valleys of these streams and it is rather the convergence of easy routes across the interfluves that gave the town its early importance as a meeting place. Long served by roads, Manchester owed much to river navigations and canals, including the Irwell navigation, the famous Bridgewater canal built to carry coal from a mine at Worsley, and especially the canals that went through the hills to Yorkshire. Railways were attracted at an early date and here, as in Birmingham, the naturally favourable position was strengthened by both canal and railway building. But the final and most valuable addition was the Ship canal, opened in 1894, which made Manchester into an ocean

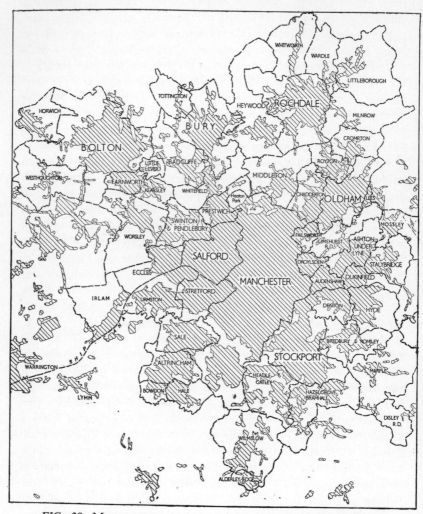

FIG. 28. MANCHESTER, BUILT-UP AREA, EARLY NINETEEN-FIFTIES

FIG. 28. Apparently there are numerous gaps in the north part of the conurbation but some have been filled up in the past three or four years and others are difficult sites due to mining subsidence. The dangers of ribbon growth are clear.

port—though oddly enough the canal's main terminal docks are in Salford.

Historical

Manchester had a Roman fort on a sandstone bluff at Knott Mill, the south end of Deansgate:[8] the Roman road from London to Chester corresponded closely to the present A6, and went through Derby and Buxton with a connecting road to Chester. But there is no clear evidence of continuous occupation and in Norman times the sandstone bluff at the north end of Deansgate became the main part of a trading town which acquired a weekly market and a fair: a charter for the market was given in 1301 and the fair probably dates from 1227, though there may have been earlier markets. Manchester became the centre of a parish covering 60 square miles,[9] with a daughter-church at Ashton but in the thirteenth century Salford acquired a charter and became a separate borough.[10] Although Manchester grew into a more vigorous trading town than its neighbour, Salford has remained unabsorbed to this day. Here at the very heart of the conurbation there is a striking example of one of its major problems—the administrative division into a number of separate units.

Slowly the mediaeval town grew. In 1538, Leland found it 'the fairest, best builded, quickest and most populous town of all Lancashire'[11] and Camden at the end of the sixteenth century found that 'it surpassed all the towns hereabouts in its building, populousness, market place and church'.[12] By the sixteenth century, the trading activity of Manchester was considerable: here linen fabrics, woven partly from Irish yarn, and woollen goods too were collected and sent to Liverpool, Chester, Hull and London for export.[13] And from the first half of the seventeenth century, Manchester merchants dealt in the woollen goods manufactured in the east of the county (the part nearest to Yorkshire), in the fustians made to the north deep into Rossendale, and in the linen manufactured in the Ribble valley and other parts of Lancashire.[14] Basically the trade of the town was in textiles, of which cotton was first introduced and treated in mixtures with flax about 1600: although cotton eventually predominated here, wool, linen, silk and—in recent times—synthetic fibres such as rayon and nylon have been used in various ways.

Defoe found Manchester[15]

one of the greatest, if not the greatest ever Village in England. It is neither a wall'd Town, City or Corporation; they send no Members to

Parliament; and the highest Magistrate they have is a Constable or Headborough; and yet it has a Collegiate Church, several Parishes, takes up a large space of Ground, and, including the Suburb, or that part of the Town called . . .*a* over the Bridge; it is said to contain about fifty thousand people.

Defoe goes on to explain that the trade had recently increased very much, that a fine new church (St. Ann's) had recently been built, but he adds that the government was inadequate for the needs of so large a town. Much of the industry was domestic, but there was cotton manufacture in Bolton—'nothing remarkable in this town'[16]— but in Bury, 'a small market town on the River Roch', cotton manufacture was replaced by the manufacture of coarse woollens 'called half-thickes and kersies'.[17] And the surrounding villages were also busily engaged in similar manufactures. At Rochdale, woollen goods were made also . . . 'the market for them is very great, tho' otherwise the Town is situated so remote, so out of the Way, and so at the very Foot of the Mountains that we may suppose it would be but little frequented'.[18]

Long before the period commonly called 'the Industrial Revolution', industry was firmly established in the Manchester area. But from the middle of the eighteenth century the cotton industry became more strongly entrenched here than anywhere else as there were a number of factors favourable to the industry: of these not the least significant was the abundant supplies of soft water, tapped in large numbers of private reservoirs for the mills.[19] Water from the Millstone grit formation of the Pennines was more suitable for cotton than the harder water from the Triassic rocks of the lowland: it was also more abundant as the high rainfalls of the Pennines (50–60 in. and more) gave a sure supply of stream water, used not only for washing the cotton but also for driving the water-wheels. The high humidity of southeast Lancashire has often been regarded as a favourable factor because it lessened the tendency of the fibre to break; and humid conditions inside the mills are generally regarded as good. But most of Lancashire is equally humid as Ogden demonstrated, and the localization of cotton here was due rather to a less direct influence—the plentiful existence of water for power and processing.[20] And when steam engines were introduced, the area maintained—even strengthened—its commercial power for there was coal available in considerable quantity.

a Presumably Salford. Possibly Defoe would have been helped by a secretary to look up the details he missed.

Communications

In its present form the communications system of the conurbation seems highly complicated, for there are numerous canals that are partially or wholly derelict, a complex system of railways that lead to Manchester's four passenger stations and other goods stations, and a road network that, though including a number of excellent modern trunk routes, such as the East Lancashire road, still appears to belong largely to a more leisured age. All the planners regard a number of new roads as essential to the conurbation; but until the East Lancashire road was built, the road to Liverpool followed a modernized series of country lanes used from mediaeval times.[21] Many of the new housing schemes have incorporated modern roads, notably the parkways of Wythenshawe, which are not only attractive in appearance but finely designed for a large volume of traffic. Wythenshawe depends entirely on road transport for the conveyance of its workers and the problem of the time involved has been solved partly by providing express bus ('limited stop') services. On the railways, electrification was limited to the lines from Manchester to Bury and to Altrincham until 1954, when the line to Glossop and Sheffield was also electrified.

The first navigation in the district was the Mersey and Irwell, which was already used to Warrington at the beginning of the eighteenth century: under an act of 1720 further improvements were made between Manchester and Liverpool.[22] The Bridgewater canal was planned shortly before 1760, and was much admired by Arthur Young ten years later,[23] who thought it an ingenious idea to drain surplus water from the mine at Worsley and make it into a canal at the same time. The canal crossed the Irwell at Barton by an aqueduct 200 yards long and 36 ft. wide and the Mersey at Sale by a bridge of one span 70 ft. long. The carriage of goods by road cost 40*s.* a ton but on the river-navigation from Manchester to Liverpool only 12*s.* a ton, and half this sum on the Bridgewater canal.[24] Love noted[25] that the canal transport 'lowered the price of coals in Manchester to half its previous amount, and supplied a speedy, cheap, and regular channel of communications between that town and its port'. Passenger boats also ran along the canal, '. . . two elegant passage-boats between Manchester and Runcorn daily'. The boat left Manchester at 8 a.m. and reached Runcorn at 4 p.m.[26]

In 1794 the Rochdale canal from Sowerby Bridge to Manchester through Todmorden was sanctioned in parliament but it was not formally opened until 1804. At Littleborough there was a branch to Rochdale.[27] Meanwhile acts of 1792 and 1793 sanctioned the building of the Ashton canal which runs parallel to the Tame, passes through Stalybridge and Saddleworth to the famous Standedge tunnel, to connect with the Huddersfield canal.[28] In the same decade, a canal to Bolton and Bury was planned under an act[29] of 1791. By the turn of the century, the rising manufacturing towns were linked to Manchester and a number of other canals and branches were also dug, so that in 1797, Aiken[30] could comment on the marvels of the age:

> At the beginning of this century it was thought a most arduous task to make a *highroad* practicable for carriages over the hills and moors which separate Yorkshire from Lancashire; and now they are pierced through by *three navigable canals!* Long may it remain the centre of a trade capable of maintaining these mighty works!

And it was also commented that Manchester was as well provided as any commercial town in the Low Countries. Interest in canals declined when the prospectus for the Manchester–Liverpool railway was issued in October 1824, and it was not for sixty years that a ship canal scheme was taken seriously again.[31]

On September 15, 1830, the railway from Manchester to Liverpool was opened from a terminus in Liverpool road which is now used as a goods station.[32] In 1838, Salford was linked with Bolton and in the following year, the Manchester and Leeds railway, later the Lancashire and Yorkshire, was built from a station in Oldham road, now a goods depot only.[33] In 1839 the line reached Littleborough and in 1840 the line from Leeds reached Hebden Bridge, and the whole route was opened in 1841.[34] Meanwhile a link was made to London, for in 1842 the Manchester and Birmingham railway through Stockport and Crewe southwards was opened from Store street,[35] which later became the well-known London road. From this same terminus the Sheffield and Lincolnshire railway began its difficult course and the Woodhead tunnel 5,300 yards long (used for over a century) was opened in 1845.[36] Four years later the line to Huddersfield through the Tame valley and Standedge tunnel was completed, and in 1849 the locally-important line to Altrincham was completed.[37] Other lines were added later, but one effect of the intricate commercial organization was that as early as 1842 Manchester had four terminal stations, one each for Liverpool, Bolton, Leeds and London. Exchange station dates from 1844 and Victoria from 1845, but both were enlarged later and linked by a long connecting platform:

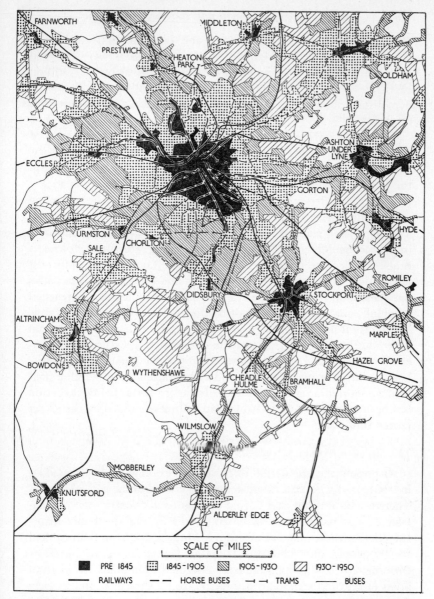

FIG. 29. THE EXTENSION OF SETTLEMENTS IN MANCHESTER AND DISTRICT

The conurbation grew to its present extent by the addition of houses around manufacturing towns and villages. Some of these towns, notably Oldham, Ashton, Stockport, Altrincham and others not shown have remained, indeed become very strong local centres. Each period has its own transport: the horse-buses were noted in Love's guide (1842). The recent expansion on the south is clearly shown here.

Thanks are due to Mr. H. B. Rodgers, M.A., who prepared this map and allowed its reproduction here.

K

Central Station was begun in 1867 and London road maintained from the beginning.[38] Originally small, the stations were enlarged at various times and the approaches were extended by the addition of engine sheds, sidings and all the other essentials of railways by demolishing houses—a form of slum clearance due to economic factors.

Canal and railway building opened this district for the marked commercial expansion of the second half of the nineteenth century. Towns that had seemed to Defoe and others remotely situated in the Pennines with hills brooding darkly over them, were no longer remote, for their supplies of water and coal, and their expanding textile mills attracted workers from the countryside and from Ireland. This expansion stamped upon these towns the apparently indelible imprint of middle and late Victorian building, with small houses in drab straight streets, the stark chapels of a largely Nonconformist population, the pseudo-Gothic churches and the utilitarian factories and workshops.[39] And so many of the Lancashire towns had reached their full economic development by the end of the century and grew hardly at all in population afterwards, many of them have changed little since then. The origins of the commercial greatness of South-east Lancashire are rooted in the activity of the domestic industries, but the effective use of canals and railways made the development of the conurbation certain. In its full modern form, the conurbation has been made by an outward spread of housing aided by the use of motor transport.

The nineteenth-century conurbation

At present the population of the conurbation is 2,421,000 (1951); in 1801, so far as can be estimated, the same area had 322,000.[40] There are indications that during the eighteenth century the population of Lancashire had increased markedly and probably quadrupled: in 1801, the townships of Manchester and Salford had 84,000 people, more than the 78,000 of Liverpool or the 74,000 of Birmingham. Flourishing industry attracted immigrants from rural areas of England, including leadminers from Derbyshire and paupers from the south[41] and the Irish[42] too—by 1841, the 30,304 Irish-born in Manchester numbered more than one-tenth of the city's people and in neighbouring towns, such as Salford, Stockport, Dukinfield and Ashton-under-Lyne, the Irish-born numbered more than 5 per cent of the population.[43] In time many handloom weavers became town-living factory workers. During the first fifty years of the nineteenth century, natural increase was marked with considerable immigration[44]—1801–1811, + 25 per cent, 1811–1821, + 29 per cent, 1821–1831, + 35 per cent, 1831–1841, + 25 per cent, 1841–1851, + 20 per cent. The whole area now covered by the conurbation had 1,063,000 people by 1851 and the growth was heavy not only in Manchester, Salford and other cotton towns but also in outlying places,[45] including those near the new railway stations in Cheshire, such as Altrincham, Sale and Cheadle.

In the eighteen-forties the cotton and other textile industries were concentrated in factories though domestic working survived. The first 6 in. to 1 mile maps issued show that cotton was the dominant industry in the area, both in the towns and outside them, for many mills were on sites beside streams or adjacent to private reservoirs.[46] Bleach and dye works, and 'print works' were placed beside rivers and there were various 'tenter grounds' where the cloth was stretched and dried. Many of the mills and works were located outside the towns and villages far from any houses and the mill-owner who added cottages under the shadow of the mill at least removed the strain of a long daily walk to work. Rapidly the population increased, and rapidly new houses were built: Ashton[47] has drawn attention to the character of the new housing in this 'barrack of industry'.

> The rapid natural increase of population was intensified by the influx of migrants from the rural areas and from across the Irish sea. No town could build quickly enough to provide the proper homes for the new comers. They crowded into the houses that the middle classes vacated as they moved to the green fields and purer air of the outskirts. They packed into cellar dwellings along the banks of the Irwell and Medlock—open sewers that bore to the sea the refuse of many towns on a stream so slow that the sparrows could find footing on the filth that encrusted its surface.

Manchester had warehouses and factories in the city, and other factories along the rivers and canals, almost inextricably mixed up with houses.[48] The 'Manchester steel works' at Newton Heath, the ironworks at Gorton, the iron foundries or ironworks at Oldham, Rochdale, Bury, Bolton and Dukinfield, all indicate the growth of the metallurgical trades that now survive more effectively than the textile industries. Woollen mills were located primarily in the Rochdale area, including outlying places such as Shaw Clough, Whitworth, Littleborough, Wardle and Milnrow, and there were also two woollen mills at Bury and one 'wool and cotton' mill. Paper was manufactured in works on the rivers at Bolton, Farnworth and

Bury, and bleaching was prominent also on various streams flowing from the Rossendales, for example on the Irwell at Bury, on the Croal and Tonge at Bolton, on the Irwell at Radcliffe and Whitefield, and on the Roch at Rochdale. By the middle of the nineteenth century the textile industry, in varied forms, was strongly established in factories throughout most of the area now covered by the Manchester conurbation. In the Oldham area, for example, there were several cotton mills and small coal pits, and in Lees too there were cotton mills. At Shaw, to the north, there were six cotton mills with others in the neighbourhood and there were several in Royton. Middleton had numerous cotton mills with print and dyeworks on various rivers and streams, and Rhodes had a calico print works and a bleach works. Two small places, Birch and Top of Hebers, have survived little changed as mill villages to this day. In the southwest, Stockport already had its numerous mills beside the Mersey and other towns of this area, such as Ashton, Denton and Stalybridge were thriving cotton centres: hat making was established in Stockport, Oldham and Denton.

In the middle of the nineteenth century the conurbation's population was 1,063,000 (1851), but within the next fifty years the number was doubled, to 2,149,000, of whom 1,930,000 were in Lancashire. The outward movement of population, made possible by the railways and by the horse omnibuses to the suburbs, began in earnest, with the result that practically all the outer residential districts of Manchester have a nucleus of Victorian houses, public buildings and

FIG. 30. Made by personal observation, this map covers some 350 acres in the centre of the city, between the major railway stations, Exchange, Victoria, London road (not shown, but a short distance east of Piccadilly) and Central. There is hardly a house surviving within this area but there are numerous churches and other public buildings. The warehouse quarter interpenetrates with the main office quarter towards the heart of the city and with the factory belt on its outer margins: many of the shops, except for larger stores near Piccadilly and in Deansgate, are small and not a few have offices on the upper floors. The main office quarter lies between the Town Hall and Market street, especially in the narrow streets close to (Upper) King street which has several major banks. These office streets commonly have small shops, especially men's hairdressers, stationers, tobacconists and cafés on the ground floor. Rebuilding is now covering the bombed areas with large blocks, some of as many as eighteen storeys: a notable addition is the 'northern Whitehall'. There are some fine buildings in the city centre, but they suffer from their impregnation with soot and from their enclosure by other property of less architectural merit. The boundary between Manchester and Salford follows the river Irwell, but the main shopping and commercial quarter is entirely on the Manchester side.

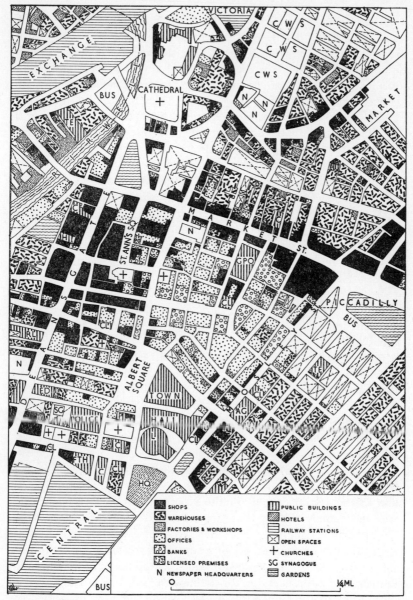

FIG. 30. PRESENT LAND USE IN CENTRAL MANCHESTER

AG, Art Gallery; C, Cinema; CL, Club; CWS, Co-operative Wholesale Society; ED, Education offices; FTH, Free Trade Hall; H, Public Hall; L, Library; P, PO, GPO, Post offices; RL, Rylands Library; T, Telephone exchanges (two shown).

churches. The movement to Sale, Altrincham, Cheadle, Bramhall, and other places in Cheshire was noted in the 1861 and 1871 census reports[49] with such comments as 'since the opening of railway communications houses have been erected for the accommodation of merchants, manufacturers and clerks from Manchester'. Nearer suburbs such as Chorlton-cum-Hardy, Moss Side, Withington and Didsbury were also growing residential districts and on the north side there were similar developments in Broughton and Cheetham Hill. The first sign of population decline in the centre of the city was recorded in the Market street subdistrict[50] which had 27,067 inhabitants in 1851 compared with 27,834 in 1841, but only 17,389 by 1871. The neighbouring Deansgate subdistrict[51] had 33,219 people in 1851 but only 24,173 in 1871. These two areas, with the London Road area, had 92,176 people in 1851 but only one-third of this number fifty years later.[52] The loss of population was ascribed to the demolition of existing buildings for erecting business premises, warehouses, factories or extensions to the railways: between 1861 and 1871 for example, 600 houses were pulled down to make a goods station at London road, in Portland Street houses were pulled down for warehouses, and in Deansgate for new warehouses and for a 'town hall' (the present Education Offices).[53] The centre of the city is now almost entirely non-residential (Fig. 30). Similarly in Salford the building and extension of the Lancashire and Yorkshire railway, the erection of mills, warehouses and the like all resulted in the demolition of houses, though at this time Salford was growing steadily due to industrial expansion.[54]

It seemed that nothing could shake the prosperity of this area, dependent primarily on cotton, but having also other textile industries and a growing metallurgical industry. But there were two sources of danger: first, the difficulty of acquiring the raw material and second, the dependence on the export market.[55] Of these the first was felt acutely during the American civil war, the time of the 'cotton famine' and the second, long recognized, became serious after the 1914–1918 war when it became impossible to regain the volume of the 1913 trade.[56] The depression came as the greater shock as the industry had been successful for so long a period. The situation would have been far worse but for two main factors; first the expansion of engineering as a major industrial activity in the area, and second, the building of the Manchester Ship canal which gave the city the position of a major port[57] and encouraged the growth of Britain's first and largest trading estate, Trafford Park, which in time had over 50,000 workers and is still expanding sixty years after its foundation. The population history bears a close relation to the industrial development of the nineteenth century, which was aided by the provision of transport by canal and railway in spite of considerable physical difficulties.

The later Expansion and Reconstruction

The numerical growth of the conurbation virtually ceased in 1914 but since 1918 there has been so remarkable a territorial expansion that it has almost been made anew, through the fusion of one town into another by re-housing from various centres. The problem of slum clearance still remains very partially solved and a further period of reconstruction is only just beginning. The conurbation area had 2,150,000 people in 1901, and 2,350,000 in 1911, an increase of 9 per cent, little more than the excess of births over deaths: in 1921 the population was 2,361,000; in 1931, 2,427,000, but 6,000 less in 1951. But in spite of this decline, within this same twenty years the number of occupied houses increased by 22 per cent from 600,600 to 738,400.[58]

In 1914 Didsbury and Withington were suburban villages partially surrounded by green fields but twenty-five years later almost all this land had been used for housing and other town features such as parks and playing fields: the city of Manchester had in 1951, 703,000 inhabitants compared with 736,000 in 1921, yet the area occupied by buildings was approximately twice as large. Clearly this is due in part to the efforts to wipe out part of the evil nineteenth-century heritage of workers' homes, some of them 'brick boxes divided into four compartments'.[59] The worst types of houses were the cellar dwellings and the back-to-back houses, but it is to the credit of nineteenth-century Manchester that legislation to remove such dwellings was provided long before it came in other cities (cf. pp. 85, 174). Powers to abolish cellar dwellings were given in 1853 and in 1874 it was said that all save 108 inhabited by old people had been closed.[60] Back-to-back houses[b] were not built after 1844 within the city, but long after this in Bradford and Openshaw, which were not brought within the city boundaries until 1885 and 1890 respectively.[61] Gradually these were converted into 'through' houses and by 1900 there were only 5,000 instead of 10,000—the last disappeared before the 1939–1945 war. But the real evil in Manchester, and hardly if at all less in the surrounding towns, is the inheritance of endless rows of drab workers' homes, especially those built during the first forty

[b] These were not prohibited by general legislation until 1925!

years of the nineteenth century,[62] close to the centre of the city, in what is known as the 'industrial collar'.

Since 1911 there has been no marked increase of population in the conurbation. Several of the towns that are primarily industrial, such as Bolton, Bury, Rochdale and Ashton, declined in population during the twenties, to a slightly greater extent than the figures suggest, for the 1921 Census was taken in June and therefore the numbers recorded are less than those in March, the normal census time. Some towns, such as Bury, Rochdale, Oldham, Ashton, Stalybridge, have grown little in numbers for many years[63]—for example Oldham with four neighbouring urban districts[c] grew steadily to a peak population of 212,500 in 1911, of whom 147,500 were in Oldham but there was a decrease to 210,700 in 1921, 204,000 in 1931 and only 183,800 in 1951. These figures are clearly related to the loss of employment in cotton mills, from 73,500 in 1929 to 51,300 in 1939 and 33,500 in 1947: textile engineering also has fewer workers now than before the war of 1939–1945 though it is still a large industry: the main increases in employment are in the aircraft industry and in the making of electrical goods. Coal mining, once widespread, has now ceased altogether in the Oldham district. Unemployment was heavy here during the depression years: the Oldham, Chadderton and Royton exchanges had more than 50 per cent unemployed in the worst months and there was much underemployment as many people were on 'short time'. Having for many decades ceased to absorb its natural increase of populations, the Oldham area is typical of others in which the phase of numerical expansion is apparently over for the present. This does not mean, however, that the various towns will remain as they now are in appearance for there are large areas covered with new houses, mainly erected during the inter-war phase and after 1945, and the re-housing regarded as necessary is by no means complete.[64] In fact the Oldham area is not untypical of many of the long-established industrial areas of the Pennines and the Rossendales which, having developed industrially during the early nineteenth century, have remained stable in population for fifty or sixty years and recently faced industrial difficulties through the contraction of cotton textiles, only partially offset by the introduction of new industries.

After the war of 1914–1918 there was a redistribution of the population of the conurbation which almost doubled the built-up area:

[c] Area 21·2 square miles. Oldham C.B., 121; Chadderton U.D., 31; Royton U.D., 15; Crompton U.D., 13; Lees U.D., 4 (1951).

housing estates, both publicly and privately financed, and new suburban roads were added on the fringes of Manchester and beside many other places that, though close to the city, were separate administrative units. Mrs. J. L. Stocks[65] has described the development in the Wilbraham Road district of south Manchester some 4 miles from the city centre:

> Manchester had in earlier times expanded starfish-wise along its main roads, the intervening spaces remaining unbuilt, except for old established country cottages and farms . . . with the operation of the post-war Addison Housing Act in full swing . . . Wilbraham road was 'adopted'; Corporation trams began to run on smooth concrete . . . trees were felled with a ruthlessness which later town-planners were to deplore; and on the fields through which Wilbraham Road ran a large new Corporation housing estate of semi-detached cottages arose. In due course it was furnished with a church, a chapel, a school encircled by a spacious playground . . . a branch library.

And this went on so steadily that only three years after the Armistice of 1918 it was clear that Manchester must extend its bounds into Cheshire.[66] In 1921, the City Council agreed to buy the land for the Wythenshawe estate though the purchase was not made until 1926, and in 1930, three Cheshire parishes, Northenden (a village with some suburban houses dating back to the nineteenth century), Baguley and Newtown Etchells, covering nearly 9 square miles, were added to the city and to Lancashire.[67] By 1958 the building of Wythenshawe, inhabited by some 85,000 people, was almost complete. Those who view this area are apt to assume that the population of Manchester is increasing but between 1931 and 1951 there was a decline of − 8 per cent, from 766,300 to 703,100.[68] Even more marked was the decline of population in Salford's 8 square miles from 234,000 in 1921 to 223,400 in 1931 (− 4·5 per cent) and 178,200 in 1951 (− 20·3 per cent).[69]

Between 1921 and 1951, the areas that have become, in part at least, residential all showed marked increases of population. This was seen notably in Whitefield which increased from 7,300 to 12,900 (+ 77 per cent), Prestwich from 18,750 to 34,500 (+ 82 per cent), Stretford from 46,600 to 61,900 (+ 35 per cent) and Urmston from 15,400 to 39,200 (+ 156 per cent), all of which are at least in parts residential.[70] All the above are in Lancashire, but from 1921 to 1931 this section of the conurbation had an increase of only + 2 per cent, followed by a decrease of − 4 per cent (1931–1951). Since 1918, the main residential expansion has been seen in the Cheshire part of the

conurbation, which from 1921 to 1931 increased in population by
+ 8 per cent and by 21 per cent in the following twenty years.[71]
Consequently there are now (1951) 421,000 people in the Cheshire
administrative areas, 100,000 more than in 1921: from 1921 to 1951
there were heavy increases in the Cheshire residential districts—thus
at Altrincham from 25,500 to 39,800 (+ 55 per cent), at Sale from
24,100 to 43,200 (+ 79 per cent), Cheadle and Gatley from 11,000
to 31,500 (+ 186 per cent) Wilmslow from 10,300 to 19,500 (+ 90
per cent), Hazel Grove and Bramhall from 9,800 to 19,700 (+ 100
per cent), Bredbury and Romiley 10,000 to 17,800 (+ 78 per cent).
Some of the outer suburbs such as Bowdon, Hale, Alderley Edge and
Marple showed smaller increases partly because they had grown
gradually through the years but they, too, were increasing in
numbers and still are. On the other hand places that are primarily
industrial, such as Dukinfield, Hyde and Stalybridge showed declines
though Stockport, covering an area of 12 square miles continued
to expand in numbers.

All this has resulted in a vast spread of houses only too apparent
to the eye. On the southwest, the towns of Altrincham and Sale,
were completely joined by the building of new houses between them
during the inter-war period in what is now Timperley and Brook-
lands (Fig. 29). Cheshire villages such as Gatley, Cheadle, Cheadle
Hulme, Handforth, Styal are swamped by suburban growth and the
old town of Wilmslow has also become the centre of a favoured
residential neighbourhood. On the east side old industrial villages
have been partially overlaid by houses of the interwar period though
considerable areas remain unused for building which are not agricultural lands of the first quality, some of which are now providing
'overspill' land for Manchester.

It is to Cheshire, partially at least an area with good agricultural
land (certainly better than on the flanks of the Pennines and Rossendales) that people able to choose naturally turn for a new house site.
There are comparable problems on Merseyside (see p. 118). The
reasons why a southward position is favoured are varied: first, there
is the attraction of open country within easy reach combined with
rapid transport to the city, for example on the railway line to
Altrincham, electrified in 1929; the private car and the express bus
service were complementary factors. Second, Cheshire is favoured for
the slightly negative reason that it is climatically drier and less smoky
than areas closer to Manchester on the north and east. On the south
and southwest side the average rainfall is some 30 in. per annum,

but on the northeast 45 in. or more. In experience this means that the clouds are frequently banked up against the Pennines and the Rossendales, and smoke drifts towards the hills under the influence of the prevailing winds. Fogs have become less frequent in recent years, though they still cause severe transport problems on occasion. A few hundred acres in the city centre now form a smokeless zone that is being gradually extended and will, it is hoped, eventually cover a large part of the city.[72]

As a result of inter-war building, four Cheshire places, Sale, Altrincham, Bowdon and Hale, have in all a population of *c*. 100,000. Similarly, Cheadle joins Stockport on one side and Bramhall on another, and there is uninterrupted building through Manchester to Prestwich, Whitefield and Radcliffe, with little break here to Bury. As Fig. 28 shows, in some parts of the conurbation the junction of one town and another is effected only along certain main roads by ribbon development but behind these ribbons there are areas not as yet used for building sites. Not all can be used as some areas are liable to subsidence. But Manchester has built the Langley estate in Middleton M.B. since 1950 and Salford has met some of its housing problems by the development of an estate at Worsley. This was the pioneer Town Development Scheme: the Worsley U.D.C. with the approval of the Lancashire County Council, began building houses for Salford.[73] The scheme is to provide houses for 15,000 people over a period of ten years and already several factories have been built. Manchester, so far thwarted of any major scheme, has made arrangements with six authorities for some 30,000–35,000 people to live in Heywood (1,175 houses). Whitefield (1,550), Stalybridge (850) and Wilmslow (800), with 4,000 houses in a scheme shared by Hyde and Longdendale. The last, which is outside the conurbation, is also providing land for another 1,000 houses.[74]

No provincial conurbation has so involved an administrative structure as this, with its fifty-two separate units, discussed below. As an area of bricks and mortar, it reached its frontier a century ago when the outer suburbs on the south, such as Altrincham, Bowdon, Wilmslow, Alderley Edge, began to grow actively through the patronage of railway travellers.[75] On the east and north what the 1951 Census called the 'crescent of industrial towns'[76] from Ashton to Oldham, Rochdale, Bury and Bolton, was well established by the year 1851. These towns, with Stockport, have maintained considerable significance as shopping and general service centres and all of them, except for Ashton, are county boroughs. In the view of many of their residents, they are scarcely parts of the conurbation at all, but rather possible nuclei of separate subconurbations, such as a greater Oldham, including its neighbours mentioned on p. 140, an enlarged Bolton, or an Ashton united with Stalybridge and possibly Dukinfield.[77] In 1932, C. B. Fawcett said that this conurbation consisted of the central city, Manchester, with its immediate neighbours Salford C.B. and Stretford M.B., and an outer girdle of towns from Altrincham to Bolton.[78] This is still so, but the most marked change of the years since he wrote has been the addition of so many houses in the areas then vacant: in its present form the conurbation is a product of 'infilling' rather than recent outward expansion.

Fawcett's view of the strength both of the central city and the outer towns was confirmed by the 1951 Census of Retail Trade,[79] which showed that the total trade of this type was valued at £300m., an average of £124 a head. Two-fifths of this trade was in Manchester (average £179 a head), and the average per head of population in the outer towns was Bolton, £123; Bury, £124; Rochdale, £124; Oldham, £125; Ashton, £135; Stockport, £119 and Altrincham, £148— the last traditionally a rural market, but now having also a strong artisan and suburban trade. Even Salford has an average of only £92 a head, and many of the minor industrial parts of the conurbation much less—for example, Failsworth, £69, Droylesden, £67, Audenshaw, £73 and Denton, £67. Not unexpectedly, however, Wilmslow at £123 a head and Alderley Edge at £143, have the high purchasing power of wealthy suburbs. It would be possible to speak of the municipal magnificence of Rochdale's nineteenth-century town hall,[80] or of the recent creation of a civic centre in the heart of Bolton, and of its fine technical college.

Administrative Aspects (Figs 31–35)

All the conurbation is now under some kind of urban government except for Disley rural district, though Limehurst R.D. was extinguished only in 1951 and 1954 by its absorption into five neighbouring towns, Oldham, Ashton, Mossley, Droylesden and Failsworth.[81] The former rural districts of Bolton, Bury and Barton have gone, and so has part of the Bucklow R.D. (Cheshire). But in 1851, only six places were municipal boroughs, Manchester, Salford, Bolton, Stockport, Oldham and Ashton-under-Lyne, though other places regarded as 'towns' were Bury, Rochdale, Stalybridge, Heywood, Hyde, Middleton, Radcliffe, Eccles and Altrincham,[82] of which all except the last were industrial centres (Altrincham acquired

FIG. 31. MANCHESTER CONURBATION, ADMINISTRATIVE UNITS, 1888

Manchester occupied a relatively small area, and has since absorbed many urban districts such as Moss Side, Gorton, Levenshulme, Openshaw, Newton Heath and Crumpsall. As yet a considerable area ranked as rural districts.

some large factories later). By 1871, a number of other places had grown so markedly that they were regarded by the Census Commissioners as towns,[83] including four, Stretford, Droylesden, Failsworth and above all Salford (124,800 in 1871) which have managed to maintain an identity independent of Manchester but others, such as Gorton (21,616 in 1871), Newton Heath (18,103), Openshaw (11,108), Rusholme (7,430), Crumpsall, Moss Side and Levenshulme have since been absorbed into Manchester. Rusholme, for example, finished its brief career as an urban district in 1885 and Harpurhey and Bradford were added to the city in the same year.[84] In 1890 the city was extended on the north and northeast by the inclusion of West Gorton, Openshaw, Clayton, Newton Heath, Blackley, Moston and Crumpsall:[85] these extensions were indicative of the direction of growth at the time for as noted on p. 141, the main phase of southward movement came later. In fact, the 1890 extensions gave the city most of its northern and eastern boundaries, which have survived little changed except for the addition in 1903 of Heaton Park.[86]

Salford has remained apart from Manchester since its first development though separated from its neighbour only by a bridged river: if any hope of union ever existed, it was removed when Salford became a city by Letters Patent in 1926.[87] It is equally unlikely that Stretford will ever be absorbed: in 1885 and in 1890, Manchester unsuccessfully approached Stretford with a view to union and in 1900 Stretford applied for borough status (to protect her interests against Manchester) but this was refused.[88] Manchester was far less successful in its territorial expansion than Birmingham (see p. 87), though in 1904 the urban districts of Moss Side and Withington were acquired and in 1909 further additions were the urban districts of Levenshulme and Gorton.[89] The addition of Withington meant that the city acquired a frontier on the Mersey, and included the residential areas of Fallowfield, Burnage and Didsbury, in which some of the housing estates of the inter-war period were built. The inclusion of Levenshulme gave a common boundary with Stockport, which was gradually extended to an area of 12½ square miles by the absorption in 1901 of the Reddish U.D. (1881–1901) and parts of the neighbouring urban districts as well as of the rural district.[90] Heaton Norris U.D. was added in 1913 (except for 45 acres given to Manchester) but Handforth C.P., all that now remained of Stockport R.D., became itself an urban district from 1904 to 1936, when most of it was united to Wilmslow, apparently to avoid inclusion in Manchester.[91]

FIG. 32. MANCHESTER CONURBATION, ADMINISTRATIVE UNITS, 1900

Manchester has now been considerably extended by the absorption of Crumpsall, Newton Heath, Openshaw and some rural areas, but Moss Side and Withington survive on the south. Alderley Edge and Chorley are one and the same place: to the northwest, note the great expansion of Bolton, primarily through the elimination of the rural districts and of Astley Bridge U.D.

FIG. 33. Manchester Conurbation, Administrative Units, 1906

By this time Manchester reached the Mersey through its acquisition of Withington and Moss Side; Stockport was expanding also but had not achieved a common frontier with Manchester and on the north Rochdale had absorbed Castleton. Some new urban districts had been created in the southwest. The Poor Law Unions of the time are shown.

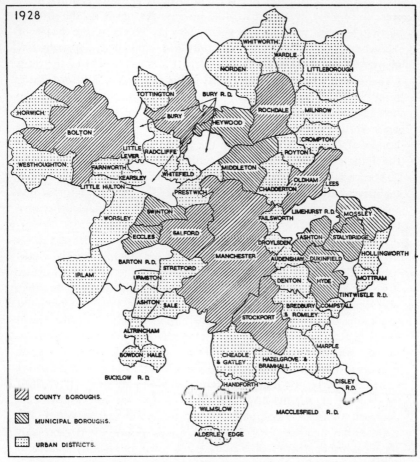

FIG. 34. MANCHESTER CONURBATION, ADMINISTRATIVE UNITS, 1928

The line of urban districts flanking Manchester and Stockport reminds one of a group of buffer states. Stockport now has Heaton Norris, and Manchester both Levenshulme and Gorton. The last relics of the rural districts are obviously ripe for slaughter.

L

Although various towns in the heart of the conurbation had grown into one another long before the end of the nineteenth century, they were not united by administrative unions: the result on the ground is that visitors who regard themselves as being in the heart of Manchester find that they have only just entered it, for even Exchange Station is in Salford. Similarly, the major docks of the Ship Canal are in Salford and the great industrial estate, Trafford Park, is in Stretford and Urmston. Another effect is that some of the housing estates extend to the very boundary of the city and then cease abruptly (Fig. 28) though on the north side Manchester-built houses at Bowlee extend across the frontier into Middleton, where the Langley estate, now being built, will eventually house some 20,000 people from Manchester. A third curious effect is that on the main road from Stockport there is a large group of factories just within the Stockport county borough, said to be so located because the rates are invariably lower than those of Manchester.

Meanwhile the term 'urban district' was applied to defined areas in which suburban housing had been added, mainly beside established villages, such as Cheadle and Gatley, made in 1886 an urban district covering 9 square miles, later modified in detail.[92] Another was Hazel Grove and Bramhall,[93] constituted in 1900 and extended to an area of 8·5 square miles in 1901, an ill-matched pair for Hazel Grove is an industrial village surrounded by modern suburban houses, and Bramhall is a suburban neighbourhood which grew initially around the railway station and later in ribbons along various roads. Similarly, Bredbury and Romiley U.D., an area suburban to a number of neighbouring towns, has by various adjustments acquired an area of 7½ square miles.[94] Its neighbour, Marple U.D., with similar qualities now covers 11 square miles.[95] It is clear that the term 'urban district' does not mean a town, but merely an area in which certain services are provided and in present circumstances it is to such areas as those named that the authorities of cities unable to rehouse their population on modern standards must turn.

Several Lancashire towns were expanded before the end of the nineteenth century. Bolton, having incorporated several rural parishes and the urban district of Astley Bridge in 1898, is one of the few major centres having no great need of 'overspill' sites.[96] Irlam, created an urban district in 1894 was extended in 1896 by the inclusion of part of Flixton parish.[97] Three other places were made into urban districts—Urmston and Worsley in 1894 and Tottington in 1899.[98] Apart from the dissolution of Castleton U.D. in 1900,[99] and its division between Rochdale C.B. and Heywood M.B., there were few major changes until 1933 when the Bury rural district was extinguished.[100] In this year, Bury's area was extended to 11½ square miles,[101] that of Whitefield to 5 square miles and Radcliffe to 7¾ square miles.[102] But perhaps the most interesting is the case of Heywood, now carried far into the Rossendales with an area of 13½ square miles:[103] the greater Rochdale, now 15 square miles, acquired most of a former urban district, Norden, including all the built-up area.[104] Ashton-under-Lyne, having absorbed Hurst U.D. in 1927 (in fact its main residential suburb) also added part of the Limehurst R.D.,[105] Barton R.D. was divided between Eccles, Swinton and Pendlebury, Worsley (which was also given Little Hulton), and Kearsley.[106] The effect of all this was to give the northern towns control over the entire area on the flanks of the Rossendales (where in fact they meet urban districts centred on towns deep in the Rossendale towns). But even so, some of the towns are not satisfied for Oldham patriots[107] argue that their problems of re-housing can only be solved if they can add to their territory such areas as Lees, Chadderton, Royton and Crompton urban districts: if there is a greater Oldham, there may legitimately be a greater Rochdale, including Whitworth, Wardle, Littleborough and Milnrow. The essential point is that on the northern side there are a number of major towns, Bolton, Bury, Rochdale, Oldham, each sufficiently strong to regard itself as in some ways a minor metropolis. Similarly Ashton, with its neighbours, Stalybridge and Dukinfield, united by building as long ago as 1850, are a group of towns which have remained independent though the first-named is the major shopping centre.

Although numerous urban districts have been incorporated by Manchester, four survive on the east side, Failsworth, Droylsden, Audenshaw and Denton. All are in part industrial centres—and Denton is widely known for felt hat manufacture, now menaced by the numbers of hatless men. ('If you want to get ahead, get a hat!') Failsworth stretches along a couple of miles of the main road to Oldham, having a line of mills along the canal which runs parallel to the road, Droylsden has numerous old mills along a canal, Audenshaw is an industrial centre close to the Ashton canal and the locally well-known Guide Bridge station, and Denton is a crossroads town with various mills. All four had 55,000 people in 1931 but 83,000 in 1951, and the large increase was due largely to the addition of new houses in the vacant land beyond the old settlements. All are

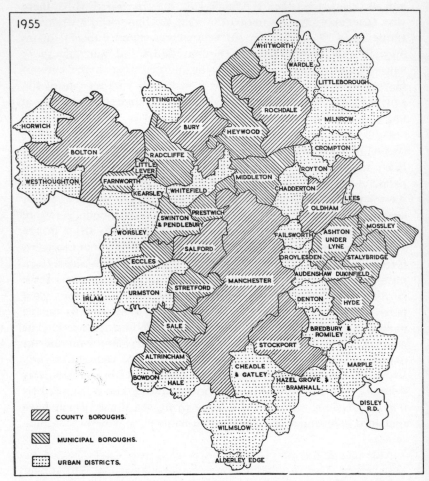

FIG. 35. MANCHESTER CONURBATION, ADMINISTRATIVE UNITS, 1955

Except for Disley rural district, all the conurbation area is under urban government but in fifty-two units. The division between Salford and Manchester goes back for more than seven centuries and many smaller places, such as the line of urban districts from Chadderton to Denton, have survived through all changes. It may be that this map will be changed within a few years as various towns in the east of the conurbation are negotiating about a possible union.

in some sense suburban to Manchester, but Failsworth to Oldham also, Droylesden and Audenshaw to Ashton, Denton to its neighbour Hyde. These places are located between the outer 'crescent' of industrial towns and the heart of the conurbation in Manchester, with Salford and Stretford and other places similarly located are Chadderton U.D. (31,100 in 1951: 1931–1951, + 13 per cent) and Middleton M.B. (32,600, + 12 per cent), both of which are still growing in numbers.

Four administrative areas in the southwest, the boroughs of Sale and Altrincham and the urban districts of Bowdon and Hale, now fused together by continuous building have in all some 100,000 people. Sale,[108] now primarily residential for Manchester, absorbed Ashton-on-Mersey in 1930 and became a borough in 1935. Altrincham, an historic market town and still the main shopping centre of the district, has grown partly as a residential centre and partly through industrialization, almost entirely in engineering, with some 10,000 factory workers. It became a municipal borough in 1937.[109] Hale, made an urban district in 1900, and Bowdon U.D., one of the smallest in population in the conurbation (3,500), helped to share part of the Bucklow R.D. in 1936.[110] At present there is only a narrow 'green belt' between these towns and Wythenshawe, but the area left free includes some excellent market gardening land. On the east side of Wythenshawe, building in the Cheadle and Gatley U.D. is steadily filling up the remaining land to Wilmslow and Alderley Edge. Many may deplore this spread of housing but it seems likely that the conurbation will have a reasonably well-defined edge and not sprawl on indefinitely into the countryside.

CHAPTER 6

WEST YORKSHIRE

THIRTY-THREE boroughs and urban districts covering an area of 481 square miles form this conurbation. Neatly parcelled up into administrative districts, it really consists of a large number of industrial villages and towns, of which only a few are of considerable size. And no single town dominates the conurbation, though Leeds can well claim to be the obvious regional capital and its neighbour Bradford occupies a special position as the great mart for wool. Compared with other conurbations, West Yorkshire is far more varied in appearance for over much of its extent there is an interpenetration of farmland and villages, of field and factory, of moorland and valley. Its major industry, wool, springs from the sheep rearing on its moors and 'intake' fields which cover the hillsides to 1,000 ft. and more: its farmsteads and villages were built of stone quarried from the hillsides where the scars may still be seen and roofed with flagstones apparently strong enough to stand any mountain wind. How far back the mining of coal and iron goes, one cannot say, though it is commonly supposed to have been practised in Roman times.

The rugged individuality for which the inhabitants are justly famed is seen also in the landscape. In parts of the upper Calder valley and in many remote tributary valleys there are still patches of natural woodland, generally of oak and birch, on slopes at all times too steep to clear for fields and houses. The improvement of the rivers to make 'navigations' from the seventeenth century and the building of canals a few decades later stimulated the growth of towns and villages in the valleys, and brought the home workers down from their farmhouses and cottages to the new factories and workshops. In the nineteenth century the railways traversed these same valleys and mining became more adequately organized than ever before, along with engineering. Inevitably mining shared the eastward movement characteristic of the whole of the Pennine coalfield, so that the largest pits are now well out in the Vale of York and the older workings are recognizable only by the scars left behind. But of all the qualities of this conurbation, perhaps the most striking is the virtual fossilization of many of its towns and villages which have grown little or even declined in population for thirty years or more, a characteristic shared by many

154

cotton towns of the Pennines and the Rossendales. True, there are new housing estates to replace worn-out dwellings, but fortunately almost all these are stone-faced to harmonize with the older buildings. Only to the east, in and around Leeds and Wakefield, are towns built largely of red brick to mark, as it were, the approach to the lowland from the Pennines.

C. B. Fawcett's definition of this conurbation, based on the 1931 Census, covered a smaller area than that given in 1951. Fawcett chose an area of 280 square miles, then divided between five county boroughs and forty-two municipal boroughs and urban districts, of which a large number were extinguished by the administrative changes of the nineteen-thirties.[1] The 'Fawcett conurbation' in 1931 had 1,433,000, but the 1951 Census conurbation had, in 1931, 1,655,000 people. The conurbation, lacking the degree of unity to be found in others, covers the Pennine foothills of the coalfield, having towns and villages in the valleys of the Aire and Calder and of some of their tributaries, with the interfluves between them. Some of this higher ground has provided attractive building sites for new houses but to this day the conurbation does not possess what Fawcett called a 'brick-and-mortar unity'; he described 'the whole urban area' as

in the form of a very irregular oval, the longer axis of which stretches from northeast to southwest for about twenty miles through Leeds and Huddersfield and the transverse axis through Bradford and Dewsbury for nearly twelve miles.[2]

The 1951 definition[3] possibly extends farther south than some would wish, but as the conurbation includes the northern part of the largest British coalfield any boundary is bound to be a compromise.

The West Yorkshire Scene

On the east side of the Pennines there are long gently-graded east-ward slopes, made up of sandstones and shales of Millstone Grit, largely peat-covered above the upper limits of farming. Dull for much of the year, these moors are flecked in summer by cotton grass and in autumn by heather. The Coal Measures extend eastwards from Huddersfield and Halifax and slope towards the Vale of York, where they dip beneath the Permian and later rocks to form the concealed coalfield. Ironstones within the coalfield have given rise to some long-established metal industries, of which some survive on imported ore. Most of the mines in the western part of the coalfield have gone though there are some opencast workings. Initially, it was not coal but water that provided the main motive power for the woollen industry and many of the old textile villages such as those in the Keighley district, including Haworth, or places such as Sowerby Bridge and Brighouse in the Calder valley, are some miles west of the mining districts. But packhorses, barges on the river navigations, canals and later the railways brought coal to the riverside mills that became so numerous in the nineteenth century.

There is a marked contrast between the Aire and the Calder valleys, both of which must have possessed such beauty before they were industrialized that even now they have managed to keep something of their former charm and grace. Approaching Keighley from the west, the Aire is a broad valley studded with mill villages but having fine large fields in the valley with wooded agricultural hill-slopes on either side. The Calder valley is narrower, and was apparently scoured by glacial meltwaters poured through the Little-borough gap to Todmorden and Hebden Bridge, thence onwards through Sowerby Bridge, Elland, Brighouse, Mirfield and other towns which are separated by two or three miles of comparatively open country, with woods on the steeper slopes. Leeds owes much to its control of the Aire crossing but the three other large towns, Bradford, Huddersfield and Halifax, are all in tributary valleys, Bradford's 'beck' to the Aire and the others to the Calder. In all these towns the valleys have been used for industry and the main shopping centres are placed on rising ground with suburbs rising to 500 ft. in Leeds, to 700-800 ft. and more in Huddersfield and Bradford and to over 1,000 ft. in Halifax.

Various novelists have described west Yorkshire, and readers of Emily Brontë's *Wuthering Heights* could hardly forget the grim setting of a magnificently-built farm, approached by tracks stone-walled on each side with deep winter snowdrifts which accentuated an isolation felt at all times. In *Shirley*, Charlotte Brontë has written of the uneasy advance of new inventions in woollen mills of the early nineteenth century. More recently, Phyllis Bentley has drawn inspiration from the inner towns of the woollen district to show the rise and fall of various families, and especially the devastating effects of the world crisis early in the nineteen-thirties. Many of Miss Bentley's descriptions of mills, of houses inhabited by her characters at varying stages of their lives, give a vivid impression of a landscape that, if lacking in charm, is certainly not without character.

West Yorkshire proved equally intriguing to Mrs. Gaskell, who on her visits to Haworth, saw Keighley as a rising industrial town possessing a relatively new railway. She described the neat stone houses, so carefully tended, that lined the road from Keighley to Haworth and do so, almost unchanged, still.[4]

The town of Keighley never quite melts into country on the road from Keighley to Haworth, although the houses become more sparse as the traveller journeys upward to the grey round hills that seem to bound his journey in a westerly direction . . . The distance is about four miles; and, as I have said, what with villas, great worsted factories, rows of workmen's houses, with here and there an old fashioned farm-house and outbuildings, it can hardly be called 'country' any part of the way. . . . The air is dim and lightless from all these habitations and places of business. The soil in the valley (or 'bottom' to use the local term) is rich; but, as the road begins to ascend, the vegetation becomes poorer; it does not flourish, it merely exists; and, instead of trees, there are only bushes and shrubs around the dwellings. Stone dykes are everywhere used in place of hedges; and what crops there are, on the patches of arable land, consist of pale hungry-looking, grey-green oats. . . Haworth . . . has a background of dun and purple moors . . . All round the horizon there is this same line of sinuous wave-like hills, the scoops into which they fall only revealing other hills beyond, of similar colour and shape, crowned with wild, bleak moors . . .

In this landscape the native yellow Millstone Grit has given an excellent building material, noted vividly by Lady Chorley:[5]

the towns of the Pennines, old and new alike, are, or should be built of stone . . . Even accumulated layers of smoke cannot overlay the fundamental unity of the Pennine towns with the country from which they spring . . . The Pennine towns are not *at one* with their surrounding country, they are one with it. And because the Pennine country is stark and resistant, the Pennine towns are stark. Nature not man made them so. These characteristics are implicit in the medium of which they are built.

The appearance of West Yorkshire is eloquent of its economic history. Defoe[6] spoke of the western part of this area as one in which holdings of a few acres abounded: by fearless effort, the limit of cultivation had been pushed steadily higher towards the unconquerable cotton-grass moors. The upper limit of improved land averages 900–1,000 ft., but in places is as low as 600 ft. or as high as 1,300 ft., and although some high-lying fields have been allowed to revert to rough pasture, the general level of agricultural occupation still remains high. On the hillsides lived the farmer-manufacturers of the day,

the nearer we came to Hallifax [*sic*] we found the Houses thicker and the Villages greater in every Bottom; and not only so, but the sides of the Hills, which were very steep in every way, were spread with houses, and that very thick; for the land being divided into small enclosures, that is to say, from two acres to five or six acres each, seldom more, every three or four pieces of land had a house belonging to it.

The austerity of the scene was clear to Defoe, who said that 'such is the bounty of nature in this otherwise frightful country' that two things abounded, 'coals and running water upon the tops of the highest hills'.[7] Coal was mined in outcrops, and the plentiful waters were led to every house, '. . . the little streams were so parted and guided by gutters or pipes . . . that none' of the houses was 'without a river, running into and through their work-houses'. Every clothier had to keep a horse or two to fetch his wool and provisions from the market, to take his yarn to the spinners, to the fulling mill or to the market.[8] Generally he kept cows also and some hens and achieved that combination of domestic manufacture with farming that was also found in Lancashire and in Ireland, and Defoe ascribed the fertility of the fields to the water impregnated with 'the dregs of the dying fat, and with the oil, the soap, the tallow and other ingredients used by the clothiers in dressing and scouring'.

The Growth of the Woollen Industries

Having an origin in the farmsteads, the woollen industry long retained its domestic character. On the rivers fulling mills were set up to serve the clothiers and in some cases corn milling and dyeing were carried on in the same premises. At the end of the eighteenth century these mills were expanded into scribbling mills where wool was carded for the spinners.[9] Groups of cottages were built around the mills and places like Sowerby Bridge now expanded and in time sprawled up the hillsides. Many of the mills became the nuclei of villages in the valleys, and upland centres in the west grew into villages as certain enterprising families extended modest warehouses into large mills and weaving sheds, for example at Shipley, Shelley, Skelmanthorpe, Lepton, Netherton and Holme.[10] The worsted trade of the western areas was dominated by strong merchants but the woollen area in the east had a far larger number of small merchants who eventually became employers.[11] Throughout the area, villages developed as centres of industry during the seventeenth and eighteenth century: these included, Woodhouse, Beeston, Armley, Hunslet and Holbeck, all now swamped by the growth of Leeds, or Churwell and Morley just beyond the city.[12] To summarize, whatever the form of industry, it was rooted in the homes of the farmer-spinners and weavers, though villages developed around the fulling mills and dyeworks—but there were scarcely twenty factories in Yorkshire in 1800, and the power-loom, used in the western—or worsted section of the area by the 1830's, was not general in the woollen section until twenty years later.[13]

Long-continued domestic and village industry has left a deep mark on West Yorkshire. Mill towns such as those of Lancashire and Cheshire did not exist: most of the places recognizably towns were small in 1801, except for Leeds which, with 53,000 inhabitants, was the seventh town of England.[14] Nevertheless, the major towns of today were already significant market centres by the end of the eighteenth century.[15] Leeds had a cloth market on the bridge in the seventeenth century, which was moved to Briggate in June 1684, and by 1725 the value of the daily sales was estimated at £30,000, and on occasion as much as £60,000: cloth halls were built in 1711, 1755, 1758 and 1775. At Wakefield, another ancient market town, a cloth hall was built in 1710, and there were others at Halifax 1708 (or earlier) and 1779, at Bradford, 1773, Huddersfield, 1776—and also at Colne.[16] These towns remain the chief mercantile and—in varying degrees—manufacturing centres to this day; and their cloth halls survived the gradual rise of the merchant who bought direct from the weaver and in time became himself the manufacturer. The character of the settlement pattern laid down by the early industrial growth has been overlaid by later growths, conspicuously through the marked rise of towns in the nineteenth century and their outward spread in the twentieth, but the West Riding still has an intricate interpenetration of town and countryside, most quaintly so to the immediate south of Leeds where between a number of towns there exists the major rhubarb-growing district of Britain. In spite of all the current needs for re-housing which, under modern schemes, must inevitably mean a vast allocation of rural land for 'development' there seems to be little sign that the West Yorkshire conurbation will ever become as dominantly urban as its analogue on the other side of the Pennines.

Canals opened up many parts of the Pennines to trade and industry: the preliminary move was to improve the rivers. The Leeds and Liverpool canal was authorized by an act of 1770 but not finished until 1816:[17] the building of the Aire and Calder canal was authorized in 1699 and later works included the Huddersfield canal, completed to Marsden at the head of the Colne valley in 1804, which was linked with the Aire and Calder system by Sir John Ramsden's canal built under an Act of 1774.[18] The Bradford canal was sanctioned in 1771 and finished in 1774, [19] and the Calder-Hebble navigation from Sowerby wharf to the Aire was constructed under an act of 1758: an extension to Halifax was made after 1825.[20] Much of the pre-railway movement was by canals in association with turnpike roads, but once the canals were made factories were built in the valleys: the Colne valley, for example, previously a backwater, was gradually dotted with mills.[21] In the Huddersfield area 'canals, turnpike roads and railways all in turn contributed to the congestion of the narrow valleys. This initiated the ribbon development of mills so characteristic of the Pennines'.[22] Having originated in the Pennine upland, the woollen industry was never restricted to the coalfield as the canals and railways carried coal to the factories beside them.

Even so, the main towns of the Conurbation are within the coal-field area, and although the valleys had obvious advantages as industrial sites, industry never left the uplands where it had been so long established. The initial advantages were 'coal and water on the hilltops': throughout the seventeenth and eighteenth centuries, coal was dug in increasing quantities in the heart of the woollen districts, for example at Queensbury, west of Bradford, 1,100 ft., where an industrial village survives to this day.[23] During the nineteenth century coal mining increased rapidly: at the beginning of the century, there were twenty pits between Huddersfield and Holmfirth and by 1860 one-quarter of the Yorkshire output came from the areas around Halifax, Dewsbury, Huddersfield and Holmfirth. As late as 1871 there were still some fifty collieries in the Bradford district, from which nearly 2,000,000 tons of coal were produced annually.[24] Inevitably coalmining spread eastward so that now the main col-lieries are to the east of Leeds and Wakefield, many of them outside the Conurbation as here defined, but water remained a crucial need and so the woollen industry has shown no tendency to move east-wards with the mining. The true mining village and town appears only in the east of the conurbation in such places as Rothwell, Methley, and many more as far as Doncaster and beyond.

It has been wisely said that 'once a textile industry is established, based initially perhaps on local materials, it changes its character comparatively easily with changes in demand for particular fabrics'.[25] This change of character may perhaps include the emergence of such activities as the manufacture of ready-made clothing in Leeds, there much more prominent than the manufacture of fabrics. But local specialization is traditional in Yorkshire, even though it is subject to change. Heaton has shown that at the beginning of the nineteenth century, there was a clear division between the woollen cloth and worsted districts.[26] In the west, worsteds were made in the upper valleys of the Aire and Calder, including Halifax, Keighley, Haworth and—in Lancashire—Colne. The woollen area to the east was bounded by a line from Leeds to Alverthorpe, and round to Brighouse, Bradford, Shipley and Guiseley. Outside both areas was Huddersfield, the centre of the 'fancy' trade, of dyeing and general finishing, as well as a powerful market. Even greater as a market was Leeds, which in 1797 was 'the home of over 1,400 merchants and traders, whose genteel residences lined Hunslet Lane, Boar Lane, Meadow Lane and Albion Street'.[27] Leeds (Fig. 36), already the largest town at the beginning of the nineteenth century, retained its power through the enterprise of its merchants and manufacturers and became a regional capital for the whole Conurbation and a large area beyond it.[28] At the same time, its dominance was never equal to that of Manchester or Birmingham, for in Bradford, Leeds had a strong, if always smaller rival which became significant as a mart of the commercial and manufacturing sides of the wool industry. Marginally placed on the coalfield and wholly non-industrial to the north of the city, Leeds' destiny was to acquire a variety of manufactures and especially the ready-made clothing trade, and to state, somewhat complacently, that not all its eggs were in one basket.

So far as can be estimated, the population of the area of 480 square miles now called the Conurbation was 290,000 in 1801, a density approaching 600 per square mile:[29] within the next fifty years there was an increase to 792,000: accounts written during this time show that local specialization was already marked and that towns and villages were growing noticeably. Parsons speaks of Halifax as a vigorous town with a strong market every Saturday, helped in its growth by the quarrying of flags and slates at Southowram, and of coal there also as well as at Northowram and Shelf.[30] Huddersfield's trade was 'immense' and its manufactures included cloths, serges, kerseys, cords and a variety of fancy goods for shawls and waistcoats, some of which were made for worsted and silk or other materials.[31] In neighbouring villages such as those of the Colne valley, water wheels and steam engines gave power to mills which produced cloth at Marsden, Golcar and Milnsbridge, and Slaithwaite also had cotton spinning and machine making; similarly in the Holme valley (south of Huddersfield) industrial villages were numerous. At Honley and South Crossland fancy and other woollen goods were made, and there were also scribbling and fulling mills and dyeworks. Within two miles

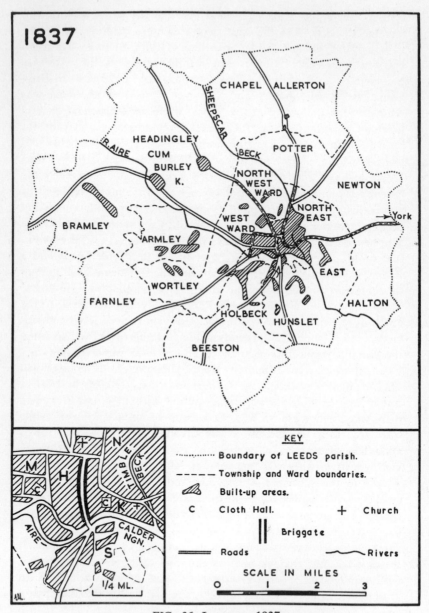

FIG. 36. LEEDS IN 1837

of Holmfirth, it was estimated, there were thirty-nine woollen mills, and at New Mill there were also stone quarries and coalmines, a brewery and a pottery.[32] In many respects this area has changed little for beyond Huddersfield, the villages are still industrial centres, with stone-built mills and houses. Between Huddersfield and Mirfield there were factories for velveteens and woollen cords at Deighton and Sheepridge on the river, and at Kirkheaton and Lepton on higher ground there were mills for fancy goods, chiefly woollen cloths and fabrics.[33] For all this area Huddersfield was the chief—in some cases the only—market and goods were sent forward for sale through its cloth halls and merchants' warehouses. In 1851, Huddersfield was described as 'a busy clothing town and the centre of a cluster of clothing villages'.[34]

Bradford had become the main market for an extensive area to the west of the town though there were subsidiary markets at Bingley and at Keighley.[35] At Keighley the main manufactures were of worsted yarns for the Bradford market but there were also some cotton mills, and machinery and other materials were made for both trades. At Bingley worsted spinning was dominant, but here too there were cotton mills—at this time the trades interlocked even more complexly than now. Remote Haworth[36] had worsted spinning and weaving, Denholme and Thornton[37] woollen goods; and the industrial villages closer to Bradford included Clayton, Allerton, Horton and Wibsey, the last described as 'on a lofty hill, which in every direction is perforated with coal mines'.[38] Bradford was a wool-marketing centre for all this district, and its turnover in worsted yarns and materials was larger than in any other market except Leeds,[39] though for cloth, Huddersfield was second only to Leeds.[40] Halifax also grew industrially during this phase, and combined activity in manufacturing woollen and worsted goods with the maintenance of a market which in 1851, had 'rather more business . . .

FIG. 36. The main streets of the town still survive and the parishes included in the borough are shown: attention is called in the text to the decline of population in the central wards during the eighteen-forties. Leeds parish included the townships named (the Leeds township covering eight wards—West, North (N), Northwest, Northeast, East, South (S), Mill Hill (MH) and Kirkgate). The boundary of the parish became also the municipal and parliamentary borough boundary.

Based on maps in *Report of the Commissioners appointed to report and advise upon the boundaries and wards of certain boroughs and corporate towns in England and Wales*, Pt. II, 1837.

of late years than formerly, when the stuff manufacture had migrated to Bradford'.[41] The competition of Bradford was felt also at Wakefield, a town always on the margins of the wool textile area whose growth towards the end of the nineteenth century was associated with coalmining and engineering rather than with wool.[42] Dewsbury and Heckmondwike were already centres of blanket production[43]—and in time the shoddy trade was located in these towns and also in Batley and Ossett. In the mid-nineteenth century, Leeds was still a major wool manufacturing centre: Dodd states that 'it presents marked evidence by the numerous tall chimneys visible on every side, of the extensive manufactures carried on'.[44] In 1838, it was estimated that Leeds had 106 woollen mills at which nearly 10,000 people, over a quarter of them women, were employed. Many of the mills were on the River Aire.

Industrial change within a few decades is well shown in the Ossett and Horbury district, between Wakefield and Dewsbury and still—somewhat tenuously—administratively independent of both.[45] In the early part of the nineteenth century, both Ossett and Horbury were 'hilltop' villages (comparatively speaking) in which a number of domestic workers lived, with mills on the rivers and streams though weaving was brought into the mills only after 1840. In Ossett all the woollen mills were closed between 1860 and 1890, and most were used for shoddy and mungo manufacture. This trade has continued to grow, and with it there has developed engineering serving the main industry, for example by the assembly and repair of machines used in the 'rag industry', and the making of fans and dust-extractors. All these firms are small and specialized. In Horbury, the woollen trade collapsed in the nineteen-twenties, and now survives only in the making of knitting wools, though oddly enough a cotton firm was established here in 1920, as the proprietors thought it would be profitable to bring the raw material to Yorkshire and sell it in the Leeds and Bradford market. But the most remarkable development at Horbury has been in engineering, including car springs, industrial equipment of a wide range (hardly at all for textiles) and the repairing of railway stock. And another industry has grown here through the chance circumstance that Mr. Sykes, an eighteenth-century cobbler, was very successful in making leather sports goods: now some 1,500 people are so engaged, primarily in a one-time woollen mill at Horbury.

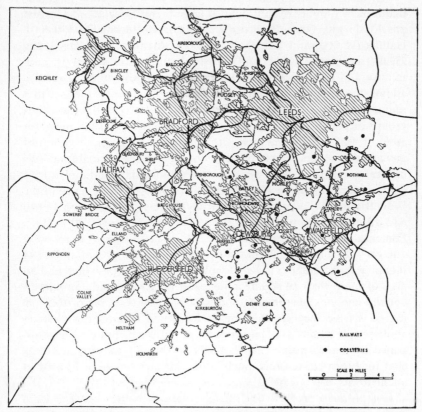

FIG. 37. BUILT-UP AREAS IN WEST YORKSHIRE, 1950

As explained in the text, the conurbation lacks the continuity of others in the country. Ribbon development is well shown: the surviving collieries are marked. There are several examples of administrative areas obviously made for convenience rather than as a recognition of the existence of well-defined towns, notably Rothwell, Morley, Spenborough, Pudsey and Elland. It is hard to see why Denby Dale, Kirkburton, Holmfirth and Meltham were included at all.

M

The Character of the Conurbation

The distinctive character of the West Yorkshire conurbation is that it has a number of well-defined large towns, of which the largest are Leeds (505,000), Bradford (292,000), Huddersfield (129,000), Halifax (98,000) and Wakefield (60,000). All these, and Dewsbury (53,000) are strong market and industrial centres, well served by road, railway and canal.[45] But the neat division of the entire area into administrative districts—thirty-three of them—conceals the fact that municipal boroughs and urban districts are not necessarily towns but groups of villages or small towns linked together for such purposes as control of sewage, public health and provision or preservation of any amenities there may happen to be—that is, the normal functions of local government (Fig. 37). In its present form, the administrative districts date only from 1939 when the number of urban areas in the West Riding (excluding county boroughs) was reduced from 119 to 68: within the conurbation, the number fell from over 90 to 33.[47] Some of these 'urban districts' existing before 1939 were mere villages—one, Scammonden, now in Colne valley, had only 394 inhabitants in a remote Pennine valley and Rishworth, which had an area of more than 10 square miles, had only 838 inhabitants in an equally remote valley to the southwest of Halifax. Some of the new divisions have the very mixture of town and country areas which some people regard as ideal for local government. But this has happened by chance rather than by design—through the circumstances that for historical reasons much of its industry has been located in small towns and villages.

Compromises worked out through various battles between local authorities have resulted in the present arrangement by which thirty-three administrative districts divide up 481 square miles which have a population of 1,692,000 (Figs. 38, 39). Leeds C.B. has managed to extend itself over 59 square miles, Bradford C.B. over 40 square miles but Pudsey M.B. staunchly preserves its 8·3 square miles between them. These boundaries have been extended gradually in a series of acts: and by their successive aggrandisements Huddersfield C.B. and Halifax C.B. have each extended to 22 square miles,

---

FIG. 38. No part of England had a more complex system of urban districts than this and the intricate parish boundaries will be noted, especially in the south. Clearly such an arrangement of town boundaries was ludicrous, but there were slight signs of rationalization by 1899.

FIG. 38. WEST YORKSHIRE, ADMINISTRATIVE AREAS, 1888 AND 1899

Dewsbury C.B. to 10 square miles and Wakefield to almost as much. There are six municipal boroughs, of which the smallest, Ossett, 5 square miles, has a population of 14,600 and the largest, Keighley, has 37 square miles and 57,000 people, but this includes several places that are in fact separate industrial villages such as Haworth and Oakworth. And much the same phenomena are seen among the twenty-one urban districts, with Ripponden, having 21 square miles and 5,000 people as perhaps an extreme example. Few of the urban districts are simple straightforward 'towns', though one may note Heckmondwike, with slightly over one square mile and 8,700 in-habitants, which has somehow managed to keep out of the union of three towns, Cleckheaton, Liversedge and Gomersal into Spen-borough in 1915, with 8 square miles and (1911) 31,000 people;[48] to this two more urban districts, Birkenshaw and Hunsworth, with parts of the Halifax R.D. were added in 1939 to give an area of 13 square miles with over 36,000 people.[49] Spenborough was incor-porated as a municipal borough on 23 May, 1955. Three administra-tive phenomena are represented here—first the union of a number of remote industrial villages and hamlets into an urban district as in Ripponden, and second the union of a number of small towns into one large urban district, and third a single town that is defined as an urban district—almost a rarity in these parts. In this process of administrative rationalization, the old rural districts have been com-pletely eliminated from the West Yorkshire conurbation area, and thanks to similar developments in Lancashire, there is now some form of urban administration all the way from Pontefract and Knottingley to the Mersey.

Local autonomy was the guiding principle when urban (sanitary) districts were first distinguished in 1872, but very soon after this the major towns began to extend their boundaries. Bradford, in 1882 acquired Thornbury and part of Calverley U.D., in 1899, four entire urban districts, Eccleshill, Idle, Thornton and Tong, and part of North Brierley U.D., in 1930, Clayton U.D., and in 1939 part of Yeadon U.D. with a few hundred acres of the rural district of

FIG. 39. The whole pattern was gradually simplified by uniting urban and rural districts into larger units. The expansion of Leeds will be noted, but there is only a short stretch of common frontier between Leeds and Brad-ford. As a result of the County Review Orders, the pattern of administra-tion districts is simpler than in other conurbations. Note also the more restricted, and in some ways more logical, definition of the conurbation by C. B. Fawcett, though Wakefield might well have been included even in 1931.

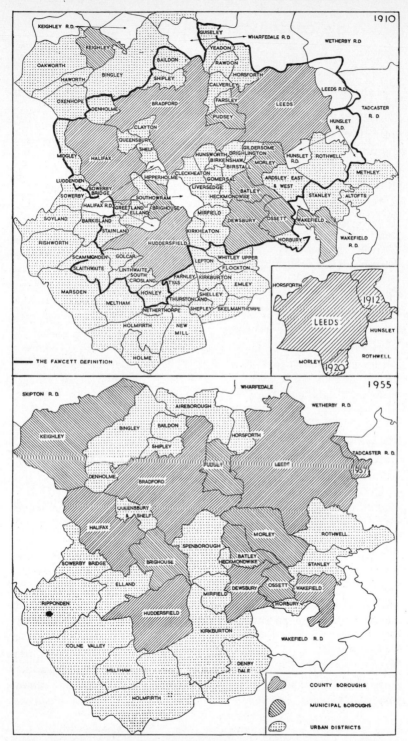

FIG. 39. WEST YORKSHIRE, ADMINISTRATIVE AREAS, 1910 AND 1955–7

Wharfedale.[50] Leeds was extended in 1912 by 7 square miles on the north and east, the civil parishes of Roundhay, Seacroft, Barwick-in-Elmet and Shadwell, in 1920 by the parish of Middleton on the south, which was immediately used for a housing scheme, in 1927 by 12½ square miles more on the east, conspicuously Templenewsam, and the north—Alwoodley and (part of) Eccup.[51] Those who know these cities will realize that the housing developments of the inter-War period were made possible only by these territorial extensions—and this applies both to Corporation and privately-financed housing.

Neither city has reason to feel that it has had more than its due, for the neighbours have shown the same tendency to fortify themselves against encroachment that was noted in the Manchester district. Morley, now having 15 square miles and a population of 39,800, became a borough in 1885, acquired the Churwell U.D. and part of West Ardsley parish in 1891, and in 1939 absorbed the urban districts of Drighlington, Gildersome and practically all of Ardsley East and West.[52] In consequence it became a long expanse of territory, partly rural, partly urban, between Leeds and Batley. Pudsey, apparently destined to absorb rather than to be absorbed, became a municipal borough in 1899, and in 1939 acquired the whole of the urban districts of Calverley and Farsley, two industrial villages between Leeds and Bradford that might well have been absorbed by either.[53] Horsforth U.D., adjacent to Leeds, has maintained its identity throughout all the changes, and had in 1951 an area of 4 square miles and 14,100 inhabitants, and beyond it, in the Aire valley, three small industrial towns, Guiseley, Rawdon and Yeadon, with part of Wharfedale rural district were in 1939 made into one urban district of nearly 11 square miles and 27,500 people.[54] It is significant that only four 'towns' have shown substantial increases of population during the past thirty years—the three just mentioned, Pudsey, Horsforth and Aireborough with Baildon, a suburb of Bradford. Leeds, successfully adding to itself on the rural north and east, has not managed to acquire extensions of consequence on the south and west, that is in areas which already had well-established industrial towns and villages by the last quarter of the nineteenth century. And the success of Pudsey is spectacular and not unhumorous.

Other towns have had a similar administrative history. Batley M.B., extended to include part of Upper Soothill in 1910, added Birstall in 1939, making its population more than 40,000 in 7 square miles.[55] Wakefield, a county borough since 1913, having absorbed

Sandal Magna U.D. in 1909, part of Lupset in 1931, part of Stanley in 1939 and 500 acres from Wakefield R.D. in 1951 consisted of 9 square miles with 60,400 people.[56] And Dewsbury, which became a county borough in 1915, was extended in 1910 to 10½ square miles by the absorption of the entire urban districts of Ravensthorpe, Soothill Nether and Thornhill, with the part of Soothill Upper not given to Batley.[57] There has been in fact no change in this case since 1910, but for any further extension both Dewsbury and Wakefield look to the area between them, including Ossett M.B. and Horbury U.D. Inevitably, Dewsbury interlocks complexly with Batley and with Heckmondwike, but further unions would meet considerable local opposition. And, as shown on p. 174, it cannot be argued that these towns have had recently, or are likely to have in the near future, any considerable increase in population as with the exception of Wakefield all of them appear to have been stationary in numbers for fifty years. The main problem is re-housing in such a way that the valuable agricultural land of the district is not entirely removed from its present use. Within the present administrative system, clearly the result of a series of compromises, there is an intermingling of country and town of such a character that most of West Yorkshire's towns have land on which new houses can be built. One curious specialization is rhubarb-growing which between Bradford, Leeds, Wakefield and Dewsbury covers over half the country's total area given to this crop. Roots are taken into long, low and dark sheds in the autumn, and the fresh pink stalks pulled from December to April. More than one-third of the arable acreage in some parishes is used for rhubarb.[58]

Population Developments

In this conurbation, as in its neighbour on the west side of the Pennines, the imprint of nineteenth-century industrial and architectural enterprise is all too clear, especially in the town centres. The population rose from 292,000 in 1801 to 792,000 in 1851 and 1,527,000 in 1901, after which the increase was slight, to 1,614,000 in 1921 and 1,655,000 in 1931 (+ 2·6 per cent), and 1,692,000 in 1951 (+2·2 per cent).[59] There is little indication that the conurbation is inadequately defined, for only 33,400 of its 834,300 workers (4 per cent) come from outside areas, over half of them to Leeds, and only 15,500 people are resident in the conurbation but working outside it.[60]

The Pennine textile areas had a prominent share in the modern industrialization of Britain. But here, as to the west, there has been little increase of population since 1900, though from 1931 to 1951 there was an increase of 18 per cent in the number of occupied dwellings.[61] The population doubled from 1801–1841, and doubled again within the next fifty years: during the decade 1861–1871, for example, there were reports of industrial expansion and related population increase almost everywhere.[62] In Morley, there was extension of the woollen cloth trade, coal mining and stone quarrying, at Batley 'extension of the trade of the district', and at Ossett, Dewsbury, Mirfield similar developments.[63] At East Ardsley 'large iron works' were established and at West Ardsley new collieries and stone quarries were opened: in Wakefield, ironworks were extended, rope, twine, thread and other factories opened, and general trade prosperity reported.[64] Everywhere the reports were similar and the increases were all ascribed to industrial prosperity though at Sandal Magna, a small increase was due to suburban expansion from Wakefield. But the phenomenon—seen also in other cities such as Manchester (p. 138) and Liverpool (p. 109)—of decline in central wards was also seen in Leeds and Bradford. The Kirkgate ward in Leeds had a decrease from 3,411 in 1841 to 3,337 in 1851 due to the removal to the suburbs of families who had formerly lived over the shop,[65] and further declines in this ward and in the South ward after 1861 were due to the conversion of dwellings into warehouses, demolitions for building 'the Northeast railway', and to the removal of labourers to adjoining districts.[66] But the population was still increasing in the East ward of Leeds, until recently a highly congested area of back-to-back houses. Mill Hill ward had a sharp decline (from 5,312 to 3,902) from 1861 to 1871, but this was due to street improvements, railway building and the use of land for warehouses instead of dwellings.[67] In Bradford, the first similar sign of decrease was in the West End ward (365 acres) from 23,138 in 1871 to 18,143 in 1881 and 15,999 in 1891.[68] These decreases were the first clear signs of the outward spread of population from the centres of towns, and the removal of people as the town centre became filled with shops, warehouses, offices, banks, railway stations and lines—and all that makes up the heart of a city. And here, as in other towns, this grew where slums had been before.

But the main difficulty in 1851 was to define the towns of the West Riding at all, and the Census commissioners only succeeded in recognizing nine.[69] Of these Leeds and Bradford, which had identical boundaries as parliamentary and municipal boroughs, were the largest—Bradford had 103,800 people in 10 square miles and Leeds 172,300 in 32 square miles. It will be noted that the definition was comparatively generous—for example (see Fig. 36) Leeds borough included the central township and those of Armley, Beeston, Bramley, Chapel-Allerton, Farnley, Headingley, Holbeck, Wortley, Hunslet and Potternewton—all of which in time became residential or industrial parts of the city. And in Bradford, the boundary was drawn so that Manningham, Great Horton and Bowling were within the borough. Halifax (33,600 in 1851), Huddersfield (30,900 in 1851) and Wakefield (22,100 in 1851) were parliamentary boroughs; Halifax and Wakefield were also municipal boroughs. Other places recognized as towns, though not possessing corporations nor a parliamentary seat, were Bingley (5,000), Dewsbury (5,000), Keighley (13,000) and Sowerby Bridge (4,400). This oddly short list includes the main commercial centres of the Conurbation, but not the somewhat formless industrial villages and residential areas that were ultimately neatly tied up into administrative parcels labelled boroughs and urban districts.

The Conurbation Today

Definition by administrative units makes a conurbation only for statistical purposes but even if it is true, as Fawcett commented, that there is little feeling of unity within this area,[70] there is certainly great local loyalty in its numerous towns and villages. Any overriding unity possessed is derived from its industrial character, with wool textiles as the main trade, combined with mining and engineering. Fundamentally there has been little change for in 1951, 293,000 out of 831,000 were employed in textile trades with paper, 103,000 in the metal and engineering group and 16,000 in mining.[71] There are some cotton mills in Yorkshire and some woollen mills in Lancashire but the main differentiation remains . . . 'although the wool textile industry is . . . widely diffused over the north and west of Great Britain . . . by far the greater part of the industry is focused in West Yorkshire with approximately three-quarters of the machine equipment and of numbers employed.'[72] At present no marked expansion of the wool industries seems likely, but there has been no heavy decline and Yorkshire has therefore avoided the acute unemployment problem characteristic of Lancashire. Thanks to a wide range of industry, it would seem probable that virtual stability may be achieved.

Fawcett's pre-1939 prognostications that no great expansion but only stability could be expected in the north, have been justified.[73]

Leeds, having increased by + 4·6 per cent in 1931–1951, had 505,000 people: but Bradford's population, 292,000 in 1951, has changed little in the past thirty years. Between these cities there has been a marked increase in the area covered by Pudsey M.B., Horsforth U.D., Aireborough U.D. and Baildon U.D. which, grouped together, had 58,400 people in 1921, 64,600 in 1931 and 82,000 in 1951. These areas are by no means wholly 'residential' in the usual sense of the term but include within their wide bounds areas regarded as good residential sites, especially on the north and non-industrial side of the conurbation. On the other hand, many towns in the heart of the industrial area are declining in numbers, such as (1931–1951) Dewsbury (− 1·5 per cent), Batley (− 3·8 per cent), Ossett (−1·8 per cent), Mirfield (− 1·9 per cent) and Heckmondwike (− 3·8 per cent). And a number of western areas have even more marked declines, such as Colne valley (− 9·1 per cent), Meltham (− 7·5 per cent), Sowerby Bridge (− 8·7 per cent), Ripponden (− 4·3 per cent) and—in lesser degree—Elland and Denholme. Most parts of the conurbation show little change of population for at least fifty years. In the south Holmfirth (− 5·6 per cent), Denby Dale (− 9·9 per cent), two adjoining urban districts covering 43½ square miles and with a population of less than 30,000, show conspicuous decreases after declining slightly since 1914.

Preservation of rural amenities and—equally important—of rich agricultural areas that have no particular scenic charm is clearly necessary, but rehousing has encroached on many countrysides. In Wakefield, for example, there are altogether 18,695 houses of which 7,826 (1957) have been built in housing estates[74], and in Ossett, on the other hand, some solid, stone-built houses dating back as far as the seventeenth century, have been modernized, but over 700 houses have been added since 1945,[75] Huddersfield's housing schemes are located mostly on heights on the edge of its morland, yet within a couple of miles of the town centre. But perhaps the severest housing problem of all is in Leeds.[76] In Leeds there are 154,140 dwellings— houses and flats, of which 90,000 are regarded as 'obsolescent' due to age, congestion, bad arrangement and general lack of amenities. Over 56,000 of these are 'back-to-back' houses, of three types, first, 16,000 built before 1844, second, 28,000 built from 1844 to 1874 and third, 12,000 built mainly from 1874 to 1909. In the year 1925, a housing act prohibited the erection of this type of house unless the street plan was already approved but the last back-to-back house was completed in July 1937! In the years 1934–1939, 14,000 houses were demolished but even now over half of the city's houses must be pulled down. And inevitably this must mean still further outward expansion of the city as the density of houses in back-to-back housing districts was as much as 80–90 per acre compared with a fraction of this in new houses or even blocks of flats. Leeds in time will be a city having a central area of flats, some of as many as eight or nine storeys, and a vast outer area of typical housing estate, built mostly by the city but including some private enterprise. In one respect, Leeds is fortunate, as within its boundaries there is almost 60 square miles, far more than the 43 square miles of Liverpool or the almost exactly similar area of Manchester.

The 1951 Census volume includes a map of land use for the Conurbation area. The first category, 'industrial, commercial and older residential districts of the larger towns', includes central Leeds, Bradford, Shipley, Keighley, Halifax, Huddersfield, Wakefield and Dewsbury—the last with an extension into Batley. The second grouping, 'transitional areas of mixed development: smaller towns' seems vague but it shows fairly convincingly the areas in which old industrial villages have gradually become towns, either individually or as parts of modern urban districts. Thirdly, the 'suburban fringe of the larger towns' is defined as an area around Leeds from Middleton on the south to Horsforth on the northwest, together with the northern suburbs of Bradford. The fourth and last group, 'rural-residential districts and smaller industrial centres', apparently shows those parts of the Conurbation which have a number of small industrial settlements and a somewhat amorphous spread of housing. (It is not perhaps too far-fetched to regard this last area as—in modern terminology—a less 'developed' form of the second type noted above.) Clearly this fourfold division can hardly be regarded as the *ne plus ultra* of town land use classification in the Conurbation, but it shows a distinct appreciation of the personality of the area.

Some years ago R. E. Dickinson drew attention to the retail and wholesale trade of Leeds and Bradford:[77] the 1951 Census of Distribution showed that in value Leeds had one-third of the Conurbation's retail trade and Bradford one-fifth.[78] Nevertheless a number of other towns can rightly claim to be strong shopping centres: for example, a Mayor of Huddersfield claims that 'although the population is only about 130,000 the shopping facilities . . . provide for a population of approximately 250,000, including outlying districts'.[79] There may be some pardonable civic pride here, but a few towns have clearly risen above others as major shopping centres—most of which are places recognized as towns in 1851. On the statistical basis provided by the 1951 investigation, the average trade per head throughout the Conurbation was £128 but only six towns have an average per head higher than this, namely, Bradford, £159, Halifax, £149, Heckmondwike, £151, Huddersfield, £148, Leeds, £148 and Wakefield, £151—next follow Dewsbury, £127 and Keighley, £121.[80] Of these towns, Heckmondwike may need some explanation: having survived all the amalgamations that have made up Spenborough, it remains a good shopping town with a strong market. The others are the major towns which have both the greater part of the trade and the highest per head of population. In many of the other places the trade per head is substantially less—for example £81 at Batley, £73 at Morley, £88 at Bingley and only £39 at Stanley. One must not press this evidence too far but it would at least suggest that within certain towns strong shopping quarters are established. It cannot, for example, be without significance that more money (£1,332,000 as compared with £1,261,000) is taken in the shops of Heckmondwike (8,900) than those of Horsforth (14,300).

There are at present two main tendencies perceptible in the outward spread of the population—but neither is new. In the first place, coal mining has been pushed eastwards with the result that most of the major pits are now east of Leeds and Wakefield and many in the centre and west of the Conurbation are now abandoned. Therefore places such as Pontefract (23,200 in 1951; 19,900 in 1931) and Knottingley (10,000; 8,500) are now increasing in population, and further eastward movement is certain. Secondly, towns within easy reach of the Conurbation, such as Ilkley, Otley and Harrogate and various villages have increased steadily in population ever since they were first reached by the railways in the middle of the nineteenth century. And this outward movement seems likely to continue but there appears to be little reason to expect any substantial increase of population within the Conurbation, so that any problems of land use will arise from re-housing rather than industrial expansion.

CHAPTER 7

TYNESIDE

TYNESIDE has a population of 835,000, a quarter of a million less than Birmingham, in an area of 90 square miles divided between thirteen separate administrative units. Of these all the six in Co. Durham with four in Northumberland—Tynemouth, Wallsend, Newcastle and Newburn—have the river as a boundary: the other three, Gosforth, Longbenton and Whitley Bay, are outlying residential areas. In 1937, a Royal Commission[1] suggested that all these thirteen authorities with two others (Blaydon U.D. and Ryton U.D.) should be united into one borough, partly because 'the river Tyne is not now a suitable boundary between administrative areas' (Fig. 42). The conurbation's essential unity lies in its dependence on the river and in the possession of one main commercial and administrative centre at the river's first bridge-point, Newcastle-upon-Tyne, used by the Great North road and in modern times by the railway from London to Edinburgh. For centuries this city has been traversed by north-bound traffic and not unnaturally it has become the regional capital for the northeast of England.

The 1951 definition of this conurbation might be criticized as restricted but Fig. 42 shows that it corresponds fairly closely to the present built-up areas, subject to the inevitable use of administrative boundaries. But Fawcett[2] in 1931 included far more as Tyneside, conspicuously Sunderland C.B. (186,000 in 1931), the rural districts of South Shields and Sunderland on the Wear, as well as the urban districts of Blaydon and Felling. The Fawcett definition carried the conurbation much farther into Co. Durham than the 1951 definition, perhaps reasonably, for there is little open country between the Tyne towns and Sunderland, though this town on the Wear is sufficiently strong to be a major centre in its own right. In its present restricted, and possibly logical form the conurbation is the industrial and commercial area of Tyneside, having on both the north and the south a mining area that, though divided into urban districts, is in fact an agricultural landscape dotted at intervals with mining villages and towns. As in other mining areas, it is hard to regard many of the colliery settlements as in fact towns even though the 'urban districts' have, within areas ranging from a few square miles to as much as

20 square miles, a population of 15,000–50,000 or even more. But around Tyneside there is in fact continuity of built-up area, because here mining has been linked to a variety of other industries as well as to shipbuilding and overseas trade.

Site and Situation

Newcastle-upon-Tyne, the one natural focus of Tyneside, is excellently served by rail and road and more fortunate than most major British cities in the possession of only one major railway station. A strong industrial centre, Newcastle is also a trading and residential town, with an attractive shopping quarter, an interesting market, and pleasant suburbs close to the town centre though here, as elsewhere, housing has spread farther and farther outward, to the coast at Whitley Bay, northwards into Gosforth, an urban district unabsorbed by the parent city, and even to villages along the Tyne valley. Gateshead remains separate, and is sometimes regarded as a 'twin' town, which grew in population partly by overflow from Newcastle but was at all times more obviously industrial. Newcastle is a social centre not only for Northumberland but for a considerable part of Durham and was described in 1928 by H. A. Mess as possessing 'a quasi metropolitan character for all the country between the Cheviots and the Pennines on the west, and the North Sea on the east and from the Border to the Tees'.[3]

The lower Tyne now has 30 ft. of water at high tide to Scotswood bridge but in its present form it is, like the Clyde and the Mersey, largely the product of modern improvements. The valley has a flat floor not generally more than half-a-mile wide, but in places as much as 2 miles wide, bordered by steep banks rising from 50 to 150 ft. above the river: as Fig. 43 shows, much of the industrial area is in the valley and almost all the residential area on higher ground. At Jarrow Slake and above Newcastle, for example, the flood-plain is wide and the land rises gently from it but normally industry is confined to the restricted riverside sites. Unfortunately some valuable sites are derelict, for example at Felling where the shore is occupied by an abandoned chemical works and dilapidated cottages. At Newcastle, ten miles from the sea, the valley narrows, the river could be forded and the high ground on either side approached by roads which traversed tributary valleys. The original site of Newcastle was the high bluff on the north bank, used by the Romans for their station of Pons Elii. Defoe[4] found the town

a spacious, extended, infinitely populous Place: 'tis seated upon the

River Tyne, which is here a noble, large and deep River, and Ships of any reasonable Burthen may come safely up to the very Town.

Defoe also mentions the 'strong and stately stone Bridge of seven very great Arches, rather larger than the Arches of London Bridge' and like its rival covered with houses. In the journey to the river, there were noted 'prodigious Heaps, I might say mountains of Coals, which are dug up at every Pit'. Newcastle stood on the 'declivity of two exceeding high Hills (north and south of the river) which, together with the Smoke of the Coals, make it not the pleasantest place in the World to live in', but the 'goodness of the River' made amends.

Coal and Communications

In modern times the Northumberland and Durham coalfield extends for some 20 miles north and south of the Tyne, having as its characteristic feature a large number of colliery villages in a dominantly agricultural landscape. At present some of the old mining villages consist of decayed houses around abandoned mines, especially on the west side, while farther east large new collieries are expanding in production and are in need of labour. Whatever happens, it is clear that substantial changes in the distribution of population may be expected. Tyneside is inevitably part of this coalfield but distinct from it in two ways, first in the possession of advantages for overseas trade, realized from mediaeval times onward, and second in its long industrial tradition, conspicuously in salt, glass and ultimately in shipbuilding and engineering. Tyneside's natural advantages included a river accessible to shipping in mediaeval times, coal mined in adits or shallow mines close to the waterfront, and the growth in Newcastle of a mercantile town at the first bridge-point of the river. Defoe[5] recognized in Newcastle that 'the River . . . bringing Ships up to the very Keys, and fetching the Coals down from the Country, make it a place of very great Business'. He notes also that coal was carried to (South) Shields to evaporate sea-salt, and that so much was used that smoke ascended in clouds for many miles round: in fact six tons of coal were needed to make one ton of salt, and there were pans along the coast from Sunderland to Blyth.[6]

Many of the advantages possesses by Tyneside were shared by Sunderland at the mouth of the Wear, by the Hartlepools developed as railway ports, and by Middlesbrough on Tees-side, all of which are possible competitors with the Tyneside towns as ports and industrial centres. A. E. Smailes has pointed out that the coal-mining areas inland from Sunderland and new ports at Seaham Harbour, the Hartlepools and on Tees-side, were opened up by railways long before the middle of the nineteenth century.[7] These ports gained trade at the expense of the Tyne, which was hard to navigate until improvements were made from 1860 onwards. Although Newcastle and its neighbours have clear natural advantages of site and situation, industrial strength could be maintained only by enterprise, conspicuously seen now in the development of trading estates to increase and diversify employment, and a century ago by the improvement of the river which like the Mersey and the Clyde was provided with quays and docks. Earlier, in the second quarter of the nineteenth century, the construction of railways was equally necessary to maintain the strength of Tyneside: here[8] the mineral lines were preceded by wagon ways which were introduced early in the seventeenth century and had come into general use by 1670.

As Defoe said of Newcastle,[9] 'It is not only enriched by the Coal Trade; but there are also very considerable merchants in it, who carry on foreign Trade to divers Parts of the World, especially to Holland, Hamburgh, Norway and the Baltick.' And he continues by explaining that ships are built 'to Perfection, I mean as to Strength, and Firmness, and to bear the Sea; and as the Coal Trade occasions a demand for such strong Ships, a great many are built here'. Various trades arose to fit out ships; and in addition there was 'a considerable Manufacture of Hard Ware, or Wrought Iron, lately erected after the manner of Sheffield, which is very helpful for employing the Poor, of which this Town has always a prodigious Number'. All the main features of the local industrial development are implied by Defoe. In the first place, coal could be mined close to the river and conveyed to the staithes by carts or along the wagonways, so that here alone in Britain was it economic to ship coal in mediaeval times both to east coast ports, including London, and to Flemish, Dutch and occasionally other ports. Secondly, the association of coal with maritime trade meant that merchants bought food and—in time—industrial raw materials advantageously: in 1652, the Newcastle Merchant Adventurers[10] said that 'By Providence they are seated in a barren and poore country, which commonly requires great supply of corne and other necessaryes', brought by sea, 'which they were better able to doe by reason of the advantage and opportunity they have above other places in the commodity of cole, by which they commonly make their voyages, and bring home their returns for small freight'. Agricultural produce, for example, was brought from Bedfordshire, Cambridgeshire, Huntingdonshire and Northamptonshire, including the upper Ouse valley. Thirdly, other industries were directly stimulated by the expanding coal-trade, and small coal unsuited for shipment was sold cheaply for the making of salt, glass, pottery and chemicals.[11] In short, it was the association of mining with shipping that proved to be the basis of Tyneside's industrial growth though it is only within the past few decades that a 'conurbation' has developed.

On Tyneside, coal-mining has been carried on from the thirteenth century, and exports from the last quarter of the fourteenth century to c. 1515 averaged 2,000–7,000 tons annually.[12] During the sixteenth and seventeenth centuries the amount of coal mined increased markedly from c. 65,000 tons a year in 1551–1560 to 1,225,000 tons in 1681–1690 and it was estimated that over 600,000 tons were shipped in 1684–1685. At the end of the reign of Henry VIII, almost all the 'ship's coal' came from pits in the manors of Whickham and Gateshead, that is on the south side of the river from the Tyne bridge to the mouth of the Derwent, but in Elizabethan times other pits were sunk at Winlanton, Stella and Ryton: and in the first decade of the seventeenth century, mining was extended to Newburn, Denton, Elswick and Benwell.[13] Mining began at Jarrow in 1617 and at Walker in 1654 and coal was brought to a wharf at the junction of the Tyne and the Ouseburn. During the seventeenth century there was a movement of mining away from the river, for example to Fenham in 1651; by 1700, the coal for shipment came from collieries as much as 8–10 miles away but there was no marked expansion until the nineteenth century. Originally adits were used but by the middle of the sixteenth century one mine at Gateshead was said to be 36 fathoms deep, and by 1700, some of the pits near the Tyne and the Wear were as much as 300–400 ft. deep.[14]

Industrial Variety

In 1698, the steam engine was invented and in 1710 so improved that it could be used for pumping. Within a few years, engines were used at the Heaton, Benton and Jesmond collieries, but by c. 1760 most of the pits in the central Tyne area were drowned out and a number of pits were sunk farther east, for example at Walker in 1762, Willington in 1775 and Wallsend in 1780 and at places on the south side of the river.[15] These newer deep pits each had as many as 300–400 workers, many of whom lived in mining villages, the nuclei of Wallsend, Hebburn and other places.[16] The salt industry prospered

N

throughout the seventeenth century but although at one time 1,000 men were employed, the seasalt industry declined gradually during the eighteenth century.[17] Nevertheless, other industries developed, including glass and pottery. The first glassworks was at St. Lawrence just to the east of the Tyne-Ouseburn confluence (c. 1616) and for over two centuries this industry flourished on both sides of the river.[18]

The iron industry was established on Tyneside during the seventeenth century but the main developments in metallurgical work came much later; for example in 1747 the Gateshead ironworks (Hawks Crawshay) was founded and blast-furnaces were built early in the nineteenth century on the Tyne at Lemington, Newburn and Wylam.[19] Out of the ironworking, shipbuilding and mechanical engineering developed. R. Stephenson made the *Rocket* in Newcastle and eight engines used on the Manchester and Liverpool railway were built at his works, which were founded in 1823.[20] Unfortunately this industry is not now located on Tyneside, and in 1936, the lament was made that 'the almost complete absence of vehicular construction is . . . a matter to be regretted'.[21] Although Tyneside was well-established as an iron and steel and engineering area, such trades as the making of aeroplanes, motor-cars and bicycles had not been attracted and ship-building met with vicissitudes that became notorious in the case of Jarrow, where the closing of Palmer's Yard in 1934 reduced almost the entire town to unemployment. When this yard was opened in 1851, Jarrow grew from a small industrial centre of c. 7,000 people to a town five times as populous, but virtually dependent on this one industry. Nevertheless, shipbuilding has remained a significant industry and up to 1930, approximately two-fifths of the merchant tonnage launched in the United Kingdom (including Belfast) came from the northeast coast, and half of this from Tyneside.[22] Some famous liners were built here, including the *Mauretania* and the *Monarch of Bermuda*, but Tyneside has never been able to rival Belfast or the Clyde in the number of liners built and its contribution has been ordinary cargo boats, oil tankers and —conspicuously—warships.[23] A further contribution to national needs is made by the ordnance factory at Elswick, Newcastle, which has a wide range of products including naval guns.

Distinguished contributions to mechanical and electrical engineering have been made on Tyneside, notably at Elswick works, for example, where cranes, warehouse hoists, and dock gates, all hydraulically operated, were made from 1846. This firm provided the hydraulic mechanism for the Tyne Swing Bridge, completed in 1876, and the compound steam-driven pumping engines, the hydraulic accumulators and engines for the Tower Bridge, in 1894.[24] A Gateshead firm has provided boilers for coalmining and shipping and a firm at Heaton supplied the first steam turbine to the Cambridge power station in 1891.[25] In electricity the first incandescent lamp was demonstrated in 1880 but in 1885 the Edison-Swan company was moved to London.[26] Other important advances include the making of the first electric winch at Gateshead in 1886 and the first electric light plant in 1884: steam generators were made here also, and later at Heaton, Newcastle.[27] From 1901, many special types of metal switchgear, including one that is flame-proof for coal mines, have been made at Hebburn, which also has the only factory in Great Britain where mineral-insulated, copper-covered cables are made.[28]

Unfortunately, although many industries were begun on Tyneside a number of them either failed to develop or were even abandoned altogether. Early in the nineteenth century, the chemical industry[29] was strongly established and by 1867, half the alkali produced in the country was made here. At Walker the le Blanc process of making carbonate of lime from common salt was first worked in 1816; Jarrow chemical works were opened in 1823. Many other chemical works were opened, and sulphuric acid was made from 1812, but the main chemical centre of northeast England is now at Billingham on Tees. From the historic glass industry, there are three main survivals, including electric lamp bulbs at Newington, press glass at Gateshead and thermal glass at Wallsend, in a factory established in 1903.[30] Paint making, established in the eighteenth century, now survives in two large concerns which have absorbed many small ones and soap making is chiefly represented by a firm founded in 1837 which, as every housewife knows, is now fighting the battle of the detergents.[31] And mention must be made of a product manufactured in Newcastle and valued by some persons—Andrews Liver Salts.

Although Tyneside has always had a variety of industries, the essential problem of the inter-war period was that it failed to attract a sufficient number of new concerns. A government report of 1934 noted that new factories opened in 1932 and 1933 provided work for 83,250 persons but of these only 900 found employment in Northumberland, Durham and the North Riding of Yorkshire, as most of the new firms in expanding industries such as the electrical group were set up in Greater London, in the West Midlands or in Lancashire and Cheshire.[32] True, the record of invention on the

Tyne was distinguished, but it was said to be 'geographically too remote from what is regarded as the largest market for the sale of those goods which the new light industries are principally engaged in producing', in other words from London, the Home counties and to some extent the Midlands with Lancashire and Cheshire.[33] The very high rates of unemployment (Tyneside and Durham, 27 per cent, Jarrow, 57 per cent, compared with a national average of 16 per cent in 1934) were noted[34] and the solution favoured was to establish trading estates, of which the first—and largest—in this area was opened at Team valley in 1936. The aim of this enterprise was threefold: first to give employment; second to provide more employment for women[a] in an area where the established industries were primarily for men; and third, to attract a wider range of industry so that in any future depression the evils of 'all the eggs in one basket' might be avoided. The fate of Jarrow, proclaimed far and wide by its friends, at least showed that nowhere in the country was the need for industrial planning greater. Jarrow is the classic case of a 'one industry town', now generally regarded as inherently precarious. But the main argument for industrial diversification rests on the dangers common to any coalfield through the eventual exhaustion of supplies. Some success has attended vigorous efforts to bring new works to the trading estates, though remoteness remains an adverse factor, especially as road transport acquires growing dominance. On the other hand, it could well be agreed that the indefinite growth of industry in the London area, the Home counties and the Midlands—especially the West Midland area—is greatly to be deprecated and that provided articles can be sold at home and abroad as cheaply if manufactured in Gateshead rather than in Coventry, Luton, Birmingham, or London, they should be manufactured in Gateshead.

Tyneside became a 'conurbation' by the beginning of the twentieth century, largely because the work of making the river navigable for big ships was carried out relatively recently—much later than on Merseyside (p. 97) or Clydeside (p. 310). Various consequences followed from this relatively late development. In the first place, there are on Tyneside a number of industrial towns and villages sharply conscious of their individuality, not at all favourably inclined to the suggestions of the 1937 Royal Commission that a new borough on Tyneside should unite them all.[35] Secondly, on each side of the river,

[a] 7,000 girls were sent out from Co. Durham and Tyneside as domestic servants in the depression years by an organization run by a committee of ladies.

there is no lack of suitable land for rehousing and industrial purposes, including some patches of derelict ground such as those on the river at Felling and Hebburn. Thirdly, the total population has remained virtually unchanged for approximately thirty years and there is no reason to anticipate any considerable increase in the immediate future. This trait is shared with other conurbations—notably Merseyside, Manchester and West Yorkshire.

River and Rail Transport

Railway construction in the northeast preceded the river improvement so necessary to maintain the long-established export trade in coal. The care of the tidal reaches of the river was vested in the corporation of Newcastle, which had various charters dating back to the reign of Henry II.[36] At the beginning of the nineteenth century, the river was in a bad state: ' . . . there are many large sands grown up . . . in some parts there was not water enough, when the tide was out, to cross in a sculler'. The Rennie report of 1816 on possible improvements was implemented only by the removal of one shoal and in 1833 complaints were made by shipowners, coalowners and by the town of Gateshead that Newcastle did not care properly for the river.[37] In 1837, the Cubitt report led to the construction by the Corporation of the quay at Newcastle, with various jetties at Wallsend and elsewhere.[38] Meanwhile in 1833, the Stanhope and Tyne railway, of which the lower sections were recently completed, obtained a licence to build at South Shields a quay wall 2–3 ft. above the highest spring tides along the front of three small docks which now became one large wet dock; later, other railway companies sought powers to build docks.[39]

Several railways were built before 1850, including the Carlisle and Newcastle line, 1839, the York and Newcastle line, 1836–1843, the Newcastle and Darlington Junction, 1844, the Newcastle and Berwick line, authorized in 1845 and completed in 1847. Many others were built, including that from Newcastle to North Shields in 1839, which bridged the Ouseburn valley at 108 ft. above stream level and also crossed Willington Dene.[40] In 1847, the York–Newcastle and the Newcastle–Berwick lines were amalgamated under the names of the three towns and seven years later this line, together with the York and North Midland and the Leeds Northern became the Northeastern railway. This meant that one company now had all the major lines from Hull and Leeds northwards to the Border, to which they added the Newcastle-Carlisle railway in 1862.[41] In 1850

Newcastle's one main station, Central, was opened,[42] a feature that travellers in cities with three or four main stations may well envy. The high-level bridge (112 ft. above H.W.M.) across the Tyne, opened in 1849, is almost unique in Britain in its possession of a roadway also.[43]

The early railway history was more fortunate than that of the river. In 1849, no ship of more than 400 tons could use the river as the depth of water over the Bar was only 6 ft., the shoals from the entrance to Newcastle were extending and the harbour at South Shields was becoming almost useless. The Tyne Commissioners, who included representatives from Newcastle, Gateshead, Tynemouth and South Shields, were first appointed by an Act of 1850 to control the river with the financial resource of various coal and ballast dues.[44] At first progress was slow, but signs of improvement came from 1854 in the building of entrance piers at Tynemouth and South Shields and of the Northumberland dock.[45] In 1855 a Royal Commission stated that it would be good

> if all the members might be induced to believe that the interest of New-castle and Shields were identical and inseparable; and to bury in oblivion those local jealousies and animosities which could only prejudice the community to which they belong.[46]

Even so, in 1860, the Tyne was 'at its very lowest point of decadence as a navigable river' relative to its trade,[47] and ships of very moderate size were unable on occasion to leave for several weeks. Apart from the competition of major ports such as Hull, nearer ports such as Sunderland and the Hartlepools could menace the economic growth of the Tyne. But improvements after 1860 included the removal by dredgers of millions of tons of sand, the construction of quays, docks and coal staithes and, from 1872, of the timber ponds in Jarrow Slake.[48]

Administrative difficulties proved almost fatal at a crucial time, but the work of the Commission has been successful. And much is owed to the railways. The Blyth and Tyne railway, described in 1855 as 'little better than a waggonway carrying a few passengers in low-roofed springless carriages' was galvanized into such enterprise that it even aspired to compete with the great N.E.R., by which it was absorbed in 1874.[49] The Blyth railway company acquired mineral lines, built shipping staithes, extended its line to Newcastle, to Tynemouth and to Monkseaton in 1864, and conveyed immense quantities of coal to the Northumberland dock.[50] Tyne dock on the other side of the river at Jarrow, was constructed by the N.E.R. from 1855 to 1859 and used for coal shipping.[51] In 1868, the railway line known as the Team valley branch was opened, and in 1872 this became the main line.[52] Other railways were added, including the expensive Riverside line, opened in 1879, which ran largely through tunnels, bridges, cuttings, embankments and along retaining walls.[53] Partly to face the competition of the trams, two railways were electrified, to Whitley Bay and Tynemouth in 1904, and to South Shields in 1938.[54]

Population

So far as can be estimated,[b] the population of the area now covered by the Tyneside conurbation was *c.* 86,000 in 1801, 174,000 in 1841, 212,000 in 1851, and 271,000 in 1861, after which the main period of growth began. Between 1871 and 1901, the population doubled, from 328,000 to 667,000. During the twentieth century there was a further increase but only to 751, 000 in 1911 and 816,000 in 1921 and there has been little change since the 1914–1918 war. The counties of Northumberland and Durham had only a slight increase of population of *c.* 18,000, from 1931 to 1951. True, such towns as Whitley Bay (+ 25 per cent), Longbenton (+ 36 per cent) and Gosforth (+ 34 per cent) had increases of population from 1931 to 1951 but this merely represents the type of outward suburban spread characteristic of its time (Fig. 40). Much more significant is that for the entire conurbation, the population increase was only + 1·4 per cent from 1921 to 1931 and + 1·0 per cent from 1931 to 1951.

Newcastle, by far the largest town on Tyneside during the first half of the nineteenth century, was by 1851 a parliamentary and municipal borough having 87,784 people compared with 33,048 in 1801. In the city parish of St. Nicholas there were only slight increases after 1831, and in St. John's parish, there were increases to 1851, followed by decreases, mentioned in the 1871 Census as due to the removal of houses for business premises and the transformation of private dwellings into warehouses.[55] Westgate township, on the other hand, had only *c.* 700 people in 1801, but 16,500 in 1851 when the increase was ascribed to 'its locality as a suburb of Newcastle' and to the opening of coalmines and stone quarries.[56] In 1851, Newcastle was

[b] Exact comparison is impossible, owing to changes in administrative areas; for 1801–1871, the areas included are the Registration sub-districts of Newcastle, Wallsend, North Shields, Tynemouth and Longbenton in Northumberland and the sub-districts of Westoe (excluding Boldon parish), South Shields, Heworth, Gateshead and Whickham in Co. Durham, with the areas that became Newburn.

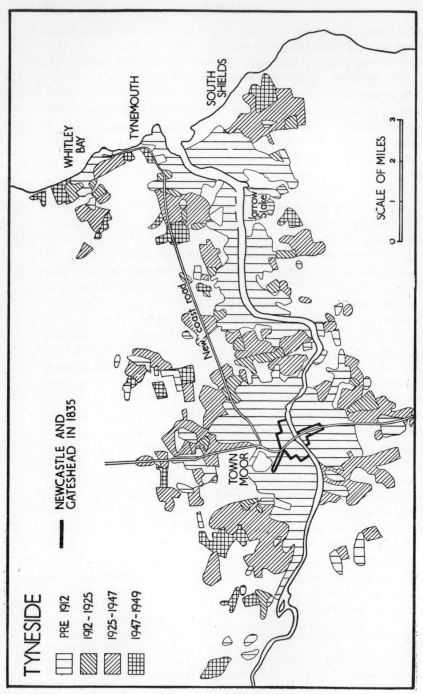

FIG. 40. THE GROWTH OF THE TYNESIDE CONURBATION, 1835–1949

still a compact town, in which Elswick had only 3,500 people compared with 59,000 in 1901: Heaton and Jesmond grew only in the last
quarter of the nineteenth century. But from 1851 to 1901, the population of Newcastle more than doubled to 215,000. In 1871,[57] the
increase was said to be due to 'the increase of manufactures in iron,
steam engines, lead, chemicals and pottery, and especially in iron
shipbuilding': then follows the significant remark 'the population of
the whole of the banks of the river Tyne, on both sides, from Newcastle to North Shields, is rapidly increasing. The coal trade, the
staple trade of the district, is and has been for some time in a very
prosperous condition'. At Byker, there was 'general commercial
prosperity' and at Elswick the long river frontage had 'great facilities
for trade' and for the 'erection and extension of manufactories and
blast furnaces'.

Other towns on the north side of the river were increasing in
population during the first half of the nineteenth century: in Tynemouth township, which covered c. 3 square miles, the population
increased from 3,856 in 1801 to 14,650 in 1851 though its neighbour,
North Shields, had varied fortunes and its population increased only
from 7,280 in 1801 to 8,882 in 1851. But there were already changes
resulting from the closing of coalmines, for example in the Chirton
township (now part of Tynemouth) where a decrease of population[58]
from 1841 to 1851 was said to be 'due to the exhaustion of some of
the collieries'. Cullercoats, Whitley and Monkseaton, having in 1851
only some 1,500 people, had declines due to the closing of a colliery
and a quarry but at Cullercoats there were fifty people recorded who
had come for the sea-bathing. Longbenton and Walker had an increasing population during this time, due to the employment available at mines in the district. By 1871, the increases were more marked
and those in the Tynemouth sub-District were ascribed to the
'extreme briskness of the steam coal trade' and to the success of 'iron
manufactures and iron shipbuilding'.[59] In North Shields, the population declined after 1861, because many of the dilapidated buildings
in this early nineteenth-century port were pulled down; but the
population in Chirton township doubled from 1851 to 1871 and

FIG. 40. The nuclear areas of Newcastle and Gateshead are taken from the
*Report of the Commissioners appointed to report and advise upon the
boundaries and wards of certain boroughs and corporate towns in England
and Wales*, Pt. II, 1837. The later limits of the built-up area were extracted
from O.S. maps.

there were considerable increases in Wallsend (which included Willington and Howdon Pans). This sub-district had 5,721 inhabitants in 1851, 10,458 in 1871 and 20,113 in 1891—a not untypical late nineteenth-century story. In Cullercoats and Whitley it was reported in 1871 that 'large quantities of land' were being laid out and used for building but Monkseaton was still rural at the end of the century. Longbenton parish in 1871 had new coalmines, employment in the shipyards, and 'improved railway facilities' given by the Blyth and Tyne railway which enabled a number of merchants to settle there. The main growth at Whitley, which came after 1891, was ascribed to settlement of an outer suburban character and to the town's popularity as a holiday resort.[60]

On the south side of the river, both Gateshead and South Shields were well-established at the beginning of the nineteenth century. Gateshead had 8,579 people in 1801, 24,805 fifty years later and 109,888 in 1901, and the large increase from 32,749 in 1861 to 47,848 in 1871 was due to 'the great development of industry', notably in the railway workshops, ironworks, chemical and cement manufacture.[61] In Fellside and Lowside a new colliery and other works were opened and a marked increase of population noted before 1851.[62] After 1851, similar trends were noted everywhere except at South Shields, where a decrease from 1861 to 1871 was due to the demolition of private houses for the erection of 'extensive glass and iron manufactures' in the 'old part of the town'.[63] South Shields was recognized as a municipal borough in 1851, with 28,974 people compared with 78,391 in 1891. Around Jarrow, shipbuilding yards, chemical works, metalworks and brickyards and a colliery all gave employment. But most of the Durham towns reached their peak population at the 1921 Census and have been declining ever since.

The slight increase on Tyneside from 815,637 people in 1921 to 827,086 in 1931 and 835,332 in 1951 indicates considerable migration from the area: even before the world economic crisis it was said that the Tyneside area was accumulating a population for which employment was unlikely to be sufficient. Between the middle of 1921 and the middle of 1926, the loss by migration was 1,800 a year but from mid-1926 to mid-1929, 35,000 left: by this time there was said to be general spirit of pessimism due to increasing trade depression. In the next five years, from mid-1929 the outward movement averaged only 6,000 a year, partly because it was hard to find jobs anywhere.[64] In the Census decade, 1921–1931, the only parts of Tyneside showing a net immigration were Whitley-Monkseaton (+ 7 per cent),

Earsdon (+ 3 per cent), Gosforth (+ 11 per cent) and Whickham
(+ 2 per cent): in the Durham towns the net emigration was heavy,
as in South Shields (— 13 per cent), Jarrow (— 20 per cent), Hebburn
(— 14 per cent), Felling (— 8 per cent) and Gateshead (— 12 per
cent). From 1931 to 1951 there were increases of population in all
the towns on the north side of the river, ranging from + 2 per cent in
Newcastle and + 1 per cent in Tynemouth to increases of more than
one-third in Gosforth and Longbenton, but on the south side of the
river, every administrative division had a decrease except for
Whickham (+ 7 per cent). Indeed the Durham towns of the conurbation as a whole lost by 7 per cent from 1931 to 1951 with a loss of
— 20 per cent in Jarrow. Some redistribution of population is likely
to continue, but most of this movement so far has been absorbed by
places already within the conurbation.

Administrative Divisions

Fig. 41 shows that the proposed new borough of Newcastle in 1937
differed from the present conurbation only by the omission of Longbenton and the southern part of Whickham and by the inclusion of
parts of Blaydon and Ryton in Co. Durham. It was said that the
Tyne was no longer a suitable frontier between administrative
areas,[65] and that a union of this type would deal effectively with
cross-river traffic, sewage (much of which went into the Tyne), the
provision of water, gas and electricity; and the rates would be more
equitably distributed over the whole area.[c] It was suggested that the
Tyne Commissioners should take over the full control of the river,
except for the fish quay at North Shields. The authors of the report
clearly regarded it as outrageous that there should be sixteen authorities in an area little larger than Birmingham and in fact having a
smaller population and they drew attention to the fact that public
utilities were shared in a complicated manner: Hebburn, for example, had water from the Sunderland and South Shields company,
gas from South Shields and from the Newcastle-Gateshead company,
the services of the Gateshead fire brigade, and almost half its

[c] In spite of the industrial derating of 1929, it was said that the higher rates in
certain boroughs were a deterrent to industrial enterprise. And there were dis-
parities: in Jarrow the rate for 1935–1936 was 19s. 6d.; in Wallsend 13s. 10d; in
Newburn 9s. 6d. (excluding exchequer grants). Assessments were, however,
generally low and the rate question was only one contributory factor to the lack
of new industries. A new borough could provide more effectively for education,
police, fire brigades, roads—and also for the health and poor law services since
taken over by the State. See *Survey of Industrial Facilities* 1936, pp. 60–2.

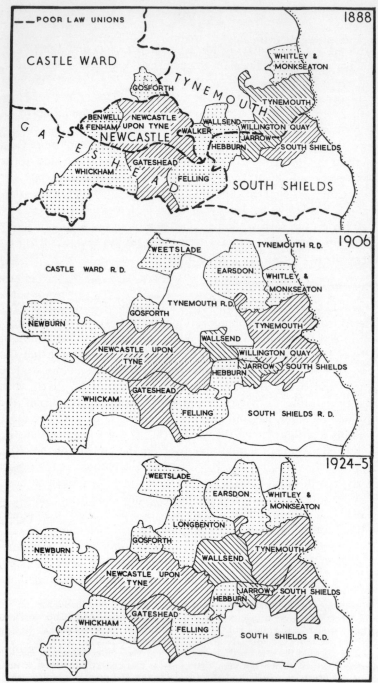

FIG. 41. TYNESIDE, ADMINISTRATIVE UNITS, 1888–1925

Newcastle was at all times the major town but the ports of Tynemouth (including North Shields) and South Shields and a number of industrial settlements became the nuclei of urban districts and boroughs.

workpeople came from Jarrow, then in the full throes of unemployment. On the other hand, Newcastle like other similar towns that are regional capitals, provided many services for people living outside its boundaries.

All that was said about administrative problems here has been said in other parts of the country, but it was said here with special point because various attempts to unite existing urban districts had failed and joint agreements for gas, water, fire brigade and other services were suspected to be arguments for eventual unions or absorptions. And the point about the Tyne Commission was especially interesting, as it was only after this body managed to control the river as an entity that the area flourished (see pp. 186–7). The Royal Commission's report followed the rearrangements made under acts of parliament and Review orders in the nineteen-thirties, by which most of the administrative units were enlarged by the absorption of small urban districts and some rural areas. In other words, this report made it clear that here the administrative revisions of the nineteen-thirties only tinkered with the problems involved: what the commissioners had in mind was the recognition that a conurbation existed by a federation similar to that which created Stoke-on-Trent in 1910.

In the middle of the nineteenth century, only four places within the present conurbation, Newcastle, Tynemouth, Gateshead and South Shields, were recognized as towns, all of which were parliamentary and municipal boroughs, with the same boundaries for both purposes.[66] Presumably all the remaining places were industrial villages rather than towns according to the judgement of the Clerks of the Peace in the counties. But Newcastle and Gateshead had boundaries defined under the Municipal Corporations Act of 1835 (see Fig. 40).[67] Newcastle consisted of some 2,000 acres regarded as the old municipal borough and five adjacent townships, Elswick, Westgate, Jesmond, Heaton and Byker, which were included in the parliamentary and municipal borough of 1851. In 1835, it was noted that the main improvements were in the town centre (St. Andrew's parish), where 'the Corporation are at present erecting a large and handsome market-house, and individuals are at the same time building, on speculation, entire streets of a superior description in the immediate neighbourhood'. This presumably refers to the work of Robert Grainger[68] who, mainly between 1826 and 1836, completely rebuilt the centre of the town using 'waste land of irregular contours' and the site of old property. The plan of the centre included several new streets, markets, a Central Exchange, a theatre, a music-hall, a dispensary, two chapels, two auction marts, ten inns, twelve public houses, four banks and over three hundred houses with shops. A contemporary writer said that only Edinburgh and Bath were comparable. It was noted also that houses 'of a superior description' were being built in the northern part of the town, for example in Jesmond. Newcastle was administratively defined on such spacious lines in 1835 that no change was made until 1904 (v.i.); Gateshead's parish of 5 square miles became in 1835 the parliamentary borough and though the town was still small (see Fig. 40), it was regarded as having strong potentialities

> not only from its proximity to, and commercial connexion with, Newcastle, from which it is separated only by the river Tyne, but more particularly from the numerous glass manufactories and iron works with the town, and from the coal-pits in the immediate neighbourhood.[69]

But the town was a poor relation for its inhabitants were workmen and colliers and there was 'not any appearance of wealth, or houses belonging to the richer class' except to a very limited extent on the southern margins in High Fell and Low Fell. In fact many of the 'master manufacturers or proprietors of the coal-pits' lived on the other side of the river.

Newcastle[70] became a city in 1882, a county borough in 1888, and its first citizen became a Lord Mayor in 1906. In 1904, it absorbed two urban districts, Benwell and Fenham, and Walker, together with a couple of square miles in Kenton parish, and now covered over 13 square miles. Later extensions of 1935 added another 4 square miles, primarily from Castle Ward rural district, but only 3,000 people (at the 1931 Census). Tynemouth[71] became a municipal borough in 1850, and a county borough in 1904: in 1935, small boundary adjustments were made, in which the Earsdon U.D. was eliminated—the rest went to Whitley-Monkseaton. The other towns north of the river included Wallsend[72] which acquired a local board of health in 1867, became an urban district in 1894 and a municipal borough in 1901: Wallsend was extended in 1910 to include part of Tynemouth R.D. and also Willington Quay, which had, in 1894, acquired what was surely one of the strangest urban disticts ever created, Howdon, with 9 acres and 1,099 people in 1891. Newburn U.D.,[73] created in 1893, and subjected only to minor boundary adjustments in the 1935 review and revision, was made from a number of rural parishes studded with mining and industrial villages.

Northward extension of settlement away from the river was noted in 1835 and has continued ever since. Gosforth U.D. and Whitley-

Monkseaton U.D. have each had some semblance of town government for over eighty years, but Longbenton U.D.,[74] now included
in the conurbation, was created in 1912 out of three civil parishes
having in 1901, 8,561 people and in 1911, 12,443 inhabitants (28,071

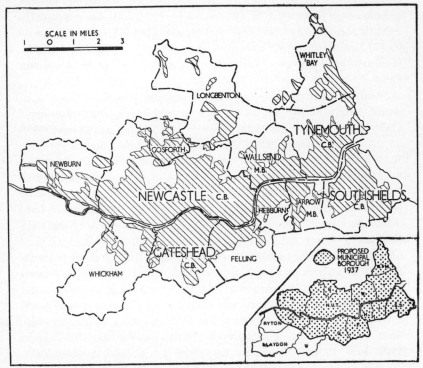

FIG. 42. TYNESIDE, ADMINISTRATIVE UNITS AND BUILT-UP AREA

This shows the present area of the conurbation, with the administrative
units as now defined, almost all of them laid down under the County
Review Order of the nineteen-thirties. The upper map includes the 1951
addition to South Shields: its previous boundary was the limit of the
built-up area. The municipal borough proposed by the 1937 *Royal Commission on Tyneside* (Cmd. 5402) is shown as an inset map.

in 1951) and enlarged in 1935 by the addition of Weetslade U.D.
(created in 1894), to an area of 10½ square miles. Gosforth acquired
a local board of health in 1872 and therefore became an urban district automatically in 1894: in 1935 it was extended by the addition
of 434 acres from Castle Ward R.D., to 1,737 acres.[75] In 1904 and in
1909 Newcastle's efforts to absorb Gosforth were successfully resisted

and in 1933 it was agreed that no parliamentary bill should be promoted for ten years except with the concurrence of the Northumberland county council;[76] consequently it remains independent though primarily a residential outgrowth of the city. Whitley-Monkseaton[77] began as small mining villages with some catering for holiday visitors on the coast. Having a health board in 1873, Whitley became an urban district in 1894 and was slightly extended (by some 300 acres) in 1912 and still further enlarged, to 5 square miles, in 1935 by the elimination of Earsdon[d] and the acquisition of part of Seaton Delavel.[e]

South of the river, changes in administrative boundaries have consisted mainly of the addition of rural parishes to the town units. Gateshead[78] became a county borough in 1904, and in 1933 and 1936 added 2 square miles from Whickham U.D. and Chester-le-Street R.D. Whickham,[79] having its first health board in 1875, managed to avoid complete absorption by Gateshead in 1931 (with the help of Durham county council) and in 1936 compensated for its loss of territory to Gateshead by acquiring enough of the adjacent rural district to cover 9 square miles; it is the only area south of the river showing a recent marked increase of population. Felling U.D.,[80] having its first board in 1868, added 1 square mile of rural territory in 1936 to give its present 5 square miles and Hebburn, with its first board in 1873, also acquired adjacent rural land in 1936. And Jarrow,[81] whose story differs only in that its first board was convened earlier, in 1863, became a borough in 1875 and was extended in 1936. South Shields,[82] having acquired a charter in 1850, was enlarged in 1901, 1921, 1936 by extension into rural districts and finally in 1951, 760 acres were taken from the Boldon urban district. Before this last extension South Shields was the only town having buildings to its boundaries.

Difficulties that arise through the multiplicity of administrative units are of two types, first those that involve co-operation between two or more areas and second those that arise within the urban district or borough. Of the former, classic examples were given when Wallsend accepted Newcastle trams to pass through only on the understanding that it did not constitute an argument for union: there was also difficulty in making the coast road through Wallsend.[83] Of the second group of difficulties, there have been numerous examples,

[d] Divided between Longbenton, Whitley-Monkseaton and the new Seaton Valley U.D. (outside the Conurbation).

[e] Most of this U.D. was incorporated in Seaton Valley U.D.

not least the depression of Jarrow when the Palmer shipyard closed in 1934. As Mess has pointed out, most of the small industrial towns are 'one-class towns'; he argued that in Newcastle the inhabitants of Jesmond were conscious of their duty to the poorer areas of the city but that 'Hebburn, Felling or Jarrow have no Jesmond'.[84] The argument was that for housing and other purposes unions would be fruitful as sites controlled by one authority might be jealously guarded against another, whereas if all were in one large county borough of Tyneside, a comprehensive housing policy could be designed. Further, some 'urban districts' were hardly effective local government units: Whickham U.D., for example, consisted of a few mining villages of which only one had any resemblance to a town, and was in fact a mining and rural area having possible housing sites of interest to neighbouring authorities. Close by, in Gateshead, acute problems existed.

Gateshead's M.O.H. has said[85] that 'many of the houses built over a hundred years ago are approaching the end of their useful life' and that before 1939, over 4,000 houses were 'considered fit only for demolition'. Of roughly 32,000 houses, 20,211 are below modern standards of habitability. The Borough, one of the most congested in the country, with 113,500 inhabitants, housed in 4,470 acres, is so completely built up that in 1953 an Extension Bill was promoted to incorporate 829 acres of Felling U.D. which had (1951) 3,405 acres for 26,020 people. This land would have been used for 3,700 houses accommodating some 13,000 people, but all the usual arguments were raised and Gateshead acquired only some 89 acres on which less than 700 houses have so far been planned. As it is not possible even to build homes to replace the 4,000 century-old houses, the suggestion has been made that Gateshead should absorb adjacent urban districts (Felling and Whickham) with the 'underdeveloped' land lying to the south of all three towns. This greater Gateshead, having a population of c. 200,000 people, would be similar in area to the Poor Law Union (abolished 1929) and would, says the M.O.H., 'be able to provide for itself . . . efficiently and economically in matters of education, health, housing, roads and many other public services'. This suggestion, though of minor scope, bears an interesting resemblance to ideas put forward in the London area after the 1914–1918 war (see p. 59).

A recent investigation, on retail trade,[86] has shown that more than half is centred in Newcastle, which has an average trade of £187 a head, compared with £123 for the entire Conurbation. Out of £103,597,000 spent in shops and certain services, £56,472,000 was

o

spent in Newcastle and only £10,191,000 in Gateshead, an average of £88 a head. Whitley Bay had an average of £122 a head, and Tyne-mouth £96 but Longbenton only £53 and Newburn £58: of the towns on the south side, South Shields's trade, valued at £10,835,000, averaged £99 a head but in the smaller industrial centres it was far less—for example, Felling, £63, Hebburn, £62 and Whickham, £58. The shopping dominance of Newcastle is clearly shown by these figures: people of the other towns contribute to its commercial prosperity.

Land Use in the Conurbation

Tyneside, like other conurbations, is highly mixed in land use.[87] The clearest-marked focus is central Newcastle, where the major shops, the retail market, the railway station, hospitals and the University buildings are concentrated. Around the centre on the east and west there are nineteenth-century houses in a gridiron street pattern but to the north there are wider roads and larger houses of Jesmond. On the south side the same gridiron pattern with small workers' houses is markedly developed in Gateshead, which has larger houses only in the Gateshead Fell area. Generally on Tyneside the various towns and villages having grown sharply during the late nineteenth century, each have a nuclear gridiron of streets and inter-war housing areas in the intervening areas, for example, around Walker. But the major recent expansion has been westward in Scotswood, Benwell and Fenham. On the south side, conditions are similar: the largest single area of a residential character is on the south side of South Shields. The towns are thickly settled, and in 1928, Dr. Mess noted that 'Tynesiders . . . class for class . . . live in houses smaller by 30 per cent or so than those in which most Englishmen live'.[88] Traditionally the houses of Co. Durham are smaller than those else-where in England and a vast amount of rebuilding is necessary: at the 1951 Census[89] it appeared that in spite of improvements since 1928, 46 per cent of all the dwellings within the conurbation consisted of three rooms or less, compared with 35 per cent in West Yorkshire and 13 per cent or less in the other conurbations. The proportion of 'houses' of three rooms or less was in Newcastle, 48 per cent,

---

FIG. 43. This is based primarily on the splendid 'Regional Settlement Map' by M. R. G. Conzen, given in the *British Association Scientific Survey of North-eastern England*, 1949, supplemented by reference to modern O.S. maps on various scales.

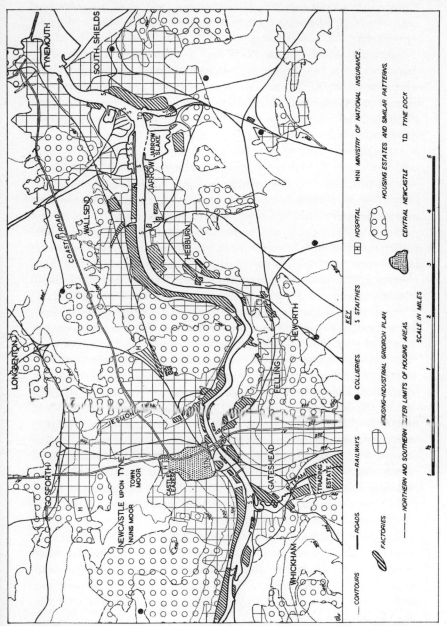

KEY

CONTOURS ····   ROADS ▬▬   RAILWAYS ⊞

FACTORIES ▨   COLLIERIES ●   S STAITHES   H HOSPITAL   MNI MINISTRY OF NATIONAL INSURANCE.

HOUSING-INDUSTRIAL GRIDIRON PLAN   HOUSING ESTATES AND SIMILAR PATTERNS.

NORTHERN AND SOUTHERN OUTER LIMITS OF HOUSING AREAS   CENTRAL NEWCASTLE   T.D. TYNE DOCK

SCALE IN MILES

¼   0   1   2   3   4   5

FIG. 43. INDUSTRIAL AND HOUSING AREAS ON TYNESIDE

Tynemouth, 42 per cent, Wallsend, 53 per cent, Gateshead, 54 per cent, Hebburn, 54 per cent, Felling, 51 per cent and South Shields, 47 per cent.

Industrial quarters flank the Tyne on both sides, together with quays, dry docks, ship-repairing and shipbuilding yards. Such stretches of riverside as the old chemical works at Felling and some disused shipyards were regarded as a dreary advertisement in days when the vital need was to attract new industries.[90] In some cases, such as the Team valley trading estate at Gateshead and the Bede estate at Jarrow, derelict sites have been turned into flourishing and neat modern industrial areas; and at Palmer's shipyard, in Jarrow, derelict from 1934 to 1941, where wartime needs brought renewed activity in ship repairing, works have been established at which heavy machinery, steel boxes and scaffolding are made. At this ship-yard some 700 people are employed, and there are some 1,600 workers at the Bede estate where machinery, textiles (Celanese), locks, paper articles, electrical parts, even mineral waters and pharmaceutical products are manufactured. Jarrow, having suffered from its concentration on one industry, now has more than a score.

Team valley, the first and still the largest of the trading estates here, has some 12,000 workers in a hundred firms. The site was a dreary stretch of river flood-plain, visible to travellers on the East Coast route but not sufficiently attractive for many to look twice. Now it is an area of factories, canteens, banks and roads, neatly laid out but by no means completely occupied. Work began here in August 1936 and by the outbreak of the 1939–1945 war some 3,000 people were making a wide variety of goods—the list is worth quoting—'clothing, safety glass, mining machinery, fibre-board boxes, milk cartons, tools, pumps, food products, radio components, moulded plastics, light engineering products, furnishing fabrics, buttons and leather bags'. Not only is the aim to produce a considerable volume of employment but to give a wide range of jobs, especially for women[f] as in this area many were obliged to move elsewhere.

The Bede estate at Jarrow occupies a site that was abandoned *c.* 1930, and consisted of a mountain of chemical refuse, derelict reservoirs, old foundations, tunnels and a network of drains and old services, but in March 1946, 250,000 tons of refuse were cleared and used as a foundation for railway sidings and six months later the

[f] In the whole area covered by the North-east Trading Estates Company (thirty-six estates and sites from Guisborough to Ashington) there were in September 1958, 52,840 employees, including nearly 30,000 women.

construction of roads, railways, factories and the provision of such services as water, gas, electricity, telephones and drainage began. The first factory was opened in May 1947. At West Chirton, Tynemouth, a vast government store became the nucleus for a trading estate where some 2,500 people are now employed, largely in engineering trades but also in textiles and confectionery; and the Corporation of Tynemouth welded this trading estate into a new housing scheme. At South Shields there is another trading estate in which the products are batteries, radio and electric parts and men's readymade clothing.

On the ground the trading estates stand out as markedly modern features in an area where many of the industrial plants are far from modern. They add to the variety of Tyneside which is in fact more complex than Figs 40 and 43 would suggest. In 1951[91] the Census divided it into three types of areas, first the commercial and administrative centre of Newcastle—which everyone agrees to be a distinct feature, second the main industrial and older residential areas, and third the 'newer residential centres, holiday centres and rural mining villages' (see Fig. 3, p. 12), 'older areas' include most of Newcastle, except on the west side and a small area towards Wallsend, and a belt of town from Dunston to South Shields on the south and through Wallsend and Tynemouth on the north side. Beyond all this lie the newer areas with some colliery villages long established. The two versions of land use given (Figs. 40, 43) are in reasonable accord, but inevitably they are generalizations, for each place is varied.[91] Tynemouth, for example, has coal staithes at Howdon shore, a mining village at Percy Main, a seaport, ship-repairing centre, steamtrawler and fishcuring port and a shopping centre at North Shields, an old established town in Tynemouth on the river mouth, and a fishing village with seaside town around it in Cullercoats and even a trading estate. South Shields has mining, a seaport, a shipyard and is also a residential town for much of mid-Tyneside and even a holiday resort. But variety of land use is to be expected in an area of complicated economic history, closely connected with mining and overseas trade, and having had a somewhat involved series of industrial changes of which the contemporary diversification of occupation is not the least interesting.

CHAPTER 8

THE MINOR CONURBATIONS

SEVEN out of every ten people in England and Wales live in urban areas having more than 50,000 people, either in single towns or in two or more towns that have fused into one on the ground. This is a nation of townspeople, and of people living in towns of some size: even so, the landscape is dominantly rural. The six major conurbations and the eighty-nine smaller ones include most of the industrial areas of England and Wales, together with all the major ports and many of the 'amenity' towns for holidays or residence. The towns considered here are of varied types, ranging from places almost wholly industrial to others that are hardly industrial at all. The statistical framework (50,000 +) here used includes both the industrial towns of central Lancashire and the coast towns of Blackpool, Fleetwood and Lytham St. Annes, and also some of the larger county capitals, such as Chester, York and Lincoln, at once major route and market centres for large rural areas, cathedral cities, and industrial towns.

Although the need for accurate definition of the areas of towns has been recognized for over a century, in places this problem remains acute today. In the next few pages, attention is given to the definition of towns and briefly to their administrative bounds from the middle of the nineteenth century. As long ago as 1851, the Census Commissioners recognized that considerable problems were raised by the growth of towns, stimulated by the influence of the new railways.[1] It was not easy in 1851 to decide which places were towns and which were not, but the Commissioners had ideas still relevant today on the grading of towns by size and by function.

The Territory of a Town

When the Census Commissioners in 1851 drew attention to the fact that a majority of the British population (10,556,288 out of 20,959,477) were living in towns, they rightly regarded it as a development of immense significance.[2] Never before had this been known, in any country at any time, but since 1851 the same phenomenon had been seen in various countries, not only in Europe, but also in the United States, Australia and New Zealand. At no period of human history has the town population of the world been as numerous as now, nor relatively so great a proportion of the whole, and the trend of the present is for town populations to increase, not inevitably at the expense of the rural community, but rather at a greater rate than the countryside. And in most cases, growth of towns has been associated with the increase of extractive or manufacturing industry, the developing complexity of commercial organization, the greater provision of cultural and administrative services, the wider demand for entertainment, and the emergence of *rentier* populations, living on pensions or investments. For more than a century towns have been the subject of parliamentary legislation. In 1837 the old boroughs were investigated and given defined boundaries,[3] and from 1848 various Public Health Acts gave towns boards of health,[4] charged with the duty of providing water, sewerage, refuse collection, street paving and the like. Some towns acquired improvement commissioners under local Acts of Parliament and the number of urban sanitary authorities, as they became known, steadily increased. In 1872, the Public Health Act made definite rural and urban sanitary authorities[5] and therefore made a distinct break between town and country; in 1888 and 1894, parliamentary acts gave English local government the 'island' system, by which county boroughs[6] were taken out of the counties to become equal in powers to the counties in which they were situated, and municipal boroughs and urban districts were taken out of the rural districts.

A full review of the administrative arrangements under these and other parliamentary Acts is beyond the scope of this book, but several excellent texts have been produced on the subject:[7] through the years many mistakes, such as the creation of too many small places as urban sanitary districts from 1862 to 1863,[8] have been rectified. Similarly there have been provisions for changes of boundary, partly through the work of the Local Government Board from 1871 to 1947. But it could hardly be maintained that a satisfactory line has ever been drawn between town and country: indeed, it is probable that no such line could ever be drawn: one aspect of the problem was excellently stated in 1851,[9] when the challenging fact of town growth was fully appreciated. The Census commissioners called attention to the fact that

a large proportion of the population in the market-towns, the country-towns, the manufacturing towns and the metropolis was born in the country ... town and country are bound together, not only by the intercourse of commerce but by a thousand ties of blood and affection. ... The vast system of towns in which half the population lives, has its peculiar dangers, which the high mortality and the recent epidemics reveal. Extensive sanitary arrangements, and all the appliances of physical as well as of social science, are necessary to preserve the material vigour of the population.

Improvements have been vast since 1851, but one could not say that all the problems of living in towns have been solved. But the passing of three succeeding generations since that time has meant the growth of a population that never knew the countryside as its home but only as a place to visit. Even so, the wish of multitudes to have a garden may show that the rural past is not completely obliterated.

After the 1914–1918 war, the rapid building of housing estates by local authorities and by private enterprise began the process of town expansion which, interrupted only by the 1939–1945 war, has continued ever since. Three government reports have dealt with the problems involved.[10] Reviewing the past administrative history, these show that there were 66 boroughs and 302 urban districts in which the population was less than 5,000, and it was recommended that small urban districts, financially weak, should be reabsorbed into rural districts: this has made some very small country towns 'rural' once more. The greater problem was the growth of the larger towns, and the commissioners were vague on the principles admissible for territorial expansion, though relevant factors included the outward spread of population, especially in housing estates built in outlying parishes. On the other hand, if a county borough provided gas, water, or electricity to a neighbouring authority, that should not give it any claim to absorb the neighbouring area, nor should land be absorbed merely for a town planning scheme. How any town was to cope with its re-housing problems without having land available to build on, no-one satisfactorily explained. The general conclusion was that there was need for a general review of the areas of all administrative divisions, achieved later under the County Review Orders of the nineteen-thirties. The suggestion was also made that these reviews should take place at 'suitable intervals', but since the nineteen-thirties there have only been local reviews, some of considerable significance.

An Urban Hierarchy?

Various attempts have been made to classify towns into groups, of which the most famous is the Christaller classification in Germany: A. E. Smailes[11] has grouped the towns of England and Wales into a 'hierarchy' of four grades, London, the one metropolitan centre, at all times unique; the major regional capitals such as Birmingham, Cardiff, Manchester, Leeds, Liverpool; the larger county centres and market towns; and finally the simpler type of market towns. In full admiration of the work done, one must recognize that the problems even of the definition of towns, as well as of their functions has become increasingly complicated with the progressive industrialization of Britain. As long ago as 1840, the Select Committee on the Health of Towns recognized that a variety of towns existed in the country.[12] These included London, the metropolis, manufacturing towns, populous seaport towns, the great watering places, and 'country and other inland towns not the seat of any particular manufacture'. Like many later workers the committee found it hard to classify mining district which, though clearly not rural in the sense of being non-industrial, did not conveniently fit into any town classification. In 1851, the Census Commissioners reported that there were in Great Britain 17,150 villages 'with defined boundaries' and 815 towns (580 in England and Wales, 225 in Scotland, 10 in the Channel Islands).[13] Villages were regarded as centres at which 'men, women and children can assemble weekly'; and the towns were divisible into three main categories, first, market towns, at which men could meet weekly and return home within one day; second, county towns, where the heads of the chief families could congregate periodically; and third, large towns around the capital. They found that on the average there was one town to each twenty-one villages, placed in the middle of a square of 110 square miles or a circle with a 6-mile radius, and that the average distance between towns was 10·8 miles.[14]

So far the plan is neat, perhaps even convincing: in fact it strongly resembles the Christaller scheme, though his plans were based on hexagons rather than squares or circles.[15] But in 1851, almost all the towns of the country were growing rapidly and their classification into types became steadily more difficult to make, as the Census Commissioners realized. Some county towns, which served 'the same purposes as the villages and the market-town, with others super-added', were becoming industrialized, notably Carlisle, Derby, Nottingham, Leicester, Northampton and Norwich.[16] And by 1851, three other groups of towns claimed attention, not only for their size but also for the rapidity of their growth, which had averaged + 22–26 per cent during the previous ten years and was clearly only just beginning.[17] All the three groups, classified as watering-places, ports, and mining and/or manufacturing towns, were regarded as 'adventitious', not perhaps a happy choice of a word as their growth was rooted in some local advantages such as mineral resources, tidal estuaries, or even spa waters. To these one might add accessibility, though with the reservation that the promoters of railways were naturally anxious to serve places already showing signs of strength and possible growth. On the other hand, railway companies did much to stimulate the growth of certain ports, such as Grimsby (p. 262), seaside towns such as Bournemouth (p. 279) and mining areas such as the Rhondda valleys (p. 289). Of the 'adventitious' towns in 1851 the first group, watering-places, included Brighton, Bath and Cheltenham; the second, ports, Plymouth, Portsmouth and Southampton, and the third, mining and manufacturing towns, Birmingham, Wolverhampton, Liverpool, Manchester and other Lancashire towns, Sheffield, Leeds, Bradford, Hull, Newcastle-upon-Tyne, Merthyr Tydfil and Glasgow. All these three groups of towns were regarded as 'of an inferior order' in their 'local relations' though in their industry, commerce and wealth they had 'almost acquired a metropolitan character'.[18] Many of these towns have in fact become strong market centres through the years: perusal of the above list will show that it includes almost all the towns regarded by A. E. Smailes as major 'regional capitals' ninety-odd years later.

Town and Countryside

Statistically, the rural districts of England and Wales have 19 per cent of the entire population.[19] But this in no way represents the agricultural community, not even with the addition of the village shopkeepers and others providing services for the rural population, as in many places there has been an outward spread of townspeople into rural parishes, in other places mining villages are recorded with the population of 'rural' parishes and certain areas of the countryside have a considerable 'retired' population. Some planners appear to believe that it will be possible to 'direct' the retired into parts of the countryside where so far such people are few: their argument apparently rests on the assumption that there is a reasonable, or desirable balance to be achieved in rural areas, such as 50 per cent farm workers, 25 per cent service workers, and 25 per cent 'adventitious' population, consisting either of people employed in neighbouring towns or of the retired.[20] That a steadily increasing number of people from rural areas work in towns is common knowledge but to expect to 'direct' retired people into certain areas is to hope for more power than a democratic nation is likely to allow. An old village near a large town, a village in some scenically attractive area in the

Home counties, or in the Cotswolds, the Yorkshire Dales or the Lake District, is far more likely to attract the retired than a village in the flatter areas of Lincolnshire or the Fenlands. This voluntary settlement in the countryside became marked during the inter-war period, due to the two factors jointly operative: first, private cars and motor buses made a home beside fields possible and second, many of the landowners were only too willing to sell off their 'desirable' sites beside roads as farming was not prosperous.

There is no need to labour the point that a threat to the countryside exists; but it has existed for generations. One might wish that the administrative structure of local government bore a closer relation to the distribution of the townspeople and was sufficiently malleable to allow adjustment to change as it occurs. The essential fact is that the urban population of the country is being spread over a larger area year by year for even in places where the population is declining, rehousing after slum clearance can be achieved only by settling some people in new housing estates, as well as in modern city flats. Far more serious problems emerge in expanding industrial areas such as Slough, Buckinghamshire which before the 1914–1918 war was a market town of some 15,000 inhabitants having a limited amount of industry. Although Slough has been spared a serious smoke menace, the town has grown to its present size in an apparently haphazard manner and the same comment could be made of many of the newer industrial areas in the neighbourhood of London—as elsewhere. New industrial and mining settlements do not necessarily arise where no place existed before, though many mining places have grown up with no clear focus except the colliery, and some have acquired no definite shopping centre. The houses, varying in type according to the standards of the time when they were built, range from the poor cottages of three rooms or less in the older parts of Durham coalfield to the bright housing estates of the newer parts of the Yorkshire coalfield. Much of the mining in this country has not been associated with town growth, rather with the addition of colliery 'villages' at intervals of a couple of miles or so through the countryside. In some cases, a number of these have been grouped into an 'urban district' but in others they have not. In the Lancashire coalfield many of the urban districts are merely sprawls of miners' cottages known to the residents by a number of local names and not by the over-riding urban authority. Where other industries exist, as at Wigan, St. Helens, Leigh, Atherton and Tyldesley, a more definitely recognizable town has developed. Nor is the situation different in the Yorkshire,

Nottingham and Derby coalfield, where the main towns, such as Barnsley, Doncaster, Mansfield and Chesterfield, have a variety of industries (v.i.). And this situation is by no means confined to coalfields for, as shown in Chapter 6, the West Yorkshire conurbation has never lost its basic historical character of a congeries of industrial villages.

The developments of the past, and those likely in the near future combine to make the current definition of towns difficult. An old town islanded in a countryside may offer no greater problem of definition than the periodical revision of boundaries but an area that is a kind of no man's land between agriculture and industry offers far greater problems. When the Census commissioners of 1851 tried to separate town from country, they were obviously puzzled by the status of many new industrial areas,[21] but one by one these places acquired Public Health boards or bodies of Improvement Commissioners, and in due course became urban sanitary districts, boroughs or (from 1888) county boroughs. Until 1947, the Local Government Board or, for the larger places, local acts of Parliament, made adjustments of boundaries.[22] Some places experienced revision of boundaries on several occasions, others hardly at all; for example, Bolton, Lancashire still has the boundaries laid down in 1898. The greatest single work of revision was done under the County Review Orders of the nineteen-thirties, after the careful local investigations under the provisions of the 1929 Local Government Act.[23] Many compromises were made. In some cases a number of small industrial towns and villages were tied into a neat urban parcel and labelled with the name of the largest member, as in Morley, Yorkshire, or even of a convenient river as in Colne Valley near Huddersfield.

Since 1945, there have been comparatively few administrative changes of significance. The post-war effort to make a series of new counties,[24] some with c. 200,000 people and some with c. 1,000,000 people, of which the latter were to have complete self-government and the former a measure of it, met with no general acceptance: such a scheme (published in a White Paper having no map) cut across too many existing loyalties, notably by uniting Worcestershire and Herefordshire into one county, but perhaps the greatest cause of its failure was the excessive veneration shown for population statistics. The distribution of the urban population on the ground has changed rapidly and presumably will continue to do so. In 1947 the Local Government Board was dissolved and the responsibility for boundary changes was transferred to the Minister of Housing and Local Government and the local authorities.[25] During the first half of the period since 1947, the only major boundary changes were made for urgent housing needs and in the later period changes were made for various reasons, though all these were of limited scope. Many interesting and apparently logical proposals were refused. In 1950–1951, a bill to extend Sheffield northwards into the West Riding and southwards into Derbyshire was rejected, although the West Riding County Council were willing to allow the housing estate areas—already built-up—to be included. In the 1951–1952 sessions, a proposal to amalgamate Hartlepool and West Hartlepool was refused. And for several years Luton unsuccessfully put forward a bill to acquire County Borough status.[26] Presumably some general directive is foreshadowed by the famous 1956 White Paper,[27] cautious as its wording appears to be, and the appointment of a Royal Commission in 1957.

Definition of the Lesser Conurbations

Here the lesser conurbations have been regarded as including areas under town administration only and no rural districts have been included, though some note is made of cases where towns are overflowing their bounds. The Fawcett conception of a conurbation as a continuous urban area has been followed but now, as when he wrote, a town apparently a unit on the ground may or may not happen to be within one administrative boundary, according to the local circumstances.[28] Each case has been examined on the O.S. 1 in to the mile map (seventh and eighth editions) and a uniform treatment preserved as far as possible. With Leicester, for example, the contiguous small urban districts of Oadby and Wigston have been included; with Hull, Haltemprice; with Cardiff, Penarth. But in the case of Oxford, there is no contiguous urban district but a great deal of continuous residential property outside the city boundary, though efforts to extend these boundaries in 1953 were rejected by the House of Lords, having been opposed by the county councils of Oxfordshire and Berkshire.[39] At the end of the 1939–1945 war, Oxford had a population of over 100,000, and, says E. W. Gilbert, 'the population of the continuous urban area, which sprawled beyond the city's boundaries, probably numbered between 115,000 and 120,000'.[30] There are other cases of like nature throughout the country. It would therefore be a reasonable assumption that the population associated with these lesser conurbations is even greater than 13,213,000, possibly nearer 14,000,000.

Some of the so-called 'minor' conurbations differ little from the major conurbations, except by having a smaller population. Some consist of a single industrial town such as Crewe (52,400), a fishing port and holiday centre such as Yarmouth (51,000), a cathedral city having some industry such as Worcester (59,700) or even Scarborough with Scalby (50,200), a holiday and residential centre. But all have one thing in common: directly or indirectly they depend on industry in a way that the small market town does not. The residential and holiday towns such as Harrogate and Cheltenham, and still more obviously Blackpool and Brighton, grew to their considerable size with the help of the railways, drawing residents as well as holiday visitors primarily from the ever-increasing town populations. Old cathedral and market centres, such as Carlisle, Chester and Gloucester, attracted industries partly because they were road and railway junctions. And York, even larger, and from Roman times a strategic site, has become a great railway centre with a considerable industrial development.

Marked changes of population distribution are a commonplace of recent economic history. In the preceding chapters of this book, examples have been given of major industrial areas now apparently static, or even declining, in population (cf. pp. 140, 187). Similarly, in certain minor as in certain major conurbations, industrial growth has not been, and in the future, will not be continuous; some areas depending largely on coal, cotton or shipbuilding, for example, have had considerable losses of population. The county of Glamorgan declined in population by 51,000 from 1921 to 1951 (and lost 250,000 by net outward migration),[31] but the town of Coventry added over 100,000 people to its numbers in the same thirty years and Dagenham increased from 9,000 in 1921 to 115,000 in 1951. There are three types of population trend seen: first, decline, second, rapid increase, and third, stability or slight increase, depending or local circumstances. And the modern ease of movement has favoured two types of internal migration, one of short range to new suburban areas and the second of longer range to towns requiring more workers.

Areas of Rapid Increase (Fig. 44)

The lesser conurbations showed varying rates of population change from 1931 to 1951. A few, such as Watford and Rickmansworth (102,000; + 40 per cent), and even more Romford, Hornchurch and Brentwood (222,000; + 120 per cent), were so obviously

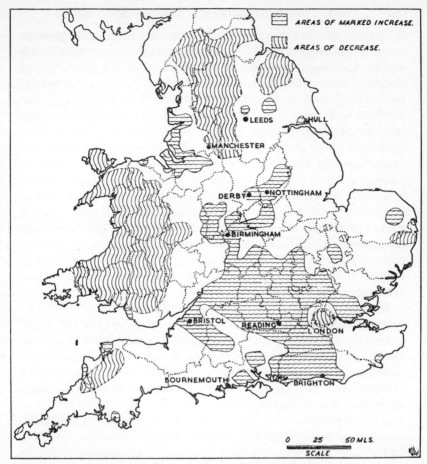

FIG. 44. ENGLAND AND WALES—MAIN AREAS OF POPULATION INCREASE
AND DECREASE, 1931–1951

This map is heavily generalized and purposely avoids mapping the changes by administrative units. The areas of decrease correspond to the major uplands: in the Pennines there are decreases in the textile towns of both Lancashire and Yorkshire. As far as possible the areas shown as having 'marked increases' are those where the population added at least 25 per cent within the twenty years considered. Clearly the major fear must be the continued attraction of the counties to the northwest of London, Buckinghamshire, Oxfordshire and Berkshire as well as the permanent threat to Surrey and Sussex. Similarly there is marked expansion from Bristol northwards to Gloucester and Cheltenham: note the growth around the industrial centres of Birmingham, Leicester, Nottingham and Derby. In the Northwest, there is every sign of continued expansion in a belt of country from the Wirral peninsula to Lymm, in the area inland from the coast near Liverpool and Southport, in the Fylde, based on Blackpool and its neighbours and around Preston.

affected by the outward spread of London that they should perhaps now be regarded as part of the London conurbation as they are fused with it. And the phenomenon of industrial expansion is widespread in the southeast, especially within a radius of 60 miles from London: Luton and Dunstable, for example, increased from 80,000 in 1931 to 127,000 (+ 59 per cent) by 1951, and at Slough, with New Windsor and Eton, there was a rise from 57,000 in 1931 to 93,000 in 1951 (+ 79 per cent). Similar trends are seen on the north side of the Thames estuary where large industrial as well as residential communities are growing up at the present time for the economic attraction of the metropolitan area remain powerful. And much the same situation is found in the areas around the West Midland conurbation where further growth is no longer desired, though towns within easy reach may acquire industries that might have been located at Birmingham. A notable example of growth is the rise of Coventry, now linked with Bedworth and Nuneaton (337,000; + 38 per cent, 1931-1951), and the same process may be seen in smaller towns such as Stafford (40,000; + 31 per cent), or Rugby (45,000; + 32 per cent). Fawcett in 1932 pointed out that the major increases of population were found in the southeast and in the West Midlands and the tendencies of that time are still marked.[32] It has in fact become almost a social problem, which some would solve by restricting building in the effort to prevent any further increase of population, but such efforts might not be successful.

Many residential and holiday towns have shown an increase similar to that of the growing industrial areas from 1931 to 1951. Of these, perhaps the most interesting are Brighton with its neighbours, having 333,000 people in 1951 (+ 21 per cent), or Bournemouth with Poole and Christchurch, 248,000 (+ 32 per cent). Such increases are not confined to the southeast and south, for the Fylde coast towns (Blackpool, etc.) with 230,000, had an increase of + 33 per cent, and similar inland towns showed comparable rates of growth, notably Cheltenham with Charlton Kings, 69,000, increased by + 25 per cent, Bath, 79,000, by + 15 per cent, and Harrogate, now joined to Knaresborough, 59,000, by + 17 per cent. As E. W. Gilbert[33] has shown such towns are of three types: first, inland spas such as Bath, Cheltenham and Harrogate, developed before the railway age; second, old ports or fishing harbours converted into seaside resorts, such as Brighton, Scarborough and Margate, and third, 'new' towns founded on land previously unoccupied or occupied only by a few houses, such as Bournemouth, Blackpool, Southport and Southend. All have in common a linear extension along the sea far greater than their inland depth; though in some, notably Blackpool, inland expansion is now marked, partly through the development of light industries, and the attraction to permanent residents of areas some distance from the sea front.

Areas of Decline

By contrast, many of the older industrial areas of the coalfields have populations that are stationary or declining. Two main factors are operative here: first, areas such as South Wales and Durham, which grew on the fruits of the coal seams and little else except iron and steel in the few places where ores occurred, inevitably suffered when the seams were exhausted or export coal no longer in full demand (pp. 284–91). Secondly, areas such as the cotton towns from Blackburn to Colne, the so-called 'weaving district', which had more than half their working population in cotton mills, suffered by the decline of the export trade from the nineteen-twenties, especially as the output of their coalmines was declining at the same time (pp. 236–7). It is in such areas that some of the heaviest decreases of population were recorded from 1931 to 1951, following declines in the previous ten years. The Lancashire cotton areas' decline of c. 10 per cent in 1931–1951 would have been greater but for the entry of various new industries and the transference of many women from mill-work to ordinary household duties as men's wages rose. The South Wales coalfield as defined on p. 236, had 666,000 people in 1951, compared with 758,000 in 1931 and 833,000 in 1921, a decline of − 20 per cent (1921–1951) in spite of the introduction of new industries and the renewed prosperity of coal mining. Durham mining towns had decreases of slightly less intensity and here a most vigorous campaign to attract new industry is in full swing (see p. 222). In such areas the problem of the industrial community is sharply seen: the county of Glamorgan[34] had a population of only 71,000 in 1801, but this was almost doubled by 1831, and more than quadrupled by 1861, after which there were further substantial increases to 860,000 by 1901. In every inter-censal decade from 1801 to 1911, the increase of population was at least + 20 per cent, and in some almost + 40 per cent, but from 1911 to 1921, the rise was only + 12 per cent and from 1921 to 1931, there was a decrease of − 2 per cent, followed by a similar decline from 1931 to 1951. What had been an area of immigration became one of outward migration, estimated at 135,000 from 1921 to 1931, and 125,000 from 1931 to 1951, a

P

heavy movement because the rate of natural increase remains high (+ 8·7, 1921–1931, + 8·2, 1931–1951). It is such examples that demonstrate the precarious structure of the mining community which has little supplementary industry. Almost the only mining areas now increasing in population are those in the newer, eastern parts of the Yorkshire-Nottingham and Derby coalfield.

Areas of Stability

Between the extremes of rapid increase and heavy decline, there are various examples of industrial areas which appear at present to be practically stable. The West Riding conurbation is perhaps the best example: the woollen textile trade has not experienced slumps comparable to those in cotton. The main coal mining area has gradually moved eastward through the Pennines so that now it has reached the wide lowlands on the east side, marginal to the conurbation; as one industry declined, others came in (see e.g. pp. 160–4). And in Central Lancashire, the mining areas between the two great conurbations, having an intermingling of the cotton, engineering, chemical and glass industries (in St. Helens) remained as a whole practically stable in population from 1931 to 1951 (1931, 446,000; 1951, 460,000, + 3 per cent). The Potteries, taken to include the towns adjoining Stoke, had 372,000 people in 1951, an increase of + 4 per cent: this distinctive industrial area shows neither a marked expansion nor contraction of its economic activity.

Areas of rapid increase, areas of decline, and areas that appear to be stable, all have in common the need for rehousing of a proportion of their population varying from one place to another: even the towns of South Wales, though declining so sharply in population, have new housing estates. In Co. Durham it is proposed to remove a number of mining villages and to develop the new towns of Aycliffe and Peterlee as homes for people who travel to neighbouring mines or work on new industrial estates.[35] But the removal of even a small mining village, still less a decayed mining town, is likely to be a rare phenomenon, especially as people can travel by bus to their work—in many cases by specially chartered buses provided by employers. And this may result in a distribution of the working population which is vestigial—related rather to a past distribution of employment than to that of the present day. Examples are numerous. In Lancashire there are large new coalmines on the southern flank of the coalfield, but they are not surrounded by houses, as the workers are brought in by buses from older centres such as Wigan, where the mines are almost exhausted. No longer need the distribution of population follow closely the distribution of workplaces: there is a time lag between one and the other. Under modern conditions a better development than the multiplication of colliery villages is to build a town possessing other industries from which workers can travel to various mines. Yet many towns must depend largely on one industry, such as Scunthorpe, Lincolnshire (34,000 in 1931 but 54,200 in 1951) which has become a steel-making town using the local ores and the coal from the neighbouring Yorkshire field. Many—not all—industrialists have a wide choice of possible locations for their works and the availability of labour and building land—even convertible premises—will influence siting. The old mill village, or the colliery village, is less likely to be chosen than a town capable of expansions and possessing good communications. It would seem therefore that these lesser conurbations are an important element in English life, and that various towns now having less than 50,000 people may increase numerically—but all our towns, through re-housing, must increase in area.

Conurbations 250,000–700,000

Approximately five and a half million people live in the fourteen conurbations of this group: the two greatest examples, the South Wales coalfield (666,000) and Sheffield with Rotherham and Rawmarsh (614,000) were regarded by Patrick Geddes as clearly-marked conurbations, to which he gave the suggestive names of Waleston and South Riding.[00] Three other conurbations have populations approaching half-a-million, the Nottingham area (489,000), Bristol and its satellites (487,000) and the Lancashire coalfield (460,000): next in order come the Potteries (372,000), Portsmouth and district (367,000), Coventry with Bedworth and Nuneaton (337,000), Hull with Haltemprice (335,000), Teesmouth (330,000), and one conurbation, based on Brighton (263,000) that deserves separate comment from the circumstance that unlike the others it is not primarily industrial in its life. Barnsley and its neighbours (252,000), Leicester with Oadby and Wigston (307,000) and Cardiff with Penarth (262,000) also come within this conurbation category.

In defining these conurbations the Fawcett criterion 'continuous town' has been followed as far as possible.[37] But the distribution of houses and factories is now changing so rapidly that any definition has elements of compromise. Only a narrow belt of open country separates the colliery towns and villages of the South Wales valleys from its great port and commercial centre of Cardiff, from Newport-Caerleon (110,000), from Neath and Port Talbot (76,000), or Swansea and Llwchwr (187,000): if all these towns were taken into one Geddesian Waleston, their total population would be 1,138,000 but on the Fawcett scheme the remaining precious belts of open country divide them into separate parts. Similarly the emergence of a major conurbation based on Nottingham, Derby and the towns and increasingly urbanized rural districts of the Erewash valley seems imminent.[38] This 'quasi-conurbation', says R. H. Osborne, consists of 'an equilateral triangle with sides of about fifteen miles in length, the apex . . . in the Alfreton district and the base lying along the Derby-Nottingham axis'. Within this area, there are some 850,000 people. What Dr. Osborne calls 'conurban linkage' is an unfortunate but probably inevitable development: but it is neither new nor unique. From Sheffield and Rotherham, a string of large mining villages extends from Rawmarsh into the Dearne valley (Fig. 46) to Barnsley and beyond: so little open land separates these places that they could be regarded as in fact one conurbation, having in all 854,000 people. And in the Don valley there is a string of mining settlements from Conisbrough to Doncaster and farther east, hardly yet one continuous ribbon of settlement, but in danger of becoming one. Examples of building along roads such as those given for Manchester (Figs. 28, 29) could be multiplied over the country: 'development' on or near a main road is natural because convenient to the population living in new houses. At present, the Lancashire coalfield conurbation meets the two major conurbations—Merseyside and Manchester—at each end, so that by choosing certain roads it is possible to travel through continuously built-up areas from Manchester to Liverpool.

Of the fourteen conurbations now under review, three showed population increases of 20 per cent or more from 1931 to 1951, four had increases of 10–19 per cent, five were virtually stable in population and the South Wales coalfield had a decline of − 13 per cent. Of the increases, the greatest was + 38 per cent in Coventry with Bedworth and Nuneaton, a classic example of an industrial area in the full tide of growth, as South Wales is of an industrial area in decline. It is in line with population history to state that various areas have been populated by immigrants, rapidly drawn from rural areas, from other and dying industrial areas, from Ireland, even from abroad, but a period of immense population increase may be followed by one of stability, and even—if the main industries be mining

and textiles—of decline. The main areas now expanding in population are those depending largely on mechanical and electrical
engineering, vehicles and aircraft, as well as on a wide variety of
other trades commonly regarded as light industries and there is no
longer an inevitable and close connexion between high population
densities and coalfields. Indeed, one may well ask whether this is not
merely an outworn textbook generalization never completely true.
Some coalfields never attracted industry, and were marked by colliery
villages 2–3 miles apart, as in Leicestershire today, or even in much
of the Durham-Northumberland or the Yorkshire-Nottingham and
Derby coalfields.

The Smaller Conurbations and Towns (50,000–250,000)

The seventy-five towns, or groups of towns, within this group have
7,600,000 people, almost one-fifth of the country's total population.
Fig. 66 shows that they are widely distributed and include a great
variety of places, many of which have increased markedly in the past
twenty years or so. In Chapters 9 and 10 these towns are considered
under regional headings but they are discussed briefly here under a
type classification.

First, *old towns industrialized.* The 1851 Census made a distinction
between the ordinary country market towns and the 'carriage towns'
that were centres of county administration and, in many cases,
Cathedral cities, and vital route junctions[39] (pp. 205–06). Among them
are Carlisle, York, Lincoln, Norwich, Chester, Worcester, Gloucester and Exeter, all of which preserve the atmosphere of an historic
town but also possess industries combined with a strong commercial
life.

Second, *ports and naval centres.* These include Plymouth and
Southampton on the south coast, Gillingham with Rochester and
Chatham in the Thames estuary, the fishing ports of Yarmouth and
Grimsby and various others. Such places do not depend solely on
one main activity: for example Yarmouth has a strong holiday
traffic and Cleethorpes (Grimsby) has similar attractions.

Third, *railway towns.* Crewe is a type-specimen of note, having
arisen at a crossing of lines in the middle of lowland Cheshire, where
no town existed before. Swindon grew around a railway works that
was successfully prevented by the learned from finding a location in
Oxford (p. 274). Derby, Darlington and Doncaster are in some way
comparable, though in these cases the expansion associated with the
railways was around an existing town.

Fourth, *older industrial areas*. Long-established industrial areas are typified by the coal and cotton towns such as Blackburn, Burnley or those of Rossendale in Lancashire, and also by similar woollen towns of Yorkshire. Having grown almost to their present size by the middle of the nineteenth century, these places have remained almost stable in population for several decades and are now declining numerically, though they have a variety of new industries which provides employment supplementary to cotton-working, now much diminished. Comparable phenomena of recent population decline are seen in some of the older coal-mining areas such as the urban district focused on Bishop Auckland.

Fifth, *newer and expanding industrial areas*. Examples such as the steel town of Scunthorpe, are the clearest at the present day, but these are merely passing through a phase seen in such places as Blackburn and Burnley a century or more ago. Towns like Watford, Luton, Reading and Slough have shared in the recent industrial expansion characteristic of London and its not easily definable surrounding area and towns round the West Midlands conurbation have seen a comparable marked expansion of population. But in both cases, residential growth is intricately mixed with local industrial development, for example in Warwick and Leamington (52,000 in 1951) which have an increasing amount of industry but remain largely residential. The industrial town rising from nothing is a rarity but the decanting of factories into existing towns a widespread phenomenon, especially around London and the West Midlands (see also pp. 252-4, 266-7).

Sixth, *residential and holiday towns*. The French geographer, Demangeon, drew attention to the great development of these towns in England and Wales and E. W. Gilbert, working also on this theme, has shown that the spas developed in the eighteenth century and the seaside resorts later, especially when easy access was given by railways.[40] All holiday towns attract in varying degrees a residential population ranging in type from those wishing to add to a slender income by catering for visitors to wealthy retired people. The more successful of these towns, such as Brighton, have become large and from their very size have inevitably developed into strong market and commercial centres. Bournemouth, Brighton and Blackpool are major examples: and smaller places such as Torquay and Paignton, or Hastings and Bexhill, also come within this category of coastal conurbations. Inland the best example is Harrogate, now effectively joined to Knaresborough, at once a holiday and conference centre, a town favoured by the leisured and retired, and to a limited extent a dormitory for workers in Leeds and Bradford. An interesting recent development has been the settlement of certain government departments in towns such as Blackpool, Southport, and Harrogate, begun during wartime evacuation.

Seventh, *London overspill towns*. These include some areas which are virtually joined to the London conurbation as now officially defined but, as noted on pp. 65–70, this definition is open to the criticism of inadequacy. Heavy increases of population were recorded from 1931 to 1951 in such continuous town areas as Romford, Hornchurch and Brentwood (+ 120 per cent), the four Surrey urban districts of Egham, Chertsey, Woking, Walton-Weybridge (+ 50 per cent), and Watford M.B. with Rickmansworth and Chorleywood (+ 40 per cent). But the problem is of wider extent: good communications are in part responsible for the growth of Reigate M.B. and Caterham-Warlingham (+ 31 per cent) and, for different reasons, various places along the Essex shore of the Thames estuary such as Thurrock (+ 33 per cent). The problem seen here is the expansion of suburban populations and in places also of industry farther into adjoining counties in two ways; first by direct outward growth and second by the addition of houses to towns and villages already existing. Everywhere suburban growth in Britain has shown both these characteristics but in the London area it is shown on a much vaster scale than elsewhere.

The last comment raises the whole question of administrative definition both of conurbations and of the individual boroughs and urban districts of which they are formed. In 1921, the issue before the Royal Commission on London was whether such areas as suburban growths in Middlesex were really part of Greater London (pp. 56–61): the question now is whether areas 5, 10 or more miles 'further out' beyond Greater London are part of a wider metropolitan area. This outward spread of towns beyond defined boundaries is found all over the country and the time is ripe for a redefinition of our towns. At present many have boundaries laid down some twenty-five years ago in the County Review Orders of the nineteen-thirties, but have grown considerably since then. Norwich, Reading, Oxford, Leicester, Crewe, Chester and others have long spread far beyond their bounds, in some cases into another county. Warrington, Lancashire, has its main suburb, Stockton Heath, in Cheshire within the Runcorn rural district, and has also spread around a number of other villages in both counties. In other cases, such as Preston (119,000), two other urban districts, Fulwood and Walton-le-Dale (28,000) join the main town and appear to be part of it: so too does Charlton Kings (6,000) beside Cheltenham (63,000), or Old Fletton (9,000) beside Peterborough (53,000). But some such districts have been united with larger centres, for example in 1954 Hoole (9,000) was joined administratively to Chester (48,000) but even now Chester's boundaries do not include Upton parish (over 6,000), nor other suburban areas. Whereas Chester apparently has a population of 57,000, a better estimate would be 78,000 (p. 244). In many such places it is possible to draw a reasonably sharp line on the ground between the areas of town and country: all that seems necessary is to revise boundaries at appropriate intervals. But that begs many questions.

CHAPTER 9

THE MINOR CONURBATIONS OF THE NORTH OF ENGLAND

THE north of England consists of three of the present Standard Regions: the first, the Northern, covers the counties of Cumberland, Westmorland, Northumberland, Durham and the North Riding of Yorkshire; the second covers the East and West Ridings of Yorkshire; and the third, the Northwest, Lancashire, Cheshire and the small part of Derbyshire nearest to the Manchester area. For purposes of convenient arrangement, the minor conurbations will be considered here under the Standard Regions, though there are some curious anomalies such as the Furness area of Lancashire, 'beyond the Sands', which clearly belongs geographically to the Lake District and its margins rather than to the remainder of Lancashire. Within the whole of the 'north', there is a population of 13,680,000, of whom 10,708,000, or 78 per cent, live in four major and twenty-eight minor conurbations, which are discussed in the following pages.

NORTHERN STANDARD REGION

Though including the greater part of the Lake District, the North Pennines and the North York moors, three of the country's national parks, this area has less than a quarter of its inhabitants living in rural districts. Nearly one million live in eight minor conurbations of which the largest is Teesmouth (330,000) and the next Sunderland with Boldon (197,000), so close to Tyneside (Chapter 7) that to some the separation seems artificial. Except for Carlisle, all the industrial towns of this area are on the Northumberland and Durham coalfield or the allied manufacturing areas on its southern flank, Teesmouth and Darlington: on the coast, Scarborough represents a different element, but one well developed in the north of England—the holiday and residential centre. Scarborough and Carlisle have increased considerably in population since 1931, but the mining areas of Durham and Northumberland have declines shared by other mining areas, notably South Wales (p. 286). The position of Teesmouth as in part the heir to Tyneside industries is noted: statistically the table overleaf shows the proportion of the population in conurbations and other towns.

221

TABLE 3

NORTHERN STANDARD REGION: CONURBATION POPULATION, 1951

	Population 000's, 1951	%
Tyneside	835	26
Miner conurbations (8) . .	999	32
Other towns	622	20
Rural districts	684	22
Total	3,140	100

Cumberland

Carlisle alone, 68,000 (+ 18 per cent, 1931–1951) has more than 50,000 people. Historically of immense strategic significance as a fortified bastion against incursions from the north, in more peaceful times it is a route centre, major market and cathedral city with a modern and varied industrial life.[1] Good railway communications have been beneficial to industry and enterprises associated with farming include eight breweries, a bacon factory and the manufacture of agricultural machinery. Engineering is represented also by metal box manufacture and the making of cranes from components brought by rail from Workington and Sheffield. Calico-printing survives and there is a famous furnishing fabrics works, originally brought here from Ayrshire. But the number of workers in service trades is almost twice as numerous as those in factory production, with railway employees as a main group, and fundamentally, Carlisle is a regional capital, now as in previous centuries.

Northumberland and Durham

In no area has the problem of attracting new industries received more attention than this for the dependence on mining raises obvious problems. Within the Northumberland-Durham coalfield, including Tyneside, the North Eastern Trading Estates company has aided the establishment of factories employing nearly 53,000 people by 1958, including nearly 30,000 women.[2] Apart from the conurbations of Tyneside and Teesmouth, mining settlement predominates with towns and villages built around pits and characteristic small ports such as Newbiggin, Blyth and Seaham Harbour on the coast:

Sunderland and the Hartlepools are larger ports, with an interest in coal shipment but also in shipbuilding and timber import.

Most of the mining villages have a monotonous gridiron pattern with some modern housing estates in the newer eastern parts of the coalfield. In the Northumberland part of the coalfield, the five towns of Seaton Valley, Blyth, Bedlingtonshire, Newbiggin and Ashington cover an administrative area of 55 square miles with a population of 128,000 (+ 2 per cent since 1931): this is a loosely defined conurbation with interlocking ribbons of town in a landscape still predominantly agricultural. Three small trading estates, with six factories and c. 1,500 workers have been established here.[3] In the Co. Durham section of the coalfield, there are three conurbations, Sunderland with Boldon (197,000, − 2 per cent, 1931–1951), the Hartlepools (90,000, − 1 per cent, 1931–1951) and Bishop Auckland-Shildon (51,000, − 7 per cent, 1931–1951). Of these three, the last shows the population decline characteristic of most parts of the Durham coalfield: but new trading estates already employ some 3,000 people, notably in clothing factories and in the electrical and leather trades.[4] On the coast at Sunderland and Hartlepool new industries include clothing factories, various metal trades and—at Hartlepool, cotton yarn doubling, worsted manufacture, and button-making.[5] The Pallion estate at Sunderland and the Hartlepool estate each have more than 3,000 workers.[6] Coalmining, shipbuilding and overseas trade remain the basic concerns of the northeast, but there is an interesting new range of industries; even so, further deline of population here seems as probable as in the inner Pennine area or the Rossendale and coal–cotton areas of Lancashire.

Darlington, in the extreme south of Co. Durham, beyond the limits of the coalfield, has remained prosperous and showed an increase in population of + 18 per cent to 85,000 from 1931 to 1951.[7] Iron and steel is the basis of the modern industrial growth, and railway construction employs several thousand people, both in the railway workshops and in private enterprises, including the original Stephenson firm, which chose Darlington for an extension of its works from Newcastle some sixty years ago and, like others, supplies engines and other railway needs in the export as well as the home market. A Darlington firm has made several of the greatest bridges in the world, and other industries include pressed steel, chemical insulation, joinery and timber, and hand-knitting yarns. At present the developments at the new town of Newtown Aycliffe to the north, are bringing a still wider industrial range to the district.

Teesmouth (330,000) has become a great industrial area in the past hundred years: the main town, Middlesbrough, had 7,431 people in 1851 but grew rapidly into a port and steel centre after the discovery (or re-discovery) of the Cleveland Jurassic ores in 1849 close to the Durham coking coals.[8] Even though the few surviving iron mines here yield less than a million tons a year and the reserves can last only for some forty years, steel has survived on imported ores (83 per cent in 1954) and those from the English Midlands and Furness (8 per cent in 1954). In 1954, the northeast steel area, including West Hartlepool and Consett and Skinningrove near Saltburn, produced one quarter of the United Kingdom's pig iron and one-fifth of its steel. The vast I.C.I. plant at Billingham, which covers 1,000 acres and has 15,000 employees, has developed to its present size since 1917: most of its sixty different products are made from five simple raw materials —air, water, coal, anhydrite and salt. The first three are obviously close at hand: the anhydrite (calcium sulphate) comes from a large deposit which lies some 700 ft. below the site and the salt is obtained by brine-pumping from the extensive rock-salt beds some 1,000 ft. below the surface, nearer the coast.[9] Teesmouth has an obvious affinity with Tyneside in its industrial character, partly because there too chemical-working is a long-established industry. And one may add that this area shares only to a minor degree the difficulties of other industrial areas in the northeast as its major industries, steel and chemicals, are conspicuously prosperous.

As a county boundary, the River Tees is one of many appropriate rather to the conditions of past centuries than of the present. Several of the wartime and post-war schemes of regionalization suggested that all of Teesmouth should be included with Co. Durham, partly because it appears to belong to the same industrial province.[10] To this a Yorkshire patriot would retort that of the 330,000 people of Teesmouth, only 98,000 live in Co. Durham, 24,000 in Billingham and 74,000 in Stockton: the North Riding has the main towns, Middlesbrough C.B. (147,000), Eston U.D. (33,000), Thornaby-on-Tees M.B. (23,000) and Redcar M.B. (28,000). Beyond these towns lie the mining centres, such as Skelton, Brotton, Guisborough and Loftus, which have shared the problems of other declining areas of extractive industry, now eased by the introduction of new factories.

Along the coast, at Marske and Saltburn, and in a number of villages to Whitby and beyond, residential and holiday settlements have grown up, and inland, the North York moors have now been made into a national park. The North Riding is industrial only at its northern extremity, and its largest holiday resort, Scarborough, has with Scalby more than 50,000 people.[11] As early as the seventeenth century, it was favoured for its beneficial spa waters and its sheltered position, and by 1835 the borough had 8,750 inhabitants, depending almost entirely on 'the resort of visitors' in the summer season. The town grew towards Falsgrave, which had ceased to be an isolated village by 1835 and also extended southwards from its main nucleus near the castle towards the spa. Many of the amenities were provided by the Cliff Bridge Company, formed in 1826 by some local residents and others from York. These attractions included promenades, handsome shops, a theatre, Italian terraces and balconies, and a carriage drive along the undercliff. The Corporation, following a similar policy from the eighteen-seventies, added more gardens, developed the cliff property on the north side as a health resort, and built a number of roads including a Marine Drive between 1897 and 1908. Though some of its interesting old streets recall its development before the railway age, its main growth is recent and apparently still continuing as in spite of its vulnerable position during the war of 1939–1945 there was a population increase of + 12 per cent from 1931 to 1951.

YORKSHIRE, EAST AND WEST RIDINGS

Nearly two-thirds of the population of the East Riding lives in Hull with Haltemprice, and four-fifths of the people of the West

TABLE 4

YORKSHIRE EAST AND WEST RIDINGS: CONURBATION POPULATION, 1951

	West Riding		East Riding		East and West Ridings	
	Total 000's	%	Total 000's	%	Total 000's	%
West Yorkshire conurbation . . .	1,692	49	—	—	1,692	42
Other conurbations .	1,046	31	335	65	1,381	35
Small towns . . .	315	8	69	14	384	10
Rural districts . . .	427	12	107	21	534	13
Total	3,480	100	511	100	3,991	100

Riding reside in conurbations of more than 50,000 people. Apart from Hull, the East Riding is agricultural, with no town of more than 25,000 people, and the West Yorkshire conurbation is a mixture of urban and rural areas rather than one continuous town. And this quality of the landscape persists throughout the mining and metallurgical areas southwards to the Derbyshire border. The population in 1951 is shown in Table 4. In fact many parishes in the rural areas are either mining areas or covered by housing estates from neighbouring towns, notably from Sheffield. The apparent increase of + 14 per cent in the rural districts from 1931 to 1951 is due to the spread of this form of settlement rather than to any increase in the agricultural population.

Greater Hull

Hull[12] with Haltemprice (335,000, + 1 per cent, 1931–1951) has a strong port trade in timber, fish, chemicals, oil-seeds and grain and its main industries are associated with these imports. The main part of the town is built on a bank of alluvium which did not exist in Roman times and the first settlement was probably on an island between two arms of the river Hull, at its junction with the Humber. Once described as 'no Edwardian mushroom', Hull was given a royal charter in 1299 and became a walled town in the fourteenth century. As a town site, it had three main advantages: first, the Hull creeks and in time the main river, could be used for quays; second, the land was flat or virtually so, and third, local brickclays were available and used so extensively that in the eighteenth century the town was almost entirely brick built. As early as 1274, it was mentioned as a port from which wool was smuggled to Flanders; its fishing trade is of great antiquity. Its modern growth precedes the railway era, for during the eighteenth century the woollen goods of Yorkshire were brought for shipment by the river navigations and canals, notably the Aire and Calder, begun in 1698.

In 1778 the first (Queen's) dock, now filled, was built; and many more were added during the nineteenth century so that by 1914, when the King George dock was opened, Hull had 5 miles of port facilities along the river. Meanwhile the railway from Leeds had reached Hull in 1840. By the end of the nineteenth century port industries had become firmly established, and steadily trade has grown so that Hull is the third port of Britain, and by far the largest fishery centre. It is not, however, prominent as a wool-importing town for the main woollen market is in London: much more significant is its grain trade, with a large milling industry and brewing, its timber trade, shipbuilding and engineering, seed-crushing with oil-extraction and the manufacture of feeding-cake, tanning and a famous chemical industry. Fishing and derived industries, ship-building and repairing are other port trades. The heavy bombing of the 1939–1945 war did not obliterate all the older part of the city, though the modern shopping quarter was virtually eliminated and rebuilt only in the nineteen-fifties after a classic struggle on the re-planning of the town. There is now an active campaign for the attraction of new industries as the town had a higher rate of un-employment than the national average before the 1939–1945 war, and was regarded as having a 'permanent surplus of labour'. Its problems are perhaps similar to those of Merseyside. Much of the modern residential development is taking place outside the adminis-trative boundary of Hull, especially in Haltemprice, which includes Hessle and Cottingham: and the favoured residential sites are on the lower slopes of the Wolds. Around Hull, there is rich arable-farming country with attractive old villages: so far it seems improbable that building will line the road all the way to the old market town of Beverley, 8 miles distant.

York (Fig. 45)

Belonging to none of the three Ridings, and governed as a county borough, York enjoys the advantage of a strategic position in the north of England: here morainic ridges gave easy access to the Ouse crossing, and here also a river port developed. Traditionally a strong market town, it is also a garrison and ecclesiastical centre. The natural strategic advantages influenced railway developments so that York became the headquarters of the Northeastern railway which, as shown on p. 185, successfully absorbed a number of other lines. But the famous chocolate industries were introduced for reasons of personal choice rather than any factor of local raw materials. Though still a tourist centre and shopping town for its rich countryside, York is hardly a regional capital, having been overshadowed by Hull to the east and Leeds to the west. In 1951, its population was 105,000, an increase of + 12 per cent over 1931: including a number of surround-ing villages beyond the city boundary, the population has increased by 20 per cent from 105,000 in 1931 to 126,000 in 1951.

At York, the West Riding begins. Its major conurbation is con-sidered in Chapter 6, so that here the main concern is with the minor conurbations of the coalfield. One of the clearest lines of regional division is the edge of the coalfield, which runs through the northern suburbs of Leeds and Bradford: north of this line, suburban developments are the main witness to the nearness of the great indus-

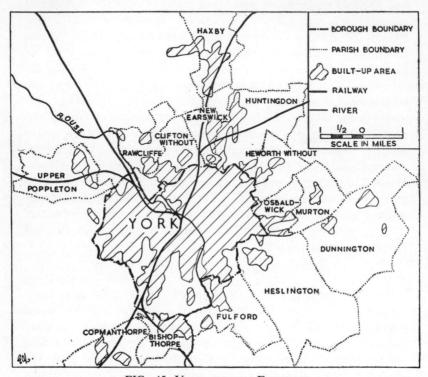

FIG. 45. YORK AND ITS ENVIRONS

York is one of the many towns where the administrative units are in need of readjustment as there has been a considerable movement into neighbouring villages.

trial area to the south. Hardly an outer suburb of the West Riding, yet partly so, Harrogate grew first as a spa in the eighteenth century and gradually became the epitome of a holiday and residential town

FIG. 46. Doncaster is within the newer and expanding part of the coalfield, has excellent road and rail communications and has become a strong industrial town: Barnsley is a long-established mining and factory centre. As in other mining areas, many urban districts consist of a number of mining villages set in an agricultural countryside.

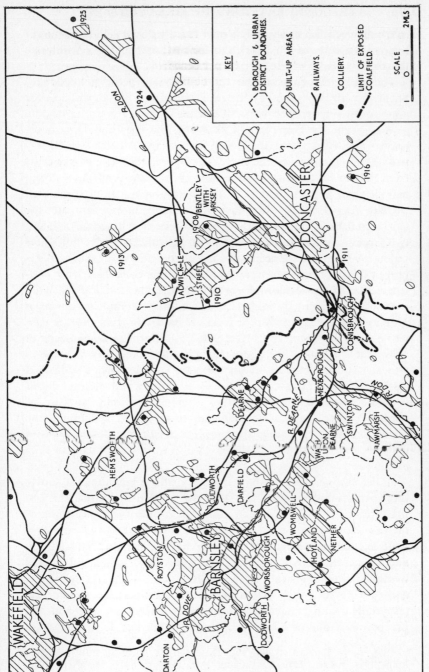

Q

FIG. 46. The Yorkshire Mining Area, with Barnsley and Doncaster

in the nineteenth century. It has now fused with the delightful market town of Knaresborough, 3 miles to the east: with 59,000 inhabitants, these places had increased by 17 per cent from 1931.

The coalfield areas straddle the countryside between Leeds and Sheffield with large mining villages grouped into urban districts for administrative purposes but with few places that are strong trading towns, except for Pontefract, Castleford, Barnsley and Doncaster: only around Doncaster, which with Bentley and Adwick has 121,000 people, was there a notable increase of population (+ 19 per cent) from 1931 to 1951. Doncaster[13] is now as for many centuries a strong market town and its modern industrialization has been stimulated by the railways and the fortunate circumstance of excellent sites for works on flat ground. The railway works was established in 1852 and two large brass foundries have an output which includes hot water piping. A ropeworks concentrates mainly on steel wire: this works is part of a large combine. Many industries have come here from elsewhere: for example, the ropeworks from Cleckheaton, a motorbody works from Dagenham in 1941, a lubricating equipment firm from Hull in 1941, an electric motor works from Bradford in 1907, a glass works from St. Helens in 1921, a wholesale clothiers from Leeds in 1949 and a woollen mill from Cleckheaton some fifty years ago. Other industries include nylon spinning on the town's industrial estate, flour milling, a cement works at Bentley and the making of combine harvesters. In fact almost an embarrassing number of industries have been attracted to this area, partly to employ the female labour of a mining district. The local mines[a] were opened from 1908 to 1913—those to the east in 1916, 1924 and finally in 1925 at Thorne.

In the *Dearne valley*, with its tributary valleys including the Dove, there are a number of colliery villages grouped into some thirteen urban districts and the county borough of Barnsley; these places increased in population by + 2 per cent from 1931 to 1951 and now have 252,000 people. Barnsley (76,000) has a long industrial tradition and was described by Defoe[14] as 'Black Barnsley, eminent still for the working in iron and steel . . . the town looks as black and smoaky as if they were all smiths that lived in it'. Glass-making, engineering (especially mining machinery) and paper-making are old and still prosperous industries, but linen manufacture has declined though

[a] See Fig. 46. Dates of opening were Bentley, 1908, Bullcroft, 1910, Yorkshire Main, 1911, Askern, 1913, Rossington, 1916, Hatfield, 1916, Markham, 1924, Harworth, 1924, Thorne, 1925.

textile trades survive in the making of eiderdowns, shirts, towels and even lifebelts. Newer industries include tar distilling for various chemical by-products of coal and a number of trades brought to the district recently with government aid, including rubber hot-water bottles and other articles, sports goods, wool textiles, handbags and raincoats and hosiery (at Worsborough). The fear of economic stringency once the coal is exhausted, of 'no mines, no work' is removed by the introduction of new factories.

Fusion of one place with another has almost resulted in a line of industrial settlement all the way from Darton west of Barnsley, to the village of Barnby Dun, east of Doncaster, a distance of nearly 20 miles. And at Conisbrough, where the Dearne flows into the greater Don, there is a similar coalescence of one place with another all the way to Rotherham and Sheffield. Fig. 46 shows that there is a gap in the built-up area east of Conisbrough—the justification for the consideration of Doncaster and its neighbouring towns as a separate entity—and shows also that on either side of the Don valley various colliery villages are outside town administration.

Sheffield and Rotherham, inseparably linked on the ground but both county boroughs, have increased little in population since 1921: in Rawmarsh U.D., with *c.* 19,000 people, there has also been little change in numbers. Successive administrative expansions of Sheffield in 1901, 1912, 1921 (an addition of over 10 square miles which included Handsworth), 1928 (4 square miles of Derbyshire) and 1938 (9 square miles from Derbyshire added) have given the city an area of over 62 square miles[15] (Fig. 47). Similar extensions in Rotherham have expanded the town's bounds to nearly 15 square miles. Although Sheffield's population declined by 5,400 (− 1 per cent) to 513,000, Rotherham's population increased by 10 per cent to 82,000 and there were substantial increases in the surrounding areas: in all these two county boroughs, with Rawmarsh, Dronfield U.D. in Derbyshire (7,600 in 1951, + 19 per cent) and the seven 'rural' parishes now receiving migrants from the towns,[b] had in all 707,000 inhabitants compared with 674,000 in 1931. It would be misleading therefore to regard this area as stationary in population: with the surrounding rural districts already mentioned there was an increase of + 5 per cent from 1931 to 1951. The current prosperity of the steel trade and associated industries has removed for the present the fears of

[b] These are, in Yorkshire, Ecclesfield and Bradfield parishes (Wortley R.D.), Aston cum Aughton, Brinsworth and Dalton in Rotherham R.D.; in Derbyshire, Beighton and Eckington in Chesterfield R.D. 622,000 without these rural parishes.

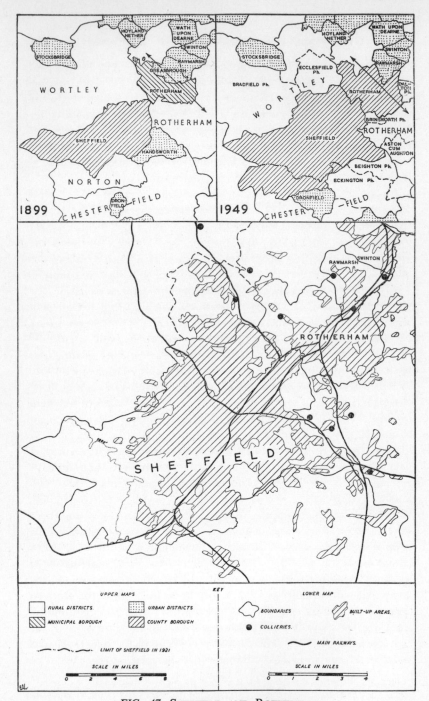

FIG. 47. SHEFFIELD AND ROTHERHAM

The past administrative development is shown but some of the most
modern housing estates are beyond the present boundaries and the Sheffield boundary runs almost through the middle of the Parson Cross estate,
on the north side of the city.

unemployment: confronted with the necessity for re-housing slum populations a considerable expansion of the built-up area is inevitable. The city of Sheffield, having built homes to its northern limit but deliberately preserving an inner green belt, has already extended its Parson Cross estate into Ecclesfield and the main development is now in Derbyshire, within the parishes of Beighton and Eckington.[e] [16] The more fortunately-placed financially have settled on the hill-slopes of the Pennines, sites not unlike those favoured in similarly situated towns such as Halifax and Huddersfield but perhaps even more attractive: Sheffield residents have also settled in villages such as Dore, Totley, Beauchief and Norton on the south side of the city, and even in Derbyshire villages such as Grindleford, Hathersage, Bamford and Hope. Like Hull and its satellites, Sheffield has a measure of isolation that helps to give it a strong degree of regional consciousness:[17] not until 1870 was a main railway line from London brought to the town, though the line to Manchester through Woodhead was opened in 1845.

Having a long tradition of home and workshop crafts, depending for centuries largely on imported ores, using first water power from mountain streams and then steam for power, Sheffield has kept both the cutlery and the heavy steel trades. Rudmose Brown said of the town:[18]

> It is still essentially a great workshop in a nook of the Pennines, essentially an industrial town in which surface relief, alternation of ridge and valley, led in the period of prosperity in the nineteenth century to a great crowding in the valleys and somewhat later growth over the ridges. No city has a more beautiful site, scarcely any city a more dreary appearance. Yet its western suburbs extending on to the gritstone moors and swept by clean winds are in striking contrast to the grimy monotony of its central part and eastern valley areas.

The wartime destruction of part of the central city area emphasizes the need for re-planning much of the town. But no fundamental change in industrial location is likely for the steel industry is both strongly and suitably developed on the limited areas of low-lying ground. Before the war, the shopping area was surprisingly small:[19] in 1939, the 'first-class' shopping quarter covered 19 acres and the second class only 15 acres. It was not expected by the anonymous

---

[e] In the 1950–1951 Session of parliament, a bill was presented and rejected, by which Sheffield should acquire more land in the West Riding and in Derbyshire, even though the county council of the West Riding was willing to allow the housing area to be included.

authors of 'Sheffield replanned' that any larger area would be required: the planners modestly explained that the city, with Rotherham, is 'a comparatively isolated industrial unit of high density', and not a shopping centre for a region like Manchester, Leeds, or Liverpool. Much of the area close to Sheffield is sparsely populated, though it draws customers from some of the surrounding mining areas. One wonders if the planners were not over-modest and whether the current prosperity of the metallurgical industry and mining, combined with the ease of communication from the growing coalfield areas to the east, might not give Sheffield the chance of further development in the near future. This surmise is perhaps justified by a visible expansion of the shopping centre in the rebuilding of the town.

LANCASHIRE AND CHESHIRE (THE NORTHWEST)

The northwest standard region includes the counties of Lancashire and Cheshire, and the parts of Derbyshire most closely influenced by the Manchester conurbation:[d] the entire population was 6,445,000 in 1951, an increase of + 4 per cent over the 6,197,000 of 1931. This increase represents a loss by migration of 128,000 or − 2·1 per cent (against a natural increase of + 6·1 per cent). As shown in the following pages, the older Pennine industrial areas now have declining populations comparable to those noted in the West Yorkshire conurbation but these decreases are balanced by increases of three types: first, in outer suburban districts such as the Wirral and the lowland south of Manchester; second, in some growing chemical and engineering towns such as Warrington and Northwich and third, in the coast towns of the Fylde or Morecambe–Heysham. Further, there has been a considerable suburban spread into some rural districts not yet absorbed into the towns from which the population came: developments of this type are marked around Chester (p. 244), Crewe (p. 245), Preston (p. 239) and Warrington (p. 244). As long ago as 1851, 66 per cent of the population of Lancashire and 48 per cent of Cheshire's was urban:[20] in 1951, only 15 per cent of Cheshire's population (189,000 out of 1,258,000) and 6 per cent of Lancashire's population (309,000 out of 5,116,000) was rural—and probably at least one-fifth of this was rural only in name. Even so, lowland Cheshire and Lancashire are rich agricultural areas, though the great

[d] Buxton M.B., Glossop M.B., New Mills U.D., Whaley Bridge U.D., Chapel-en-le-Frith, R.D.

arable farming belt between Manchester and Liverpool is complexly broken by the interlocking towns of the coalfield: in the Pennines pastoral farming still exists beyond the towns. The population may be grouped as follows:

TABLE 5

NORTHWEST STANDARD REGION: CONURBATION POPULATION, 1951

	1951	%
Major conurbations (Manchester and Merseyside)	3,804	59
Minor conurbations	1,808	28
Other towns	329	5
Rural	506[e]	8
Total	6,447	100

Minor conurbations in the northwest fall into five groups: of these the first, and most remote, Barrow-in-Furness with its immediate neighbour, Dalton (78,000, + 2 per cent), has grown during the past hundred years through the exploitation of local haematite ores into a great iron and steel centre, together with armaments works on Walney island.[21] The Furness district of Lancashire, 'beyond the Sands', belongs rather to the Cumbrian dome or Lake District area, with such iron-working towns as Barrow, Whitehaven and Working-ton on its coastal margins. More truly Lancastrian, the second group consists of the coal-cotton towns of Rossendale and the Calder-Darwen valleys to the north: here grouped into four small conurba-tions, the nineteen towns had a total population of 460,000 in 1951 but 517,000 in 1931 (− 12 per cent). Preston is not a coal town, though it has long shared in the fortunes of the cotton trade; nor is it strictly coastal though it has a long history as a port. A great route centre, it stands between the cotton towns just mentioned and the coast, and also on the major line of road and rail communication from London to Carlisle. In the third group, coast towns, including Lancaster with Morecambe, the Fylde coast towns, and Southport with Formby, there have been some large increases of population,

e Actually *c.* 12,000 more, but the two rural districts of Limehurst, Lancashire, and Disley, Cheshire, were included as part of the Manchester conurbation in the 1951 Census: Limehurst has now been absorbed into five neighbouring towns (Figs. 31–35).

notably by + 33 per cent in the Fylde towns. The fourth group, the Lancashire coalfield, with some 460,000 people, is now increasing only slightly in population: as shown on pp. 241-4, there is considerable industrial variety in this area. Lastly, south of the coalfield, four towns differing markedly from one another in appearance, Runcorn-Widnes, Warrington, Crewe and Chester, have in common a varied and recent industrialization.

The 'weaving area' Towns and Rossendale

Burnley (85,000) and Blackburn (111,000) are the largest of the fifteen town units in what is commonly called the 'weaving area' of Lancashire: although weaving predominates over spinning, this term is an over-simplification as many mills have both the low weaving sheds and the spinning rooms on several floors.[22] Factories, public buildings and almost all the older houses are stone-built, solidly if not decoratively, and the background of smooth-topped ridges 1,300-1,400 ft. high gives a scene similar to that in the extreme west of Yorkshire. Reduction of the number of cotton workers to less than half the figure of 1921, combined with the exhaustion of some of the mines, has been responsible for the population decline, which would have been much greater but for two factors, first, the introduction of new industries—especially metal trades—and second, the rise of wages which has meant that married women were able to cease work in the mills. Even so, the loss of population has been $c. - 10$ per cent everywhere and there is no increase concealed by movement to adjacent rural districts. The four groups of towns are here separately considered.

I. *Burnley*, and Padiham to the west, are in the Calder valley, which opens one of the easiest but least-used routes through the Pennines to Todmorden in Yorkshire. The valley north of Burnley is drained by the Pendle water and traversed by the Leeds and Liverpool canal in its southward passage from the Aire gap. In Burnley, numerous mills and factories are placed beside the canal though mills are also scattered through these towns and surrounded by houses.[23] Along the road and canal through Brierfield to Nelson and Barrowford, there is continuous town, with a further extension to Colne, in the Colne water valley, and finally up a steep valley in Trawden. Here, as elsewhere in Lancashire, many mills are now used for electrical and general engineering and for the footwear and clothing industries. Stone-built, these towns have a grim dignity: far from beautiful in themselves, their suburbs are built on the flanks of the Rossendales, for example on the south side of Burnley, or on Pennine slopes, for example on the north edge of Colne. In all this group of towns had 164,000 people in 1951 compared with 187,000 in 1931.

II. *Accrington* and its adjoining towns Clayton-le-Moors, Church, Greet Harwood, Rishton, Oswaldtwistle had 81,000 in 1951 but 91,000 in 1931. Here, as in the Burnley area, the main industry, cotton, has declined, and there are now only a few hundred miners, though Accrington has a brickworks of some renown. Accrington has long possessed a greater variety of industries than its neighbours and its trades include calico-printing, textile and general engineering.[24] Places such as Great Harwood, where over four-fifths of the employed population were cotton workers in 1929, suffered sharply during the nineteen-thirties. Although some new industries have come here, many old cotton mills have been demolished.

III. *Blackburn and Darwen* with 142,000 people in 1951 (159,000 in 1931) have famous paper-making and engineering industries as well as cotton.[25] Blackburn, at the junction of the Calder and Darwen valleys, is the largest of the towns in this part of Lancashire, with excellent road, rail and canal communications. Around the town there is hilly ground with a line of suburbs penetrating the countryside to the north. In Blackburn some of the mills no longer needed for cotton were used for other trades, notably electrical and general engineering and clothing, and at Darwen a useful development has been the growth of the paint industry, in association with the wallpaper factory.

IV. *The Inner Rossendale area* consists of four towns, Ramsbottom, Haslingden, Rawtenstall and Bacup, now having 73,000 people but 81,000 in 1931. The older parts of these towns are tightly clustered in the valleys with a regrettably large number of back-to-back houses but newer estates are located on the hillsides. Here an enterprising man developed the slipper industry, having observed the use of felt slippers in the mills, which in time also became a boot and shoe trade that has absorbed former cotton workers. The slipper and footwear trades, and other even newer industries, occupy old cotton mills.

Preston, an old port and market centre and the county town, had 147,000 inhabitants in 1951, including Fulwood U.D. and Walton U.D., compared with 141,000 in 1931, but there has been an outward spread of population into a number of parishes still technically rural, such as Penwortham which almost doubled its population, from 5,722 to 10,893, between 1931 and 1951. And this expansion is linking

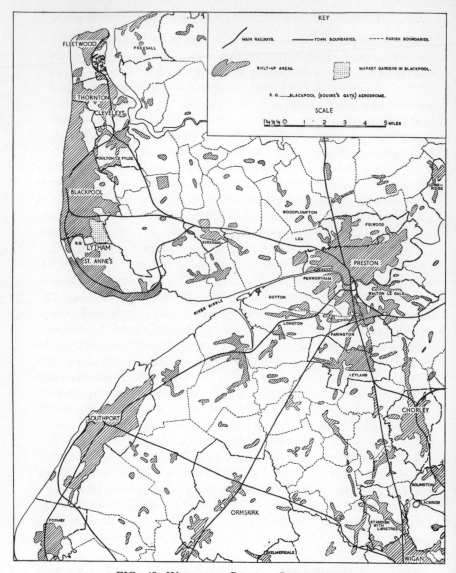

FIG. 48. WEST AND CENTRAL LANCASHIRE

Southport and Formby, Blackpool and its coastal neighbours, and Preston
with its unabsorbed adjacent urban districts are all minor conurbations.
The seaside towns, like Brighton and Bournemouth, spread for miles along
the coast. There are many examples of 'overspill' into nominally rural
areas, especially along roads. Indeed, there is an almost continuous line of
houses along the main road from Preston to Chorley and Manchester, and
the ribbon development around Wigan is marked.

Preston with Leyland, famous for its vehicle manufacture. If all the parishes clearly affected by this movement, with Leyland, are included, the population increased from 168,000 in 1931 to 189,000 in 1951, + 12 per cent. Travelling through this area along the main road from Preston to Chorley, there is now little break in housing and the dangers of further town spread are clear. Preston's major industries[26] are cotton, textile machinery and electrical engineering; and Leyland has far-famed vehicle and aircraft works (Fig. 48).

The Coast Towns

Decline of population in the older industrial areas of the Pennines and Rossendales contrasts with the marked increases of the coastal area. From 1929 to 1947, there was a decrease of − 24 per cent in the number of employed workers in the weaving areas (those discussed above) but an increase of + 63 per cent in the coastal areas from Formby to Morecambe. This area was regarded as 'not only attractive for residents but also . . . for industrial development', indeed, to some extent comparable with the newer industrial areas of the south.[27] And during the inter-war period, some authorities took advantage of low building costs to undertake public works. Miles of golden sands may be provided by nature, but nearness to a vast industrial market of holiday-makers is exploited with the aid of advertisement, including the encouragement of holiday traffic outside the main 'season' by illuminations and other allurements. The very size of the Fylde coast conurbation, a dozen miles of town from Fleetwood and Preesall through Thornton Cleveleys to Blackpool and Lytham St. Annes with Poulton, is impressive, and its population increased from 80,000 in 1901 to 172,000 in 1931 and 233,000 in 1951 (+ 33 per cent). Similarly, Morecambe-Heysham, with Lancaster, increased by + 30 per cent from 68,000 in 1931 to 89,000 in 1951 and Southport and Formby increased by + 9 per cent to 94,000 in 1951. Along the Lancashire coast there are some 400,000 people.

In 1838, Baines wrote that Lytham had been frequented by visitors for two centuries and had an esplanade, and that Blackpool had a 'parade' by the sea,[28] the forerunner of the famous promenades. From 1820, Manchester visitors went by canal to Wigan and thence by coach. The first Fylde railway, to Fleetwood, was built in 1840 and the lines to Lytham and Blackpool were added in 1846. From the beginning, the railways have invested heavily in improvements, including the connecting line from Lytham to Blackpool in

1861 and the provision of special facilities for excursion traffic at Talbot road in 1883. Large hotels, boarding houses and lodgings are there for the thousands: various private companies have provided attractions such as the Tower and the piers. Growth, however, was slow in the early railway days, and Blackpool had only 10,000 people when it became a borough in 1876. Three years later a parliamentary act gave the council power to spend part of its rates on advertising, and from that time its policy was the attraction of the industrial masses—'the more we are together the merrier we shall be'. Many close-packed terraces had been built as 'homes from homes' for Lancashire workers and from the eighteen-nineties Blackpool and its neighbours surged ahead.[29] But one problem remained, the shortness of the season, with winter unemployment. Advertising made a 'congress city' out of what was already a 'city of health and pleasure', and there has also been industrial development, including confectionery and two large biscuit works at Blackpool ('baked in breezy Blackpool'), with motor coach building and some other light engineering and aircraft construction. Fleetwood has become the major fishing port of the west coast, having one-tenth of the national catch in 1949, with a wharf built in 1841 and a dock built in 1877, and there is also marine engineering.[30] But a modern development has been the manufacture of nylon and terylene, with plastics; and the salt deposits of Preesall are exploited to give one-tenth of the national output. Nearly 30 per cent of the insured population are engaged in miscellaneous services including entertainment and sport, catering and the hotel trade, laundries and domestic service, and Lytham St. Annes, strongly residential in tone, has one of the highest proportions of domestic servants in the country[31] (8 per cent of the total insured population, cf. Southport, 7 per cent).

Lancaster, Morecambe and Heysham have now fused into a single small conurbation. Early in the nineteenth century, Morecambe was favoured for its sea-bathing and its views across the bay, but the main growth came with the railway in 1850, used especially by Yorkshire visitors. The Midland Railway dock was built in 1904 for the Belfast service.[32] By 1901, Morecambe and Heysham had 15,000 people and Lancaster 40,000, but by 1951 Morecambe-Heysham had 37,000 and Lancaster 52,000. Lancaster is a fine old market town having flour milling and milk processing plants, linoleum and furniture works and, since 1929, a rayon and plastics factory. Morecambe has razor blade and plastics factories but its main occupation is catering for tourists.

Facing much the same problems as Blackpool, Morecambe has extended its season by the lavish use of electricity.

Southport's first hotel was built in 1792 to accommodate visitors who came for seabathing and in 1812, a sea-bathing infirmary was opened. Rapid expansion followed[33] the opening of the railway line from Waterloo (Liverpool) in 1848, and the line to Wigan and Manchester in 1855. Southport was designed as a garden city, with a checker-board pattern of tree-lined streets and no terraces, due to the wishes of the two lords of the manor.[34] Up to the 1901 Census its population, then 64,000, was greater than the 48,000 of Blackpool, but by 1951, Southport had increased only to 84,000 compared with Blackpool's 147,000. As a result of a different policy Southport has become a residential centre for Liverpool[35] and—thanks to rapid train services—Manchester, a fine shopping centre, a favourite place for the retired and a holiday town for a more restricted public than Blackpool. Southport has a number of small industries, especially in the food and clothing trades, but there is also a large engineering works;[36] such enterprise has been welcomed by many as a remedy for seasonal unemployment but others complain that it removes the very domestic labour on which the comfort of the population rests. Having become a borough in 1867, Southport absorbed Birkdale U.D. in 1912: Formby U.D., though fusing with the larger town, remains independent.[37] For reasons discussed on p. 96, fusion with the Merseyside conurbation is unlikely.

The *Lancashire coalfield* consists of twenty separate administrative divisions covering in all 122 square miles: of these only two, St. Helens (110,000) and Wigan (85,000), are county boroughs and only one, Leigh (49,000) a municipal borough. In all the population was 460,000 in 1951 and 446,000 in 1931. This area certainly qualifies as a conurbation on the original Geddes criterion (pp. 1–2) and was in his view separated neither from Liverpool on the west side nor from southeast Lancashire.[38] In the forty years since Geddes wrote, the trend towards fusion of these places with one another has become steadily more marked, and never more so than now. But this should not conceal the fact that interlocking with the mining villages and towns of this area there is one of the richest agricultural districts of the country, its intensity of farming stimulated by the proximity of town markets. Coal is the basis of this area's economic development, combined with cotton in towns such as Wigan, Leigh, Atherton and Tyldesley, and also with engineering in Wigan, and wagons and locomotives at Newton-le-Willows. Other industries came into this area, such as electrical engineering at Prescot and Leigh, food industries and clothing at Wigan but by far the most famous industry is the glass-making of St. Helens which has some 19,000 employees, one-quarter of the country's total.[39]

As a whole this coalfield lacks the pulsating prosperity seen to the north in the Leyland area, based on vehicles, and to the south in Warrington and district, based on chemicals and metal trades. In the Wigan area, for example, unemployment was consistently high during the nineteen-thirties, due to the dependence on coalmining, textiles and steel manufacture, all then declining industries. Since the 1939–1945 war, the main trend in coalmining has been the organization of large pits, all with more than 1,000 workers, which include Chisnall Hall (between Chorley and Wigan), Lea Green (St. Helens), Bold (St. Helens), Sutton Manor and Cronton (near St. Helens) and Mosley Common (Tyldesley).[40] Although the Wigan area still has mining, the chief area of current development is on the southern fringe around St. Helens, Leigh and Atherton. No extension into the concealed field on the scale seen on the east side of the Pennines is likely as the coal measures dip at a sharp angle beneath the Triassic rocks to the south. Dreary relics of past mining are seen in the large flashes around Wigan, Hindley and Leigh and the numerous spoil-heaps (including the 'Wigan Alps'):[41] equally typical of mining areas are the groups of brick-built cottages in rows, or ribbons along roads with agricultural land behind them. Unfortunately some of the limited areas available for industrial development, and not subject to subsidence, are encumbered by derelict plant expensive to remove. The abandoned steel plant at Wigan has a network of subterranean brick flues and various other cavities that make the initial cost of preparing the site for other uses (at 1950 prices) £1,000,000.[42] Happily there are already signs that some of the dreary eyesores in central Lancashire will be transformed by the tipping of industrial and household waste—indeed it is estimated that within the next twenty years some 10,000 acres will be used in this way.[43] But this can be done only with the help of government grants made available under the 1947 Planning Acts, as the cost to local authorities would be prohibitive. One authority, for example, was found to have two-fifths of its area derelict and reclamation would have added 5s. in the £ to the rates. The flashes are a problem, though they have some recreational use. But here as in the Black Country, derelict land will be available for farmland, housing, schools, new industries and open spaces: under the National Parks Act, financial assistance is given for tree planting on spoil heaps, already carried out in places with some success.

The neat division of this area into urban districts hardly means that a number of towns exists, rather that groups of amorphous mining settlements have had a line drawn round them for administrative purposes. But Wigan, St. Helens, Leigh, the three boroughs, all have strongly developed shopping centres. The 1950 Census of retail trade showed that the total retail sales were £43m., an average of £93 a head, but Wigan's share was £12,337,000, an average of £146 a head, St. Helens' £10,633,000, an average of £95 a head.[44] Wigan was therefore a stronger town for retail trade than any other, though in sales compared to population the closest rival was Leigh, with sales of £5,587,000 (average £114). Many urban districts of the coalfield had sales that averaged as little as £40–50 per head, hardly more than the national average expenditure for groceries and confectionery. To those unacquainted with central Lancashire, the commercial strength of Wigan may seem surprising, but it is a market town attractive to the population of the surrounding industrial and rural areas and sufficiently far from its main shopping rivals, Liverpool, Manchester and Southport, to show resistance to their stimulating competition.

The social problems of dreary landscapes, poor nineteenth-century housing and lack of town centres now seem acute here. Having an evil record of unemployment, most of the urban districts were made a Development Area in 1946 to provide work,[45] primarily in the Wigan district as many government factories had been closed. Three sites were cleared and developed, at Lamberhead and Goose Green, Wigan, and also at Parr, St. Helens, but so far, the developments on these trading estates have been slight. There is little unemployment, because of movements to work which include the transport of many hundreds of men to the newer collieries on the south side. The 1951 workplace Census showed a daily outward movement of 15,500 workers from Wigan compared with an inward movement of 10,700.[46] Similarly, the prosperity of vehicle industry to the north at Leyland, and of chemical and engineering industries at Warrington, as well as the demand for workers in the Manchester area, including the Irlam steelworks, all provide opportunities for workers from the coalfield. Warrington imports workers drawn from areas where the principal industries have declined, for example coal, cotton and steel at Wigan and Leigh: the 1951 Census showed that Warrington had a daily net inward movement of 7,000 workers.[47]

Similarly, there is a great deal of daily travel from places where mines have been closed, such as Skelmersdale, Upholland, Westhoughton and Aspull to new mining areas, for example those south and south-east of St. Helens.[48] There are indications that the distribution of employment is changing markedly but that the population distribution is a survival of an earlier phase.

Warrington, Widnes and the Cheshire Towns

On the Cheshire border, the twin towns of Runcorn and Widnes (59,000, + 17 per cent) have increased even more in population than these figures would suggest as in each case there has been considerable settlement in adjacent rural districts. At Warrington (81,000, − 1 per cent), the Ship canal forms the county boundary with the result that Stockton Heath and other residential areas are outside the borough: if these and similar areas around the town are included, the population was 110,000 in 1931 and 131,000 in 1951 (+ 20 per cent). Warrington is a town of many industries including metal trades, leather, brewing, sawmilling, paper, and clothing: like Widnes and Runcorn it is a significant centre for chemical products though at Warrington only some 6 per cent of the employed population are engaged in the chemical trade (here soap) compared with some 40 per cent in Runcorn and Widnes.[49] Increasingly the Ship canal is becoming what its founders hoped it would be—a magnet for industry, and especially industry depending on imported products, though most of the firms are located beside the older canals such as the Bridgewater at Runcorn. Even so, an area possessing chemical and engineering industries seems likely to prosper under modern conditions.

Chester and Crewe are towns comparable in size but vastly different in history and appearance. Chester has been a route centre from Roman times: Crewe is a product of the railway epoch for the main road junction of south Cheshire is four miles to the south, at Nantwich. Chester with Hoole has 57,000 people, Crewe 53,000, but in both cases there are several thousand more in areas nominally rural beyond the town boundaries. With Nantwich and the intervening parishes such as Willaston and Wistaston, with a few other villages in process of suburbanization, there is here a population of 71,000 in 1951 (64,000 in 1931). Similarly Chester with its outer suburban fringe now has 78,000 people, an increase of 26 per cent from the 61,500 of 1931. Chester has the attraction of Tudor and eighteenth-century streets: Crewe the dull buildings of the latter half of the nineteenth century. Chester has a variety of industries, chiefly in metals: Crewe the great railway and aircraft engine works with a growing clothing industry. But the real difference lies in the continued maintenance of Chester as a county town having over three

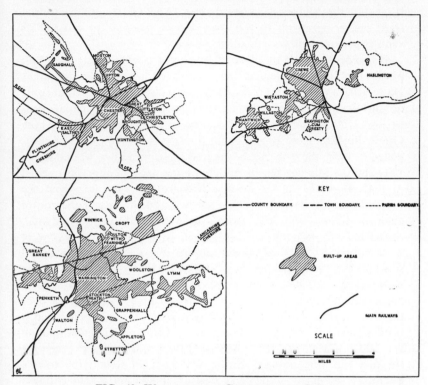

FIG. 49. WARRINGTON, CHESTER AND CREWE

In all three cases there is a considerable population in areas norminally rural, including in the case of Warrington (Lancashire) the Cheshire suburb of Stockton Heath. Lymm has been proposed as a possible overspill town for Manchester, but it has become largely suburban to Warrington.

times the national average of persons in local government service: in addition it is the headquarters of the Crosville bus services which serve Cheshire and the whole of North Wales.[50] Chester has maintained a vigorous commercial life for in 1951 the sales in its shops were valued at nearly £16,000,000 compared with £6,300,000 in

R

Crewe: over 7,000 full-time workers were employed in the shops of Chester compared with 2,800 in Crewe.[51] Crewe's good communications have not made it into a strong commercial town but Chester remains a market and shopping centre for the adjacent countryside, for visitors from the Flintshire towns and for the Wirral fringes of the Merseyside conurbation. And Chester has a tourist trade that brings profit to the town: Crewe has not, for most of its visitors are on their way to other places.

It has been argued that Crewe developed largely by chance:[52] no physical obstacle prevented the growth of a railway junction at Nantwich, but there is some evidence—hardly conclusive—that some of the landowners, partly under the influence of canal proprietors, refused to sell. The first line to pass through Crewe, the Grand Junction from Birmingham to Newton-le-Willows, was completed in 1837; the Crewe, Chester and Birkenhead line was added in 1840 and the Manchester–Birmingham line to Stockport was opened in 1842. In 1848, the Crewe and Kidsgrove branch line from the North Staffordshire railway was finished and the last of the routes entering Crewe, the line from Shrewsbury through Nantwich, completed the six-point railway star in 1858. The first works were built from 1840, but in 1841 the population of Monks Coppenhall was only 200 rising to 4,600 in 1851 and 42,000 by 1901. Steadily the works expanded, with 6,000 employed by 1877 and over 10,000 in 1920. At first the railway company exercised a paternal influence over the town's growth, but a Local Board was set up in 1860, and a borough in 1877. The greater part of the Church Coppenhall parish was added to the borough in 1892 and the residue in 1936, when for the first time the railway station was brought within the town's boundary. As early as the 1871 Census, it was noted that cottages for work-people had been built in surrounding villages, such as Haslington, Willaston and Shavington, but in 1882 it was ruled that no company workman should live more than $2\frac{1}{2}$ miles from the works so Nantwich could not be used as a dormitory centre. But the nearer villages such as Willaston on the railway line continued to grow, though one suburb, Wistaston, developed little until after the 1914–1918 war and is still unabsorbed. Only on the west side is there a reasonably clear limit to Crewe, for here the main railway works have been built and there is little residential attraction; consequently some of the finest Cheshire farms survive untouched very close to the town. Fig. 49 perhaps makes clear what is still more obvious on the ground—that there is a threat of town expansion in this part of Cheshire. Indeed, at the moment of writing, there is a press report that Crewe is willing to accept residents and new industries from the Manchester area, to be settled on the north side of the town.

CHAPTER 10

THE MINOR CONURBATIONS: THE MIDLANDS, THE SOUTH AND WALES

THIRTY million people live in these seven Standard Regions of England and Wales, 35 per cent of them in the London and West Midland conurbations (Chapters 2 and 3), 29 per cent in sixty-one minor conurbations, and 23 per cent in rural districts. As shown in the following pages, and in Fig. 44, some rural districts—in the strict administrative sense of areas so defined—are now stationary or declining in population, as for example in most of Wales, but others have large increases. On Fig. 44 an attempt has been made to show those areas of marked increase, due not to increased employment in agriculture but almost everywhere to the outward movement of townspeople into adjacent villages. Such a process is described for Derby (p. 259), Leicester (p. 261), Cambridge (p. 263), and Norwich (p. 265) and it is widespread in the southeast and in the 'Southern' Standard Region. The rural districts in the three counties of Kent, Surrey and Sussex had an increase from 619,000 to 777,000 (+ 24 per cent) from 1931 to 1951, and in the 'rural districts' of counties on the west side of London the increases were even greater, for example Hertfordshire, + 69 per cent, Buckinghamshire, + 35 per cent, Berkshire, + 35 per cent, Oxfordshire, + 41 per cent and Hampshire, + 38 per cent. Only Dorset (+ 19 per cent) and the Isle of Wight (+ 8 per cent) are apparently sufficiently far away from metropolitan influence for the countryward movement to be slighter.[1]

Argument of this general character may conceal the fact that many of these outward spreads are confined to comparatively small areas. The suburbanization of villages near Oxford and Cambridge should not induce the thought that all the villages and countrysides of Berkshire, Oxfordshire or East Anglia are about to be engulfed. Yet the movement is insidious. In a careful study of recent population changes in Leicestershire, A. G. Powell[2] has shown that there are heavy increases of population in the part of the county closest to the Warwickshire border, that is towards the West Midlands conurbation, and also in market towns such as Melton Mowbray (14,000 in 1951, + 33 per cent) and the industrialized centres of Hinckley

248

(39,000, + 35 per cent) and Loughborough (35,000, + 19 per cent). A similar development is the gradual infiltration of industry and private housing into villages, for example between Leicester and Loughborough or Leicester and Coventry; there is a danger that a continuous urban belt may soon exist in the Soar valley. And from 1931 to 1951, the population increase of + 16·5 per cent in Leicester-shire meant an increase of + 33·6 per cent, or 41,042, in the number of 'structurally separate households',[3] even though more people were sharing houses in 1951 than in 1931. Leicestershire shows features seen in other Midland areas though the county still has a countryside hardly touched by these trends.

On the basis of existing administrative divisions, the population of the various Standard Regions falls into the main categories given in the following table:

TABLE 6

POPULATION IN CONURBATIONS, OTHER TOWNS AND RURAL DISTRICTS:
THE MIDLANDS, THE SOUTH AND WALES, 1951

	Population in thousands	Major con.	%	Other con.	No.	%	Smaller towns	Rural districts	%
Midland . .	4,422	2,237	51	984	7	22	186	1,015	23
North Midland .	3,378	—	—	1,735	11	51	530	1,113	33
Eastern . .	3,096	—	—	1,174	12	38	771	1,151	37
London and Southeast .	10,906	8,348	77	1,266	11	12	513	779	7
Southern . .	2,649	—	—	1,214	7	46	429	1,006	38
Southwestern .	3,020	—	—	1,140	8	38	721	1,151	38
Wales and Mon.	2,599	—	—	1,301	5	50	510	788	31
Total	30,070	10,585	35	8,822	61	29	3,660	7,003	23

THE MIDLAND S.R.

Over half the population live in the West Midlands conurbation (Chapter 3), and more than one-fifth in seven lesser conurbations that include areas of considerable variety. The Potteries (p. 250), one of the most isolated industrial areas of Britain, have a devastatingly rich range of land use problems through past and present mining and clay extraction. Another mining area, Cannock Chase (p. 252), has at present no general industrial development, but it lies sufficiently close to the West Midlands conurbation for its economic prospects to appear good. Stourport and Kidderminster, Warwick and Leamington and above all Coventry and its neighbours, are examples of towns belonging to the great manufacturing area of the West Midlands, though separated from its major conurbation. All these have marked individuality for in Warwick and in Leamington, for example, industry has not submerged the traditional character of the two towns. Worcester is an example of an old cathedral town that, like Lincoln, York, Chester and Gloucester, has acquired an interesting group of factories. Burton-on-Trent, the main brewing centre of the country, and a town unique in its atmosphere, fuses into the mining and manufacturing districts—one could hardly say towns—of the South Derbyshire coalfield.

The Potteries (372,000)

Marginal perhaps to the north of England, the Potteries area[4] is located approximately half-way between Manchester and Birmingham. Stoke-on-Trent was made by the administrative union of six towns into one county borough in 1910 and became a city in 1925 (Fig. 50). But on the ground Tunstall, Burslem, Hanley, Fenton, Longton and Stoke are still recognizable as towns for each has its own shopping centre and even its own town hall. In spite of a grimness rarely equalled, except in parts of the Black Country, each town has its own social life and yet is near enough to other towns for fruitful contacts, and in the whole area the population is sufficient for the support of first class music and a theatre. Stoke itself, though centrally placed, is by no means the largest of the component towns though there are schemes for a new and dignified civic centre. Readers of Arnold Bennett's novels will recall some of his remarkable descriptions of the industrial scene, and the struggle for supremacy as a shopping centre between the pushing but successful Hanley and the sedately-minded Burslem. The battle fought for federation of the separate towns is made the climax of the plot in *The Old Wives' Tale*, and in the Clayhanger series the outward movement to the suburbs is excellently described. Of these, Newcastle M.B. (70,000 in 1951, compared with 54,800 in 1931, + 28 per cent) still remains apart, though having within its bounds much of the suburban property that belongs to the conurbation as a whole, and on the north, Kidsgrove and Biddulph also retain their administrative independence.

The very isolation of the Potteries may account in part for its regional consciousness, making it a small industrial *pays* in a district

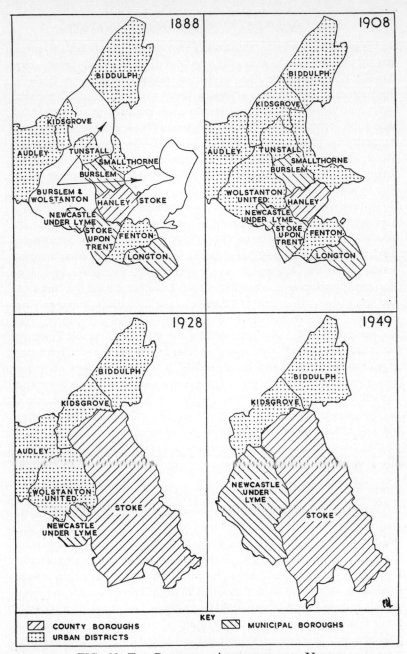

FIG. 50. THE POTTERIES, ADMINISTRATIVE UNITS

Behind this map lies the struggle for the federation of the Potteries towns into Stoke and the continued separation of Newcastle but the administrative picture is neater than that on the ground, one of the untidiest and most depressing areas in Britain, if also one of the most interesting. Audley ceased to be an urban district in 1932.

that is predominantly agricultural. The movement outwards to more attractive suburban scenes has continued on a wider front since Arnold Bennett wrote, for residential property has been built in the Pennine fringes to the east and in the rural lowlands on the south, west and north. The most spectacular indication of industrial migration is the building of the Wedgwood factory at Barlaston, with its many hundred workers coming mainly by special train from Stoke. Trentham on the south, long regarded as dedicated to fortunate commuters, now has some new factories, a trading estate that so far has attracted little new industry, and even a new coalmine. By its very situation, the Potteries area is not hampered in its outward expansion, and its crucial problems are at its core rather than its circumference. Approximately one-third of the central area has been made derelict by mining subsidence, by the dumping of industrial waste, or by the digging of clay workings. Mining subsidence has sterilized considerable areas that might have been used for housing, and has caused considerable damage to public buildings and private property. A recent newspaper headline, 'Water in the church, but the baths run dry',[5] was followed by the news that in the Longton swimming baths, all the water vanished and that a church congregation in Etruria had been startled by sudden rushes of water which sent tiles flying about. Vast tip heaps still continue to grow and the potteries have large waste dumps for disposing of breakages, plaster casts and saggers, though in some cases these are dumped into old clay holes. Apparently the cost of removing coal tip heaps, or of placing either old or new mining refuse in the clay holes, is economically prohibitive.

Towns near the West Midland Conurbation

Three small conurbations and the single town of Worcester all share significantly in the growth of population characteristic of the West Midlands. Cannock and Brownhills lie immediately north of the conurbation with 62,000 people (+ 16 per cent) in part of the Cannock Chase coalfield, which is almost exclusively a mining area,[6] used on a small scale from mediaeval times where seams were exposed, but developed from 1840 over the whole exposed area and from 1900 in the concealed field. Much of the southern part has no coal left, but there has been no loss of population as workers are needed both in the north part of the field and in the Black Country. Unfortunately coal mining is almost the only local occupation, and the population lives in typical formless and ugly mining villages and housing sprawls. To the southwest of the main conurbation, the three towns of Stourport, Kidderminster and Bewdley have now coalesced into a small conurbation of 52,000 people (+ 27 per cent) with carpet making as the major industry, and a tinplate works at Stourport. On the west side, Worcester (60,000, + 16 per cent), 25 miles from Birmingham, has doubled its population within the past century.[7] Primarily a cathedral, administrative and market town, it has famed glove and porcelain industries, to which various forms of metal and engineering works have been added since 1850: this last group now has over half the factory workers of the town. Located neither at the exact source of raw materials nor at the centre of a market, Worcester is reasonably accessible to both, for the metal-box industry, for example, uses tinplates made in South Wales and sells the finished products partly in the West Midlands. Material for tanning comes from India and Africa through Liverpool and Avonmouth, and the leather is used both in the city's own glove factories and in the foot-wear industries of Leicester and Northampton. Such factors help to explain the industrial developments at Worcester and comparable towns of the English Midlands and the founding of branch works in various centres as much as 50 miles away by Birmingham manu-facturers would appear also to be a likely peacetime development.

Warwick and Leamington together[8] have 52,000 people. Warwick is the ancient centre, Leamington a spa and residential town attract-ive both to the retired and to those seeking an escape from the West Midlands conurbation. Many of its residents work in Coventry and some, chiefly of the professional classes, in Birmingham, so that in some ways it is comparable in position and function with Harro-gate, in relation to the West Riding industrial area. Like Harrogate, Leamington developed in the early part of the nineteenth century and has some Regency buildings but it was never able to attract as many visitors to consume its medicinal waters. In 1801 its population was 315 but by 1821, it had 2,000 people, and continuous expansion followed. The New Town on the north bank of the river was laid out from 1808 onwards with wide parades, streets, crescents, circuses and gardens, and though Leamington preserves something of its stately atmosphere, it has a large factory producing motor-car parts, various other engineering firms, and a number of light industries, including some new ones located on a trading estate. In Warwick also the largest concerns are producers of motor car and aeroplane components.

The Coventry Area

No area shows more dramatically the process of industrial expansion around old towns than this.[9] Coventry has added to itself 100,000 people within thirty years and now has (1951) 258,000 inhabitants, and Bedworth and Nuneaton to the north have also increased in population, so that the three places now have 337,000 inhabitants. Suburban expansion on the south is already penetrating beyond the city boundary and becoming noticeable at various villages, such as Ryton, and less than 2 miles now separates the edge of Coventry from Kenilworth. One is tempted to see in this growth a twentieth-century expression of what was so marked in the nineteenth century—the rapid expansion of an area endowed with flourishing industries, but in this case industries connected primarily with road transport. The old industries were two—silk and ribbon, begun in the early seventeenth century, and watch and clock making, dating from the middle of the seventeenth century. Both of these have been the progenitors of vast modern industries—the textile trades for rayon, established here in 1904, and for sewing machine manufacture, and the watchmaking for machine tools. The making of a primitive velocipede here in 1865 a fruitful new beginning, though the bicycle trade is now comparatively small and modern Coventry owes much more to the motor-car manufacturers, whose work became the basis of the aeroplane industry during the 1914–1918 war. With these the electrical engineering trades grew rapidly, and there was also a stimulus to general engineering. Since 1919, the number of the employed population has almost doubled, and by 1948, 37 per cent of the insured workers were in the vehicle works, 20 per cent in general engineering, 8 per cent in the metal industries but less than 5 per cent in textiles.

Many factors have favoured this development. Nearness to Birmingham and the Black Country, local coal mining with four large pits, a good road network, a long industrial tradition and the availability of land for large motor engineering and other works, have all been influential. The older and smaller industries are found close to the town centre, the newer ones on sites that were on the edge at the time they were built. And there is still land available: in 1952, some 1,350 acres of Coventry was used for industrial purposes and another 650 acres allocated to expansion, some of it already begun. Two trading estates have been laid out, at Longford and Stonebridge Highway, chiefly for light and electrical engineering. In

all the circumstances it would seem that further expansion is likely
and present housing developments are linking Coventry firmly with
Bedworth and Nuneaton, which has a wide range of industry, closely
similar to that of Coventry, but also indicative of a relationship with
the East Midlands.

Nuneaton, a town of venerable history, has had coal mining at
least from the fourteenth century and stone quarrying of sandstones,
dolerites and quartzites, also for many centuries.[10] Quarrying is now
limited by the difficulty of finding workers but the hard rocks are
still valued for road metal to the southeast and the local clays are
used for tiles, bricks, pipes and chimney pots. Wool and silk weaving
were established here in the seventeenth century, and the textile
industry now includes the spinning of worsted yarns, silk-weaving
and hosiery manufacture. The yarn factory was established by a
Bradford firm seeking new premises and female labour, the silk-
weaving came from Coventry and hosiery from south Leicestershire.
Clothing trades include a hat and cap factory, introduced from
Atherstone *c.* 1870, and tailoring. But the largest textile enterprise
is rayon-making. Engineering too is well represented in the town; a
firm of special interest provides hosiery needles, and there are also
works for alloy castings (with over 1,000 employees), for heating and
cooking appliances, for mattress springs, as well as firms providing
machine tools and precision instruments. Various other industries
include jam making, boot and shoe manufacture, and box and carton
making. Clearly the range of occupations is wide, and equally clearly
this area is likely to increase in economic strength and population.

A less favourable picture comes from the Burton-Ashby area
which has 80,000 people (+ 2 per cent, 1931-1951) and consists of the
line of buildings from the brewing centre of Burton to the historic
country town of Ashby. Burton breweries use the local hard water
from Keuper marl. On the local coal measures, an area of some 20
square miles, the two urban districts of Ashby Woulds and Swadlincote show acute problems of subsidence, of derelict land and of bad
housing—in short the area is comparable to Stoke-on-Trent.[11]
Mining is combined with earthenware manufacture, for which clay
pits have been worked locally, and the population is grouped into a
number of industrial villages with houses spread between them.
Much of the area cannot be used for housing and therefore some of
the new estates are located outside the bounds of the urban districts,
with a well-marked ribbon of expensive houses along the road to
Ashby on elevated ground. Ashby itself is a market town outside

the workable area of the coalfield and showing no apparent trace of its propinquity. To the southeast of Ashby there are several important mines but this Leicestershire section of the field (around Coalville, on the margins of Charnwood Forest) has no industry associated with the mining and gives an excellent example of a rural landscape studded with a few colliery villages.[12]

THE NORTH MIDLAND S.R.

In its officially defined form, this standard region stretches from the southern part of the Yorkshire-Nottingham and Derby coalfield through Lincolnshire to the coast and through Leicestershire into Northamptonshire. Attempts to define the Midlands have been numerous, but one must be mentioned: the East Midland Geographer, in its first number, defined the area as 'that part of the country drained by the middle Trent and its tributaries' with 'the adjoining parts of the basins of the Witham, Welland and Nene', or again the kingdom of Mercia, divided later into the five shires of Derby, Nottingham, Lincoln, Leicester and Northampton, with tiny Rutland also.[13] To a geographer 'North Midland' seems a less fortunate term than 'East Midland'. As a whole the region has a diversity of industries, with textiles, footwear, hosiery and engineering as the main manufactured products, and the workers include 64 per cent of the national total in lace-making, 61 per cent of those in the hosiery and knitwear trades, 54 per cent of those in footwear, 14 per cent of the miners and 11 per cent of the iron and steel workers.[14] Marked industrial expansion is seen around Nottingham, Derby and Leicester, but to the south in Northamptonshire or the east in Lincolnshire, one enters a countryside primarily agricultural, though possessing also Jurassic iron ore deposits, exploited in Lincolnshire, especially at Scunthorpe, and in Northamptonshire. Another deposit of great value is the brick clays of the Peterborough area. Peterborough and Lincoln, both cathedral cities, have acquired some industries without losing their essential character, but Scunthorpe and Grimsby are both towns of newer vintage and far less character. The first conurbation areas to be considered here are those in the southern section of the Yorkshire, Nottingham and Derby coalfield (Fig. 51), then the major midland cities, and finally the major towns of Lincolnshire, with Peterborough.

Chesterfield[15] with Staveley and Bolsover had in 1951 a population of 97,000 (+ 5 per cent over 1931). Traditionally dependent on coal

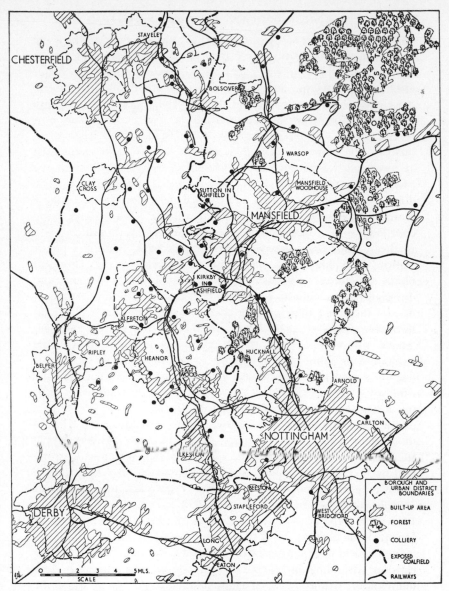

FIG. 51. THE COALFIELD FROM DERBY AND NOTTINGHAM TO
CHESTERFIELD

Nottingham is the chief town of one of the most vigorous of the minor
conurbations of Britain, with numerous mining and industrial settlements
to the north. Derby has spread beyond its bounds: the other major towns
are Mansfield and Chesterfield. Many of the collieries are in the concealed
part of the coalfield and there are numerous mining villages, of which the
older type is splendidly described by D. H. Lawrence's *Sons and Lovers*.
Fortunately the amenities of Sherwood Forest are still preserved.

and iron from local sources, Chesterfield has steelworks which use scrap iron and haematite pig iron from the Furness district, and make steel primarily for railway stock. Engineering is now the major industrial occupation, and the products include mining equipment, gas engineering plant and a great variety of pipes, of iron, steel, with other minerals and alloys. Although all the major collieries are now to the east of Chesterfield, coal is still a fundamental basis of industrial development in the town and its vicinity: coke ovens exist at three collieries in the neighbourhood, Grosvenor, Williamthorpe and Holmewood, and coalite is manufactured at Bolsover. In 1956 a large new coke-oven plant was opened in Wingerworth, beside a main railway line on the site of an old colliery.[16] Branch lines bring coal from several mines to the north, east and south and the river Rother is used for water. Beside the coke-ovens, there is a power station, a sulphuric acid plant and a by-product plant. The local mines are efficiently mechanized, with a high output per man and one-eighth of the country's opencast coal comes from this neighbourhood. One could therefore say that coal and iron are still fundamental resources here, but there are also interesting pottery and glass works now concerned mainly with electrical supplies, and a textile works having some 3,000 employees, which has medical supplies as one of its chief lines. Chesterfield, a good shopping centre with a long tradition as a market, has met the challenge of industrialization without losing the atmosphere of an historic town.

Mansfield, Mansfield Woodhouse, Sutton-in-Ashfield and Kirkby-in-Ashfield form another group of towns with 141,000 people (+ 12 per cent from 1931). The prosperity here is due to a strong industrial tradition,[17] combined with the opening of several pits in the concealed coalfield within the past fifty years, for example at Mansfield (Crown Farm) in 1905, at Rufford in 1913, Clipstone in 1922, Bilsthorpe in 1923 and Thoresby in 1925. In the borough of Mansfield, almost two-fifths of the employed population are miners, many of them working some distance away. But there are also textile factories, including thirty separate works in various types of hosiery manufacture with some 4,000 employees, cotton-doubling works for the lace and hosiery trades and a woollen clothing works. Metal works employ almost as many as textiles, and range from iron and brass foundries to a small works providing precision instruments; the main form of engineering is the making of textile and other machinery, steam and water condensers, pipes and many more products. There are various other industries, including radio equipment and footwear.

A mining area that developed around an old market and industrial town like Mansfield or Chesterfield, is economically stronger than a rash of mining villages in an otherwise entirely agricultural countryside, or a group of mining towns of the South Wales coalfield type.

In the Erewash valley four towns, Alfreton, Ripley, Heanor and Ilkeston, together with Eastwood, and also Belper in the Derwent valley, have 125,000 people (+ 6 per cent): mining is combined with iron and steel working at Ilkeston and is the basic industry also of all the other towns except Belper, which has metal trades, a famous cotton mill and hosiery works. All of this area is partly suburban to Derby and Nottingham.[18] Derby (141,000) had a decline of − 1 per cent from 1931 to 1951, but this was due to the outward movement from the congested core of the town into the neighbouring rural parishes of Chaddesden, Spondon, Allestree, Littleover, Alvaston and Boulton. If these places are included, Greater Derby had 166,000 people in 1931 and over 200,000 in 1951, an increase of more than 20 per cent. Clearly the present administrative definition of the town is inadequate, for its aero-engine, engineering and rayon industries are growing considerably and the area is attractive to immigrants. Few towns have a greater inflow of workers, which in 1951 numbered more than 36,000 compared with an outward movement of only 3,800. Over 20,000 came in to Derby from the neighbouring 'rural' district of Shardlow, 1,400 from Belper U.D., over 4,000 from Belper R.D., and even 1,750 from Nottingham.[19]

Greater Nottingham

The question whether Nottingham with Derby forms one single middle Trent conurbation was raised on p. 216. C. B. Fawcett apparently thought so but the P.E.P. Report on the location of industry called it a mere 'urban region' and not an 'urban cluster' or conurbation.[20] Some delicate distinction appears to exist here but in fact there is a break between Long Eaton and Derby though it is clear that a mid-Trent conurbation is likely to exist shortly, if it does not already exist. Nottingham's long history goes back at least to Saxon times and the Danes saw the significance of a head of navigation, where road and river traffic would naturally meet: under the Normans, the main growth was on the fine sandstone bluff.[21] For centuries, the Trent has been a much-used waterway. In its modern growth, the Nottingham area owes much to four main occupations: hosiery manufacture, lace-making, engineering and mining. The first of these is widely developed in the Midlands, especially in the

Leicester area, but also in Long Eaton, and in the neighbouring towns of Ilkeston and Mansfield. Having an initial stimulus given by the invention of the stocking frame in 1589 at Calverton, this industry has its roots in the domestic work carried on in the Pennine valleys. Towards the end of the eighteenth century, the introduction of steam power, for which suitable coal was available locally, stimulated the textile industry, previously handicapped by the lack of suitable streams: the first steam-driven cotton mill was opened at Papplewick in 1785.[22] Lace making was also located here through the happy accident of local inventions: originally dependent on local cotton mills, the manufacturers bought much of their yarn in the Manchester market once railways were built. Though still surviving strongly, this industry has had to meet rigorous foreign competition and a declining demand, but the introduction of new lines, some partly of artificial silk, has maintained this historic and interesting industry. Engineering, associated originally with the making of the intricate machines needed for local industries, has increased markedly. Coal mining too is strongly developed in the area, and there are four collieries within the city boundaries, of which Wollaton and Radford, are on the exposed coalfield but Cinderhill and Clifton are beneath Bunter Pebble beds. The Gilding and Bestwood pits are just outside the city boundary and eastward expansion was seen in the sinking of a shaft at Calverton in 1939, where a large new colliery was made in 1952. A new pit is being sunk at Cotgrove, near Bingham, in an area so far entirely rural, and the first coal will be supplied in 1958. In all, the seven existing mines produce $3\frac{1}{2}$ million tons a year, as much as the Cumberland, Kent and Bristol fields combined, and the coal is sold for household and steam power, notably for the electricity generating stations beside the Trent.[23] But perhaps a major reason for the modern prosperity of the Nottingham area has been the success of a wide range of industries including pharmaceutical chemicals, tobacco and a variety of others, including service trades. In 1951, the population of Nottingham with its immediate neighbours was 489,000, + 20 per cent compared with 1931.

Greater Leicester (Fig. 52)

Leicester, Oadby and Wigston had 307,000 people in 1951, 13 per cent more than in 1931, but recent estimates suggest that this central part of the county has some 358,000 inhabitants, 18 per cent more than in 1931.[24] The long-established hosiery and footwear industries were prosperous before the 1939–1945 war, but engineering was growing markedly in new factories built on the outskirts of the city. Naturally these engineering works were expanded during the war

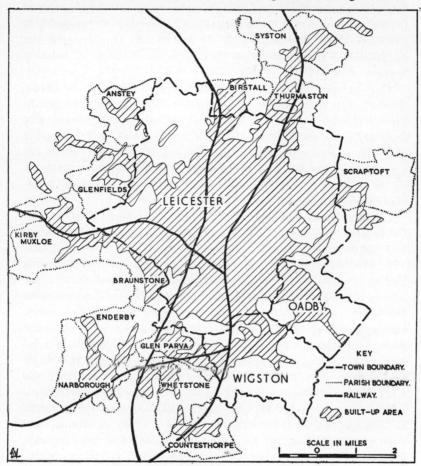

FIG. 52. LEICESTER AND ITS ENVIRONS

The economic prosperity of the three historic Midland cities, Leicester, Nottingham and Derby, is reflected in their outward spread, seen here and in Fig. 51, p. 257.

but this industry remained strong afterwards, partly because so many skilled men were available; similarly the footwear and hosiery industries have done well both in home and foreign trade since the war. Various consequences have followed from the fortunate

s

economic position, including an acute shortage of labour and immigration limited only by the lack of living accommodation. Some manufacturers, especially in hosiery and footwear, have built branch factories in other towns and villages of the county. Industrial spread from a major centre is by no means unique, for it is seen notably in the West Midlands (see pp. 252-5) and in the London area (see pp. 266-8). A general comment on this feature of industrial location is given on p. 212.

Throughout the area of England commonly regarded as 'Midland' there is every sign of economic progress. Developments similar to those at Scunthorpe are seen in the smaller, but rapidly growing, new town of Corby, and in the well-established towns of Wellingborough and Kettering. But the major town of Northamptonshire is the old county town (104,000, + 8 per cent, 1931-1951), which has footwear as its main industry, combined with the manufacture of boot-making machinery and other forms of engineering.

Lincolnshire has only three centres with more than 50,000 people. Of these the largest is Grimsby which with its neighbour, Cleethorpes, had 124,000 inhabitants in 1951, an increase of + 2 per cent over 1931. It could be said that the town, associated primarily with fishing and the timber trade, belongs rather to the Humber than to the county of which it is a part, for its development was almost entirely due to the enterprise of the Manchester, Sheffield and Lincolnshire railway company (later the Great Central and L.N.E.R.) which built docks that stimulated the growth of a fishing village into a large town.[25] Scunthorpe has doubled its population within thirty years, to 54,000 in 1951 largely due to the expansion during both world wars of the steelworks (with their cokeries) using the local Jurassic ores. The workplaces volume of the 1951 Census showed that Scunthorpe had 24,113 resident occupied workers of whom 1,061 went outside the borough for employment; but 7,014 came inwards, primarily from rural areas though there were 500 from Grimsby, 390 from Brigg and even 250 from Goole.[26] Lincoln (69,000, + 5 per cent) was a route centre of significance both in Roman and Danish times, and acquired considerable prosperity from the twelfth century due to the wool trade. The historic route along the Lincoln wolds inevitably comes to the crossing of the River Witham, and the town grew on a commanding site on the north side of the gap. Having had a long career as a cathedral town and a market centre, it has emerged also as an administrative and industrial town and has now spread far beyond its well-defined late eighteenth-century limits.

Its main industries are engineering, including agricultural machinery, but the manufactures also include fertilizers, timber and leather.[27]

On the margins of East Anglia, Peterborough with Old Fletton has 62,000 inhabitants (+ 23 per cent since 1931). Like other cathedral towns, Peterborough is a strong market centre, having a favourable position in the rich Fenland area. At Old Fletton, the fourteen brickworks which use the excellent raw materials of the Oxford clays have expanded steadily since the first was established c. 1890.[28] But the recent industrial growth has been associated primarily with engineering, including a diesel engine works established in 1932 now employing over 4,000 people and older firms, which manufacture a wide range of machinery and other goods down to hearthrug needles and fish slices. Footwear is represented only by a firm making laces, and also braid ties, and other industries include canvas goods, materials for home handicrafts, and boiled sweets. There is also a strong printing trade.

THE EASTERN S.R.

As now defined, this includes East Anglia, with Essex and Cambridgeshire, Huntingdon, the Isle of Ely, Bedfordshire and Hertfordshire, though no part of the Greater London conurbation is included (see Fig. 66). One feature of special interest is that the outer suburban spread of London is likely increasingly to affect large parts of Essex and Hertfordshire. But to many brought up in the north, England east of the main line to York seems a gentler land, knowing little of the harsh realities of the industrial scene, less threatened by the inevitable spread of towns than the north and the midlands. Even though Cambridge has some of the worst examples of ribbon development in the country and also has more than half the population of the county, one still has the feeling that the countryside is not far away. More than half the population of Norfolk and Suffolk is in rural districts and in these counties most of the towns are country market centres placed at intervals of a dozen miles or so one from another, though a few towns have grown larger for a variety of reasons (Fig. 53).

Cambridge (81,000, + 16 per cent) still preserves the atmosphere of a country town to a far greater extent than Oxford and industry has entered only to a small extent, notably in a radio works.[29] The first modern industries were a jam-making factory established in 1873 and a scientific instruments works in 1881. The county town, it was

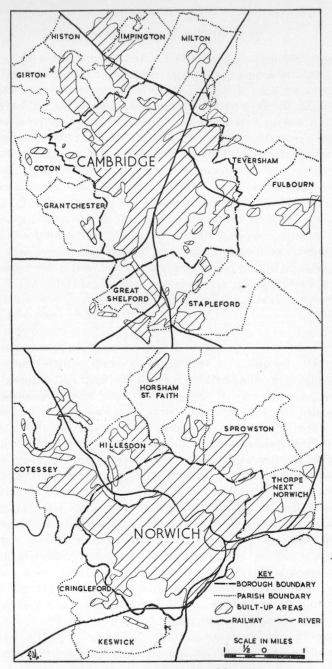

FIG. 53. CAMBRIDGE AND NORWICH

Both these East Anglian towns, though of considerable size, retain something of the atmosphere of a country town but both have expanded considerably during the past forty years. Villages near Cambridge have been linked with the town by ribbons of housing along the main roads but the comparable outward movement from Norwich has been of a more fortunate character.

chosen as the regional centre for East Anglia during the 1939–1945 war, and may grow rapidly in the near future, for as Holford and Wright point out, it has numerous attractions. It is, for example, a suitable centre for modern scientific industries, and for other firms trying to find sites close to but not within London, and it is also a suitable centre for contractors relying on custom from the headquarters of the Eastern region. University expansion through new research institutions, especially in science and agriculture, and the continued attraction of a residential population, may also contribute to the town's growth. During the inter-war period, its growth took a singularly unfortunate form, for the expansion of outlying villages such as Girton, Shelford, Histon-Impington, gave the town a ribbon of houses over 8 miles long from north to south (see Fig. 53). Including the villages outside the borough that are effectively joined to it, the population is approximately 92,000[a] (78,000 in 1931).

Norwich (121,000) apparently declined by − 3 per cent from 1931 to 1951, or more accurately from 1931 to 1939, since when the population has remained static: though there has been an outward spread beyond boundaries clearly in need of revision and its population is approximately 155,000 in fact. Norwich has the atmosphere of a major market town, with its castle, its large cattle market and fine shopping centre, and above all its magnificent cathedral and old parish churches. It is easy to realize that its greatest relative importance was reached in the eighteenth century, and that in 1801, with 37,000 people, it was the eighth town of England.[30] Manufacturing industry is connected with agriculture, especially in the famous mustard and malt trades, and in milling. Engineering is represented by the making of wire-netting, wrought-iron goods and timber-framed buildings and on the electrical side by the making of engines and heating appliances. There are also boot and shoe firms, clothing factories, and a confectionery works famous also for Christmas crackers.[31] Twenty miles away, Great Yarmouth has its traditional association with herring fishing and a strong holiday trade, but here the population has declined from 61,000 in 1921 to 57,000 in 1931 and 51,000 in 1951, partly due to the diminution of the (herring) fishing trade but also to its vulnerable position during wartime.[32]

Ipswich (105,000 in 1951, + 20 per cent) has remained prosperous, partly through its port facilities used especially for handling coal,

[a] Including the parishes of Impington, Histon, Girton, Great Shelford, Fulbourn.

combined with milling, brewing and a famous agricultural machine industry with recent additions that include vegetable and fish canning and sugar beet processing.[33] As in many other places, the engineering industry has been widened in scope, and now includes the manufacture of cranes, excavators, railway material and electric road vehicles. At Colchester (with Wivenhoe, 60,000, + 16 per cent), agricultural machinery is also made, together with boilers and gas engines: other industries include clothing and printing. In the last two it is not difficult to see the influence of London for various firms have chosen sites conveniently near the metropolitan market. But a different metropolitan influence is seen in Southend-on-Sea (152,000, + 17 per cent), which has grown steadily as a holiday and residential town, near enough to London to be a dormitory and to attract enormous numbers of day visitors. According to the 1951 Workplaces Census, 19,200 Southend residents left daily to work elsewhere, 11,902 in London and 7,500 in Essex, including 1,800 in Thurrock.[34] conversely, only 5,300 came in to Southend for work.

Metropolitan influence is seen also in such towns as Bedford and Luton, both of which have grown rapidly during the past thirty years. Bedford (with Kempston, 62,000, + 28 per cent) has considerable fame as an educational centre due to the provision of ancient trusts: there are also engineering works and in the vicinity some of the country's largest brickworks. Luton's growth is even more striking. It had 61,000 inhabitants in 1921, 70,000 in 1931 and 110,000 in 1951, and Dunstable's growth by + 74 per cent to 17,000 from 1931 to 1951 carried its built-up area to the fringes of the larger town. Luton's traditional straw-plaiting industry has developed into a more sophisticated hat manufacture, but the recent growth is associated more with the vast development of the motor car, refrigerator and other engineering trades.

Some criticism of the definition of Greater London is given on pp. 65-70. In Hertfordshire, Watford, Rickmansworth and Chorleywood (102,000 + 40 per cent) are undergoing the same expansion that was seen nearer the centre in earlier decades. Having excellent communications Watford has acquired various industries, many of them located on a munitions site made available after the 1914–1918 war: of these printing with paper and ink making is long established but others include various forms of engineering, notably lorries, vans, steel furniture, precision instruments, electrical equipment, asbestos, cement, and various foods.[35] On the east side, Dagenham is no longer the effective limit of the continuously built-up area, for

Romford, Hornchurch and Brentwood had 222,000 people in 1951 (and 257,000 in 1955), an increase of + 120 per cent within twenty years—Hornchurch had 17,500 people in 1921, 39,400 in 1931, 81,400 in 1939 and 104,100 in 1951. Brentwood is basically a country town now being brought within the London orbit. To the south, the somewhat amorphous urban district of Thurrock had 82,000 people in 1951 (101,000 in 1954), having increased by + 33 per cent from 1931 to 1951 following an increase of + 27 per cent from 1921 to 1931. Within this area of almost 63 square miles, constituted an urban district in 1936 by the union of Grays, Tilbury and Purfleet, with the Orsett rural district,[36] the main asset is a frontage of 20 miles on the Thames estuary.[37] Shell Haven is a large oil port, recently expanded, East Tilbury has a footwear works with 3,000 workers, and Purfleet a margarine works with its own jetty and the Thames Board mills with 2,500 workers. There are also various timber yards and cement works beside the river. But the main expanding area is the West Thurrock Estate, which has 2 miles of river frontage (on which tenants can build their own jetties), two main railway lines and the main Southend road, A13, through the centre. Much industrial expansion is certain here.

LONDON AND THE SOUTHEAST S.R.

This standard region includes the whole of the Greater London conurbation and the remaining parts of Kent and Surrey with the whole of Sussex. As in the eastern region, metropolitan influence is seen in a variety of ways. Some of the Kent towns, such as Gravesend and its neighbours, or the Medway towns, show industrial growth similar to that in Essex on the north side of the Thames estuary (v.s.). Other places on the coast, from Margate to Worthing, have grown into considerable towns through the attraction of visitors and residents, and on the south of Greater London, a number of towns such as Reigate and Redhill have become outer suburbs. Of this the most notable example is the group of suburbs in the attractive country to the southwest of London where Chertsey and its neighbouring towns had a quarter of a million inhabitants in 1951. As noted on p. 65, the Census definition of the conurbation was unrealistic here.

Gravesend, with Northfleet and Swanscombe, which have 72,000 people, an increase of 16 per cent over 1931, in fact join Greater London. Here there are paper works and cement works beside the river.[38] The Medway towns, Chatham, Rochester and Gillingham, also have cement and paper industries, located here as on other Thames-side sites partly because chalk and good water are available, supplies can be brought in by sea, and the finished product sold in the great metropolitan market: Chatham also has its famous naval dockyard. These towns increased by + 16 per cent to 159,000 in 1951. As Southend has grown on the north side of the entrance to the Thames, so on the south, four interlocking towns, Margate, Broadstairs, Ramsgate and Sandwich have developed as residential and holiday centres, catering for a wide variety of visitors. These places together have 97,000 people, an increase of + 7 per cent from 1931 to 1951.

Growth continues apace on the southwest side of London, and is nowhere better seen than in a group of Surrey suburbs with 249,000 inhabitants (Egham, Chertsey, Woking, Walton and Weybridge, Esher, Leatherhead and Dorking) which are growing around former independent towns and villages. All are increasing rapidly in population, and added + 50 per cent from 1931 to 1951. But the most interesting development in Kent is the expansion of the line of gap towns on the south side of the North Downs: on pp. 26, 64–5 reference was made to the growth of London suburbs on the north flank of the Downs but there is an increasing invasion of the other side. From west to east, the line is Dorking, mentioned above; Reigate, with Redhill within its bounds and fusing into Caterham on the Downs (74,000, + 31 per cent), all of which are in fact linked by ribbons of housing to Croydon; Sevenoaks still a small town of 15,000 but growing rapidly; and Maidstone (54,000, + 20 per cent), the county town placed in the heart of so rich an apple orchard and hop-growing area that it is difficult for the town to expand except by building on first-class land. Here on the Medway the main industry is papermaking and there are three large breweries. Two large industries have developed from grocers' shops, of which one, producing toffee (Sharpe), grew slowly from 1876–1910 then rapidly after the war and the other (Foster Clark) began when a grocer's assistant made baking powder and bun flour in 1889 and set up a factory with a capital of £100.[39] Development is expected at Ashford, still comparatively small but having excellent communications by road and rail. In the deep Wealden heart of the county, Tunbridge Wells has a long-established reputation as a spa, and is now linked by housing with Southborough and the market town of Tonbridge is a town-cluster of 66,000 people (+ 11 per cent, 1931–1951).

The South Coast

Not all the towns of the south coast have been equally fortunate in their recent history. Brighton and its neighbours have prospered in spite of a vulnerable position during the 1939–1945 war, but Folkestone and Hythe remained virtually stationary with 54,400 and their near neighbour, Dover, declined from 41,000 to 35,000. Similarly Eastbourne (58,000) has decreased by − 1 per cent since 1931 but has in fact been declining since the 1914–1918 war. And in Hastings with Bexhill (91,000) there was an increase only of + 4 per cent from 1931 to 1951. Some local observers incline to the view that in this southeastern corner of the country, towns with a fast electric train service to London are likely to prosper more than those with slower services: if this be so, the advantage lies with Brighton rather than with the others.

Brighton is now the main town (156,000) of a coastal conurbation that extends for 8 miles of Sussex coast from the River Adur from Old Shoreham bridge to the end of Kemp Town, and 3 miles beyond it to Rottingdean and Saltdean which, with Woodingdean, are now inside Brighton C.B.[40] These five towns (Figs. 54, 55), says E. W. Gilbert, with a population of 263,000 are effectively one unit as there is no perceptible break between Brighton, Hove, Portslade, Southwick and Shoreham. Indeed, there is virtual continuity of settlement as far west as Worthing and even further to Little-hampton. From the eighteenth century, Brighton has been a holiday and residential centre, fully aware of its health-giving qualities, and favoured for this and other reasons by an increasing number of visitors, including royalty. Gilbert has shown that the first period of Brighton's modern growth began in 1754, when Dr. Russell began to attract patients to take his famous 'cures'. Growth, slow at first, brought the population to some 3,500 at the time of the Prince of Wales's first visit in 1783. Royal favour helped and the rapid increase which more than doubled the population during the Regency years (from 7,000 in 1801 to 24,000 in 1821), has left both a tradition of good planning and some distinctive architectural marks in central Brighton. When the railway came in 1841, the population was over 46,000, and in the following thirty years the population doubled, for the journey to the coast for holidays, even for days, was made possible for everyone. Apart from its natural advantages of a fine downland site, Brighton owes much to the fact that it is the nearest and most accessible place on the south coast from London. Having

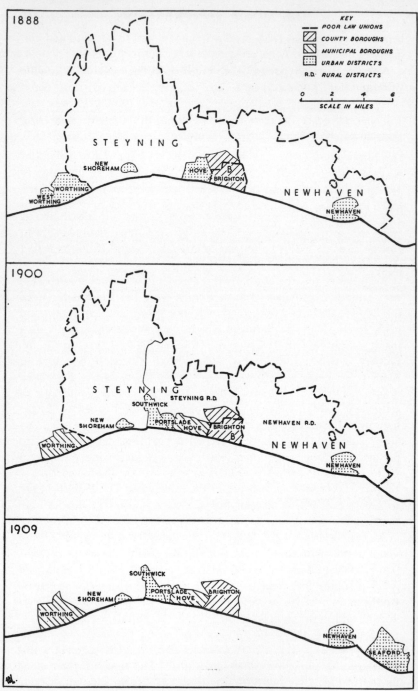

KEY
- - - POOR LAW UNIONS
COUNTY BOROUGHS
MUNICIPAL BOROUGHS
URBAN DISTRICTS
R.D. RURAL DISTRICTS

0   2   4   6
SCALE IN MILES

1888

STEYNING

NEW
SHOREHAM

HOVE
B
BRIGHTON

WORTHING

WEST
WORTHING

NEWHAVEN

NEWHAVEN

1900

STEYNING

STEYNING R.D.

SOUTHWICK

NEW
SHOREHAM

PORTSLADE
HOVE

BRIGHTON
B

NEWHAVEN R.D.

WORTHING

NEWHAVEN

NEWHAVEN

1909

SOUTHWICK

NEW
SHOREHAM

PORTSLADE
HOVE

BRIGHTON

WORTHING

NEWHAVEN

SEAFORD

FIG. 54. BRIGHTON AND DISTRICT, ADMINISTRATIVE AREAS, 1888–1909

become a borough in 1854, it grew from strength to strength and like many more seaside towns, attracted a large number of retired people.

A writer of 1897 spoke of the people of Hove as living in a cultivated but mildly athletic ease.

> Life in Hove is tranquil and ornate . . . the residents spend their days at golf, bicycling, or At-Homes. The sound of a concertina in Hove would paralyse the local police with horror.

Doubtless customs have changed but the very success of Brighton, Hove and their neighbours has attracted a commercial community providing insurance and other specialized services. Brighton is the most important banking and insurance centre east of Portsmouth and south of London and until 1956 five newspapers were published in the town of which one was the only evening paper published in Sussex, though unfortunately the local daily morning paper ceased publication in that year. Further, Brighton with the adjacent streets in Hove, is a strong and attractive shopping centre.[b]

In 1951, the retired population was 11·6 per cent of all males in Brighton and 12·7 per cent in Hove (compared with a national average of 8·5 per cent).[41] In 1939 Brighton had 2,100 recognized lodging- and apartment-houses and 205 hotels in the centre of the town, and 110 public houses within half a mile of Palace Pier. In 1948, over 9,000 persons were engaged in the hotel and catering industries and a further 2,700 in entertainment and sport. Almost twice as many were engaged in the manufacture of metal goods, vehicles, and in general or electrical engineering. The railway works originally established to serve the old London, Brighton and South Coast railway, are still used for the assembly of engines, though the

[b] In the 1950 Census of Retail Distribution, these figures were given for the retail and services group:

	Retail establishments	Number employed		Sales £000's
		Whole-time	Part-time	
Brighton . . .	2,861	12,344	2,682	26,924
Hove	1,046	4,150	1,046	9,241
Worthing . . .	1,154	5,274	2,433	11,717

FIG. 54. Brighton became a county borough in 1888 and Hove and Worthing were promoted to borough status later. The towns spread along the coast without any considerable inland penetration.

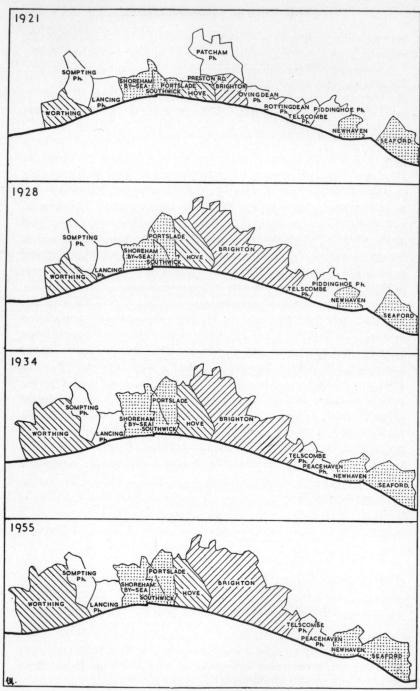

FIG. 55. BRIGHTON AND DISTRICT, ADMINISTRATIVE AREAS, 1921–1955

nautical engineering was transferred to Newhaven in 1901 and the carriage works to Lancing in 1912. The main area of heavy industry is around Shoreham harbour, close to Lancing, but other industries are placed along the railway between Brighton and Shoreham, even in Hove, and there is a wide range of industries, mostly light in character, in Brighton itself, including some in the Hollingbury valley, an amphitheatre in the Downs; among these are electrical engineering, typewriter manufacture and soda water making by a famous firm using a well 240 ft. deep, and many more. As Brighton extends outwards to the edge of the Downs, it is proposed to develop several small industrial estates. Although the expansion of industry would clearly raise problems for a district dependent for its pros- perity largely on its amenities, light industries in clean factories, worked by electricity and located away from the areas normally visited by tourists, need do little harm to the town and district. Here, as in Blackpool, there are many thousands of residents having little contact with the holiday trades, living some distance from the sea. One expression of the outward spread of London residents is that 3,800 people (1951) had season tickets to London from the Brighton and Hove stations, compared with 2,400 in 1938: fast electric services make the journey as quick as that from some outer suburbs of London. The Workplaces Census shows that 5,073 residents of Brighton and Hove work in the L.C.C. area.[42] Made largely by the railway, though already a well-favoured town early in the nineteenth century, Brighton still depends partly for its prosperity on rail com- munication and a natural fear of the planner is that the London and Brighton line may become one suburban sprawl from end to end.

The spread of housing west of Shoreham is reflected in the increase of population by 113 per cent, from 14,000 to 29,900 in the Worth- ing rural district, which is obviously due to residential rather than to agricultural development. The old village of Lancing has proved a nucleus for a good deal of modern building. Worthing (69,000 in 1951, + 49 per cent since 1931), was a small bathing resort in the middle of the eighteenth century and developed considerably in the early years of the nineteenth century.[43] When the railway reached the town in 1843 there was no immediate growth and the main expansion came from 1859 when a sewage system was provided. A new pier in

---

FIG. 55. Penetration inland became marked, but the coastal areas were filled up with houses and the nominally 'rural' parishes are by no means completely rural in appearance.

1862 also proved an attraction. West of Worthing the growth of the villages of Ferring, East Preston and Rustington threatens to make building continuous almost all the way to Littlehampton. The destruction of rural amenity along the south coast is a subject almost too well known to mention, except perhaps by noting a few classic examples.

THE SOUTHERN S.R.

This area is not aptly named, for in Buckinghamshire and Oxfordshire it includes two counties north of the Thames, regarded by H. O. Beckit as part of the southeast Midlands, which he spoke of as having an 'essentially rural character . . . a borderland, a zone of passage and in some ways of transition, between the "metropolitan" London Basin and the largely industrialized inner or true Midlands farther to the north-west'.[44] Within these counties, as also in Berkshire, a main problem of the present is the outward spread of industrial and residential settlement, conspicuously along the Thames valley. The remainder of this 'region' covers Hampshire (officially the county of Southampton) and Dorset, which have three interesting coastal conurbations centred on Portsmouth, Southampton and Bournemouth. Also in Hampshire, the two military centres of Aldershot and Farnborough with Frimley-Camberley in Surrey, increased in population by + 20 per cent, from 70,000 in 1931 to 84,000 in 1951.

Oxford (99,000, + 23 per cent, 1931–1951) is at once a cathedral city, a university town, a great market centre for a rich agricultural area, a residential and tourist town, and it now has the motor and allied steel trades added for personal rather than geographical reasons.[45] A century ago, the university authorities managed to prevent the erection of the railway works (which were established at Swindon) but no one managed to prevent the incoming of the motor trade, and the associated growth of Cowley. In 1921 Morris Garages began to assemble parts of motor cars at Cowley, in a factory 3 miles southeast of Carfax, and in 1926, the Pressed Steel Company was established to produce steel car bodies. Nearly 10,000 houses were built in Oxford during the interwar period. In 1851, Oxford's population was 28,000, but there was an increase to nearly 50,000 by 1901 and the present population is c. 110,000 (some thousands more than the vacation figure of the Census). Although the city's boundaries were extended to cover 13 square miles in 1923, it is estimated that at least 23,000 people live in suburbanized villages still technically 'rural'. Efforts to revise the city boundaries in 1953 were unsuccessful, partly because they would involve the alteration of county boundaries. Continued growth is regarded with some concern, shown for example in the suggestion by Dr. Thomas Sharp that the Nuffield works and part at least of the Pressed Steel works should be removed elsewhere,[46] but these proposals did not meet with the approval of the city council. In 1946, the city council passed a resolution 'that all possible steps be taken in an endeavour to prevent the population for which Oxford is the natural centre from increasing'; yet in 1953, the city's Development Plan estimated that the population would increase to 118,500 by 1973, of whom at least 16,000 would be re-housed outside the city boundaries. Efforts to prevent housing development in areas expanding in population, industrial, commercial and residential, may lead only to a chronic shortage of houses and inflated prices for accommodation of any description.

Reading (114,000, + 17 per cent) has grown steadily and continuously from the beginning of the nineteenth century round an ancient crossing-place of the River Kennet. Sufficiently far from London to be a strong market town, it became sufficiently near to be a residential centre when the Great Western Railway was opened in 1840. E. W. Gilbert has spoken of the town in 1830 as 'still a typical English market town . . . the appearance of modern Newbury or Abingdon . . . may help us to imagine what Reading was like before industry laid its ugly hands upon her'.[47] But one of its famous firms, Sutton's seeds, is concerned more with beauty: it was established before 1840. In 1841, Huntley and Palmer joined forces to develop the biscuit firm that at times has employed as many as 6,000 workers, and in more recent times a variety of industries have been established.

Slough, now joined to the old towns of Windsor and Eton but vastly different from them, had 20,000 people in 1921 but 66,000 in 1951, and 93,000 (+ 79 per cent since 1931), with its two dignified neighbours. Development came here through the opening of a large trading estate after the 1914–1918 war, encouraged partly by the enterprising Great Western Railway. A further advantage of site was nearness to the main London–Bristol road. The estate of 457 acres, acquired by a commercial company in 1920 and gradually settled with industries from 1924, now has some 200 tenant firms and 25,000 workers. Some of the firms have expanded considerably and built their own factories outside the estate on the main road from

London to Bristol. This area has shared conspicuously in the industrial growth of the London area, especially in light engineering, luxury goods and patent foods. Labour was attracted from various depressed areas of Wales, Scotland and the north of England between the wars, and recently a large number of Poles have been absorbed into a community already of varied origin. The town's growth is by no means complete and at present the London County Council is building estates within it while Slough is building estates in the adjacent rural district.

Both the two largest south coast conurbations, centred on Portsmouth and Bournemouth, are now increasing markedly in population. Portsmouth[48] itself declined from 1931 to 1951 by − 8 per cent, from 252,000 to 233,000 but the conurbation of which it is a part increased by 11 per cent to 367,000, due to large increase in Fareham (42,000) and Havant-Waterloo (33,000) which cover outer suburban areas and in industrial Gosport (58,000). The initial geographical advantage possessed by the greatest naval base in the British Commonwealth is the two natural harbours on either side of Portsea island, combined with the sheltered Spithead anchorage. A dockyard was mentioned in a Pipe Roll of 1212 and from the mid-thirteenth century, Portsmouth was the assembly point for troops crossing to France. Henry VII made it a royal dockyard and a garrison town: prosperity came in the eighteenth century and in 1801 the population was 32,000. Southsea developed first in 1809, when the famous Terraces were built, but grew rapidly in the middle of the century, when the Common, once a dreary marsh, was drained and levelled. In 1864, the Royal Dockyard was greatly extended and as late as 1870, the existing fortifications to protect the island from landward attack were strengthened. From 1871 to 1911, the population was doubled (from 114,000 to 231,000) and buildings covered almost the whole of the island, and spread also to the 'mainland' villages of Widley, Wymering and Cosham, which were incorporated into the

---

FIG. 56. This is copied from a map by H. A. Garnett, described as 'from the Ordnance Survey, estate maps and other available data' (B.M. 2620(5)). As yet the shore promenade was not built but there were walks named as 'promenades' along the cliffs, 100 ft. high, sloping down to the central pier. Public gardens had been laid out and the turbary common was later transformed into Meyrick Park. The Deer Park estate was laid out with the cricket ground in the centre and the town has an interesting fusion of straight and turning streets. Some of the best nineteenth century town planning is to be seen in seaside places.

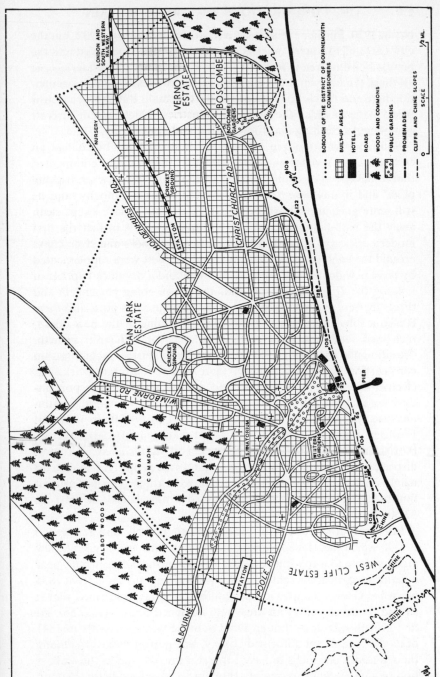

FIG. 56. BOURNEMOUTH IN 1883

T

city in 1920. Further extensions to its area were made in 1932, but the city's area of 15 square miles is now almost entirely occupied and the newest housing area is to be at Leigh Park, in Havant-Waterloo. At all times the Navy and the garrison have provided the main occupation here and the cargo trade of the port is small. But efforts are now being made to widen the range of industries, which include aircraft components, clothing and food trades, and engineering.

Southampton's modern growth has been striking, but it had an early career as a watering-place though in 1841 a writer commented that it 'never was or could be considered in the light of a sea-bathing place' and in any case 'the all-devouring railway company, and its still more grasping twin-sister, the dock company, have swept clean away the bath-buildings and the bathing-shores'.[49] In fact the first modern dock was opened in 1842. The earlier docks and river quays around the confluence of the Itchen and the Test were supplemented by large new docks built from 1926–1934, and a dry dock capable of holding the *Queen Elizabeth*. Half the ocean-going passengers and three-quarters of the United States travellers use this port, and there is also a substantial cargo trade. In the building of the new docks, reclaimed land has been made available for industrial growth. Traditionally, the major industries have been marine, including ship construction and repair though there are also aircraft works, an electric wire and cable works, and several characteristic port industries, such as tobacco, margarine, and feeding stuffs. Southampton increased in population from 66,000 in 1891 to 178,000 in 1951 and Eastleigh increased from 23,000 to 31,000 in 1931–1951. Totton, though in fact a suburb on the river Test, is included in a rural district, and there are other signs that townspeople have gone to neighbouring countrysides, for in thirteen rural parishes around Southampton the population increased from 31,700 in 1931 to 57,500 between 1931 and 1951.

Bournemouth is one of several planned holiday and residential towns which developed during the nineteenth century.[50] A few visitors came to a roadside inn and neighbouring cottages built near a mansion early in the century, but the main impetus came from 1835 when Sir George Tapps-Gervis acquired an estate and ruled that it should be developed as an area with detached houses (Fig. 56). At first growth was slow, though Dr. Granville wrote shrewdly in 1841 of its site 'and its yet unformed colony, as a perfect discovery among the sea-nooks one longs to have for a real invalid, and as the realization of a *desideratum* we mainly thought to have found elsewhere on the south coast of England'. Another writer of the time regarded it as a suitable winter resort but there were only thirty houses in 1841. Even so, the attractive plan was kept and the Improvement Commissioners appointed in 1856 built the first pier, improved the seafront, and laid out cliff walks within the next ten years. Having only

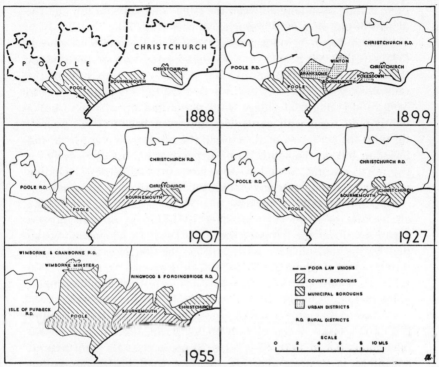

FIG. 57. ADMINISTRATIVE UNITS IN BOURNEMOUTH AND DISTRICT
FROM 1888

Here, as in Brighton and district, the marked increase of population necessitated the redefinition of the towns, including two historic places, Poole and Christchurch. As in other seaside areas, the main spread has been parallel to the coast.

1,700 inhabitants in 1861, the town grew rapidly from 1870 when the railway station was built. Private companies financed the Winter Garden 1875 and Boscombe pier 1889, but these were eventually taken over by the town council, who added various parks and pleasure grounds, including those in the Chines, and an Undercliff drive, completed in 1907. Created as a resort, it remains a holiday and residential town showing continued growth from 96,000 people in 1921 to 117,000 in 1931 and 145,000 in 1951. Spread of housing has now fused it with the old towns of Poole and Christchurch, with the result that the conurbation had 248,000 people in 1951, an increase of 32 per cent over 1931. East of Christchurch, there has been a marked spread of housing in Milton and New Milton, and on the north side there is little open land between the fringe of Bournemouth and the delightful old town of Wimborne Minster (Fig. 57).

Swindon began its modern career as a New Town of the eighteen-forties with 2,000 people in 1841, but by the turn of the century there were over 45,000 and 12,700 people were employed in the railway works.[51] The 'New Swindon' of the railway planners was to be a model industrial village with parks and open spaces, but a tightly-built town with gardenless and even back-to-back houses, thirty to the acre, was built between the railway on the north and Swindon hill on the south. Long dependent almost exclusively on the railway works, Swindon now has other industries, including engineering, radiograms and clocks, tobacco, raincoats and uniforms —especially for railway workers. In 1951, the population was 69,000, an increase of + 10 per cent over 1931, but at present there is expansion under the terms of the 1952 Town Development Act so that by the mid nineteen-sixties the population is expected to be 92,000, some of whom are to come from London. An area of 1,000 acres is to house over 20,000 people in five distinct neighbourhood units, three built by the Council and two by private enterprise.

Gloucester has grown rapidly in recent years, not least through the development of the aircraft industry: in 1931, it had 56,000 inhabitants but in 1951, 67,000 (+ 20 per cent). Its main natural advantage is strategic—here is the first road bridge across the Severn, a canal with useful docks and waterways farther inland, and good railway communications. Like other cathedral towns it has remained a strong market and route centre, attractive to industry, which includes the making of railway carriages for the home and export trade, timber working, shirt manufacture and a wide range of engineering.[52] Now that its aircraft production is so widely known, there seems to be every expectation of still greater growth both in the town and in the neighbourhood.

Cheltenham was known as a spa in the eighteenth century, but its main growth dates from the Regency period 'a time when con-temporary taste was at a high level . . . The town is one of the most attractive examples of urban development in the country . . . It is particularly famous for the wealth and elegance of its architectural iron work.' [53] Located beside the Cotswolds edge, in a rich countryside, Cheltenham was built around lawns and gardens, and one of its famous streets, the Promenade, was laid out in 1818 with limes and chestnuts. In time it became a residential and educational centre rather than a spa, growing steadily through the nineteenth century. In 1951, with its immediate neighbour, Charlton Kings, its population was 69,000, an increase of + 25 per cent from 1931. The main industries are light engineering and the making of electric clocks, but the general development of industry around Gloucester, nine miles away, may result in further increase of population, of which there are already clear indications.

Bath's renown for its waters goes back to Roman times, but as late as 1687, Celia Fiennes found that 'the ways to the Bath are all difficult, the town lies low in a bottom and its steep ascents all ways out of the town; the houses are indifferent, the streets of a good size well pitched . . . the baths in my opinion make the town unpleasant, the air thick and hot by their steam, and by its own situation so low, encompassed with high hills and woods'.[54] Some thirty years later, the building of Georgian Bath began, and the fashionable and the decrepit were so carefully considered that nothing, Jane Austen reminds us in *Northanger Abbey*, could offer greater pleasure than a visit to such a place. By 1801, it was the tenth town of England in size, with 32,000 people, and during the nineteenth century it became more and more a residential town. Steady but hardly dramatic growth brought its population to 69,000 in 1931 and 79,000 in 1951, due in part to some industrial development, chiefly in engineering and leather working.

Bristol, with its three independent neighbours, Keynsham, Kingswood and Mangotsfield, had 434,000 people in 1931 and 487,000 in 1951, an increase of + 12 per cent. For centuries the second city of the land,[55] its population of 64,000 in 1801 was exceeded only by Manchester, Liverpool, Birmingham and Southwark. Bristol's trade in mediaeval times was with home ports, Ireland and other parts of the western seaboard but from the Age of Discovery its shippers traded also with Africa, the West Indies and the American colonies in slaves, sugar and tobacco. Connexions with France, Spain and Portugal were maintained for wines and salt: wool, yarn, flax and cattle were brought from Ireland and commercial contacts with Cornwall and South Wales were preserved. Few inland towns are more obviously ports, for the Avon still flows through the city centre though part of the tributary Frome river has been built over. But the most interesting feature is the Feeder and the Floating Harbour, completed in 1809 to provide reasonable facilities for shipping: the building of modern docks at Avonmouth and Portishead dates only from 1877 to 1880. Only gradually during the nineteenth century was the industrial life of Bristol adapted to the changing conditions of the times, as it seemed that the north had now the economic power, but efforts to establish cotton working gave the city one large mill from 1837 to 1926. A tradition of non-ferrous metal working, using lead from the Mendips and copper and tin from Cornwall and Devon, dates back to mediaeval times, and the chief modern enterprises of this type are the spelter industry at Avonmouth and a galvanizing works on the Feeder. Engineering and metal trades developed during the nineteenth century, and included railway and wagon works, the making of bicycles, motor-cycles, cars and finally air-craft. At the present time the remarkable growth of the aircraft industry on the north side of the city presages further expansion. Long-established manufactures associated with the traditional West India trade are tobacco, chocolate and soap. Still the port trade is significant, especially for foodstuffs, including West Indian bananas, petrol and general merchandise; and the docks at Avon-mouth have vast stores for meat, grain and other imported foodstuffs, with a notable milling industry. At the docks, canal barges are loaded with supplies carried to various places along the Severn and a colour-ful spectacle is given by the barges waiting for the tide to enter the river. Bristol as a city has remained throughout its history a regional capital for a large part of the southwest and preserves to a greater extent than many cities interesting residential quarters close to the centre. A large new shopping centre is under construction. At present the main shopping centre fuses into a second one on the fringe of Clifton, the nineteenth-century residential district built on the Downs above the Avon gorge, which happily has not suffered the decay seen in many such residential areas of other cities, even though many large old houses have been turned into flats, hotels or offices.

Devonshire has three urban areas to be considered here. Of these Exeter is a cathedral, market, and administrative town comparable to Lincoln, Gloucester, Chester and others of its kind, and Plymouth is a long-established naval and commercial port. Torquay and Paignton are successful seaside holiday and residential towns that have developed mainly since visitors came here to watch the ships during the Napoleonic wars.[56] These towns have an enchanting site, southfacing on rising ground, and their climatic mildness has made them favoured both in winter and in summer. From 1931 to 1951, their population increased to 79,000 (+ 21 per cent).

Exeter[57] has been a see since 1050 and became a great centre of the woollen industry from the sixteenth century; in spite of the decline of this industry in the eighteenth century, the town remained important and doubled its population from 1801 to 1841. Numerous town houses were built round the turn of the century (c. 1780–1820) as the city was the centre of a large and rich agricultural district. Not all its various industries were permanently successful, but the survivors are varied, and include, paper, printing, foundries, breweries, tanning and church furnishing. Oddly enough the largest single factory is a gas meter works with 1,200 employees. The first railway to reach Exeter was the G.W.R. in 1844, followed by the L.S.W. (Southern Region) in 1860.[e] The prosperity of Exeter, which had 75,000 people in 1951 (+ 12 per cent) continues to rest largely on its market trade, on miscellaneous professional services, such as hospital provision for a population of half a million, on its administrative services, and on its transport facilities. The circulation of its evening newspapers over a wide area of Devonshire and north Cornwall is closely influenced by the available railway services.

Plymouth, perhaps the most isolated of the larger towns of England, is known chiefly as a naval port, but it is also an industrial town, and a market, shopping and distributing centre for west Devon and most of Cornwall.[58] Devonport, which with East Stonehouse was united into Plymouth in 1914, became a naval centre before the seventeenth century and was strongly fortified in the period from 1810 to 1853. The railway was opened in 1848 and the famous Saltash bridge was completed in 1859 to carry the line into Cornwall. The port has three main functions: first, the supply of materials especially coal and oil to the Devonport dockyards; second, general cargo supplies to the city and its hinterland, and third, passenger traffic. Before the war, over one-third of the insured population was employed by the Navy and here as in Portsmouth, other industries were small and varied, including clothing, foodstuffs, chemicals, timber, oil and engineering. Plymouth, which became a city in 1928, had 209,000 people in 1951, with two suburbs across the water, Torpoint and Saltash, 223,000; the population has declined very slightly since 1931.

[e] Here the southern and western railway regions of British Railways cross each other!

WALES

So far the only conurbations of Wales are in the south, and of recent growth, yet they include half the population in spite of some recent heavy declines in the coalfield. In North Wales, the coast towns from Prestatyn through Rhyl, Abergele and Colwyn Bay to Llandudno and Conway, are virtually fused one into another, but they are here excluded as this process of 'conurban linkage' is hardly complete. Geddes regarded 'Waleston' as one of the great conurbations:[59] here it is considered under four headings (a) the coalfield, pp. 284–92; (b) Cardiff, p. 292; (c) Swansea, p. 293 and (d) Neath-Port Talbot, p. 293. These areas are all part of the coalfield or have developed as ports and metallurgical centres in relation to the coalfield, but they are by no means the whole of South Wales, nor even the whole of the coalfield, which extends into remote valleys of Carmarthenshire: nor do they cover the whole of Glamorgan as between the coalfield and the Bristol channel there are agricultural lowlands. To the nineteenth-century observer, the movement of population into the upland valleys and the coast towns was so remarkable a phenomenon that apparently there could be no end to the economic growth.

The Coalfield (Fig. 59)

'Everyone thought South Wales was a gold mine', said one business man, 'but almost overnight it became a depressed area.' In 1934, some towns had half their population unemployed and it was estimated that the number of workers 'on the dole' in basic industries, here coal, iron, steel and tinplate, was 183,000 in 1927 but 125,000 in 1934.[60]

The period of economic distress began several years before the world economic crisis, and by 1931 was partly alleviated by outward migration. Many factors were contributory. Some of the older mines were nearing exhaustion, the sale of Welsh steam coal fell off once

---

FIG. 58. On the margins of the coalfield, Cardiff, Swansea and Neath were ports having industries and commercial functions: Bridgend and Cowbridge were also market towns—the latter a borough never having more than 1,500 people. (One of its mayors, hailed in London, is alleged to have replied, 'Hush—I'm travelling incognito'). Urban status was given to the new strings of colliery villages in the mining valleys, and the greater part of the upland became 'urban' as the new districts were based on the old rural parishes.

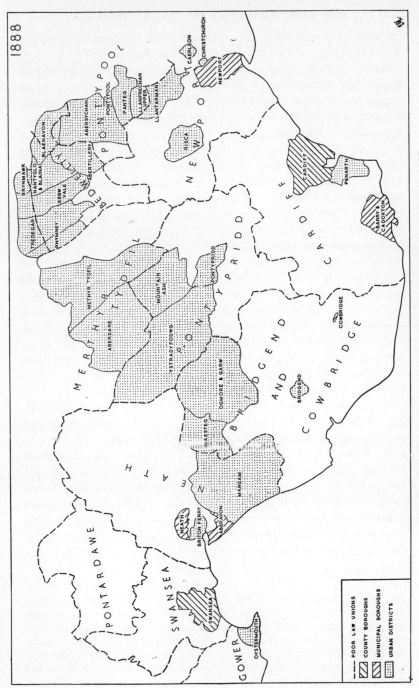

FIG. 58. THE SOUTH WALES COALFIELD, ADMINISTRATIVE UNITS, 1888

modernized power plants began to use small coal and ships turned to oil (even in the Navy); and foreign markets were lost through increased home production, both of coal and electricity. South Wales became the classic example of an industrial area having most of its eggs in one basket and lacking the resilience possible in an area having a range of industries, of which some may be declining but others expanding.[61] The mining towns and villages grouped together as Rhondda U.D. in two long deep valleys relied entirely on coal mining, and the decrease of population from 163,000 in 1921, to 141,000 in 1931 and 112,000 in 1951, was due to a net outward migration of c. 36,000 (− 21·7 per cent) from 1921 to 1931 (natural increase + 8·6 per cent; net decrease − 13·1 per cent) and a net outward migration of c. 37,000 (− 26·4 per cent) 1931–1951 (natural increase + 5·2 per cent; net decrease − 21·2 per cent). In 1921 the coalfield area shown on Fig. 59 had 833,000 inhabitants, in 1931, 758,000 and in 1951, 666,000. The decrease of population was − 20 per cent from 1921 to 1951, and − 13 per cent from 1931 to 1951. Within the area, the declines were most marked in the districts once famed and prosperous for steam coal, such as Aberdare, − 26 per cent; Mountain Ash, − 29 per cent; Rhondda, − 31 per cent; Ogmore-Garw, − 25 per cent and Maesteg − 20 per cent. But population decline, in varying degrees, has been almost universal throughout the coalfield since the 1914–1918 war.[62]

Fundamentally the main problem of South Wales is the distribution of population. During the past century and a half the deep and narrow valleys of the upland have been penetrated by roads and railways and settled by a mining and metal-working community living in villages and towns that, though administered as boroughs and urban districts based on the old hill-parishes, are deficient in urban amenities such as good shopping centres. An even more immediate problem is the poor quality of the houses, built in stark straight rows on the narrow valley floor or on steep hill-sides. True, there have been efforts to improve towns such as Pontypridd, Porth,

---

FIG. 59. The changes since 1888 have included the enlarging of Cardiff, Swansea and a few other towns, and the union of some urban districts of the coalfield under the Review Orders of the nineteen-thirties, but the historic influence of the old hill-parishes remains perfectly clear. Apart from the extension of Cardiff—inadequately it could be said—there have been no boundary changes since 1936. Rhondda became a municipal borough in 1955.

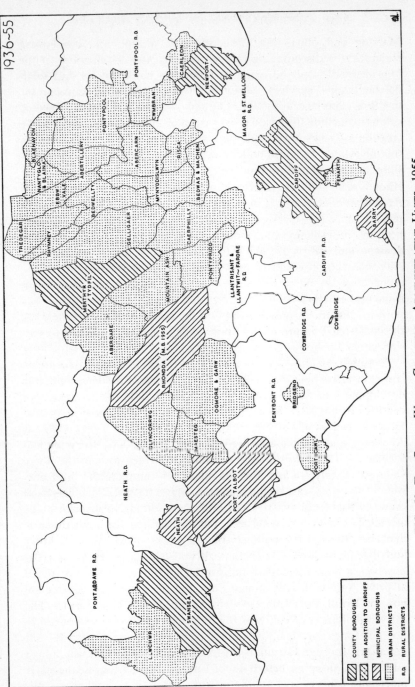

FIG. 59. The South Wales Coalfield, Administrative Units, 1955

Maesteg and others but the decline of mining and consequent emigration is discouraging to such efforts. And the memory of the long depression period, with its numerous bankruptcies and semi-derelict shops, survives. Many of these problems are comparable to those experienced in West Durham (see p. 223) where projected solutions include the gradual extinction of many mining villages, the creation of new towns and the introduction of new industries on trading estates. In South Wales one new town, Cwmbran, Monmouth-shire, is planned and trading estates have been set up, notably in the Rhondda, at Treforest, at Hirwaun, at Bridgend, and at Pontypool.[63] At present coal mining is in a stage of rationalization by which large pits are replacing smaller and presumably less efficient units. Having been in constant fear of unemployment, the miner is now in great demand and efforts are made to provide work for the womenfolk. Although the provision of new housing is difficult in some valleys, an effective beginning was made during the inter-War period, when some new estates were built on elevated sites made accessible by bus services. But this is possible only on the margins of the coalfield, as the constricted nature of the upper valleys makes it difficult to find sites either for housing or for industry.

Although coal has been mined at least from the thirteenth century, it was iron-working that initiated the remarkable modern economic development of South Wales.[64] From the middle of the eighteenth century, ironmasters from the Midlands and the north settled at Dowlais and at Cyfarthfa, both now in Merthyr Tydfil C.B., at Aberdare, and in neighbouring valleys at Ebbw Vale, Rhymney and Blaenavon. Other works were established farther west in the Tawe valley, at Ystalyfera and Ystradgynlais, but the main developments were in the northeast of the coalfield, where both the rich clayband ores and coal from quarries and adits were found. Steelworking was attracted at first to the same area, but the necessity for importing raw materials affected the remotely-placed works of Merthyr, Sirhowy and Blaenavon adversely so that all were closed by 1929. In 1936, however, a large integrated mill producing tinplate was constructed at Ebbw Vale with government help, but the main steel centres are now at Cardiff, Port Talbot, Swansea and Llanelly on the coast. The early exploitation of coal was for industrial use, for local consumption and for export, mainly from the eighteenth century onwards, but not at first through Cardiff as Swansea and Newport handled almost all the coal shipping before 1840. Cardiff's port trade in the early nineteenth century was mainly in iron, but as more and more railways were built, and especially when the Rhondda steam coals were successfully exploited from the eighteen-sixties, Cardiff became the leading coal port of the Bristol channel.[65]

Inaccessibility was a main problem of the South Wales upland when industrialization began, but a road from Merthyr to Cardiff was opened in 1767 and replaced soon afterwards by an easier way along the Taff valley. Several new roads were made in the valleys during the late eighteenth century.[66] Many years after the canals and river navigations had been engineered in England (cf. pp. 77, 102, 131), the Glamorgan canal from Cardiff to Merthyr was opened in 1794, with an extension to Aberdare in 1818. The Monmouthshire canal, opened in 1792, with later extensions promoted the growth of Newport as a coal-exporting town: other canals included the Neath, 1791 and the Swansea (Tawe valley) 1798, which were beneficial to Swansea.[67] Wagon ways constructed between 1800 and 1830 fed the canals with traffic and led also to Newport (conspicuously those of the Sirhowy and Rhymney valleys), to the small port of Porthcawl from the Llynfi valley, and to Llanelly. In all there were several hundred miles of wagon ways, the forerunners of the railways which by 1870 had almost vanquished all other forms of transport.[68] But progress was comparatively slow. The first line from Cardiff was constructed to Merthyr Tydfil in 1840–1841, and by 1851 there were trains running from Newport to Cardiff, Bridgend, Neath and Swansea along the present main line. Almost all the present lines were built during the next thirty years except for the Vale of Glamorgan line (sanctioned 1889) and the Barry railway (1884),[69] which made possible the growth of Barry from a hamlet of 100 people in 1881 to a port and holiday centre of 13,000 in 1891 and 41,000 in 1951.

Swift increases of population were a commonplace in South Wales during the nineteenth century, but the main early development was in the northeast, and conspicuously in Merthyr Tydfil, which by 1841 had 35,000 people, more than Cardiff (10,000) and Swansea (19,000) together. Such towns were then a magnet for immigrants. In 1851, Merthyr had 35,093 people aged 20 and over, of whom only 9,102 had been born in the town; of the rest, 4,146 were from other parts of the county, 2,330 from Ireland, and 21,827 (62 per cent) from other areas, 14,189 of them from the counties of Carmarthen, Brecon, Pembroke and Cardigan.[70] From the rural counties of Wales, from Cornwall, Devon, Somerset and Gloucester, from the mining and industrial areas, from Ireland, workers came to South

Wales. But as early as 1871–1881, a loss of population by migration was reported from Merthyr,[71] and as this town is in many ways an epitome of the South Wales problem, it is proposed to follow its story further. The Dowlais ironworks were producing 500 tons of iron a year by 1759, six times as much by 1800, over five times as much again by 1815 and vastly more by 1845, when there were 7,000 employees; but production ceased in 1930.[72] Similarly the great Cyfarthfa works, which in 1803 had 1,500 employees and was said to be the largest in the world, was closed in 1910, re-opened during the 1914–1918 war, closed again in 1921 and dismantled in 1928. Other and smaller works had been closed in 1859 and 1880, but the larger works had retained their strength through changing circumstances. Coal mining was prosperous up to the 1914–1918 war, and in 1913, some 24,000 men were employed but by 1924, there were only 16,000, and in 1935, only 8,000, even though the resources were estimated at 120,000,000 tons. Many other signs of decay were noted in 1935, and it was reported that 'none but Council houses have been built for years' and that the 'number of closed shops, especially in Dowlais, was very noticeable'.[73] About 1,000 men were known to work as much as 20 miles away, and only two very small factories had been opened locally. It seemed that prosperity could never return to such a place, remotely situated at 500–1,100 ft. above sea level, scarred by derelict land from abandoned enterprises with an evil record of unemployment. Having risen in population to 80,000 in 1921, it decreased to 71,000 in 1931 and 60,000 in 1951: and any revival must be hampered by the loss of a high proportion of the young and active population (see also p. 286).

Biological analogies fashionable in some geographers' teachings might lead to the view that Merthyr's story is a natural historical development in an industrial town. It is no such thing. Iron and coal made South Wales strong economically, and when they failed, the towns they created failed, and their workers went elsewhere if jobs were to be found. It was not easy, indeed it appears to have been almost impossible, to attract to such distant and unattractive places the new industries whose expansion near London and the Midlands so many deplored. But at least Merthyr has a long and by no means undistinguished industrial history: Rhondda, covering the 37 square miles of the old Ystradyfodwg parish, has not. In 1861, it had 3,000 people, in 1871, 17,000, in 1881, 56,000, in 1891, 88,000 and in 1901, 114,000. The maximum recorded was 163,000 in 1921 after which there was a decline to 112,000 in 1951: that is, within fifty years the population has increased by half and declined again by the same amount. In fifty years, 1871–1921, there was growth from an embryonic mining area to one in its full strength. A century ago, the Rhondda valleys were peaceful and pastoral, with wooded slopes, and the first coal owners, undeterred by the need to sink deeper pits than those previously known, had to offer higher wages than those prevalent elsewhere in order to attract population to so remote a dwelling,[74] but in recent times, the one desire of many people has been to get away. As part of a Development area, the Rhondda valleys have already received a number of new factories, for example a clothing works at Treorchy with 1,400 employees, on a drained and previously unused river terrace, or five factories with over 1,000 employees at Porth, providing textiles, zip fasteners and precision instruments, all built on a levelled tip heap.[75] As there are no large areas available for industry in these valleys, the development has been rather of the single factory or a small group of works. Within Rhondda M.B., the estimate is that by 1970, the number engaged in factories will be equal to the number of miners.

Elsewhere in the South Wales coalfield, the new industries include several new enterprises, some of them inspired by continental refugees, as well as extensions of existing firms elsewhere. A glass firm from St. Helens now makes plate glass at Pontypool, where there is also a vast nylon-spinning plant with several thousand workers; a West Midlands firm has a galvanized hollow-ware factory at Caerphilly; and a Canadian biscuit firm has established a works at Llantarnam. At Merthyr Tydfil there are now factories for washing machines, thermostats, electric lamps, mechanical toys, hosiery, lingerie, silk stockings and wooden buttons (the last two in Dowlais): at Ebbw Vale, corsets are now made and at Brynmawr and Blaina, notorious black spots of the nineteen-thirties, there are works providing rubber, brass, industrial felt and the attractive material known as 'candlewick'. Aberdare has cable making, and Mountain Ash, the manufacture of radio components and shopfittings. At Maesteg in the Llynfi valley there are two contrasting new factories, one for drilling machinery and the other cosmetics, and across the mountain, remote Cymmer has a plastics factory. Many more examples could be given but enough has been said to illustrate the industrial change achieved by the building of individual factories as well as of spectacular industrial estates. It will be noted that the largest trading estates are on the margins of the coalfield, due partly to the need for large areas of level land, but under modern conditions of transport, workers are drawn from the heart of the coalfield to the new factories.

Cardiff

This rise of Cardiff has been inseparably linked with the fortunes of the coalfield;[76] though a Roman site and a Norman fortified settlement, it remained small until the nineteenth century and had less than 2,000 inhabitants in 1801. The line of the Roman road through the lowland of South Wales is still followed by the main road today and the town has clear natural advantages as a bridge-point controlling the westward route and other routes from the hill-country to the north. All this meant comparatively little until the railways, and to a limited extent the canals before them, began to open up the previously unexploited riches of the country to the north. Even so, it was not until the eighteen-sixties that the supremacy of Cardiff over its rivals, Swansea and Newport, as a coal port was established and this change was due largely to the opening of the deep Rhondda mines, which had excellent steam coal. By 1872, the coal trade of Cardiff was almost twice as great as that of its two main rivals put together. In 1839 the Bute dock had been opened, and in 1855 the Bute East dock was added, only to be extended twice within the following five years. Three other docks were constructed, the Roath basin in 1874, the Roath dock in 1887 and the Queen Alexandra in 1907: meanwhile the Penarth dock was built and connected by rail with the Ely and Rhondda valleys, in 1866 (but closed in 1936). Cardiff's prosperity was built up largely on the export of coal, for up to the 1914–1918 war, it was the greatest coal port in the world. Iron ore is imported and discharged on to the stockpile for the steelworks, which were built on the East Moors in 1888–1891 as part of the Dowlais works. Heavy iron and steel is still the largest single industry, with over 7,000 employees, but there are various other metallurgical trades, including ship repairing, vehicle manufacture, the making of wire ropes and chains, and many more: flour-milling, with other food and drink enterprises, are strongly represented, and there is a wide range of minor industries. But the port is not now used to its full capacity, as coal exports have declined to a fraction of their former extent.[d] Efforts are being made by civic authorities and the National Industrial Development Council to attract new industries.

[d] In 1953, only 1,278,000 tons of coal were exported, one-quarter of the amount sent in 1938 and one-eighth of that in the peak year of 1913.

Through the gifts of the Bute family and the enterprise of its citizens, Cardiff has grown into a handsome town with some good shopping streets, and a number of fine buildings set in Cathays Park, including the National Museum, the University College, and the City Hall. Suburbs surround the town on the east, north and west, of which those to the north are close to the pleasant and varied countryside that separates the city centre from the coalfield. To the southwest, Penarth (18,500) is a seaside suburb which grew with the parent city: the population of Cardiff and Penarth in 1951 was 262,000, an increase of + 8 per cent over 1931. But if one includes Whitchurch, still 'rural' though having 20,000 people in 5 square miles, the population increased by 9 per cent from 258,000 in 1931 to 282,000 in 1951. Although depressed during the period of coal-mining decline, Cardiff managed to maintain and add to its industries, and to remain the commercial capital for South Wales. Having become a regional capital and the largest town of Wales, in 1955 it became what its inhabitants have for many years regarded it to be—the capital of Wales. But its critics say that it has only grown to such stature through coal, along with the mining area beside it, and that linguistically it is the least Welsh of towns, too new, too industrial, too commercial, perhaps even too English, to be an expression of a Wales whose spirit lies in deep countrysides and mountain valleys.

In South Wales, the three town groups of Swansea-Llwchwr, Neath-Port Talbot, and Newport-Caerleon, are all associated with ports and metallurgical industries.[77] Swansea-Llwchwr (187,000, − 3 per cent, 1931–1951) and Neath-Port Talbot (76,000, + 3 per cent) are practically joined together. Neath has for centuries been associated with the smelting of lead, copper and with silver industries and Swansea's manufactures have followed the same lines at least from the beginning of the eighteenth century, so successfully that Swansea was the centre of the world's copper trade until the eighteen-eighties. Although this trade declined, others of a similar character have developed, notably tinplate, zinc and especially steel, now represented by a vast modern plant at Margam, Port Talbot. The long history of metallurgical industry here has been combined with the import of ores by sea for little of the raw material was available from home resources. A large modern oil refinery has been established at Llandarcy, which is linked by a pipeline to the Queen's Dock at Swansea. A new post-war trading estate, the Fforestfach, has so far some 3,000 people employed in twelve factories, but there is provision for another fifty works. The main

U

trades are engineering, toys, brushes, clothing and mineral waters. Unfortunately this area has a wide variety of problems which arise from its physical features and the devastation brought by past and present industries. Port Talbot and Aberavon occupy constricted sites backed by the upland edge; Briton Ferry and Neath are placed beside the river Neath with the hill-edge a short distance away. On the north side Swansea sprawls off through the dreary industrial villages of the Tawe valley, and Llwchwr is an urban district more in name than on the ground for it too consists of a number of industrial villages. But on the west and southwest, Swansea has access to the attractive countryside of the Gower peninsula and its suburbs lie mainly on the west side of the town, beside the great sweep of the bay to Mumbles.

Newport (110,000 with Caerleon, + 8 per cent, 1931–1951) grew as a coalport drawing supplies from the Monmouthshire valleys, and for several decades seemed likely to become a larger town than Cardiff (see p. 289). It has a recently established large aluminium industry, and also has the manufacture of electric cables: it is also an import centre for iron ore feeding the Monmouthshire works (see p. 288). Inevitably the decline in coal export raises problems, and some new industries have recently come to Newport though there is not a trading estate as such: one of these, a firm making uniform clothing, established in London since 1870, came to Newport in 1947 and now has 650 workers, of whom 100 are men. The move was made because sufficient labour could not be found in the East End of London to open a new factory.[78]

CHAPTER 11

SCOTTISH CONURBATIONS

By CATHERINE P. SNODGRASS

OF Scotland's 5,096,000 people, just over one-third live within the Central Clydeside conurbation and slightly over one-fifth in six smaller conurbations of which the most notable is Edinburgh and district. Although all the major Scottish towns have long and varied histories, the remarkable economic prominence of Glasgow and district dates only from the commercial and industrial changes of the late eighteenth and the nineteenth centuries which radically altered the distribution of population. The farming of high standard that has prevailed since the Agricultural Revolution has contributed, along with industry, to the commercial strength of towns, such as Perth, Stirling and Dumfries, which are smaller than those treated in this book. Here it is possible to deal only with the one major and six lesser conurbations; and, as so much of Scotland's industrial strength is concentrated on Clydeside, that area will be considered first.

As the Scottish administrative structure differs from that in England, a brief explanation may be helpful. Historically the burghs were of two types: Royal, held directly from the Crown and governed by councils of burgesses, and burghs of Barony or Regality held from a local lord and administered by his representative, or from the Church before the Reformation. Under an Act of 1833 twelve towns which had recently expanded became Parliamentary Burghs, and later in the century many growing urban centres became Police Burghs; but some centres of population of more recent origin or expansion with many thousands of inhabitants (the largest 26,000), including industrial and residential areas in Clydeside and mining villages in the Lothians, have still no separate administrative identity and no legally defined bounds, being merely villages,—in Scotland there are no 'urban districts'. Parish government was deeply entrenched in Scotland, and the counties became administrative units only in 1889. Most parishes date from mediaeval times; from the Reformation period secular rule was largely in the hands of the Kirk Sessions, combined in some cases with the local landowners or heritors until parish councils were established by Act of Parliament in 1894. They were abolished by the Local Government (Scotland)

Act, 1929, and new County or 'landward' Districts created; 'landward' means non-burghal and should be distinguished from 'rural' which means non-urban, that is including no settlements with over 1,000 people. (Sixteen of the older burghs have less than this number.) This Act reclassified the burghs into 'large' and 'small', the dividing line being a population of some 20,000, and gave the four major cities the status and functions of counties.

THE CENTRAL CLYDESIDE CONURBATION

Definition

The conurbation covers an area of 326 square miles in N.W. Lanarkshire and adjoining parts of Renfrewshire and Dunbartonshire and contains a population of 1,758,000. The County of the City of Glasgow, with 1,090,000 inhabitants in 60 square miles, is the largest unit: the seven large burghs included have a combined population of 349,000, and the five small ones 68,000; while the seven county districts house 251,000, 223,000 in villages and towns without burghal status, and 28,000 in rural areas or villages with less than 1,000 inhabitants (see Figs. 60, 61).[1, 2] Glasgow, situated at the lowest bridging point where traffic from all directions converges to cross the Clyde, is the chief commercial, educational, ecclesiastical, medical, and social centre of southwest Scotland, the country's largest port, and its most important manufacturing centre. The city's overwhelming dominance in the economic and cultural life of the lower Clyde Basin gives the conurbation vital unity, although its sphere of influence extends much farther afield. Indeed Glasgow may justly be regarded not only as the metropolis of southwest Scotland and even of the West Highlands, but also as the industrial and commercial capital of Scotland itself.

On the southeast, the built-up areas of its ancient trading rival, the Royal Burgh of Rutherglen (24,000), and the dormitory and steel-making village of Cambuslang (26,000) are now continuous with that of the city, while on the west Paisley (94,000), an old abbey town and the largest burgh in Scotland after the four cities, was linked during the nineteen-thirties by narrow zones of bungalow and villa development to Glasgow on the east and to the textile-manufacturing and engineering town of Johnstone (16,000) on the west, and nearly so to the ancient Royal Burgh and Port of Renfrew (17,000) on the north. The open space between this burgh and the city has largely been filled since 1920 by docks, factories and a big thermal electricity generating station, while only the Clyde separates Renfrew from the former gap between Glasgow and Clydebank (45,000), a boom town of the late nineteenth and early twentieth centuries. This gap was partially converted to urban use between 1907 and 1939, with docks, railway marshalling yards, factories, and houses, and almost completely so after 1945 by extensive house-building, while the space between Clydebank and the village of Old Kilpatrick (3,000), excluded from the conurbation by the Census, has been filled since 1920 with oil storage tanks and houses. Glasgow suburbs have spread widely into rural Renfrewshire and Dunbartonshire, especially since 1920, and this justifies the inclusion of the First District of the former and the New Kilpatrick District of the latter in the conurbation, though both have considerable areas of agricultural land and even uninhabited moorland. Villages such as Kilbarchan (3,000) and Linwood (2,500) are excluded, though closely linked both on the ground and economically with their neighbours, Johnstone and Paisley. In the north the conurbation includes Milngavie (8,000), once an industrial village, but now largely a dormitory town, and Kirkintilloch (15,000), an ancient burgh of barony, and at one time a busy canal port . It has a population of commuters and retired people as well as workers employed in local industries and services. Kirkintilloch is separated from Glasgow by a two-mile wide belt of predominantly agricultural land; Milngavie is practically joined by a narrow zone of inter-war bungalows to Bearsden (10,000), a suburb which was made a burgh in 1958.

The northeast Lanarkshire area of coalmining, iron and steel working, and heavy engineering is separated from the rest of the conurbation by a strip of farmland 1–2 miles wide, dotted with some villages, collieries and other works, and institutions. Its inclusion seems reasonable, both on account of its nearness and its economic relations with Clydeside. The 1951 definition included four 'landward' districts of Lanarkshire (the Fifth, Sixth, Eighth and Ninth) and the four large burghs of Hamilton (40,000), an ancient burgh of barony, now the administrative and judicial headquarters of the Middle Ward of Lanarkshire and a distributing, social, mining and manufacturing centre, Airdrie (30,000), an old settlement near the moorland edge on a long-established route between Glasgow and Edinburgh, Coatbridge (48,000) and Motherwell–Wishaw (68,000), both mining and manufacturing towns of mid-nineteenth century creation. Unfortunately, a number of villages on the margins of the burghs, connected to them by built-up areas, are excluded, of which

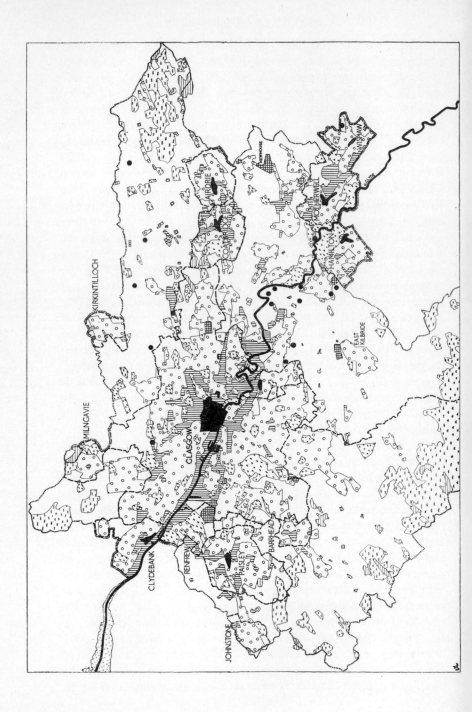

FIG. 60. Land Use in the Central Clydeside Conurbation

Only the major town centres are shown and the industrial areas have been generalized. Although there appear to be considerable areas of land available for urban expansion, factors mainly of altitude and slope in the south and possible subsidence due to coal mining in the north leave little available, if the conversion of the whole basin into one continuous built-up area is to be avoided and some of its highly productive farmland preserved.

Based on:

(*a*) Abercrombie, P., and Matthew, R. H., *The Clyde Valley Regional Plan.* Map 29 Industry, and map 30 The Clyde: Riverside Land Uses.

(*b*) Field work, with assistance from the Planning Officers of the Department of Health for Scotland.

(*c*) 1″ and 2½″ O.S. maps.

(*d*) Bartholomew's *Pocket Plan of Glasgow.* Published *c.* 1951.

(*e*) Corporation of the City of Glasgow. *Map of Main proposals in the City of Glasgow Plan approval order* (1954). Published by the Corporation in 'Written statement' (1954).

the largest, Newmains, east of Wishaw, has a population of more than 6,000.

Inevitably the Census authorities used administrative units, therefore the official definition of the conurbation may differ from one made from personal knowledge of the area. Two former definitions

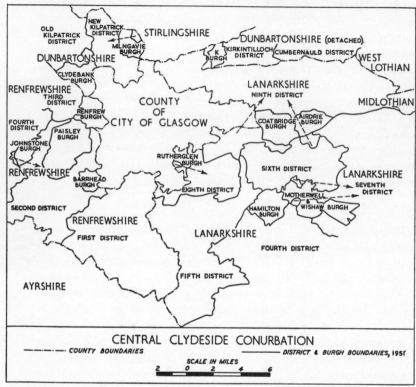

FIG. 61. THE CENTRAL CLYDESIDE CONURBATION, ADMINISTRATIVE UNITS

These are discussed on pp. 296 ff. The County Districts comprise the landward or extra-burghal areas. On Clydeside they include much suburban development and many villages, several with over 10,000 inhabitants. Less than 2 per cent of the population live in a rural environment.

made by C. B. Fawcett in 1932 and P. Geddes in 1915 also differ. Except for the landward part of Glasgow parish, Fawcett used the burgh populations only and therefore excluded several suburban areas.[3] In the west and south the burghs included were the same as in 1951 except that Johnstone was left out; in the north Kirkintilloch and Milngavie were excluded. The extent of the built-up areas in 1931 justified these choices, but in North Lanarkshire the inclusion of Hamilton and the exclusion of Motherwell–Wishaw, separated from it only by the Clyde floodplain, seemed curious. Geddes' definition, here as elsewhere, was wide. In Greater Glasgow he included all the Clyde ports and holiday centres, industrial North Ayrshire, and even Stirling, Dunblane, and Bridge of Allan where some of its 'merchants have their villas'.[4] But he also envisaged a future Clyde–Forth conurbation stretching all the way from central Ayrshire to the Midlothian coalfield and the East Lothian coast. The latter definition was partly in the nature of a warning and, with the greater general appreciation since 1940 of the need to preserve good agricultural land, it does not seem likely to materialize except in the more restricted sense of the Clyde Basin together with the Falkirk–Grangemouth industrial area (see p. 343–4). Even then it would include considerable stretches of open country both west and east of Clydeside's second new town to be built at Cumbernauld some 3 miles from the outskirts of Glasgow and 5 from Falkirk.

Physical Features

The conurbation lies in a topographical and structural basin open on the east side. The Carboniferous sandstones, shales, coals and limestones, of which it is composed, were warped down and also affected by faulting and igneous activity. The younger rocks have been preserved in the centre and east, while the thick lavas interbedded with the oldest Carboniferous sediments form a hill rim to the north, west and south. This rim, which rises to moorlands varying in altitude from about 700 ft. to 1,800 ft., has led to the canalization of the main routes into the basin through certain gaps and valleys. It has proved useful as gathering grounds for water supplies, but in many places it creates great and even insuperable obstacles to urban expansion, due to the steepness of its bordering slopes and to its height. In the west only a narrow gap cut by the Clyde connects the conurbation with the Dumbarton and Greenock areas and gives access to the West Highlands, Argyllshire, Ireland and the Atlantic. In the east, on the other hand, the Coal Measures extend from the structural basin traversed longitudinally by the middle Clyde to the Forth Basin in western Lothian and southeast Stirlingshire. Beyond the steep slopes of the mile-wide incised middle Clyde valley the surface rises gradually to moorlands lying between 600 and 900 ft., with many conical coal bings and occasional craggy hills of igneous rock.

Topographically, the area has been much affected by glaciation and subsequent changes in sea level. Most of the lower ground is covered with drumlins—small elliptical hills of till or boulder clay—trending broadly in a west–east direction, with intervening flats and hollows which have generally poor natural drainage. Two hundred years ago they were largely occupied by peat mosses or small lochs. A few survive, but some of the present lochs are artificially created (or re-created) reservoirs. In the more low-lying parts of Glasgow, and in the area between it and Paisley the drumlins rise above flat raised beaches, lying approximately 100 and 50 ft. above sea-level, which border the extensive lower terraces of alluvium through which the Clyde flows. Its tributaries usually flow on to these beaches and terraces over rapids situated in steep-sided, but shallow, gorges. The small scale topographic features have presented both opportunities and difficulties in the economic development of the region both in its former agricultural and rural and in its modern predominantly in-dustrial and urban phases. The raised beaches, river terraces, and reclaimed tidal flats were easily excavated for docks and ship-building yards, and provided suitable sites for large works and factories. While the rapids were useful for driving mills in early times, the steep sides of the gorges and of many of the drumlins have created difficul-ties for building and transport.

Scotland's largest coalfield, with an annual production reaching a peak of $17\frac{1}{2}$ million tons in 1911, laps round Glasgow, and extends from the city east and southeast for about 20 miles and northeast over to the Inner Forth Lowlands.[5] Within it there were rich deposits of Blackband iron ore, especially in the parishes of Old and New Monkland in the Ninth District and neighbouring parishes in the Sixth and Seventh Districts. The Carboniferous rocks of the coal-field also provided limestones for flux, fireclays for furnace lining, and freestones (sandstones) and bricks for building, while hard igneous 'whinstones' were available in plenty for road making and other construction work. The raised beaches give brick clays and the glacifluvial deposits sands for moulding and building.

Water resources are another valuable asset of Clydeside. The river itself gives abundant supplies for industrial cooling, for example in blast furnaces and thermal power stations. Some of its East Renfrew-shire tributaries as well as the river Leven, downstream from the conurbation, have pure water very suitable for bleaching, printing, and dyeing. Piped supplies for general purposes from the surrounding hills and moorlands have been supplemented in Glasgow since 1859 by enormous quantities of very pure, very soft water from Loch

Katrine in the Perthshire Highlands, and in the coalfield towns from reservoirs within the Southern Upland portion of the Clyde Basin. Furthermore, Glasgow Corporation supplies water at high pressure (900 lb. per square inch) to industries requiring hydraulic power.[6]

Economic Development

Prior to the early eighteenth century the Clyde Basin was a region of self-sufficient farms with a number of small burghs, largely inhabited by craftsmen and traders. The Clyde was a wide, shallow salmon river encumbered by sandbanks and islands with a low-water depth of 15 in. at Glasgow Bridge, and it was easily forded in several places, the lowest being at Dumbuck, 12 miles downstream from the city, where hard rocks outcropped in its bed only 2 ft. below low water level. In the centre of the basin, where routes through the gaps converge to cross the river, two burghs grew up on rising ground on opposite sides of the flood-plain. On the south side Rutherglen was erected into a Royal Burgh in the early twelfth century with privilege of trade and manufacture over a wide area, and for some centuries it was superior to its neighbour in trade and population. Glasgow, on the north side, was primarily a Cathedral town, governed by the local clergy, the centre of the greatest diocese in Scotland and of the second Scottish University, founded in 1451. At the end of the seventeenth century it was judged by travellers to be a pretty little town, fair and well-built, sometimes defined in retrospect as 'the St. Andrews of the west'.

The merchants of Glasgow carried on a long struggle against the greater privileges of both Rutherglen and Dumbarton, but after the Reformation, and more especially after the burgh was granted full royal status in 1611, commerce began to expand, only to be hampered later by the imposition of the English Navigation Acts at the Restoration in 1660. In spite of this setback, land was bought at Newark Castle, 18 miles down river on the south bank in 1668 and the harbour of Port Glasgow constructed. After the Incorporating Union of 1707, the merchants of the city quickly took advantage of their freedom from the English Navigation Acts to expand trade, especially with the English colonies in North America, where a few descendants of Covenanters deported to the plantations had prospered materially. Tobacco was imported from Virginia and Maryland, and by the middle of the eighteenth century Glasgow had become an entrepôt for the dispatch of tobacco to Continental ports to which the Navigation Acts still applied. Great fortunes were made, and the strutting 'tobacco lords' in their scarlet cloaks became conspicuous in the town. As return cargo the ships carried many articles in demand on the plantations, and a variety of manufactures were started or expanded to supply such goods as linen and woollen cloth, shoes, saddlery, glassware, soap, candles, nails, hammers, pick-axes, and shovels; and most of these are still made in the city.

Gradually cotton was introduced, and, after the collapse of the tobacco trade in 1775 following the Declaration of Independence, cotton manufacturing for a varied market, including Europe and later the East Indies, developed as the main economic activity of the region, largely replacing linen in the country districts. At first both the spinning and weaving were domestic industries organized by the 'manufacturers' of Glasgow and Paisley, whose sphere of influence by 1790 included areas 20–30 miles away from Girvan in the south to Stirling in the north. In the seventeen-eighties spinning became a factory industry and by the end of the century many mills were built on the rivers and rivulets, notably the mills at New Lanark, some 20 miles upstream from Glasgow, where Robert Owen carried out his famous experiments. The first steam-driven mill was erected at Tradeston in 1792 and soon many more were established, especially in Calton and other villages east of the city. Johnstone, a new, neat and regularly built village, became the principal spinning centre of Renfrewshire. Numerous printfields and bleachfields were established, while most of the towns and villages of the basin had rapidly expanding colonies of weavers. By 1793 the Glasgow 'manufacturers' were supplied with the produce of 15,000 looms, each giving employment to nine men, women, and children,[7] while about 27,000 people were engaged in the silk gauze, lawn, cambric, muslin, thread, and other textile manufactures of Paisley.[8] By 1800 the manufacture of cotton cloth was the main industry of Scotland, employing over 180,000 people in its various branches, mostly in the Clyde basin, though there were a few large mills elsewhere. As the main controlling centre Glasgow grew rapidly in wealth, influence, and population, and so to a lesser extent did Paisley. In 1775, 137 lb. of raw cotton were imported to the Clyde, in 1790, 1¾ million lb., and in 1810, almost 10 million.[9] The chemical industry developed as an auxiliary of cotton manufacture, one of its foremost scientist-organizers being Charles Macintosh, who invented the process of waterproofing cloth.

In the mid-eighteenth century bar or wrought iron was imported from Sweden for manufacturing nails, typefounding and other

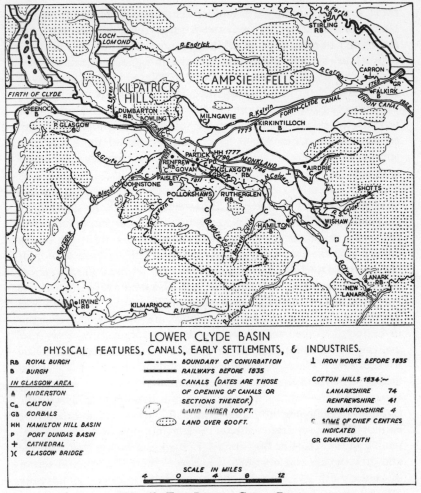

FIG. 62. THE LOWER CLYDE BASIN

Sir Patrick Geddes regarded virtually the whole lowland area shown on this map as Greater Glasgow, but the 1951 Census definition of the Central Clydeside conurbation is more restricted. This map includes the canals, railways, and ironworks constructed by 1835 and some of the historic cotton mills.

Based on the ¼-in. O.S. map.

Information for 1835 mainly from the *New Statistical Account of Scotland*, Vols. 6, 7 and 8.

purposes, and towards the end of the century the cotton manufacture and allied trades gave rise to many new manufactures and
the making of machinery 'of all kinds', which 'together with all kinds
of work in cast and malleable iron and in brass and lead are now
made in Glasgow in great quantities'.[10] The making of iron goods
thus preceded the introduction of modern iron smelting; later it
expanded concurrently with it. In Scotland iron smelting using coke
was first begun at Carron, north of Falkirk, in 1759. The first blast
furnaces in the Clyde Basin were built in 1786 at the Clyde Iron
Works, 3 miles east of Glasgow where 'there was plenty of ironstone
with coal 200 yards away'.[11]

As trade began to expand attention became focused on the dis-
advantages of transhipment at Port Glasgow, and the question of
deepening the Clyde was taken up with renewed urgency (as early as
the mid-sixteenth century combined efforts had been made by the
citizens of Glasgow, Dumbarton, and Renfrew to remove the obstruction at Dumbuck Ford). Eventually the method of 'making the
river work for them' by contracting it by jetties, blasting away the
rock obstruction, and dredging, suggested by John Golborne, was
adopted by the Town Council and sanctioned by Act of Parliament
in 1770. By 1775 vessels drawing 6 ft. of water, and by 1793 those
drawing 7½ ft., could come up to the Broomielaw, a deep pool close
to Glasgow while considerable areas of land had been reclaimed
along the banks of the river.[12] By the seventeen-sixties trade between
the east and west coats of Scotland was considerable and that with the
Baltic was developing. The canal connecting the Forth and the Clyde
was opened from Grangemouth to Kirkintilloch in 1773, and extended to the Clyde at Bowling by 1790 (Fig. 62). By that date the
Glasgow Branch had been continued from the Hamilton Hill Basin,
opened in 1777, to Port Dundas, one mile northwest of the city
centre.[13] In its day the 'Great Canal' was a difficult feat of engineering; 35 miles long, with a maximum height of 156 ft., it has twenty
locks at the Forth and nineteen at the Clyde end, and it was carried
over many roads and rivulets and two rivers, the crossing over the
Kelvin valley being a four-arched aqueduct, 275 ft. long and 68 ft.
high.[14] The Glasgow Branch was situated about 170 ft. above sea
level on rising ground skirting one of the drumlins north of the city
from which ships' masts and sails were seen on the skyline well above
fields and houses, and it was connected with the Monkland canal,
built in 1786 to carry coal to Glasgow. In 1790 the White Cart was
deepened to Paisley, and in 1811 a canal was opened from the south

side of Glasgow to Johnstone, though never extended to Ardrossan as originally intended.

Trade increased rapidly after the Clyde was made into a waterway navigable for ocean-going ships. By 1821, vessels drawing $13\frac{1}{2}$ ft. came to Glasgow harbour, and some ten years later ships of over 300 tons from America, the East and West Indies, and the continent of Europe as well as coasters were found three or four deep along its whole length. In 1834, 27,000 vessels passed Renfrew Ferry, sometimes at the rate of twenty to thirty per hour.[15] The maintenance of the deep channel was made easier and more effective after steam dredgers came into use in 1824. Ships registered at Glasgow increased in number from 24 in 1810 to 507 in 1850, and in tonnage from 2,000 to 138,000, while customs duties collected increased from £125 in 1796 and £500 in 1801 to about £60,000 in 1830 and £640,000 in 1850. Between 1831 and 1840 duties increased sixfold, from £69,000 to £427,000, and ships arriving at the harbour by about 50 per cent, from 11,500 in 1831 to 16,500 in 1840 with an increase in tonnages from 732,000 to 1,166,000 tons.[a][16] Predictions regarding urban development on the south side of the river opposite Glasgow were rapidly being fulfilled. In 1840 this area had cotton spinning and power loom weaving factories, other textile works making carpets, and satins, silks, and velvets, blast furnaces, and extensive collieries. A new 2,000-ft. long quay had been constructed at Tradeston and the Clyde widened and deepened to give the Broomielaw the 'appearance of a very capacious harbour. But the crowded state of the berths on both sides of it already shows that the accommodation provided is not adequate to the rapidly increasing trade of the river'.[17]

Iron smelting expanded slowly during the early part of the nineteenth century and engineering and coal mining fairly rapidly following the experiments of James Watt (partly carried out in Glasgow University) and others. The dominant cotton industry also expanded rapidly until in 1833 there were 119 mills in the three counties, most of them in or near Glasgow and Paisley.[18] By the mid-thirties, however, the future prominence of the iron trades seemed assured by the great iron and coal resources of the district and the peculiarly favourable position of Glasgow 'for the cheap conveyance of the bulky and heavy articles of this manufacture to every quarter of the world'.[19]

[a] The Clyde Navigation Trust, composed until 1809 of members of the Glasgow Town Council, and since then of representatives of all local authorities in the area and of trade organizations, administers the whole river from Glasgow to the sea as a non-profit making body. Its revenues rose from £147 in 1770 to £3,320 in 1800, £16,204 in 1826 and £64,234 in 1850. See ref. 16.

The two chief events which led to the dominance of the metal trades and engineering were the discovery by David Mushet of rich deposits of blackband ore, first used in the new Monkland Works in 1825, and the invention in 1828 of the hot blast by James Beaumont Neilson, engineer and manager of the Glasgow Gas Works[20]—the city was lit by gas in 1818, and cheap gas supplies aided industrial expansion. The use of the hot blast enabled the local splint coal, of which vast quantities were available, to be used in the raw state and so overcame the disadvantage occasioned by the scarcity of good coking coals. At the time of the New Statistical Account (1835–1840) iron works were springing up rapidly in the richly endowed Monkland area, then the main centre of iron working in the country. In 1840, sixty-five out of eighty-eight blast furnaces in Scotland were in the parish of Old Monkland—a major cause being the abundance of Blackband iron ore in it and the neighbouring parishes of New Monkland and Bothwell. In Old Monkland parish the tonnage of pig iron produced rose from 3,600 in 1794 to 9,000 in 1806 and 177,000 in 1839.[21] By this time several railways, at first with horse-drawn wagons, had been built to connect collieries, ironstone mines, and ironworks with navigable waterways. The earliest were two short lines connecting local collieries with the Clyde (1785) and the Glasgow–Paisley Canal (about 1820). In 1826 a 10-mile long line connected the centre of the Monklands iron industry with the Forth and Clyde Canal at Kirkintilloch, and traffic on it increased so rapidly that horses were soon replaced by steam engines. It had branches to various collieries, and in 1828 a branch 6½ miles long with feeders was opened to run from Kipps, near Airdrie through the coal and iron mining area of New Monkland. In 1831 the Kirkintilloch–Monkland line was linked to the Monkland canal just north of Glasgow Cathedral by the Glasgow and Garnkirk Railway; in 1833 a line was constructed southwards to Wishaw and Coltness, thus promoting the development of the southern part of the iron-field; Govan and Rutherglen were connected with the Broomielaw; and in 1837 Paisley and Renfrew were joined by railway.[22] In 1834 some 1½ million passengers entered and left Glasgow by coaches, steam-boats, track-boats and railroads[23]—in 1812 Henry Bell's *Comet* had inaugurated the first regular steam-boat sailings on a navigable river in Europe between Glasgow, Greenock and Helensburgh.[24]

In 1837 the first iron sea-going ship was built on the Clyde,[25] and after the mid-forties shipbuilding developed rapidly, having the advantages of nearby resources and of the skills in metal working acquired during the previous half century. This in its turn stimulated further expansion of iron-smelting and of ironstone, coal and lime-stone mining. But cotton still retained a very important place in the Clyde economy. During the period 1815 to 1850 power loom weaving gradually replaced that of the hand loom, at first only for the coarser cloths, but later for the finer as well. After the cotton famine caused by the American Civil War (1861–1865) the industry was reduced substantially, though certain types of high-quality cloth and materials for industrial use are still made today; the thread industry, begun early in the eighteenth century, and now associated largely with the Coats firm, employs many thousands in Paisley and other places.

As the iron and engineering trades flourished in the mid-nineteenth century, so the commerce of Glasgow rapidly increased; and several villages and tiny hamlets on the ironstone field, such as Coatbridge, Wishaw, and Motherwell, grew into towns with engineering works as well as blast furnaces; and coal, ironstone, and limestone mines dotted its countryside. Glasgow was linked to Ayr by railway in 1840, to Paisley, Greenock and Port Glasgow in 1841, to Edinburgh in 1842, and to Carlisle in 1848. In that year rail links were also completed between the Clyde and Forth Basins and Perth, Forfar, and Aberdeen. In the eighteen-fifties Glasgow was connected with Helensburgh and Balloch with a branch line from the latter to Stirling through the country east of Loch Lomond and the upper Forth Basin.[26] The railway boom added greatly to the demand for the products of the iron industry, and Glasgow became, and still is, an important centre of locomotive building.

Steel-making prospered after 1878, when the Gilchrist-Thomas method of eliminating phosphorus made it possible to use Scottish ores. Further stimulus came from the use of steel for shipbuilding: many yards were expanded and new ones were opened not only in Glasgow and Govan but also down the river at Renfrew, Dumbarton, Port Glasgow and Greenock. Some of the older yards were pressed for space and one of the largest Govan yards was transferred to a site on the north bank which had then 'neither house nor railway accommodation'. This was the beginning of Clydebank and in 1884 the American Singer Sewing Machine Company moved from the east end of Glasgow to a large new factory there.[27] Between 1881 and 1886 two-thirds of the tonnage produced in the United Kingdom was built or engined on the Clyde.[28] Many industries were introduced or expanded to equip ships, for shipbuilding is a vast assembly industry,

X

whose requirements cover not only coal, steel plates, engines, steering gear and nautical instruments, but also electrical fittings, sanitary ware, furniture, upholstery, bed and table linen, kitchen equipment, cutlery and crockery. Moreover Clydeside became famed for civil as well as mechanical engineering, and other industries grew, many of which used imported raw materials. Glasgow Corporation began to develop electricity in 1892, and in 1901 the Clyde Valley Electric Power Company was founded, much to the benefit of the area.

The Clyde Trust Act of 1840 authorized deepening of the river to 17 ft. at neap tides and widening in its upper reaches, which were beginning to prove too narrow for the large vessels coming into use, and the construction of a wet dock to supplement the quayage. From 1862 hopper barges were employed to take the dredged material down to the Firth and deposit it in deep waters. Traffic was not sufficiently large to justify the construction of the wet dock until the sixties. In 1867 the one-basin Kingston dock ($5\frac{1}{3}$ acres) was opened on the south side, but the increase in traffic was so great during the two following decades that quays were extended on both sides of the river and in 1880 the two-basin Queen's dock (34 acres) was opened on the north side to be followed during the nineties by the three-basin Prince's dock (35 acres) on the south. By the turn of the century the export of coal and import of ores had reached such proportions that the Rothesay dock (20 acres), specially equipped for the efficient handling of minerals, was opened in 1907 at the east end of Clydebank.[29] The size of the ships coming to Glasgow increased steadily: both in 1860 and in 1900, there were some 16,000, but their tonnage increased from 1,449,000 to 4,362,000, and meanwhile the ships registered at Glasgow increased from 660, of 212,000 tons, in 1860 to 1605, of 1,582,000 tons, in 1900. In 1904, the revenue of the Clyde Navigation Trust was over £500,000.[30]

By 1870 a close network of railways had been built in the Clyde–Forth region, with the lines from Glasgow to Edinburgh via Holytown, Shotts, and West Calder and via Coatbridge, Airdrie, and Bathgate completed during the preceding decade, as well as the inland route from Paisley via Kilmacolm to Greenock and Wemyss Bay, where connexions could be made with Clyde steamers which also sailed from Gourock and Craigendoran, and the route north to Aberfoyle by Kirtintilloch and Strathblane. During the eighteen-seventies Glasgow was linked directly to Kilmarnock via Barrhead and the Loch Libo gap, and in the nineties the West Highland line was built from Glasgow via Helensburgh to Fort William, and later extended to Mallaig where it connected with steamers to the Western Isles. In the early years of this century an additional line was built between Paisley and Ayrshire through the Lochwinnoch gap.[31] An underground railway built in 1896 in the western half of Glasgow did not become really popular or financially successful until electrified by the Corporation in 1935.[32] With the development of the railways traffic on the canals dwindled, later to reach vanishing point as motor transport became widespread. Up to 1918 Port Dundas remained an important harbour, but traffic even on the main Forth and Clyde Canal is now very limited.[33] Parts of the Paisley–Johnstone and the Monkland canals have been filled in; indeed most of the bed of the former was used decades ago for a railway.

Developments in trade and industry brought with them a great increase in population, and the urban area increased rapidly on the coalfield and on both sides of the river. For some decades means of local transport for those of lower income were practically non-existent, and the practice arose of housing the large number of industrial workers in tenements, generally of four storeys, close to, and in some cases surrounding, the factories and works. To serve the growing urban areas west of Glasgow the Clyde Trust started in 1884 a service of small passenger steamers called *Cluthas*, each carrying from 230 to 360 passengers, between the city and Whiteinch about 3 miles downriver with intermediate stopping places. In 1900 they carried almost 3 million passengers, but by 1903 they had been withdrawn as they had been superseded by the system of electric tramways introduced by Glasgow Corporation in 1902 on the main roads of the city and the surrounding country both north and south of the Clyde. (The Corporation had bought out a limited system of horse-drawn tramways from a private company in 1894.[34]) This change was soon followed by a rapid expansion of the built-up area associated with the city. The most usual type of housing built during the late nineteenth and early twentieth centuries in Glasgow and the adjacent industrial burghs and even some of what were then industrial villages was the four-storey tenement solidly and soundly constructed of white, yellow, or red sandstone; but there was an enormous range in population density, amenities, and condition, from the over-crowded, one or two-roomed houses in narrow streets, often with overbuilt backlands and few, if any, open spaces, to the seven- or eight-roomed flats in more spacious streets. Tramways enabled many of the more fortunate to settle in peripheral areas, especially in the northwest and southwest in much lower density terrace houses or detached or semi-detached villas. Decades before this the railways permitted the growth of dormitory towns or villages, such as Helensburgh and Kilmacolm, while some of the most successful merchants and captains of industry built mansion-houses close to the Gareloch and Loch Lomond, and travelled in their own carriages to the nearest railway stations.

Glasgow's site made the extension of industry, railways, and housing difficult. Once the river terraces and raised beaches had been largely occupied, the railways and large industrial premises were crowded into the intervening flat spaces between drumlins. These steep-sided hills, many of which have rock cores, were left to the house builders. The heavy four-storey tenements and the gridiron street pattern, then in vogue, were ill suited to such sites, and some very steep streets were constructed: even in the heart of the city of today there are a few too steep for vehicles. Thus in Glasgow the topography accentuated the tendency to mixed industrial and residential development that characterized nineteenth-century industrialism.

The disturbances brought by the 1914–1918 war at a time when the Blackband ore had been practically exhausted and the coalfield had just passed its zenith were followed by the world depression of the thirties in which Clydeside by the nature of its basic industries and their wide ramifications was very badly hit. In the short intervening interval dock accommodation was increased by the opening of the King George V dock in 1931 with a depth of 44 ft. at high water in open country on the western outskirts of Govan, just beyond the large Shieldhall factory area of the Scottish Co-operative Wholesale Society: until 1925 the largest ocean-going ships could sail into the heart of the city. Several electric power stations were built, and

---

FIG. 63. A comparison of these maps brings out the remarkable increase in the number and size of urban settlements on Clydeside, a process which had already been marked, especially in and west of Glasgow, for half-a-century before 1835.

Based on the *New Statistical Account of Scotland* (1835), Vols. 6, 7 and 8. Published in 1845.

Census of Scotland 1861. Report and Population Tables.

Census of Scotland 1951. Vol. I for cities and burghs. Vol. II for population of towns and larger villages (excluding burghs).

Use has also been made of Bartholomew's *Post Office Maps* of various dates.

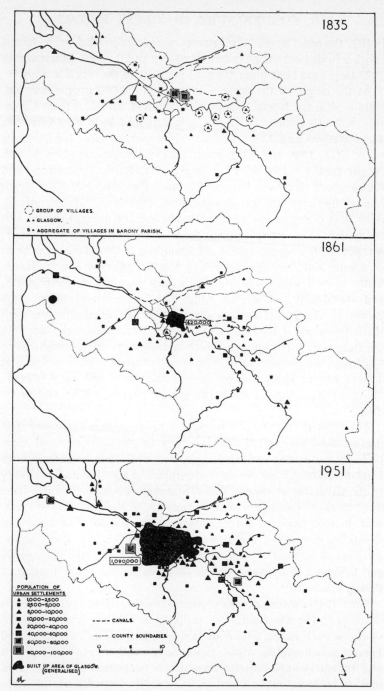

FIG. 63. Clydeside Expansion of Towns and Large Villages, 1835–1951

in 1927 the new George V bridge was completed just below the lowest existing bridge over the Clyde in the heart of Glasgow. Moreover, in 1929 the Clyde built more than 20 per cent of the world's ships.[35]

At the height of the depression in 1932, 38,000 people were unemployed in the North Lanarkshire coalfield, and 42,000 on Clydeside, with percentages of 53 in Clydebank and 46 in Port Glasgow, 44 in Wishaw and 43 in Airdrie.[36] The average rates for the three years 1932, 1936 and 1939 were: coalfield towns between 30 and 38 per cent, Clydebank, 27, Glasgow, 21, Paisley, Johnstone and Kirkintilloch between 16 and 17, and Renfrew, 8.[37] The North Lanarkshire coalfield was designated a 'Distressed'—later 'Special' Area, but Glasgow, owing to its lower rate of unemployment and the variety of its activities or to the possible damage to its prestige, was not. By this time the effects of a hundred years of feverish activity in mining and smelting had left in North Lanarkshire a landscape badly scarred with tip-heaps, water-filled quarries, rushy pastures, and abandoned and derelict mines and factories—an effect which proved in the thirties to be a severe handicap when attempts were made to induce industrialists to build new factories there. By 1936 the Industrial Estates policy, which has since proved so beneficial to Clydeside, was initiated with two small estates on the coalfield and a large one at Hillington on one of the best farms on Clydeside about a mile southeast of Renfrew and near the King George V dock.

The 1939-1945 war again brought a stress on heavy industry, and during these years Clydeside was very active as a port and ship-building, converting and repairing centre, while firms evacuated from England learned from personal experience of the skill and reliability of the Clydeside workers; others from America and elsewhere have done so since. During the war the airports of Renfrew and of Prestwick in mid-Ayrshire were enlarged, and they are now busy and expanding terminals, the latter being important for transatlantic services. A number of improvements were made for the movement, and loading and unloading of ships, including the rehabilitation of Paisley Harbour.[38]

Since 1945 a renewed spirit of vitality, optimism and enterprise has developed. The Distribution of Industry Act (1945), which included Glasgow itself in the Clydeside 'Development Area', the Industrial Estates policy, and the work of the Scottish Council (Development and Industry) have brought several new industries, especially light ones suitable for women and girls. In north Lanarkshire the addi-

tional problems brought by the impending exhaustion of the coalfield, except in the northwest and a few places in the east, have to be
faced. In the central part, which was the hub of nineteenth-century
mining, a working colliery will soon be a rarity. In spite of new developments in Lanarkshire there is apprehension that work for able-
bodied men will be insufficient when the collieries close down, but
current and potential developments may fill the gap. The most
notable and key project in hand is the £20m. integrated iron and
steel plant being built at Ravenscraig on the southeast outskirts of
Motherwell. This and other developments in the iron and steel
industry and in heavy engineering will ensure the continuance of the
traditional heavy industries along with the newer light ones on the
Industrial Estates, of which there are now seven in the county, thus
giving this part of the conurbation something of the variety in
manufactures that Glasgow itself has long possessed.[39] Furthermore
the old advantages of position for the import of raw materials and
the export of manufactured products still survives, and Clydeside is
the iron, steel, and heavy engineering region of Europe nearest to the
new ironfields being opened up in Labrador, from which the first
cargo of ore has already arrived. Quays in Glasgow harbour are
being modernized for general purposes and for handling cargoes of
ore quickly and efficiently, and Lanark County Council has just
completed the big Daer scheme for new water supplies of 14 million
gallons per day from the Upper Clyde.[40]

As in other conurbations and large cities traffic congestion is
acute, especially in the centre of Glasgow, partly due to the lack of
any road bridge below the centre of the city, the absence of easy
by-pass roads, and the unco-ordinated nature of the railway development, with four main passenger stations and no convenient public
transport links between them. An agreement was recently reached
between Glasgow Corporation and the British Transport Commission for the electrification and rationalization of lines in the city and
surrounding country, partly to induce commuters to travel by rail
rather than bus, with buses providing feeder services to the trains.
The start on the Whiteinch road tunnel under the Clyde about 5 miles
west of the city centre, suggested in the Regional Plan, has been subjected to numerous delays.

Population

The commercial, industrial, and transport developments on Clydeside in the eighteenth and nineteenth centuries were accompanied by

an enormous increase in population derived largely by immigration, but also in the mid- and late-nineteenth century from a big natural increase. The total population increased from 62,600 in 1755 to over 1¾ million in 1951, but the rate of growth varied at different times and in different parts of the conurbation. A comparison of Dr. Webster's Census of 1755[41] and the data given in the *Old Statistical Accounts* shows that the population of the conurbation had doubled between 1755 and the early seventeen-nineties: by 1801 a further 34,000 had been added. Thereafter decennial rates of increase of about 30 per cent brought the population to 350,000 by 1831. In the following decade of big industrial expansion numbers increased by 117,000, giving 1831–1841 the maximum decennial increase rate of 33 per cent. The mid-century increase was less rapid, the average decennial rate being about 20 per cent, but by 1881 the population had risen to 990,000. With the great developments of the steel period the next decade saw the greatest ever growth in numbers, namely 239,000, but the rate of increase was only 24 per cent compared with 33 per cent between 1831 and 1841. The decades 1891 to 1901 and 1901 to 1911 also saw substantial increases, but at the lower rates of 16 and 11 per cent, giving by 1911 a total population of 1,580,000. Subsequent increases have been relatively small—approximately + 3½ per cent for each of the two decades 1911 to 1921 and 1921 to 1931, and + 4½ per cent for the twenty-year period 1931–1951; giving totals of 1,640,000 in 1921, 1,690,000 in 1931, and 1,758,000 in 1951. Though there was an addition of 68,000 to the conurbation between 1931 and 1951, an area comprising the counties of Glasgow, Lanark, Renfrew, and Dunbarton together, six-sevenths of whose population is included in it, did not absorb all its natural increase. It lost about 170,000 by migration, of whom probably some 7,000 settled in the counties of Ayr, Bute and Argyll, presumably mainly on retirement. Renfrew and Dunbarton showed small net gains by migration, but Lanark lost 50,000 and Glasgow 122,000. It should be noted, however, that the natural increase rate in Lanark was high (+ 17·5 per cent) for the twenty-year period compared with a Scottish average of + 10·4 per cent and in the other counties fairly high (Renfrew, + 13·6 per cent, Dunbarton, + 12·6 per cent, and Glasgow, + 12·3 per cent).

The following table summarizes the population position. It indicates the magnitude of the changes in the last four half-centuries, and the substantial falling off in the rate of increase during the first half of the twentieth century.

TABLE 7

POPULATION OF THE CENTRAL CLYDESIDE CONURBATION: FIFTY-YEAR
CHANGES

Year	No. to nearest thousand)		Increase	
			No.	%
1755	63,000	—	—	—
1801	160,000	1755–1801	97,000	154
1851	569,000	1801–1851	409,000	253
1901	1,424,000	1851–1901	855,000	152
1951	1,760,000	1901–1951	344,000	24

The total increase between 1801 and 1951 was 1,608,000, showing
a tenfold growth. The writers of the *Clyde Valley Regional Plan*
believe that the lower Clyde Basin is super-saturated with people and
recommend that some 100,000 of them with the necessary employment should go to other parts of Scotland.[42]

Glasgow had 4,500 inhabitants at the time of the Reformation (an
estimate), 15,000 in 1660, but only 12,000 in 1688.[43] The post-
Restoration loss was not made up until the second decade of the
eighteenth century. Thereafter growth was steady for some sixty
years, and then between 1780 and 1801 the population doubled as
communications improved and trade and cotton manufacturing expanded rapidly. By 1801, over half the population of what is now the
conurbation area lived in Glasgow. Most of this growth took place
on the north side, in and around the Royal Burgh. Gorbals, a hamlet
at the south end of Glasgow Bridge, had only 500 people in 1771 and
800 in 1793; but by 1831, it had 27,000 and by 1851, over 60,000.
Decennial increase rates in the south side parishes of Govan and
Gorbals were 50–60 per cent between 1801 and 1831 and 45–48 per
cent between 1851 and 1881. The whole city and suburbs had a
population of a quarter of a million by the late eighteen-thirties, half
a million by the late eighteen-sixties, three-quarters of a million by
1900, and a million by 1921. Since then there has been redistribution
rather than increase, for decline in central wards has been compensated by increases in the suburbs. Earlier peripheral growth had
justified boundary extensions, notably that of 1912, when the areas
annexed included the police burghs of Govan (89,000), Partick
(69,000) and Pollokshaws (13,000): of these, the first had grown from

a large village and the others from hamlets associated with water-driven mills. The decreases in central wards and increases in the outer wards are by no means a new phenomenon: for example as early as 1841–1851 St. Enoch's Ward lost 800 people (— 10 per cent) due to 'the conversion of dwellings to places of business'; the 1911 Census records that Blythswood ward had declined by 29 per cent, Exchange by 24 per cent, and Broomielaw by 21 per cent, and that there were big increases in outer wards and 'a large and striking increase' (20 per cent) of population in the burghs and parishes immediately round the city, a dispersion made possible by tramway services. Ward re-arrangement unfortunately makes it impossible to give figures illustrating the changes over a long period in different parts of the city as business premises replaced dwelling houses, slums were demolished, and people moved to suburbs.

In the Lanarkshire part of the conurbation, increases in the late eighteenth and early nineteenth century were considerable, largely due to the work available in cotton manufacturing and coalmining, stimulated by the opening of the Monkland Canal, but between 1831 and 1841 the development of the iron industry led to a spectacular increase from 48,000 to 80,000 (66 per cent). In Old Monkland

the population . . . is advancing at an amazing rate . . . New villages are springing up almost every month, and it is quite impossible to keep pace with the march of prosperity and the increase of population.[44]

After a period of slower increases to 1871, the decennial increase rate rose to 45 per cent to give 175,000 people by 1881; and thereafter the population almost doubled by 1911, to 343,000. By this time Coatbridge had 43,000 inhabitants, Motherwell, 40,000, Wishaw, 25,000, Airdrie, 24,000 and Hamilton, 39,000, while Old Monkland parish had 61,000 compared with 4,000 in 1801. But the period of heavy increase ended with the 1914–1918 war, and between 1921 and 1931 this area had an increase of only 0·8 per cent, with Motherwell–Wishaw declining from 69,000 to 65,000. Between 1931 and 1951 the rate of increase rose to 8 per cent to bring the total population almost to 400,000 with 68,000 in Motherwell–Wishaw.

East Renfrewshire's population increased mainly in three periods. In the late eighteenth and early nineteenth century several cotton manufacturing and printing and bleaching centres developed. These included the new town of Johnstone and the old abbey town of Paisley, by 1830 the third largest burgh in Scotland. Slower rates of increase were recorded between 1831 and 1871 when the second major phase of expansion began. This was associated with developments in thread manufacture (which offset the decline in other cotton trades), engineering, carpet-making, shipbuilding, and other industries such as sanitary ware manufacture at Barrhead and boilermaking at Renfrew. By 1911, there were 228,000 people in this area of whom 110,000 were in Paisley. The burgh of Renfrew increased from 9,000 in 1891 to 27,000 in 1911, and suburban expansion from Glasgow affected such places as Pollokshields, Cathcart, and Scotstoun, all eventually absorbed by the city. The third phase raised the population of East Renfrewshire from 232,000 in 1921 to 390,000 in 1951 (1931–1951, 43 per cent increase). It was due partly to developments in Paisley, Johnstone and Renfrew, but primarily to a great expansion of residential areas associated with Glasgow. This affected the parishes of Paisley (13 per cent) and Renfrew (14 per cent) themselves, as well as those of Cathcart (151 per cent) and Eastwood (140 per cent), where suburbs were already established before 1914, and the higher parishes of Mearns (93 per cent) and Eaglesham (50 per cent), the latter with new houses added to an attractive old-world village, the former with a new high-amenity suburb and a large new hospital.

East Dunbartonshire showed three similar phases of marked population growth, the first reaching its peak between 1821 and 1841, when cotton manufacturing and the Forth–Clyde canal were in their heyday: increases of 28 and 37 per cent gave a population of 10,000 in 1841 (two-thirds in Kirkintilloch). A period of stability followed until spectacular increases set in from 1871 to 1911 (34, 68, 45 and 57 per cent), largely due to the removal of shipyards and other works from Glasgow and Govan to the new burgh of Clydebank, which had only 1,634 people in 1881, but 10,000 in 1891, 18,700 in 1901, 37,500 in 1911 and 46,500 in 1921. The main industrial expansion came before the 1914–1918 war, and the third phase due to residential growth overlapped it after the tramway extensions of the early twentieth century. It was greatly accelerated after 1921, with the population increasing from 72,000 in 1921 to 87,000 in 1931 (+ 22 per cent) and 114,400 in 1951 (+ 30 per cent in twenty years).

Administrative Units

In the eighteenth century there were within the conurbation area three royal burghs, Glasgow, Rutherglen, and Renfrew, and four burghs of barony, Paisley, Hamilton (which had royal status from

1548 to 1670), Kirkintilloch and East Kilbride. Under the legislation of 1833 Paisley, Hamilton and Airdrie became three of the twelve new 'parliamentary burghs' having 'all the privileges of Royal Burghs', and later Coatbridge became a municipal burgh with similar privileges except parliamentary representation. The historic dominance of the parish in Scotland meant that as towns grew they were divided into urban parishes. In 1595, Glasgow was divided into the Royalty and the Barony because 'the population has so much increased that it is inconvenient for all the inhabitants to meet in one place'; and with growth after the mid-eighteenth century the number of parishes was increased to eight by 1790, ten by 1821 and sixteen by 1851. In 1771, the built-up portion of Gorbals Barony became a separate parish, extended in 1821; and in the forties the parishes of Calton, Maryhill and Shettleston were formed from (Glasgow) Barony, with Springburn in 1854. Similar divisions gave the Abbey and three town parishes in Paisley. As their populations increased, numerous towns became police burghs, Motherwell, Wishaw, Johnstone and Kirkintilloch by 1871, Milngavie by 1881, Clydebank by 1891, and Barrhead by 1901. Others that grew up in the immediate neighbourhood of Glasgow were later annexed to the city—Crosshill, Govanhill, Maryhill, Hillhead and Pollokshields, all annexed in 1891, Kinning Park in 1905 and Govan, Partick and Pollokshaws in 1912.

FIG. 64. The small eighteenth-century town and its *immediate environs* on the west form the hub of the modern city, which has expanded over a large area during the last seventy years. The historic past of Rutherglen has given it a claim against incorporation.

Based on:

(*a*) *Scot. Geogr. Mag.*, 37, No. 1 (Glasgow number).

(*b*) *Statistical Accounts of Scotland, Old and New.*

(*c*) *Parliamentary and Municipal Map of the City of Glasgow.* H. Wilson, 1848.

(*d*) 1st edition O.S. 25 in. to 1 mile.

(*e*) Marwick, J. D., *The River Clyde and its Burghs.* Abstracts of Charters and Documents relating to the City of Glasgow (1833–1872). Renwick (1908).

(*f*) Bartholomew's *Pocket Plan of Glasgow* constructed for the Post Office Directory 1925 and 1951.

(*g*) Plan of Glasgow 1901—Bacon.

(*h*) *Map of the County of the City of Glasgow as divided into municipal wards.* A. B. McDonald 1912. Published by J. Bartholomew.

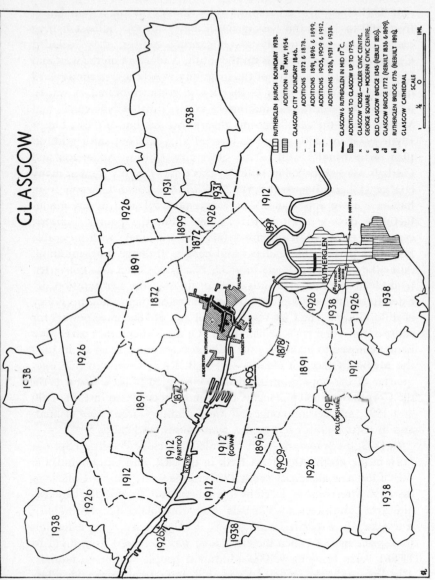

GLASGOW

RUTHERGLEN BURGH BOUNDARY 1938.
ADDITION 16TH MAY, 1954
GLASGOW CITY BOUNDARY 1846.
ADDITIONS 1872 & 1878.
ADDITIONS 1891, 1896 & 1899.
ADDITIONS 1905, 1909 & 1912.
ADDITIONS 1926, 1931 & 1938.

GLASGOW & RUTHERGLEN IN MID 17TH C.
ADDITIONS TO GLASGOW UP TO 1795.
GLASGOW CROSS — OLDER CIVIC CENTRE.
GEORGE SQUARE ~ MODERN CIVIC CENTRE.
OLD GLASGOW BRIDGE 1345 (REBUILT 1851).
GLASGOW BRIDGE 1772 (REBUILT 1836 & 1899).
RUTHERGLEN BRIDGE 1776 (REBUILT 1896).
GLASGOW CATHEDRAL

SCALE

FIG. 64. THE EXTENSION OF GLASGOW

The Growth of Glasgow

In 1791 Glasgow was surrounded by villages varying in population from 900 to 7,000 and having in all 20,000 people, almost half as many as the city; mostly manufacturing centres, they included Calton on the east, Gorbals on the south, Anderston on the west and Cowcaddens on the north of the inner city.[45] All these occur as ward names, and other villages farther away, commemorated as wards, included Woodside, near the branch of the Forth–Clyde canal, and Shettleston in the east. The first absorption was not of these, but of Blythswood in 1830, a new residential area laid out on a gridiron plan on a drumlin west of the older city. Calton, Anderston and Gorbals were absorbed in 1846. By this time Glasgow showed many contrasts. According to the *New Statistical Account* 'Glasgow from having a mean appearance is now the most splendid of any manufacturing city or town in the Empire'; but the poorer quarters, especially in the old city had wynds (narrow lanes) with miserable houses in narrow, filthy closes and neither drainage nor sanitation. After the cholera epidemic in 1832, Glasgow Green was converted from an ill-drained area into a park: in 1846 the Corporation decided to buy the worst properties and demolish them; and this policy is still followed. The City Improvement Act of 1866 gave powers for some of the worst parts to be rebuilt at a time when other parts were being removed to make way for railway extensions. Even so, in 1880 the Medical Officer of Health, Dr. J. B. Russell, showed that one-quarter of the population lived in one-roomed houses. From 1888, the Corporation had tenements built under acts passed in 1881, 1890 and 1897, and certain congested and insanitary areas were cleared, and in parts used for tenements, warehouses, and shops.[46, 47]

In 1872, the boundaries were extended to include Possil and Springburn in the north, Alexandra Park in the east, and Gilmorehill, the site of the new university (built 1879) in the west; the old College in the High Street was replaced by a goods station. In 1878 the Coplawhill area southwest of Gorbals was absorbed; like Springburn it was largely associated with railway developments. A big extension took place in 1891 when the city's area was increased from 6,111 to 11,861 acres bringing 93,000 additional people within its bounds. The areas annexed included Govanhill, both residential and industrial, Crosshill and Langside, both residential, Pollokshields, 'superior' residential, Hillhead, residential close to the University, and Maryhill, primarily industrial. Bellahouston, a residential area south of Govan, was added in 1896, Blackhill in the northeast in 1899, and Kinning Park, a police burgh containing Princes Dock and streets of tenements on the south side of the river between Gorbals and Govan, in 1905. Under the Local Government (Scotland) Act of 1889 the whole of Glasgow was included in Lanarkshire, and subsequent city annexations from Renfrewshire and Dunbartonshire transferred to that county.

In 1912 a further area of 6,000 acres (9½ square miles) with 224,000 people was added. It included docks and shipyards on both sides of the river, the burghs of Partick, Govan, and Pollokshaws all of which were industrial and residential, and the district of Cathcart. On the east, the inclusion of Tollcross and Shettleston added an area where recently-built houses surrounded earlier manufacturing villages. It is worth noting, however, that Glasgow has not so far absorbed any burgh of ancient foundation: Rutherglen remains apart in local government. During the first decade of the twentieth century the building industry ceased to find the construction of houses for letting a profitable investment, at first those for lower income groups and soon thereafter those of any type.[48] By 1919 the problem of congestion was so severe that the Corporation embarked on extensive house building projects, and in the twenties and thirties the speculative builder covered large areas on the city's outskirts with houses for sale, areas beyond the boundary being popular partly because the rates were much lower than in the city. The next extension of the city, in 1926, differed from that of 1912 in that the area acquired was largely open country, though it included some shipyards and factories: it covered 10,105 acres with 17,353 residents (see Fig. 64).

Two further extensions, in 1931 and 1938, gave Glasgow an area of 60 square miles: of these the first addition was small, but the later one foreshadowed the big development of suburbs on the east, north, west, and south that has taken place since 1945. In that year there was still a huge problem created by overcrowding—some 700,000 people still lived in 3 square miles in the centre at net densities up to 700 per acre and an average gross density of nearly 400 per acre.[49] It was estimated that the overspill from central development would be about 530,000, i.e. half the city's population, and of these 250,000 could be accommodated in what was considered desirable development on the periphery, leaving an overspill of 300,000 to be housed beyond the city boundary.[50] In the 10,000 acres, with a 1931 population of 5,000, added in the nineteen-thirties, modern housing has taken a variety of forms. Between 1920 and 1940 the Corporation generally built three-storey blocks of flats, set back a few yards from the pavement, on the margins of the older built-up areas, and two-storey blocks of four flats each, with gardens, in certain peripheral areas. The speculative builder's bungalows and semi-detached villas did much to fuse one place with another between the wars, and since 1945 the Corporation, which now has its own building staff, has colonized areas more and more distant from the city centre. After a short period of building 'pre-fabs' and two-storey blocks similar to those of the thirties, they have concentrated mainly on two-storey terraces and three- and four-storey blocks of flats. These have the traditional Scottish straight gable-end and usually brighter-coloured paint, roughcast, and curtains than before 1939. The flats—and many Glasgow people like living in flats (as in continental cities)— generally have balconies, and both flats and terrace houses have small gardens, many of which show signs of care and attention. Experiments have been made with a few very narrow, high (about nine-storey) block of flats. One curious result of the different phases of building during the last century is that one passes from central city areas with very high densities through intermediate zones of lower and decreasing densities and then comes suddenly to outer districts of Corporation-built flats having up to 120 persons to the acre net.[51]

Other burghs of the conurbation also had big problems of over-crowding and unsatisfactory housing, and all were extended in area between 1931 and 1951, mostly from 1935 to 1938 and 1946 to 1949. Their combined area was increased by 11,725 acres. Johnstone and Milngavie were increased three-fold, Paisley and Motherwell–Wishaw by four-fifths, and Clydebank by two-fifths. On the coalfield, new houses are steadily replacing drab rows of small stone or brick houses: the general effect is to improve a landscape that has already benefited by some clearing-up of unsightly derelict ground. It seems that the needs of all the burghs except Rutherglen can be met by building in directions away from the city or from closely adjacent burghs, but that Glasgow cannot house all its people within or close to its own boundaries, if some at least of the remaining agricultural land (in places very productive) is to be preserved, if valuable coking coals are not to be sterilized by over-building, and if the creation of one huge amorphous urban sprawl within this hill and moorland girt basin is to be avoided.

The Clyde Valley Regional Plan envisaged the preservation of a

Green Belt within the basin, largely of dairying and market garden land, and the grouping of new houses round existing towns and selected villages and in certain wedges round the edge of Glasgow. Though there has since been some encroachment on the Green Belt, particularly between Glasgow and Clydebank, the project still stands, and the City of Glasgow Plan (approved in 1954) ensures that a belt of agricultural land is preserved between the City and Coatbridge and an enclave of such land between Glasgow, Paisley and Barrhead.[52, 53] The suburban housing schemes are almost all completed or under way and the Corporation is now proceeding to the rebuilding of 111 acres in Gorbals and Hutchesontown to house about 10,000 people at a net density of 164 per acre (1951 population 27,000). This area will have both low terraces and blocks of flats many of ten or more storeys, arranged on a carefully designed plan with modern amenities for both domestic and community life.[54] Thus the Glasgow of the future, like that of the late nineteenth century, will resemble many continental cities, like Stockholm, Paris, and Vienna, rather than the cities of England. Meanwhile the new town of East Kilbride, which also includes three- and four-storey flats as well as two-storey terraces and some cottages, is growing and that of Cumbernauld beginning. Although no definite agreements with other local authorities to take Glasgow overspill have been announced, the County plans for Lanark and Renfrew are understood to make provision for it.[55]

The reconstitution of the Clyde Valley Regional Planning Advisory Committee is an important recognition of the interdependence of the several parts of the conurbation, and perhaps of its unity. Moreover the recent agreement between Glasgow Corporation and the British Transport Commission for the rationalization, electrification, and improvement of the railway system is a highly significant step towards increasing the efficiency and human welfare of a region where much travel to work seems inevitable in view of the 'immobility' of so many of its economic activities.

Besides its one major nucleus in Glasgow, Clydeside has many other nuclei with active local life of their own. Both in wholesale and retail trade, Glasgow is supreme. It has 53 per cent of all the wholesale trade in Scotland, five times as much as Edinburgh or Dundee and ten times as much as Aberdeen. Its wholesale trade is valued at £420m., compared with £5,600,000 in Paisley, and less than £2m. in Motherwell–Wishaw. The retail trade of the city is valued at £150m., three-quarters of that for the city and all the burghs of the

Y

conurbation, and one-quarter of that for the whole of Scotland: the average sales are £138 per head, £20 over the national (Scots) average. The only other burgh with sales of over £10m. is Paisley (£12m.), which, like the old centre of Hamilton, has per capita sales of £124–£125. Of the other burghs, on the whole the larger have greater sales per head than the smaller, the older than the newer, and the more remote from Glasgow and Paisley more than those close to them. Thus in Motherwell–Wishaw sales are valued at £109 per head, in Airdrie and Kirkintilloch at £108, while those in Johnstone realize only £79 and in Milngavie £61. The other burghs have values between £80 and £100, and here perhaps it is worth noting that the small residential and dormitory burgh of Helensburgh, outside the conurbation, but intimately connected with it economically, has sales worth £172 per head as well as one of the lowest urban population densities in Scotland.

Land Use

Generally speaking, as the Clyde Basin has become urbanized, docks, shipyards, industries, and to a lesser extent communications have had first pick of suitable sites, with housing taking second choice, and agriculture having what was left over. Since the beginning of factory production, industrial location has been strongly influenced by topography and communications. Though water is no longer a factor so far as power is concerned, some industrial settlements, such as Pollokshaws, and some existing works, like the older meal and flour mills in Partick and Paisley, had their origin where local water power could be harnessed, while the presence of pure water is important in the location of the printing, bleaching and dyeing works in east Renfrewshire. The large supplies of cooling water available from the Clyde are a key factor in the siting of many undertakings, such as the power stations at Cambuslang, Dalmarnock, Yoker and Braehead.

The river banks from Glasgow Bridge to Clydebank (or more accurately Bowling) are lined with docks and shipbuilding yards as well as industrial establishments closely related to imports, such as timber yards, flourmills, animal feeding stuffs and fertilizer works. The most recent docks, the power station, sewage disposal works, and riverside industries are in the stretch between Govan and Renfrew, where the Clyde Navigation Trust possesses land for further quayage and two additional docks; Glasgow's airport is situated on flat alluvial land southeast of Renfrew, and east of it is the large

Hillington Industrial Estate with over 150 firms in close proximity to the King George V dock. The only extensive area of flat or nearly flat land left to agriculture west of the city lies partly within the conurbation on raised beach and carse land west of Renfrew. The Clyde Valley Plan proposal to build a new town at Bishopton, some 4 miles west of Renfrew, for overspill from Glasgow and Greenock was rejected on account of the high agricultural value of the land. Fig. 60 shows the distribution of the main types of land use within the conurbation, subject to severe limitations set by smallness of scale.

Within the city, warehouses are found mainly in two areas, one near the quays and upper docks, and the other on flat land west of the High street where the fruit market and other wholesale premises are located. The main shopping and business centre lies immediately west of this and extends into the formerly largely residential zone of Blythswood, beyond which many of the Georgian houses in the terraces and crescents of the Park District have recently become offices for national and local government bodies and business concerns, nursing homes, hotels and hostels. Up-river from Glasgow the flat river terrace and raised beach sites have been used for industries and large public utility buildings. The Clyde Iron Works are linked over the river with the Clydebridge Steel Works on the south side into a large modernized integrated plant, while other steel works are situated farther east at Cambuslang. There are also chemical works, a paper mill, a ropeworks, as well as two thermal power stations and several sewage disposal works.

Flat raised beach and river terrace lands are also extensively used for marshalling yards. On the south side these are very large in the Port Eglinton and Polmadie areas, south of Gorbals and about threequarters of a mile from the Clyde, where they are associated with locomotive and other engineering works, and gas works and associated industries. On the north side analogous sites were largely built up before the railway era. The northern passenger stations were built on the edge of the mid-nineteenth-century city, but the railways penetrated to them with difficulty by tunnels, while extensive demolitions took place to enable large new stations to be built for railways from the south when bridges brought them over the Clyde. One of the goods stations immediately east of High street largely occupies the land of the older University, while extensive marshalling yards to the northeast of the older city make use of flat land between the drumlins, as do heavy engineering, gas and chemical works. A similar squeezing of railways and industry into the flat land between drumlins is seen in the case of the Hallside Steelworks and adjacent colliery and brickworks east of Cambuslang. Some of the heavy industry works, which have survived from pre-railway days, are situated on the Monkland canal (Blochairn Iron and St. Rollox Chemical Works), the Forth and Clyde canal, or in what was open country on the northern and southern fringes of the city in the mid-nineteenth century. The result of all this is to give a horse-shoe shaped belt containing numerous iron and steel, heavy engineering and chemical works stretching round the older city from south through east to northwest, where it culminates in an area of mar-shalling yards, engineering, gas and chemical works at Maryhill close by the main western lock stairway of the Forth and Clyde canal.

A variety of industries, such as distilling, the preparation of agri-cultural supplies, saw-milling, are located at Port Dundas and else-where along the Glasgow Branch of the canal, while on the main canal there are industries at Kirkintilloch (where new factories are mainly on flat land in the Kelvin valley), and at Netherton and Temple on the northwestern outskirts of Glasgow, west of Maryhill. The main textile manufactures are (1) in Paisley and Johnstone, which, like the other east Renfrewshire towns, have long had a variety of industries, thus rendering them in the nineteen-thirties less liable to unemployment than those of west Renfrewshire, Dun-bartonshire, or north Lanarkshire; and (2) in the east end of Glasgow in Calton and Bridgeton between the mediaeval town and the Clyde, north of Rutherglen—in this area of cotton factory settlements of the late eighteenth and early nineteenth-century industry and tenements are closely intermixed. From the south side of Paisley to Renfrew there is a narrow zone of industries on flat or gently sloping land beside the White Cart, and at the foot of the escarpment of the lava hills there are print and bleach works on the Levern and other streams. Several large works are situated in open country, or what was at the time of construction open country on the edge of the Renfrewshire burghs, notably the Ferguslie Thread and the Pressed Steel Mills at Paisley, the former originally served by the Glasgow–Paisley Canal, Shank's Sanitary Earthenware factory at Barr-head, and the large Elderslie carpet factory southeast of Johnstone. Within Glasgow industrial estates have recently been established at Cartyne and Queenslie in the eastern suburbs, Thornliebank in the extreme southwest, and North Cardonald (an extension of Hillington) and Craigton in the west. Hillington itself is in Renfrew-shire, just beyond the city boundary.

The pre-1914 residential areas of Glasgow were situated on certain of the flat raised beach and terrace lands adjacent to industries, shipyards and docks, and climbed up the slopes beyond them. Some of the drumlin tops have been left as open parks; some carry public buildings such as hospitals, the University, and the Teachers' Training College. In 1914 the continuously built-up area did not extend much beyond the White Cart in the south and the Glasgow branch of the Forth and Clyde canal in the north, though beyond the latter there were a number of works and railway yards with associated tenements. From about 3 miles below Glasgow Bridge urban development was largely limited to a narrow discontinuous belt on the south and to the raised beach on the north side. Since 1920 residential districts have spread over drumlin covered areas in almost every direction round the city, and in many cases the drumlins are capped by a large water tower to give sufficient head for the houses to be supplied.

Hospitals and similar institutions are a feature of the open country round Glasgow and Paisley; though some older ones are in the main built-up area. The agricultural land is chiefly devoted to intensive dairying with some cash-cropping, especially of potatoes and vegetables, and some market gardening on the lighter loams of the raised beaches and glacifluvial gravels; and much of it is highly productive. The moorlands are largely used as gathering grounds for water supplies and carry flocks of Blackface sheep.

Apart from some works on the south of Airdrie, some north of Coatbridge beside the earliest railways, and some in small villages or in open country, the main smelting, steel-making and heavy engineering works of the north Lanarkshire ironfield are in three areas of relatively flat land between the Clyde and the North and South Calder rivers. There are no works on the floor of the Clyde valley above the narrows at Bothwell, as a natural tendency to water-logging and flooding has been much accentuated by subsidence due to mining. The three relatively flat areas are: (1) north of the North Calder, the area now forming the south and west parts of Coatbridge burgh which lies at about 300 ft. and was traversed by the Monkland canal. The older associated residential areas are on rising ground to the north and on the slopes in the neighbouring burgh of Airdrie. (2) Between the North and South Calder waters an area at about 250 ft. associated with the large villages of Bellshill and Mossend. There are residential areas in these villages and in several small straggling settlements on rising ground to the east and southeast, while the west part of the interfluve overlooking the wooded Clyde gorge carries the late nineteenth-century residential village of Uddingston. To the northeast, at Tannochside there are new houses and industries, notably an American-owned caterpillar tractor works. Bothwell, to the south on the lip of the gorge, is still a residential village with an old castle and church. (3) The long narrow plateau between the South Calder and the Clyde rising gradually from 250 ft. north of Motherwell to 400 ft. south of Wishaw, on which the combined burgh grew up almost entirely within the last hundred and ten years. The new integrated coke oven, blast furnace, and steel rolling mill at Ravenscraig is being built on a partly derelict area between the present steel mills at the south end of Motherwell, which it is to supply, and the South Calder, the site being levelled by modern machinery. In Wishaw the residential areas are mainly on slopes rising to the northeast, in Motherwell on slopes on the southwest and northeast down towards the incised Clyde and South Calder valleys.

Some of the newer houses, which replace the poorer, overcrowded and often drab rows of one- and two-storey cottages of former days, have been built on higher ground towards the east and northeast as have the new industrial estates of Carfin, Chapelhall, and Newhouse, the largest in the county. Other industrial estates in Lanarkshire are at Coatbridge, Blantyre, a mining settlement now continuous with Hamilton, and the new town of East Kilbride. That in the new town of Cumbernauld will be in the detached eastern portion of Dunbartonshire. No doubt the presence of the steep sided incised valleys of the North and South Calder and the Clyde has been largely instrumental in preventing the growth of one huge amorphous urban sprawl in north Lanarkshire. The Clyde Valley Regional Plan recommends that the slopes of these and other valleys, where not built over, should be preserved as spines of woodland.

THE LESSER CONURBATIONS OF SCOTLAND

In Scotland only one of the six lesser conurbations has over 250,000 inhabitants, that is Edinburgh with 485,000. Aberdeen has 188,000 and Dundee 182,000. The three others are the Port Glasgow–Greenock–Gourock urban area with 107,000, Ayr–Prestwick with about 54,000, and the Falkirk–Grangemouth area with 53,000 in 1951, if only burghs are counted, but some 83,000, if adjacent villages are included. Together these areas account for 1,100,000 people. They are difficult to classify satisfactorily as nearly all have many functions.

Edinburgh, as the capital city, stands in a category by itself; in addition to its administrative, legal, medical, educational, financial, distributive and social functions, it has long been a strong agricultural market, its port at Leith is the third in the country, and its significance as an industrial centre is growing. It is also a favourite place with tourists and retired people. Aberdeen and Ayr are also Royal Burghs and old regional centres, agricultural markets, and ports, with a variety of industries, and they are popular with holiday makers and retired people. Dundee and Greenock–Port Glasgow are primarily ports and manufacturing centres, while Falkirk–Grangemouth is mainly industrial with both older and rapidly developing newer manufactures. None of the conurbations is now increasing heavily in population, though Ayr–Prestwick added 13 per cent. from 1931 to 1951 (Prestwick burgh, + 33 per cent) and Grangemouth burgh gained by 26 per cent in the same twenty years. The Dundee and the Greenock–Port Glasgow conurbations are virtually stable in numbers.

Aberdeen alone of the conurbations is outside the Central Lowlands, and all the rest except Dundee are within the Clyde–Forth basin. The lesser conurbations with Clydeside include most of the major mining and industrial areas and all the major ports. Yet Scottish industrial areas outside these conurbations include the expanding Fife coalfield, the manufacturing towns of Central Stirlingshire and Clackmannan, West Lothian, and the central part of the Midlothian coal basin, the numerous small manufacturing towns in North Fife, Angus and East Perthshire, the Border textile towns, and a number of individual centres with important expanding industries, the largest of which are Perth and Dumfries.

Kirkcaldy and Dunfermline grew rapidly between 1931 and 1951, by 9½ and 27½ per cent respectively, and had almost reached the 50,000 mark by 1951—Kirkcaldy, 49,000, Dunfermline, 45,000. Together with neighbouring ports and coalfield and manufacturing burghs and villages they each form part of loosely-knit urban groups with some 100,000 people.[56] Similarly the urban settlements of the Inner Forth Lowlands may be considered as a fairly loose constellation of towns and villages with northern and southern foci in Stirling and Alloa and Falkirk–Grangemouth respectively, with a total urban population of some 170,000 people. In North Ayrshire there are almost 60,000 people in the urbanized industrialized coastal triangle with apices at the ancient port and Royal Burgh of Irvine, at inland Kilwinning, and at the modern port and holiday resort of Ardrossan

–Saltcoats (burghs whose population increased by one-quarter from 1931 to 1951), and with a very large chemical industry; and another 60,000 inland in the string of manufacturing towns and villages along the Irvine valley. By far the largest of these is Kilmarnock, the main inland regional centre, market and manufacturing town of Ayrshire with a population increase of + 9 per cent between 1931 and 1951. Exclusive of adjacent villages it had reached 42,000 by 1951, and, if the suggestions in the Clyde Valley Regional Plan for further industrial development and reception of Glasgow overspill are implemented, it may soon reach the 60,000 projected therein.

At the 1951 Census, 38·8 per cent of the population of Scotland lived in the four counties of cities (Glasgow, Edinburgh, Aberdeen, Dundee), 16 per cent in the twenty large burghs (with over 20,000 inhabitants), 15·3 per cent in 172 small burghs and 13·3 per cent in 225 villages of 1,000 inhabitants or more: 16·6 per cent in the 'rural' areas. Though some two-fifths of the people of Scotland dwell in the four counties of cities, the relative importance of small and fairly small urban centres is also a notable feature of Scottish life. Included among them, but excluded from the conurbations, defined as single or contiguous towns having at least 50,000 people, are several of the major trading burghs such as Perth (40,500, increase 1931–1951, 15 per cent), Stirling (27,000, + 10 per cent), Dumfries (26,000, + 14 per cent), and Inverness (28,000, + 19 per cent), the only town with over 11,000 people in the Highlands.

Edinburgh

The Royal Burgh of Edinburgh was founded in the mid-twelfth century on the mile-long ridge running eastward from the Castle Hill towards the Abbey of Holyrood. By the mid-fourteenth century it had expanded southwards on to a neighbouring ridge, and by the mid-fifteenth it had become the capital with a consequent increase in population. With fear prevalent from the late thirteenth century onwards as a result of the destruction caused by periodic invasions, increased population was accommodated by building both upwards and on top of the cultivated plots behind the older houses. Thus a tradition of overcrowded living conditions developed with tenements, eventually of five, six and even up to twelve storeys, and the citizens lived within the wall of 1513 until the mid-eighteenth century. The city lost status, influence, and wealth when the Court moved to London in 1603, and again when the Scots Parliament was prorogued in 1707.

By 1750 building began to spread outside the walls on the southeast, and in the sixties a bold scheme for draining and bridging the Nor Loch (a narrow lake formed to protect the town by damming a swamp on the north side) and building a New Town in the grand manner on the ridge beyond it was put into execution. Similar spaciously planned Georgian streets, terraces, crescents and circles intended predominantly for the well-to-do, especially in the law and other professions, were built on its north, west and east flanks in the early nineteenth century. Although there had been an expansion of industries of old-established types, the city was 'by repute and in fact a residential city with a large population of "bankers, professional men, and capitalists", skilled craftsmen and others engaged in retail trade, personal service or general labour'.[57] Its importance as a marketing centre had increased with agricultural improvements in the Lothians, and for a number of decades it had been one of the most renowned intellectual and cultural centres of Europe. For centuries it had been the largest city in Scotland with a population of about 25,000 in 1688, 83,000 in 1801 and 162,000 in 1831; and it was not surpassed in numbers by Glasgow until 1821. By that time the poorer local people shared the Old Town with Irish and other immigrants. Living conditions deteriorated, as later the craftsmen also moved out, leaving the Old Town to become one of the worst slums in Europe with some fantastic population densities.

The financial crisis of the late eighteen-twenties and the *laissez-faire* scramble of mid-century brought the planned extension of the city to an end. Large areas were used for the railways of competing companies and, after 1875, for substantially built four storey tenements, largely of two-roomed houses 'unrelieved by open spaces or softened by amenities'.[58] These were built mostly in the westsouthwest and northeast close to the main railways, where industries also developed, while four- and five-storey blocks of larger flats, and terraces, villas, and even small mansion houses covered extensive areas, chiefly to the west and south and also on the coastal plain west of Leith. For a generation in mid-century population growth was relatively slow but after 1861 it again speeded up to give the city 317,000 inhabitants by 1901. Decline in certain central areas was noted as early as 1831, when old houses were removed to make way for new streets and public buildings and dilapidated dwellings fell into disuse. Later some were removed when Waverley Station was built in the valley of the Nor Loch. Under the Improvement Schemes of 1867 the Old Town was 'opened up' by the creation of several new

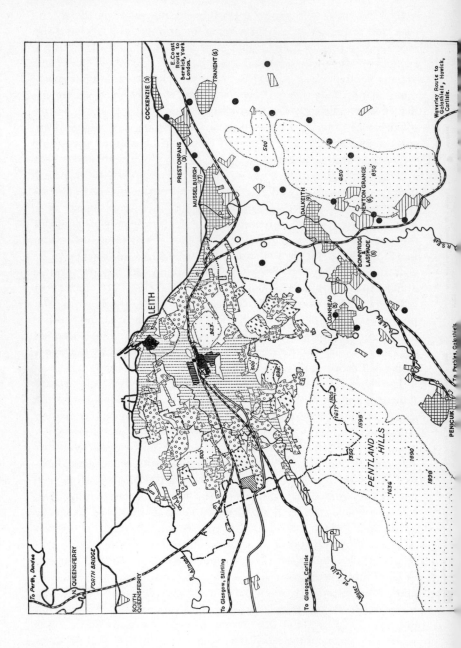

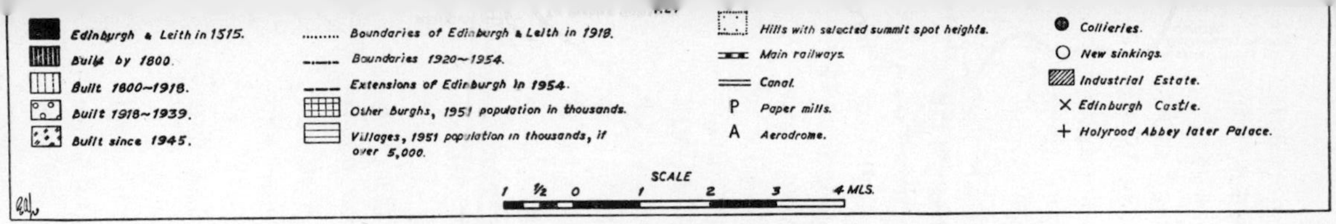

FIG. 65. The Growth of Edinburgh

The Royal Mile, from the Castle to Holyrood, formed the historic town, but the modern commercial nucleus lies to the north in the late-eighteenth century 'Georgian' town, now considerably altered.

By 1900 the greatly extended built-up area had fused with that of Leith, and since 1920 housing has spread widely on the surrounding rich farmland.

Based on:

(a) The Chronological Map of Edinburgh showing the expansion of the city from the earliest times to the present', by J. G. Bartholomew, *Scot. geogr. Mag.*, 35, 1919 (Edinburgh number).

(b) *A Civic Survey and Plan for Edinburgh*. Prepared for the Town Council by Patrick Abercrombie and Derek Plumstead, and published by Oliver and Boyd, 1949. Maps of. of inter-war development 1918/1939, facing p. 16.

(c) Bartholomew's Pocket Plan of Edinburgh.

(d) Personal knowledge.

Edinburgh & Leith in 1515.
Built by 1800.
Built 1800–1918.
Built 1918–1939.
Built since 1945.

.... Boundaries of Edinburgh & Leith in 1918.
Boundaries 1920–1954.
Extensions of Edinburgh in 1954.
Other Burghs, 1951 population in thousands.
Villages, 1951 population in thousands, if over 5,000.

Hills with selected summit spot heights.
Main railways.
Canal.
P Paper mills.
A Aerodrome.

● Collieries.
○ New sinkings.
Industrial Estate.
× Edinburgh Castle.
+ Holyrood Abbey later Palace.

SCALE
1 ½ 0 1 2 3 4 MLS.

streets flanked by new tenements.[59] The burgh was extended in 1883, 1885, 1896, 1900 and 1901, from an area of some 7,000 acres to over 10,000 acres.

Between 1901 and 1911 there was some decline in the most congested central areas and in those where commerce was extending into residential quarters, but substantial increases in Portobello—a seaside resort turned residential suburb, absorbed in 1896—and other outer wards, with much growth in neighbouring parishes. The Edinburgh Boundaries Extension and Tramways Act, 1920, which almost trebled the city's area to 32,400 acres, brought in many of these suburban places, extensive rural tracts that have since been largely built over, and even the northern slopes of the Pentland Hills. In that year the city absorbed four small parishes whose villages are now the centres of suburban districts: and the burgh of Leith was reabsorbed after an independence lasting eighty-two years. The city population increased from 320,000 in 1911 to 420,000 in 1920 almost entirely due to these extensions, the largest contribution coming from Leith (80,000), which had grown up at the mouth of the Water of Leith, as the historic port of Edinburgh. The roadstead there has been supplemented by a series of docks, the earliest in 1720, the others at intervals since the early nineteenth century when considerable expansion took place in shipbuilding and other industries. Over 400 acres have been reclaimed from tidal mud-flats for docks, wharves, and railways sidings and further improvements in hand include a large new basin on the west. Coal exports have declined since 1940, but new developments in grain and oil storage and handling facilities and in fertilizer treatment should help to maintain trade.

By 1920 Edinburgh was faced with a big problem of slum clearance and of housing to relieve over-crowding and replace sub-standard dwellings both in the older city and in Leith, whose central parts had by then become congested slums. At first the Corporation used mainly flat sites on post-glacial lake beds and raised beaches to build rather drab, but well-spaced, two-storey blocks of four flats each with gardens and three-storey tenements of modern design, while the speculative builder used more remote raised beaches and the outer ridges and less steep hill slopes for bungalows and semi-detached villas. Between 1920 and 1939 new houses under all auspices were built for about one-third of the city's population,[60] but most of the new areas had little provision for community life. Since 1945 Corporation housing has spread up the outermost ridges included in the city, forming in several places wedges between the areas of speculative building, of which many were on or near the main roads. The new buildings comprise largely two-storey terraces of more traditional and distinctive design than that of 1920–1939, with provision of space for community buildings; three-storey blocks of flats and one-storey cottages and two-storey blocks of four flats are also included, and some experimental multi-storey flats have been tried. More recently, appreciation of the need to prevent further sprawl has led to a decision to turn to central redevelopment when current peripheral schemes are completed; indeed it has already begun with rebuilding in traditional style along the historic Canongate. Two small additions to the city's area in 1954 serve to remove irregularities in the boundary.

Between 1921 and 1931, many outer wards experienced increases of 15–50 per cent, while most central ones declined by 1–8 per cent; between 1931 and 1951 the population of Leith plus what was the city before 1920 decreased from 405,000 to 352,000 (− 13 per cent), while that of the outer fringe increased from 34,000 to 114,000 (+ 238 per cent).[61] The speculative builder was largely responsible for linking the city between 1921 and 1931 to the old burgh of Musselburgh (17,000) with its wire rope, paper and net making industries. Only a few small villages are contiguous with the built-up area and outside the city boundary, so that the total conurbation population is only about 18,000 greater than that of the city itself with its 467,000 in 1951, and increases of + 4·5 and + 6·3 per cent in 1921–1931 and 1931–1951. A deliberate attempt is being made to preserve a green belt between Edinburgh and the rapidly growing coalfield towns and villages of the middle Esk Basin with aggregate population of about 32,000 in 1951; and a suggestion has been mooted for trying to put a ceiling on the city population at about half a million.

Edinburgh has relatively high percentages engaged in professions (11, cf. Glasgow, 8), public administration and defence (9, cf. Glasgow, 4), insurance and banking (3, cf. Glasgow, 2), but in the distributive trades it has 14·6 compared with Glasgow's 16·4. Its wholesale trade amounted in 1950 to £88m.; only 11 per cent of that of Scotland, and only £6m. more than that of Dundee. But its retail sales reached about £75m. one-eighth that of the country, and £154 per head, figures which reflect its relatively high proportion of well-to-do citizens, and its importance as a shopping centre for the Lothians as a whole, and for certain articles a larger area including the East Borders and much of Fife. In 1951 30·5 per cent were engaged in manufacturing and 7 per cent in building and contracting compared with 27 per cent and 5 per cent in 1931, the chief industries being food and drink (8 per cent), engineering and metal manufactures, including shipbuilding, and constructional, mechanical and electrical engineering with recent important developments in electronics (about 7 per cent), and printing and paper making (5 per cent). To encourage industrial development the Corporation have established an industrial estate on the western outskirts.

Aberdeen

The conurbation consists of the city itself (182,720) and the Donside villages of Bucksburn, largely industrial (3,800) and Bridge of Don, residential (1,500). The city developed from two mediaeval nuclei; Old Aberdeen, a quiet cathedral town near the Don with St. Machar's Cathedral, its precinct, and the formerly Catholic University of King's College; and Aberdeen, a castle town crowning a steep bank on the north side of the Dee, where it opened out into a half-mile wide basin studded with islands and sandbanks. The latter soon became the major port of the northeast, carrying on active trade with the Low Countries, France, Scandinavia, and the Baltic, and in 1593 its own Protestant University, Marischal College, was opened. Early in the following century immigrant Flemish merchants developed the domestic manufacture of woollen cloth and stockings in the county with a big export through Aberdeen.[62] In the late eighteenth and early nineteenth-century water-driven woollen, linen, cotton, and paper mills and associated villages were established, mainly along the Don, which has a fairly steep gradient in its lower reaches, modern shipbuilding and other new industries were started in the city, and harbour improvements begun: these eventually provided several large basins, a deepened channel connecting them with the sea, and reclaimed land for industrial and railway purposes. From 1850 onwards railways strengthened the position of Aberdeen as the commercial capital of northeast Scotland. Once artificial fertilizers came into common use and facilities for transport by steamboat and railway to southern cities were made available, the farming of the region became commercialized and concentrated on the production of oats and prime quality beef for sale; and Aberdeen expanded as its main trading centre, developing a whole range of related activities—slaughter-houses, hide and tallow works, a comb factory, fat refineries, meal and seed-crushing mills, fertilizer and agricultural implement works. During the nineteenth century the working and export of granite for paving stones and building and its polishing for monumental and architectural purposes expanded, and during its last two decades, following harbour improvements and the rise of steam trawling, a white fishing industry grew so rapidly that by 1900 it was of prime importance in the city.[63] Though it has declined from its peak there are still some 2,300 people engaged in fishing and about 7,000 in direct ancillary industries such as curing, box and barrel making, shipbuilding and repairing. As well as being the gateway to 'Royal Deeside', the city since the nineteen-twenties has itself become a very popular holiday resort, especially for Clydeside, and also a favourite place for the retired, and a centre of research, especially in agriculture and fisheries, as well as education (the two colleges were combined in the University of Aberdeen in 1860).

The most notable feature of the life of Aberdeen is its many-sided character, including the variety of its industries. In 1951 just under 30 per cent of its 'occupied' population were in manufacturing, the largest group in engineering, shipbuilding, and electrical goods, 7 per cent, followed by food, drink and tobacco, 5·5 per cent, and textiles, paper making and printing, and woodworking each about 3 per cent. Transport and communications accounted for 11 per cent, professional and miscellaneous services for 11 and 9 per cent respectively, public administration and defence, 5·5 per cent, and insurance and banking, 2 per cent. The city's position as a regional and commercial centre is emphasized even more by the 19·4 per cent in the distributive trades, 3 per cent more than in Glasgow, the next highest Scottish city in this respect. Its retail sales amount to over £31m.; £162 per head and 70 per cent of those of its large county. Its wholesale trade is valued at £44m. By 1952 the port had nearly recovered its pre-war trade coastwise and with Europe, North America and North Africa, and further improvements in the harbour were under way.

The population increase from c. 2,000 in the twelfth century to over 8,000 in the seventeenth was due mainly to commercial enterprise;[64] that from 10,000 in 1755 to 16,000 in 1795 within the 'strict limits' of the city 'chiefly to the rapid progress in manufactures'.[65] By 1801 the population of the town in a less restricted sense was 27,000 and by 1831, 57,000. Growth was slower in the middle decades, but by 1891 the Royal Burgh, which had been extended in 1871 and 1883, had 110,000. The municipal burgh was extended in 1891 when both Old Aberdeen (2,000) and Woodside, the nearest and largest industrial centre on Donside (5,400) were incorporated. By then Old Aberdeen had been linked to the city by housing and industrial works, the latter largely on the raised beaches; but Woodside was not linked till after 1900, and then mainly by housing. Though 11,000 houses were built between 1918 and 1939 and slums removed from its older quarters, Aberdeen still had in 1946 serious overcrowding, with much sub-standard tenement housing built in the nineteenth century. At least 15,000 new houses were then required, and in 1951 still 10,000.[66] In spite of its older tenements Aberdeen is outwardly a bright clean city since the granite retains its freshness and sparkle. In 1933 the Aberdeen and District Joint Planning Scheme provided for the controlled development of the outer parts of the city and adjacent portions of the counties of Aberdeen and Kincardine, and in 1935 the city's area was increased by 4,000 acres to 11,000, 2,000 being south of the Dee, where the satellite town of Kincorth was built in the nineteen-thirties.[67] A further extension was made in 1952. Corporation housing—blocks of flats, terraces, cottages and semi-detached bungalows—also covers large areas in the north both east and west of Old Aberdeen and on higher ground south of Woodside where the boundary was extended in 1952, while modern private building—granite bungalows, and two-storey flatted terraces—occurs largely in the west.[68] As in Edinburgh suitable peripheral areas within the city boundary are nearly used up, and central redevelopment is probable in the near future.

Dundee

Like Edinburgh, the Royal Burgh of Dundee (founded in 1184) has had a chequered history. In mediaeval times it was a flourishing collecting and distributing centre and port: in the sixteenth and early seventeenth centuries it was a 'town of riches and trade', the second in Scotland, but in 1651 it was sacked by General Monk and about two decades later its harbour was destroyed in a storm. By 1695 it had fallen to fourth place, and after the Union of 1707 its previously successful woollen industry and its trade with France and Holland were ruined. After about a hundred years of setback and stagnation, however, the town began to revive in the middle of the eighteenth century, largely by transferring hereditary skill in spinning and weaving from wool to flax. Linen manufacture and export developed rapidly and by 1770 the town was 'large and prosperous'. Its population, which had remained almost stationary for centuries, increased from about 12,000 in 1750 to 26,000 in 1801. The import trade also grew rapidly as supplies of flax and hemp from the Baltic augmented home-grown flax. The village of Lochee to the northwest became a weaving suburb and numerous bleachfields were established along the Dighty Water a few miles north and east of the town.[69] The early years of the nineteenth century saw the transfer of the linen industry to factories, the beginning of modern dock construction and land reclamation of the Tay mudflats, south and east of the town, and of shipbuilding and foundry work, and the extension of the traditional fisheries and fish trade to whaling. Coal from the Forth provided the motive power for the factories, most of which were situated on gently sloping ground along the Scoonie Burn northwest of the mediaeval town. From 1840 onwards jute largely replaced flax and hemp, and in subsequent decades manufacturing expanded rapidly, making Dundee one of the main jute manufacturing centres in the world. Population increased quickly, reaching almost 80,000 in 1851, when 15,000 immigrants from Ireland were connected with the docks and mills, and 140,000 in 1881, after which the rate of increase fell off, giving by 1911 a population of 165,000.

The original town was situated on the brow of an old cliff over-looking the harbour, and behind it the surface generally sloped steeply up to the Law (572 ft.) one mile away. The limitations of this natur-ally beautiful site affected the spread of the town and gave rise to marked social cleavages. The slopes surrounding the old centre, where not occupied by factories, warehouses, and public buildings, became closely built over mainly with drab four-storey tenements practically unrelieved by parks or gardens. The jute magnates built mansions and large villas beyond the eastern and western outskirts and on rising ground behind the neighbouring burgh of Broughty Ferry, while humbler villas and terraces appeared in that burgh and further east in Monifieth (railway to Arbroath in 1836), on the south side of the estuary in Newport, Tayport and Wormit (ferries, Tay railway bridge built in 1887), and to the north in the village of Down-field. The population of Broughty Ferry increased from 2,800 in 1851 to 11,000 in 1911, that of Monifieth from 300 in 1841 to 3,000 in 1911. The Royal Burgh of Dundee was extended in 1831 and 1876, and the municipal burgh in 1892, 1907, 1913 and 1914. The extension of 1911 incorporated Broughty Ferry, and the city's area increased from 3,600 acres in 1901 to 6,600 in 1921.

By the early twentieth century Dundee had become a typical, per-haps even an extreme, example of nineteenth-century specialization with 41 per cent of its employed population in textile manufacturing, 36·5 per cent being in jute. The development of manufacturing in

z

Bengal near the main world source of the raw material and the world depression hit the city very badly; it was designated a special area, and pervaded by an atmosphere of defeatism. The rate of population growth slowed down to 0·1 per cent between 1931 and 1951; but since 1945 a new Dundee, both physically and psychologically has emerged. Many new industries have developed on two industrial estates in the northeast and northwest beside Kingsway, a modern ring boulevard. New manufactures include watches, accounting machines, cash registers, electrical equipment, valves, hats and other ready made clothing; and the jute industry has been transformed. Extensive areas of two-storey terrace and three-storey blocks of flats have been put up by the Corporation north of Kingsway, with some even north of the Dighty Water. Inter-war house building (both Corporation and private) had linked Dundee with Broughty Ferry and extended the city westwards and northwards beyond the Law. Further extensions in 1932, 1939 and 1946 give it an area of fully 12,000 acres. With a population of 177,000 this gives an average gross density of 1,450 per 100 acres, compared with 2,568 in 1921 and 3,419 in 1911.

The predominantly industrial character of Dundee is shown by its 51 per cent in manufacturing, and its relatively low proportions in the professions (7·6 per cent), public administration and defence (4 per cent), insurance and banking (1·6 per cent), and the distributive trades (14 per cent). There are now 11 per cent in metallurgy and engineering (in 1931, 8 per cent), and only 23 per cent in textiles (jute, 18 per cent). The continued but diminished relative importance of textile manufacture helps to account for the high ratio of 66 women in employment for every 100 men, cf. Glasgow, 54, Motherwell, Clydebank and Coatbridge about 30 but Paisley, 83. Retail sales amount to almost £25m. (£140 per head), and wholesale trade to £82m., over 10 per cent of the Scottish total.

Port Glasgow—Greenock—Gourock

This urban area of 107,000 people extends for 7 miles along the narrow coastal strip between the Renfrewshire Uplands and the Firth of Clyde; its expansion to relieve overcrowding or promote new industrial development is seriously hampered by steep slopes. Urban development here is entirely a product of the Atlantic and industrial phases of Scotland's economic history. Port Glasgow (22,000) was largely eclipsed as a port when the deepened Clyde gave access to the city itself for ocean-going ships, but it continued to grow as a centre of shipbuilding and rope and canvas making. In the seventeenth century Greenock (76,000) developed from a fishing village to a port, and modern Clyde shipbuilding started there in 1711. Thereafter the town developed rapidly both as a port, trading mainly with the West Indies and North America, and industrially, with a densely peopled overcrowded central and eastern part, and a spaciously laid-out western suburb. With railway extension west-wards in 1889 the former fishing village of Gourock (9,000 in 1951) expanded, largely as a residential town with some yacht building and marine engineering, and as one of the main terminals for Clyde steamers. The major industries of Greenock are now marine en-gineering, shipbuilding and repairing, sugar refining, and worsted and hosiery manufacture; its wholesale trade is valued at £6m., its retail sales at almost £8m., or £99 per head compared with Gourock's £97 and Port Glasgow's £71.

Owing to their great dependence on shipbuilding and marine en-gineering both Greenock and Port Glasgow were badly hit during the depression, but some new factories in the former and an industrial estate in the latter now give a more varied employment structure. This estate and considerable areas of post-1945 housing have been built on the 350–400-ft. plateau behind the town and near the inland railway to Paisley and Glasgow via Kilmacolm; while a satellite settlement to Greenock with important new industry as well as extensive housing is under construction in the Spango Valley. The effect of commercial and industrial development in this area can be gauged from the fact that the population of the three parishes in-volved increased from 7,000 in 1755 to 23,000 in 1801, 47,000 in 1851, 92,000 in 1901, and 114,000 in 1921. The post-1920 setback and the subsequent stability are indicated by 1931 and 1951 populations of 109,000.

Falkirk—Grangemouth

This conurbation lies within the key 'cross roads' area of Scotland, and is now one of its chief growing points industrially. Its two major components are the burghs of Falkirk (37,500) and Grangemouth (15,400), whose administrative areas are now contiguous. Close to Falkirk on the north and east about 20,000 people live in a number of villages connected with the iron industry, while southeast of the most easterly of these are another 10,000 in several contiguous villages, mainly concerned with mining. Following the opening of the Carron Iron Works in 1759 on the Forth and Clyde canal, 1½ miles to the north, a number of iron manufacturing and mining villages grew up beside the old trading town of Falkirk. Some of these developed into straggling suburbs as the burgh itself expanded rapidly in trade with further development of iron manufacturing and coalmining in the neighbourhood, the former specializing in light castings. Falkirk's population rose from about 4,000 people in 1790 to 8,200 in 1841, 20,000 in 1891, 29,000 in 1901 and 33,000 in 1911. After a slight decline, growth was again resumed in the twenties when big house building programmes increased the demand for the main products of the area. Since 1945 aluminium rolling and casting have been added, and in 1951 they employed about 2,000 of the burgh's 20,000 'occupied' population, while the iron industry employed 4,800. The importance of Falkirk as a shopping centre is revealed in its retail sales of over £7m., i.e. £191 per head.

Founded in the late eighteenth century as the eastern terminal of the Forth and Clyde canal, and later extended partly on land reclaimed from tidal mud-flats, Grangemouth is now the second port in Scotland. Its shipyard and saw mills date from its early period, but in 1897 a new phase began, which gave rise to big developments after 1920, and is still doing so. These are concerned with various branches of the chemical industry for which the attractions are abundant supplies of water, flat land, accessibility by road, rail, and sea, and the nearby Firth for receiving the effluents. The soap and glycerine works of 1897 were followed by works for the manufacture of dyestuffs in 1919, and by a refinery for imported oil in 1924: pharmaceutical products were added in 1942. Recently the oil refinery and cracking plants have been greatly extended and a petroleum chemicals industry is being developed. Though the port still despatches the products of the refinery, the Forth is too shallow for modern tankers, and in 1951 a 60-mile pipe line capable of delivering 6,500 tons of crude oil daily was opened from a new oil port at Finnart on Loch Long.[70] The population increased from 2,000 in 1861 to 6,400 in 1891, an increase largely due to trade expansion following railway developments. From 8,400 in 1901 it grew to 10,000 in 1911, and after a setback reached nearly 12,000 in 1931.

Ayr—Prestwick

The nucleus of the present county town of Ayr is the old port, Royal Burgh (founded 1203), and market town on the south side of the mouth of the River Ayr. In the eighteenth century the harbour was improved and coal export and a number of industries developed in Newton-upon-Ayr north of the river, while terrace houses were added to the old burgh, which for a time became a gay residential centre for well-to-do families.[71] After the Glasgow–Ayr railway was opened in 1840 industry expanded and the town grew rapidly as a holiday resort,[72] its attractions being the bathing, the sea air and sunshine, and the fine views of the Firth and the Arran hills. Agricultural improvements and mining developments also contributed to trade and industrial expansion. Burgh extensions took place in 1873, when Newton was incorporated, and in 1885, and 1935, the last doubling its area to 4,650 acres and bringing in the mining village of Whitletts in the east and the villages of Doonfoot and Alloway (Burns' birthplace) in the south.[73] Just over one-quarter of the occupied population are engaged in manufacturing with 11 per cent in metallurgy and engineering, 8 per cent in textiles (threequarters of them in carpet manufacture), and 1·1 per cent in chemicals, mainly fertilizers. 'New industries are finding Ayr a good place in which to settle and some of the older firms are extending their activities.'[74] But the town's chief functions are still commercial, administrative and social; it is one of the principal agricultural markets in the country, a holiday resort of increasing popularity, and a place of residence for commuters who work in other Ayrshire towns, in neighbouring collieries (600 men), and Glasgow.[75] Its wholesale trade amounts to £6m., and its retail sales to £9m., that is £207 per head. Nearly 18 per cent are in the distributive trades, 12 per cent in both transport and miscellaneous services, 9·5 per cent in the professions, and 8 per cent in public administration and defence. The population increased from 17,600 in 1851, to 24,000 in 1891, 36,800 in 1931, and 42,400 in 1951.

In the nineteen-twenties Ayr became linked to the neighbouring burgh of Prestwick by a zone of bungalows and villas. Before its Golf Club was formed in 1851, Prestwick was a mere straggling village of 500 people; but its course on the natural links of blown sand soon attracted golfers from outside and became famous as the scene of championships. Later, as it became a popular holiday resort, three other courses and in 1931 a large bathing lake were added. Prestwick also attracted retired people and commuters to Glasgow. Between 1901 and 1951 its population quadrupled from 3,000 to nearly 12,000. But its increase recently is in large part associated with its aerodrome, opened in the late nineteen-thirties as a private venture by two Everest fliers, greatly enlarged during the war, and now one of the main international airports of northwestern Europe.[75]

CHAPTER 12

THE PROBLEM OF THE CONURBATION

ONE major problem of modern Britain is the distribution of its population. Approached from the countryside, the main concern is the preservation of agricultural land: in the major conurbations, the main need is the provision of decent homes for their citizens in new city flats at high densities, or in new housing estates, or in new towns at lower densities of population. Even a stationary population, such as that in much of the industrial north, may require more homes if the average size of family declines further from its 1951 level of 3·2 persons. Thanks to the realistic work of Best and Ward,[1] it is now widely believed that suburban gardens may produce food equal in value to the farmgate financial returns of good agricultural land—if not necessarily the best land. It may be, therefore, that England can afford to lose the 35,000 acres a year (over 50 square miles) withdrawn from agricultural use. Some people would surround every conurbation, even every major town with a green belt and move all emigrants either to new towns or to established towns whose authorities are willing to accept them and the industries upon which they depend. Undoubtedly such enterprises have had some success but they provide only partial solutions for the immense social problems that exist in our conurbations and other industrial towns, some aspects of which are noted in the following pages.

Administrative Aspects

At many points in the preceding chapters, attention has been drawn to the intricate arrangement of local government units, county boroughs, municipal boroughs, urban and rural districts that now exists in England and Wales. The Scottish system, although differing in historical origin and development, also offers problems to the administrator. Never was it harder than now to say what is a town and what is not. In Roman times, a town was a planned entity with definite social functions. The mediaeval towns of Britain grew up as centres for traders and craftsmen, at intervals of a dozen miles or so one from another throughout the land. Some of them became boroughs under the Municipal Corporations Act of 1835 and others were made parliamentary boroughs under the Reform Act of 1832, but once modern industry developed on the coalfields a new type of 'town' grew, inevitably commercial but depending for its livelihood largely on some form of industry. In 1851 the Census Commissioners found it hard to say which of these places were 'towns' as such, and timidly asked the advice of the Clerks of the Peace of the respective counties, who were 'consulted as to the places which are entitled to be deemed towns, and several places containing more than 2,000 inhabitants (were) omitted, because in the opinion of those officers, they could not in strictness be so designated'.[2] In the West Riding there had been vast increases of population though the effect on the landscape was not to add a number of new towns, but rather to induce the addition of houses around old towns and villages, or the building of mills with workers' cottages in favoured situations beside rivers and canals, or beside collieries.[3] Nor was the position markedly different in the neighbourhood of Manchester—nor in any other industrial area of the country.

Town definition meets a social need, a fact clearly realized by the Royal commissioners of 1871 who stressed the problems of public health raised by the massing of thousands of people into small areas. They wrote:[4] 'There may be districts (where) . . . urban powers are necessary for their continued well-being. It is possible that some new source of mineral wealth will shortly be developed. Unless measures be taken, an ill-built and undrained manufacturing or mining village or group of villages will cover what are now agricultural lands . . . the necessity for urban powers to regulate the plan of the future town is abundantly manifest.' During the nineteenth century, one commission or select committee after another dealt with such problems, only to find that as one social need was met, another arose. Far from becoming easier to separate town and country, it became more difficult especially in places locally known as 'mill villages' or 'mining villages': in this case one suspects that the term 'village' is used only in order to avoid the use of 'town' on the analogy that a population of a few hundreds or even a couple of thousand must form a 'village'. But it is not unusual to speak of a 'mining village' having some thousands of people, possibly because many such places are not well provided with shops, banks, or professional services and therefore depend upon the facilities provided by neighbouring towns.

An administrative boundary of a town may run through Pennine moorlands or along Oxford street. An agricultural area within a town's boundary is naturally regarded as a 'lebensraum' for eventual housing developments, although the boundary may be merely that

of an ancient parish: on the other hand, many towns have no agricultural land whatever within their boundaries, and the suburbs are
in parishes belonging to adjacent rural districts or in adjoining places
that rank as urban districts on their own account. Numerous examples have been given in this book, some of them due to the existence of a county boundary defined centuries ago for an England quite
different from that of today. One of the best examples is the separation between Lancashire and Cheshire, considered in Chapters 4
and 5, and also on pp. 243-4: only in one place, Wythenshawe,
Manchester, has the boundary been altered in a manner sufficiently
radical to allow an effective spread of housing and of industry by a
great city. In other words, the alteration made in 1931 met the needs
of a city which during the previous ten years had built housing
estates up to its southern boundaries. But the need was met only for
a time and under mid-twentieth-century conditions, it would be an
advantage to have some administrative definition of towns that bore
a clear relation to the area covered by the homes of its people,
together with some reasonable mechanism of changing these boundaries as the need arises. It is, for example, highly improbable that
Manchester will ever again be able to absorb an area comparable
to the 9 square miles of Wythenshawe for the rehousing of that
section of its population still living in derelict and semi-derelict
houses.

Administrative boundaries have been greatly changed during the
past century but are clearly anachronistic in many cases, especially in
the major conurbations. In 1887 Birmingham formulated its expan-
sionist policy (pp. 87, 90) of including all districts whose people were
connected with the city's commerce and industry and not too remote
for absorption.[5] Had this principle been efficiently applied elsewhere,
many cities would have been enlarged to include suburbs now under
other municipalities, for example, Liverpool would include Bootle,
Litherland, and Huyton-with-Roby, and perhaps also some of its
Cheshire suburbs. The West Yorkshire conurbation consists of so
many separate towns that the changes might not be great, but the
division of the Manchester conurbation into fifty-two units can
hardly be defended. Even so, the best way to make local authorities
within a conurbation combine is to raise fears of absorption by their
larger neighbours, such as 'the Manchester octopus'. In 1922, many
boroughs of outer London were anxious to show that they were not
part of any metropolitan entity but rather independent growths
worthy of perpetuation as such. But if the conurbations as now

defined are in any way unities on the ground, surely the time has
come to ask if their interests could best be served by some kind of
advisory council or planning body that could consider their problems
as a whole.

Everything has combined in the last fifty years to make the
conurbation an expanding entity, having problems inevitably shared
by the various administrative units within it, but devoid of any
central authority capable of uniting all the parts into one whole.
True, there have been special *ad hoc* organizations for transport—
notably the London Passenger Transport Board—or for the provision of water and other services.[6] Gas and electricity services are
now united under regional boards, and the national health scheme
has linked together hospital services. Many people feel that local
administration has been weakened by these recent developments as
by the earlier abolition of the Poor Law services. For a time after the
1914–1918 war, various regional planning boards met to consider the
development of housing, industry, transport and general amenities:
these boards covered far larger areas than the conurbations—for
example one based on Manchester went deep into rural Cheshire,
north to the Rossendales and into the centre of Lancashire where it
met the area covered by the planning board based on Liverpool.[7]
Since then planning has become the concern of county boroughs and
county councils, acting in co-operation with urban and rural districts
and in consultation with county boroughs. In other words, modern
planning is closely tied to existing administrative boundaries, and
any hope that the first job of planning might be to re-arrange the local
government structure has gone.

The prospect of establishing a Manchester county council, one
authority for Tyneside, or a governing body for Birmingham and the
Black Country, now seems remote: in other words, the example of
1888, when the county of London was formed, seems so unlikely to
be repeated that at times one is driven to the conclusion that the
conurbations are merely regarded as convenient statistical units and
little more. On the other hand, a White Paper of 1956[8] showed aware-
ness of the need to improve the pattern of local government within
the conurbations: two main suggestions were made. The first was to
recognize as inevitable 'the continued existence of a patchwork of
local authorities of different types and with different powers, but to
endeavour to reduce their numbers . . . by amalgamating county districts (that is municipal boroughs, urban and rural districts), by
expanding county boroughs and creating new ones, and by adjusting

county boroughs so as to reduce the number of counties involved'. A second method would be 'to reorganize the area on a uniform basis', for example by forming a group of county boroughs in the larger conurbations, or by making one large municipal borough in smaller conurbations. The former of these two suggestions was made for outer London in 1922 (p. 59), and the latter for Tyneside in 1937 (p. 191). Whatever course may be taken, there will still be a need for some co-ordination of services, for example in an entire conurbation.

Economic and Social Aspects

In Victorian times, despite a few shocks due to trade depressions, the common assumption was that population growth would continue indefinitely for every Census had a large increase to record. The warnings of Malthus were soon forgotten. One writer of 1837, in Merthyr Tydfil, clearly saw the dangers of reliance on extractive industry alone, even though the iron trade had dominated the economy of South Wales for forty years. He commented:[9] 'Would that we could induce our own ironmasters or stranger speculators to manufacture our iron into various useful things in our domestic economy . . . we surely ought to find the skill, the capital and enterprise for so desirable a consummation. Are we to go on in the same old-fashioned way subject to the ebb and flow of a very uncertain trade . . . a large encampment sent merely to exhaust the ore and coal and then to fall into ruin and decay. Or are we to have new manufactures, a greater division of labour, fresh competition, and a boundless field for ingenuity and welfare of future generations.'

Within one century the South Wales coalfield has seen an immigration both rapid and vast, and an emigration of similarly surprising extent. In the Rhondda, for example, there has been a period of quick growth which filled quiet valleys with mining towns and villages, two decades of peak prosperity followed by long years of continuing decline. These are perhaps extreme examples, yet the problems of other mining areas such as West Durham or of various cotton textile towns in Lancashire also command attention. One would argue that the town depending on one industry or exclusively on mining should never be built at all: places such as Chesterfield or Barnsley, where mining and industries have developed in association, have had their times of heavy unemployment but are obviously more stable ecomomically than Rhondda or Mountain Ash.

Ever since the nineteen-thirties, some effort has been made to control, or at least to influence the distribution of industry. Various examples are given in this book of the new industries brought into South Wales valleys or decrepit mining towns of Co. Durham under the development area policy. True, there have been difficulties: there is, for example, a story of one new Welsh factory having inside the front door a large notice, 'The Government sent us here. As soon as possible we are going back to Yorkshire.' But while economists are divided about the wisdom of the policy, it has at least provided work where it was needed and to a limited extent drawn off new industries from areas such as Greater London or the West Midlands. Prophecy is difficult: for example, the planning board which considered South-east Lancashire and its neighbouring areas shortly after the 1914–1918 war, forecast an expansion of factories and houses on the west side of Manchester far greater than that seen since then.[10] At that time, writers could not be expected to foresee the world economic crisis of the nineteen-thirties, nor the decline of the cotton industry, nor that so large a proportion of the newer industries would be established in the London area, taken in a wide sense to include towns within a radius of 60–70 miles from Charing Cross, or in the Midlands. It is one of the most ironic features of twentieth century economic history that it has become necessary to attract industry to some of the very areas on which Britain's nineteenth-century prosperity was based.

The extent to which the population of Britain, and especially the working population, is migratory is perhaps inadequately realized by many people: one detailed short-period study in the Birmingham area showed the swiftness with which population movement reacted to fluctuations in industrial employment.[11] But the motor-bus has made possible movements to work of some complexity by which, for example, new coalmines in Lancashire on the southern edge of the field draw their workers from the towns and villages where mining has declined, or the large trading estates on the margins of the South Wales coalfield have labour drawn from the mining valleys. If no work of a desired type is available within a reasonable distance, people will migrate: if jobs are provided a few miles away they can attract workers. There are signs that the movement to work is becoming steadily more intricate and for this very reason the planned outward movement of population from large towns is now generally linked with the provision of work near the homes of the people. The existing distribution of population is not something that can be maintained for all time, nor even for ten or twenty years. In 1931, C. B. Fawcett[12] drew particular attention to the population changes characteristic of the previous ten years: from 1921 to 1931, the main increases of population were in the southeast and the English Midlands, and the northern industrial areas had very slight increases of population (West Yorkshire, + 2·6 per cent; Tyneside, + 1·4 per cent; Manchester area, + 2·8 per cent; similarly Clydeside, + 3·4 per cent). From 1931 to 1951, the same tendencies were seen. The northern industrial areas still remain virtually stable in population, and the southeast, if defined as including Essex, Cambridgeshire, Berkshire, Buckinghamshire, Oxfordshire and Hampshire, still shows increases of population (Fig. 44).

The Changing Town

Various studies of towns have shown that the change in land use is comparatively rapid, as for example in London and in major provincial cities. Such changes were noted in the nineteenth century and in various major provincial cities by the decade 1841–1851. The initial steps in slum clearance were due to economic factors, especially in London where many of the finest streets and buildings rose on sites which had become too precious for houses. And similarly, many of the great railway stations with their less-commonly observed sidings and warehouses have been built partly on sites that had to be cleared of houses; the 1934 social survey of London notes the existence in Highgate of 'a well marked patch of poor streets' erected when St. Pancras was built,[13] and when Manchester's London Road station was enlarged in the eighteen-sixties, some 600 houses were pulled down.[14] More recently, between 1905 and 1936, nearly one-quarter of the city of London was rebuilt, and the new buildings produced 42 per cent of the rateable value.[15] Most buildings had two 'lives', one of thirty years and a second of equal or greater length after alteration and modernization. Even if the changes are greater in London than elsewhere, comparable features are seen in all cities. Beyond the central city area there may be attractive residential quarters or what has been called a 'blighted belt', in which old houses, once suburban, are let off in flats or in single rooms, transformed into boarding houses, or converted into factories and warehouses. In many cases the larger houses provide the greater problem as they lose their original use more readily than the smaller houses, and in an area of Manchester well known to the author, the large houses are—with few exceptions—in far worse condition than the smaller houses around them.

Decline of population is seen first in the central areas of towns and steadily farther out from the city centre. This phenomenon, though by no means new, has now reached alarming proportions in several boroughs of East London where, due to bombing as well as slum clearance, the population has been halved within twenty years. In some cities, such as Manchester, the open spaces of the inner areas are partly bombed sites and partly land cleared immediately before the 1939–1945 war, and only recently used for the new blocks of flats that are to cover large parts of the inner city. A considerable time may elapse between the clearance of sites and the building of flats: many cities now prosperous have considerable areas that appear to have suffered from some kind of scorched earth policy. That large sections of industrial cities should be rebuilt no one could doubt— at least no one who has taken the trouble to explore them on foot. Many people in conurbations (and outside them) have the idea that the councils have large building sites unoccupied while they are agitating for more land outside the city. They fail to see that a scheme of modern flat building may cover a site of 50–100 acres or more, and that the whole site must be cleared before a beginning is made. Further, not all those displaced can be settled in the new flats and in any case estimates of ultimate need are based on an assessment of the number of people who can be rehoused inside the city as well as outside it.

'Wider still and wider shall thy bounds be set' could well be the motto of any considerable industrial town. In fact its people have gone farther and farther afield in two waves, of which the first and oldest was mainly a movement of the more fortunate people financially, seeking suburban homes on the edge of the built-up area or in villages that became suburbanized and the second came mainly after the 1914–1918 war when large 12-to-the-acre housing estates were erected on the then fringes of our cities. And along with this trend, mainly during the years from 1928 onwards to 1939, there was another little different from it, the building of 'estates' for private profit, for people who did not want a 'council house' but a 'modern semi', little larger than the local authority house but slightly more pretentious, and in many cases farther from the city centre. But just as the local authority houses were placed beyond the former outer suburbs, so in time other local authority houses have been placed beyond the private estates. The net result has been that in many cities the area covered by houses and their gardens, not to mention roads, schools and public buildings, has been doubled since 1921: fig. 29 shows that in Manchester, for example, the built-up area has been vastly enlarged during this time, yet the population has declined from its peak of 766,000 in 1931 to 703,000 in 1951. Had the incorporation of Wythenshawe not been achieved, the decline would have been far greater, as in the case of its neighbour, Salford, which had 234,000 people in 1921 but only 178,000 in 1951.

All this leads to the conclusion that a town is a dynamic entity, constantly changing in its land use and in the distribution of its people. The obverse of the picture is that the location of a city's main shopping quarter may change very little, if at all, for a century, and that its markets may remain on the same site for generations, or alter only by the removal of stalls from the street to a market hall. In Manchester, the warehouse quarter has not changed its position for more than a century, though rebuilt gradually on more spacious lines. The railways helped to consolidate this warehouse area, which for some goods still profits from a central location. But can one assume that a central shopping quarter will remain strong? On the whole one may, but to an increasing extent, central stores are establishing branches in outer towns of the conurbation. Various instances have been given in this book of strong shopping centres in conurbations, such as Wolverhampton in the West Midlands, or the outer crescent of towns from Altrincham to Bolton in the Manchester conurbation. Similarly in London there are many such, notably South Kensington, Kingston-upon-Thames or Croydon. A resident in Ealing may go to the West End shopping area infrequently or never, having other excellent shopping areas close at hand. Nevertheless, it is impossible to believe that the central shopping quarters of large cities will ever cease to attract customers for the centrality of the great city is so well established that it is unlikely that its attraction can be easily reduced.

At many points in this book, the evils of nineteenth-century housing and the problems of rapid industrial growth have been noted. Our involved system of railways due to the work of competing companies and our lack of modern highways in many parts of the country, both provide major if different problems of transport: and our modern trunk roads, such as the Great West road from London or the East Lancashire road from Manchester, have proved all too attractive as factory sites. The fear of the present is the indefinite spread of towns and the further alienation of land, some of it of good quality, from agriculture. These are all problems of the distribution of population, past and future, and the need is to guide this growth so that town and countryside each preserve their amenity: to take the attitude that the Industrial Revolution is merely deplorable, misses the point that the modern strength of Britain rests on a way of life that is urban, industrial, commercial, and scientific, depending more and more on technical ability and skill as the overseas competitors become stronger, and the initial advantages of an early start in the eighteenth century based on inventions, water power, coal and iron, no longer an asset. One could in fact argue that the early beginning has been in some ways a disadvantage, for so many towns are composed largely of houses and factories that seemed reasonable and even desirable when they were built but do not conform to the standards of the mid-twentieth century. Out of the contemplation of towns in this book, the reflection comes that the main social problem for the future will lie not in the town centres of the present, nor in many of the older and better outer residential areas, but in the suburbs built since 1919. Recently the present author walked for 3 miles across a housing estate of the nineteen-twenties in a northern city. It has good roads, open spaces, fine schools, attractive churches, trees and gardens, some modern factories—but in thirty years' time, what will it be?

NOTES AND REFERENCES

The abbreviations listed here are used for some of the sources that occur frequently: the short forms for the names of periodicals are taken from the *World List of Scientific Periodicals*, 1950.

Advancement of Science	*Advanc. Sci. Lond.*
Architectural Review	*Arch. Rev. Lond.*
East Midland Geographer (not in 1950 list)	*East Mid. Geogr.*
Economic Geography	*Econ. Geogr.*
Geographical Journal	*Geogr. J.*
Geographical Review	*Geogr. Rev.*
Geography	*Geography*
Journal of the Royal Statistical Society	*J. R. statist. Soc.*
Publications of the Institute of British Geographers	*Pub. Inst. Brit. Geogr.*
Scottish Geographical Magazine	*Scot. geogr. Mag.*
Town Planning Review	*Town Plann. Rev.*
Transactions of the Manchester Statistical Society	*Trans. Manchr. statist. Soc.*

Books and articles in journals to which frequent reference is made are listed as follows:

Addison. Addison, W., *English spas* (London, 1951).

Ashworth. Ashworth, W., *Genesis of modern British planning* (London, 1954).

Darby. Darby, H. C. (ed.), *Historical geography of England before 1800* (Cambridge, 1936).

Defoe. *Defoe's Tour through the whole Island of Great Britain*, with an introduction by G. D. H. Cole (London, 1927).

Fawcett. Fawcett, C. B., 'Distribution of the urban population in Great Britain', *Geogr. J.*, 79 (1932), 100–13.

Geddes. Geddes, P., *Cities in evolution* (London, 1915).

Gilbert (1939). Gilbert, E. W., 'The growth of inland and seaside health resorts in England', *Scot. geogr. Mag.*, 55, (1939), 16–35.

Gilbert (1947). Gilbert, E. W., 'The industrialization of Oxford', *Geogr. J.*, 109 (1947), 1–22.

Gilbert (1948). Gilbert, E. W., 'The boundaries of local government areas', *Geogr. J*, 111 (1948), 172–98.

Gilbert (1954) *Brighton: old ocean's bauble* (London, 1954)

Jackman. Jackman, W. T., *The development of transportation in modern England* (Cambridge, 1916), vol. I, 1–459, vol. II, 461 ff.

L.I.D.A. Lancashire Industrial Development Association pamphlets.

Ogilvie. Ogilvie, A. G. (ed.), *Great Britain: essays in regional geography* (Cambridge, 1928).

Priestley. Priestley, J., *Historical account of the navigable rivers, canals and railways of Great Britain* (London, 1831).

Smith. Smith, W., *Economic geography of Great Britain* (London, 1949).

Official publications are listed as follows:

Cmd. 1830 (1923). Royal Commission on London government.

Cmd. 9559 (1955).   Report of the Ministry of Housing and Local Government for the period 1950/51 to 1954.
Cmd. 9876 (1956).   Report of the Ministry of Housing and Local Government for the year 1955.
Cmd. 193 (1957).   Report of the Ministry of Housing and local Government for the year 1956.
Retail.   Census of Distribution and other Service trades, 1950, vol. 1, Retail and Service trades (H.M.S.O., 1953).

The British Association Scientific Surveys are listed thus:

B.A. Norwich.   *Scientific Survey of Norwich and district*, ed. R. H. Mottram (1935).
B.A. North-eastern.   *Scientific Survey of North-eastern England*, ed. P. C. G. Isaac and Ruth E. A. Allan (1949).
B.A. Birmingham.   *Birmingham and its regional setting*, ed. M. J. Wise (1950).
B.A. Merseyside.   *A scientific survey of Merseyside*, ed. W. Smith (1953).
B.A. Oxford.   *The Oxford Region*, ed. A. F. Martin and R. W. Steel (1954).
B.A. Bristol.   *Bristol and its adjoining counties*, ed. C. M. MacInnes and W. F. Whittard (1955).
B.A. Sheffield.   *Sheffield and its region*, ed. D. L. Linton (1956).

CHAPTER 1

[1] Geddes, 31–2.
[2] *Ibid.*, 34.
[3] *Ibid.*, 39–41.
[4] *Ibid.*, 41–3.
[5] Fawcett, 100.
[6] Geddes, 35.
[7] This phrase has become conventional: it is discussed in Perry, A. C., *Housing for the Machine Age* (New York, 1939), 50–72.
[8] Census 1951. Report . . . conurbations, xxiv–xxix.
[9] Perry, A. C., *op. cit.*, 21: the symptoms are 'steadily declining property values . . . shabby, ill-kept buildings, buildings boarded up or abandoned, torn down buildings'.
[10] Ministry of Housing and Local Government, Slum Clearance (1955), Cmd. 9593, 60.
[11] Census 1951, Housing, 92.
[12] Fawcett, 102.
[13] Robson, W. A., *The Government and Misgovernment of London*, (London, 1939), 90–1.
[14] Geddes, P., *op. cit.*, 32. Similarly optimistic forecasts are found in the regional plan produced by the Manchester and District Joint Town Planning Advisory Committee with maps and texts (Manchester, 1926).
[15] Much more interest has been aroused by the major 'regions' or 'provinces' of the country—see Gilbert, E. W. *Geogr. J.* 94 (1939), 29–44.
[16] Census 1951, Report . . . conurbations, xviii–xix.
[17] Howard Spring, *A Sunset Touch* (London, 1953), 14.

CHAPTER 2

[1] Census 1951, Report . . . conurbations, xxii.
[2] Cmd. 1830 (1923), 51.

[3] Census 1851, Population Tables I, vol. 1, Div. 1, 42–5.

[4] Cmd. 1830 (1923), 146–7.

[5] Cole, Margaret, *Servant of the County* (London, 1956), 36.

[6] *Ibid.*, 35.

[7] Cmd. 1830 (1923), 51–2.

[8] Census 1921, General Report, 28–9.

[9] *County of London Plan* (1943), 1.

[10] Census 1951, Middlesex, 4; Surrey, 6; Essex, 3.

[11] Mackinder, H. J., *Geogr. J.*, 78 (1931), 268.

[12] Unstead, J. F., 'A system of regional geography', *Geography*, 18 (1933), 177–8.

[13] Jones, Ll. Rodwell, *The geography of London river* (London, 1931), 16–18.

[14] Collingwood, R. G., *Roman Britain* (Oxford, 1932), 54–9.

[15] Jones, L. R., *op. cit.*, 16.

[16] Spate, O. H. K., in Darby, 543.

[17] Ormsby, H., *London on the Thames* (London, 1924), 21.

[18] *Ibid.*, 33.

[19] Wooldridge, S. W., 'Some geographical aspects of the Greater London Plan., *Pub. Inst. Brit. Geogr.*, 11, (1946), 14.

[20] Ormsby, H., *op. cit.*, 21–4.

[21] Wooldridge, S. W., *op. cit.*, 14.

[22] Abercromby, P., *Greater London Plan 1944* (H.M.S.O., 1945), para. 42.

[23] Ormsby, H., *op. cit.*, 25–6. See also Mrs. Ormsby's chapter, 'The London basin', in Ogilvie, 1928.

[24] Collingwood, R. G., *op. cit.*, 58, and works by Sir Mortimer Wheeler; Gilbert, E. W., 'The human geography of Roman Britain', in Darby, 61–65.

[25] Gilbert, E. W., *op. cit.*, 78–81.

[26] Darby, H. C., 'The economic geography of England A.D. 1000–1250', in Darby, 222–3.

[27] Pelham, R. A., 'Medieval foreign trade: Eastern ports', in Darby, 303–4.

[28] Jones, L. R., *op. cit.*, 2.

[29] Taylor, E. G. R., 'Camden's England', in Darby, 363–4.

[30] *Ibid.*, 364–5.

[31] Baker, J. N. L., 'England in the seventeenth century', in Darby, 442.

[32] Defoe I, 327–8.

[33] *Ibid.*, 391.

[34] *Ibid.*, 318–23.

[35] *Ibid.*, 316.

[36] *Ibid.*, 349–50.

[37] *Ibid.*, 349–50.

[38] *Ibid.*, 352.

[39] *Ibid.*, 7, 381–93.

[40] *Ibid.*, 6–8.

[41] *Ibid.*, 94–6.

[42] *Ibid.*, 97–9.

[43] *Ibid.*, 96–7.

[44] *Ibid.*, 157–9.

[45] *Ibid.*, 157.

[46] *Ibid.*, 164–5.

[47] *Ibid.*, 168.

[48] *Ibid.*, 382–5.

[49] *Ibid.*, 381–3.

[50] Rasmussen, S. E., *London the unique city* (London, 1937), 177.

[51] Spate, O. H. K., in Darby, 534–6.

[52] Jones, L. R., *op. cit.*, 17.

[53] Jones, L. R., *op. cit.*, 74.

[54] Rasmussen, *op. cit.*, 190, 192.

[55] Ashworth, 36.

[56] Spate, O. H. K., in Darby, 536.

[57] Jones, L. R., *op. cit.*, 63.

[58] Spate, O. H. K., in Darby, 537.

[59] Census 1851 Population Tables I, vol. 1, xlviii.

[60] *Ibid.*, Div. 1, 2, 13–21, 24 (Southwark).

[61] The detailed comments used in this paragraph are drawn from the famous marginal notes of the 1851 census. Certain major provincial cities had a declining population between 1841–1851 in central areas, but apparently the same phenomenon was noted earlier in London. But the figures for London are given with minute dissection, as some of the parishes covered extremely small areas: it may be that some early declines in provincial cities are hidden by the statistics. Nevertheless, one would expect what is in fact shown—the decline of population due to the change from residential to other land uses to be first shown in the heart of the largest city.

[62] Ashworth 37: Rasmussen, S. E., *op. cit.*, 277–81.

[63] Ashworth 37–8.

[64] Census 1851, Div. 1, esp. pp. 22–24, 26.

[65] *Ibid.*, 1851, Div. 1, 14–18: *ibid.*, 1901, London 15–16, for areas constituting these boroughs.

[66] Jones, L. R., *op. cit.*, 74–9.

[67] *Ibid.*, 39–31, 112–59.

[68] *Ibid.*, 63.

[69] *Ibid.*, 74–5.

[70] Sekon, G. A., *Locomotion in Victorian London* (Oxford, 1938), 14–16.

[71] Jones, L. R., *op. cit.*, 78–9.

[72] Robson, W. A., *The government and misgovernment of London* (London, 1939), 196.

[73] *The new survey of London life and labour*, vol. 3 (London, 1932), 142–3; vol. 6, 1934, 242–54, 270–5.

[74] Demangeon, A., *Les Isles Britanniques* (Paris, 1927), 256 and many later writers.

[75] *Op cit.*, in note 73, vol. VI, 175–91.

[76] Munby, O. L., *Industry and planning in Stepney* (Oxford, 1951), 79.

[77] Booth, C., *Life and labour of the people of London* (1892), vol. 3, 3–42 gives a thorough survey of these dwellings.

[78] Price-Williams, H., 'The population of London, 1801–1881', *J.R. statist. Soc.*, 48 (1885), 434–5.

[79] Pick, F., 'The organization of transport with special reference to the London Passenger Transport Board', *J. Royal Society of Arts*, 84 (1936), 212.

[80] Sekon, G. A., *op. cit.*, 133–6.

[81] *Ibid.*, 139–41.

[82] Pick, F., *op. cit.*, 212: Rasmussen, *op. cit.*, 136–7.

[83] Sekon, G. A., *op. cit.*, 192–4.

[84] *Ibid.*, 92.

[85] Pick, F., *op. cit.*, 212.

[86] *Ibid.*, 212–15.

[87] Gilbert 1954, 248.

[88] Census 1951, Report on . . . workplaces, 188–9.

[89] Garrett, A. J., 'Geographical development in northwest London', *Geography*, 24 (1939), 44.

[90] Pick, F., *op. cit.*, 216.

[91] *Ibid.*, 207–11.

[92] *County of London Plan* (1943), 88–9.

[93] *Ibid.*, 85–7.

[94] *Greater London Plan, 1944* (H.M.S.O., 1945), 39–41.

[95] Bird, J., *The geography of the port of London* (London, 1957), 147–8.

[96] *Greater London Plan* 1944, 41–4.

[97] Stamp, L. D., *The Land of Britain: its use and misuse* (1947), 133, 142–3.

[98] Bird, J., *op. cit.*, 143–55.

[99] *Greater London Plan* 1944, 43.

[100] *Ibid.*, 43.

[101] *Ibid.*, 43.

[102] *Ibid.*, 43.

[103] *Ibid.*, 42–3: Garrett, A. J., *op. cit.*, 45–7.

[104] Mackinder, H. J., *Britain and the British seas* (Oxford, 1907), chs. 14 and 15, esp. pp. 231–3, 260–2.

[105] See for example Gilbert 1947, 1–25 and Griffith, E. J. L., 'Moving industry from London', *Town Plann. Rev.*, 26 (1955–1956), 51–63.

[106] Mackinder, H. J., *op. cit.*, 257.

[107] Fawcett 102.

[108] *Ibid.*, 109. The figure of nine millions 'within a fifty mile radius of Manchester Town Hall' is inaccurate. Some of the advertising matter gave figures as high as fifteen millions, but according to the author's mapping of the area within a 50-mile radius, the population was 10,435,600 in 1931 and 10,935,300 in 1951.

[109] Census 1951, Report . . . conurbations, xxiv–xxix.

[110] Cole, Margaret, *op. cit.*, 36.

[111] Cmd. 1830, (1923) 51–54, 146–7 (interesting comments in a minority report): Robson, W. A., *op. cit.* (note 72), 57–60, 80–90.

[112] *Ibid.*, 62–3.

[113] Gibbon, G. and Bell, R. W., *History of the London County Council 1889–1939* (London, 1939), 38–9.

[114] Rasmussen, S. E., *op. cit.*, 325–7.

[115] Robson, W. A., *op. cit.*, 91.

[116] Census 1921, General Report (1927), 28.

[117] *Ibid.*, 28.

[118] The London County Council 1938, 37–9, 146–7.

[119] Gibbon, G. and Bell, R. W., *op. cit.*, 39, 505, 513.

[120] Robson, W. A., *op. cit.*, 168.

[121] Gibbon, G., and Bell, R. W., *op. cit.*, 368.

[122] Young, T., *Becontree and Dagenham: a report made for the Pilgrim Trust* (London, 1934), is a full analysis of this area in its early years.

[123] Gibbon, G., and Bell, R. W., *op. cit.*, 373. See also Quigley, H., and Goldie, Ismay, *Housing and slum clearance* (London, 1934), esp. pp. 61, 65, 105, 171, 208. On pp. 60–2, these authors show that in the early years of this century, sites in Central London were still cheap enough to repay the builders of working-class tenements, but about 1907–1908 there was a glut of houses, partly through building in (then) outer London districts such as Leyton, Woolwich and Wandsworth. Rents fell and working-class tenants began to use empty middle-class houses as tenements. By 1912–1913, house building was stagnant in Central London (p. 65).

[124] *County of London Plan 1943*, 115.

[125] Census 1931, County of London, vii–ix.

[126] Cmd. 1830 (1923), 973–4.

[127] *Ibid.*, 973.

[128] *Ibid.*, 1000.

[129] *Ibid.*, 1038–9.

[130] Census 1951, London xiii–xvi.
[131] *Ibid.*, 2, 57, 61.
[132] Census 1951, Report . . . conurbations, xxiv–xxv.
[133] Census 1851, Population Tables I, vol. 1, Div. 2, 86–9; Div. 3, 82–4; Div. 4, 72.
[134] Cmd. 1830 (1923), 996.
[135] Census 1891, vol. II, Surrey, 11. Census 1931, Surrey Pt. II, 10.
[136] Cmd. 1830 (1923), 481.
[137] *Ibid.*, 479–80.
[138] *Ibid.*, 819.
[139] *Ibid.*, 821
[140] Census 1931, London and Middlesex Pt. II, 9, 10.
[141] Census 1931, Pt. II of reports for each county.
[142] Cmd. 1830 (1923), 856.
[143] *Ibid.*, 796.
[144] *Ibid.*, 798.
[145] *Ibid.*, 799.
[146] *Ibid.*, 555.
[147] *Ibid.*, 547.
[148] *Ibid.*, 606.
[149] *Ibid.*, 761.
[150] *Ibid.*, 874.
[151] *Ibid.*, 877.
[152] Census 1931, Essex Pt. I, 12, Pt. II, 9.
[153] Cmd. 1830 (1923), 622.
[154] Census 1931, Surrey Pt. II, 13: 1951, Surrey, 5.
[155] Cmd. 1830 (1923), 756.
[156] *Ibid.*, 753.
[157] *Ibid.*, 537.
[158] Census 1901, Middlesex 10: 1931, Middlesex Pt. I, 8.
[159] *Ibid.*, 1901, 11–12: 1931, Middlesex Pt. II, 12.
[160] *Ibid.*, 1911, Middlesex 220–1, 223.
[161] *Ibid.*, 1901, Surrey 9, 10.
[162] *Ibid.*, 11.
[163] *Ibid.*, 1901, Kent 14, 15: 1931, Kent Pt. II, 7.
[164] *Ibid.*, 1901, Essex 12, 14.
[165] *Ibid.*, 1931, Middlesex Pt. I, 6.
[166] *Ibid.*, 1931, London and Middlesex Pt. II, 10.
[167] *Ibid.*, 1931, Surrey Pt. II, 6, 7, 9, 12.
[168] *Ibid.*, 1921, Kent 16: 1931, Kent Pt. II, 8, 11.
[169] *Ibid.*, 1931, Middlesex Pt. I, 6.
[170] *Ibid.*, 1931, Middlesex Pt. I, 6.
[171] *Ibid.*, 7.
[172] *Ibid.*, 7.
[173] Information from Town Clerk of Harrow.
[174] Gilbert (1948), 185–6.
[175] Census 1921, Essex 13.
[176] *Ibid.*, 1911, vol. 1, 220, 221.
[177] *Ibid.*, 1931, Middlesex Pt. I, 7.
[178] *Ibid.*, 1931, London and Middlesex Pt. II, 13.
[179] *Ibid.*, 1931, Surrey Pt. II, 18: 1951, 10.
[180] *Ibid.*, 1911, vol. 1, 162.
[181] *Ibid.*, 1951, Kent 15.
[182] *Ibid.*, 1931, Essex Pt. I, 12: 1951, 23.
[183] *Ibid.*, 1951, Report . . . conurbations, 6–7.

[184] Robson, W. A., *op. cit.*, 49.
[185] Quigley, H., and Goldie, I., *op. cit.*, 86.
[186] *Ibid.*, 86.
[187] Cmd. 1830 (1923), 979.
[188] *Ibid.*, 979.

CHAPTER 3

[1] Census 1951, Report on . . . conurbations, lx–lxxvi.
[2] West Midland Group, *Conurbation: a planning scheme of Birmingham and the Black Country* (London, 1948), 26–7.
[3] *Ibid*, 87–95, 139–52.
[4] Briggs, A., *History of Birmingham*, vol. II (Oxford, 1952), 326.
[5] Allen, G. C., *The industrial development of Birmingham and the Black Country, 1860–1927* (London, 1929) and works mentioned in notes 2, 4.
[6] *Conurbation, op. cit.*, in note 2, 160.
[7] Retail 8, 60.
[8] Brennan, T., *Midland City* (London, 1948), 22.
[9] *Conurbation, op. cit.*, esp. 53–9, 182–4.
[10] Warwick, G. T., in B.A. Birmingham, 8.
[11] Wise, M. J., and Johnson, B. L. C., in *ibid.*, 162.
[12] *Ibid.*, 241.
[13] Wise, M. J., 'Some factors influencing the growth of Birmingham', *Geography*, 33 (1948), 176–90, esp. 179.
[14] Gill, C., *History of Birmingham*, vol. I, 12–19.
[15] Allen, G. C., *op. cit.*, 13 and Gill, *op. cit.*, 48.
[16] Allen, G. C., *op. cit.*, 15.
[17] Gill, C., *op. cit.*, 56–7.
[18] *Ibid.*, 58.
[19] Allen, G. C., *op. cit.*, 13.
[20] Gill, C., *op. cit.*, 66, quoting Wm. Hutton, *History of Birmingham* (1781).
[21] Gill, C., *op. cit.*, 60–70.
[22] Wise, M. J., and Johnson, B. L. C., in B.A. Birmingham, 168.
[23] *Ibid.*, 170.
[24] Gill, C., *op. cit.*, 111.
[25] *Ibid.*, 87.
[26] Priestley, 63–75, 205, 583–96, 655–7, 690, 700–1: Jackman, 367–72.
[27] Gill, C., *op. cit.*, 154–5.
[28] Census 1851, Population Tables, I, vol. I, Div. VI, 64–9, 76–85.
[29] Gill, C., *op. cit.*, 125.
[30] Wise, M. J., and Thorpe, P. O'N., in B.A. Birmingham, 214.
[31] Wise, M. J., *op. cit.* in note 13, esp. 186.
[32] *Ibid.*, 187.
[33] Gale, W. V. K., in B.A. Birmingham, 198–201.
[34] Beaver, S. H., in Stamp, L. D., *The Land of Britain, Part 61, Staffordshire* (1945), 646.
[35] Wise, M. J., *op. cit.* in note 13, 189.
[36] Allen, G. C., *op. cit.*, 103–9.
[37] Rees, H., 'Birmingham and the Black Country', *Econ. Geogr.*, 22 (1946), 137–41.
[38] Walkerdine, R. H., and Corbin, E. G., (ed.) *Guide to the Coalfields 1957*, Colliery Guardian, London, 341, 344–5.
[39] Allen, G. C., *op. cit.*, 439.
[40] Gill, C., *op. cit.*, 282–9, 388–9.

[41] Briggs, A., *op. cit.*, vol. II, 11.
[42] Gill, C., *op. cit.*, 290.
[43] Census 1851, Population Tables I, vol. I, lxviii, cciv–ccvii.
[44] Gill, C., *op. cit.*, 32, 230–1.
[45] Census 1851, I, vol. I, Div. VI, 67, 79.
[46] *Ibid.*, 67.
[47] *Ibid.*, 67.
[48] *Ibid.*, 85.
[49] Briggs, A., *op. cit.*, 138.
[50] *Ibid.*, 11.
[51] Census 1851, Population Tables I, vol. I, 78–9.
[52] Census 1871, II, 315.
[53] Gill, *op. cit.*, 367.
[54] Census 1871, II, 315.
[55] *Ibid.*, 1871, II, 308, 315–16.
[56] *Ibid.*, 1871, II, 316.
[57] *Ibid.*, 1871, II, 318.
[58] Allen, G. C.. *op. cit.*, 438.
[59] *Ibid.*, 458.
[60] Census 1871, II, 309.
[61] *Ibid.*, 1871, II, 308.
[62] *Ibid.*, 1871, II, 308.
[63] *Ibid.*, 1871, II, 308.
[64] *Ibid.*, 1871, II, 309.
[65] *Ibid.*, 1871, II, 309.
[66] *Ibid.*, 1871, II, 309.
[67] *Ibid.*, 1901, Worcester 1.3.
[68] *Ibid.*, 1901, Stafford, 31
[69] Census, 1901, Warwick, 20.
[70] Census 1871, II, 315.
[71] Wise, M. J., and Thorpe, P. O'N., 'The growth of Birmingham', in B.A. Birmingham, 213–28.
[72] Briggs, A., *op. cit.*, 53, 158–60: Ashworth 132–3.
[73] Briggs, A., *op. cit.*, 139.
[74] *Ibid.*, 138.
[75] Wise, M. J., and Thorpe, P. O'N., in B.A. Birmingham, 224.
[76] Census 1871, II, 315.
[77] Briggs, A., *op. cit.*, 13, 19.
[78] *Ibid.*, 15.
[79] *Ibid.*, 325.
[80] *Ibid.*, 77–8.
[81] *Ibid.*, 83.
[82] *Ibid.*, 86.
[83] *Conurbation, op. cit.*, 91.
[84] Briggs, A., *op. cit.*, 229–35.
[85] City of Birmingham, *Report on the health of Birmingham in 1956*, 253–68 and statement kindly provided by the City Architect in 1957. See also Briggs, A., *op. cit.*, 229–35.
[86] Fidler, A. G. S., 'Post-war housing in Birmingham', *Town Plann. Rev.*, 26 (1955–1956), 41–4.
[87] Report in note 85, 253.
[88] *Conurbation, op. cit.*, 87–93.
[89] Local information.
[90] Cmd. 9559 (1955), 72.
[91] Brown, K., *Arch. Rev. Lond.*, 119 (1956), 309–15,

[92] 'Counter Attack', in *Arch. Rev. Lond.*, 120, no. 719 (1956), 432.

[93] Cmd. 9559 (1955), 72.

[94] Briggs, A., *op. cit.*, 141.

[95] Census 1901, Warwick 12.

[96] Census 1911, Co. of Warwick 331: Briggs, A., *op. cit.*, 145.

[97] Briggs, A., *op. cit.*, 155–6.

[98] *Ibid.*, 145–56.

[99] Census 1931, Warwick Pt. I, 8.

[100] *Ibid.*, Warwick Pt. I, 9.

[101] Briggs, A., *op. cit.*, 273.

[102] *Conurbation, op. cit.*, 184.

[103] *Ibid.*, 53.

[104] Census 1931, Stafford Pt. I, 11.

[105] *Ibid.*, Stafford Pt. II, 10.

[106] *Ibid.*, Worcester Pt. II, 8.

[107] *Ibid.*, Stafford Pt. II, 7.

[108] *Ibid.*, Stafford Pt. II, 7.

[109] *Ibid.*, Warwick Pt. I, 9.

[110] *Ibid.*, Warwick Pt. I, 8.

[111] *Ibid.*, Stafford Pt. I, 11.

[112] *Conurbation, op. cit.*, 93.

[113] Census, Stafford Pt. I, 11.

[114] *Ibid.*, Stafford Pt. II, 9.

[115] Gilbert (1948), 187.

[116] *The Times* 24 November 1953: report of the West Midland Group.

[117] Walker, G., 'The growth of population in Birmingham and the Black Country between the Wars', *University of Birmingham Historical Journal*, I (1947–1948), 158–79.

[118] And many of the furnaces put out were not re-lit. See Briggs, *op. cit.*, 282.

[119] *Conurbation, op. cit.*, 121–7.

[120] Census 1951, Occupation Tables, 586.

[121] Briggs, *op. cit.*, 282.

[122] *Ibid.*, 299.

[123] *Ibid.*, 300.

CHAPTER 4

[1] Fawcett 112.

[2] Census 1951, Report . . . conurbations, cviii.

[3] B.A. Merseyside 178.

[4] Jones, D. Caradog (ed.), *Survey of Merseyside*, vol. 1, 4–8; Allison, J. E., *The Mersey estuary* (Liverpool, 1949), 5–15.

[5] Gresswell, R. K., *Sandy shores in south Lancashire* (Liverpool, 1953), 146–7.

[6] Jones, D. C., *op. cit.*, in note 4, p. 5.

[7] Darby 59 (E. W. Gilbert) and 296–7 (D. T. Williams).

[8] Hodges, R., in B.A. Merseyside 164.

[9] Gresswell, *op. cit.*, 90–7.

[10] Steers, J. A., *Coastline of England and Wales* (Cambridge, 1946), 108.

[11] Stamp, L. D., *The Land of Britain: its use and misuse* (London, 1950), 368, 271.

[12] Jones, D. C., *op. cit.*, vol. 1, 10 and Darby, 297.

[13] Williams, D. T., in Darby, 296.

[14] Taylor, E. G. R., in Darby, 376.

[15] Routledge, J. F., in B.A. Merseyside, 105.

[16] Baker, J. N. L., in Darby, 430.

[17] Smith, W., in B.A. Merseyside, 190.
[18] Marriner, Sheila, in B.A. Merseyside, 107–10 and Hodges, R., *ibid.*, 164.
[19] Defoe II, 675.
[20] Marriner, Sheila, in B.A. Merseyside, 110–13.
[21] Jones, *op. cit.*, vol. I, 21.
[22] B.A. Merseyside, 110.
[23] *Ibid.*, 110.
[24] Defoe II, 664.
[25] *Ibid.*, II, 667.
[26] Jackman, 355–70.
[27] Baker, J. N. L., in Darby, 500–1.
[28] Rideout, E. H., *The growth of Wirral* (Liverpool, 1927), 31–2.
[29] Allison, *op. cit.*, 20–25, esp. map p. 23.
[30] Rideout, *op. cit.*, 89.
[31] Jones, *op. cit.*, vol. I, 28; Marriner, S., in B.A. Merseyside, 114.
[32] Cleveland-Stevens, E., *English railways—their development and their relation to the state* (London, 1915), 27.
[33] Griffiths, E. R., *The Cheshire Lines Railway* (Oakwood Press, 1947) gives a full account of this railway.
[34] Rideout, *op. cit.*, 33–4.
[35] Hewitt, W., *The Wirral peninsula* (London, 1922), 244.
[36] *Ibid.*, 243–5.
[37] Smith, W., *Physical Survey of Merseyside* (Liverpool, 1946), 61.
[38] Allison, *op. cit.*, 23.
[39] Jones, *op. cit.*, vol. 3, 19.
[40] Allison, *op. cit.*, 28–30.
[41] On Garston, a debt is owed to D. W. Mackay, B.A., for use of his unpublished thesis (University of Manchester).
[42] A similar acknowledgement is made to M. Glazzard, B.A., who wrote a thesis on Ellesmere Port. See also Census 1871, vol. II, 394: Rideout, *op. cit.*, 58–63.
[43] Census 1851, and later censuses. See also Lawton, R., 'The population of Liverpool in the mid-nineteenth century', *Transactions of the Historic Society of Lancashire and Cheshire*, vol. 107 (1955), 89–120.
[44] Census 1951, Population Tables I, vol. 2, 31.
[45] Census 1871, vol. II, 395.
[46] Lawton, R., in B.A. Merseyside, 124–8.
[47] Census 1851, Population Tables I, vol. II, 396.
[48] Jones, *op. cit.*, Survey, vol. I, 55.
[49] Bailey, F. A., in B.A. Merseyside, 241 and Ashworth 40–1.
[50] Census 1851, Population Tables I, vol. II, 31.
[51] Hewitt, *op cit.*, 196–200: Rideout, *op. cit.*, 67–72.
[52] Census 1871, vol. II, 395.
[53] *Ibid.*, 395.
[54] *Ibid.*, 394.
[55] Rideout, *op. cit.*, 64–6.
[56] Census 1871, vol. II, 395.
[57] *Housing Progress 1848–1951*, published by the City of Liverpool, 33–5.
[58] Jones, *op. cit.*, vol. III, 20 (T. S. Simey).
[59] *Ibid.*, vol. III, 18.
[60] Rideout, *op. cit.*, 77.
[61] Census 1891, Div. viii, 72.
[62] *Ibid.*, Div. viii, 78–9.
[63] Census 1901, Co. of Lancaster 29.
[64] *Ibid.*, 177, 180.

[65] Census 1921, Co. of Lancaster 27.

[66] *Ibid.*, 22.

[67] Census 1931, Co. of Lancaster, Part 2, 7.

[68] Royal Commission on the geographical distribution of the industrial population, Cmd. 6153 (1940), Minutes of Evidence, 827.

[69] *Housing Progress*, see (7)note 5 60.

[70] *Ibid.*, 59.

[71] Census 1911, vol. I, Lancashire 175; 1951, Lancashire 24, 25, 26.

[72] *Ibid.*, 1951, 25.

[73] Rideout, *op. cit.*, 82.

[74] *Ibid.*, 85–88.

[75] Census 1931, Co. of Chester, Part II, 11.

[76] Census 1901, Co. of Chester 14: 1911, 77: 1931, Part II, 10.

[77] Census 1931, Co. of Chester, Part I, 14: 1931, Pt. II, 8.

[78] Census 1931, Co. of Chester, Part I, 14: Part II, 6–7.

[79] Census 1931, Co. of Chester, Part II, 15.

[80] Rideout, *op. cit.*, 49, 55.

[81] Census 1951, Report . . . conurbations, xcvii–ciii.

[82] Thompson, F. L., *Merseyside Plan 1944* (H.M.S.O., 1945), 17.

[83] Retail 2, 5–6.

[84] Thesis of J. G. Wilson, B.A., on the Wirral: *ibid.*, note 83.

[85] Smith, W., in B.A. Merseyside, section on 'The urban structure of Liverpool', 188–99, is an excellent study. See also Bradbury, R., 'The technique of municipal housing in England', *Town Plann. Rev.*, 22 (1951), 44–71.

[86] *Ibid.*, 179.

[87] *Ibid.*, 180.

[88] Thesis of D. W. Mackay (note 41).

[89] Smith, W., in B.A. Merseyside, 196.

[90] Rideout, *op. cit.*, 85.

CHAPTER 5

[1] Fawcett, 103, 111.

[2] Geddes, 31–2.

[3] Census 1901, Chester 18: 1921, Lancaster 27.

[4] Census 1931, Lancaster, Pt. I, 23.

[5] Census 1951, Report . . . conurbations, xliii.

[6] Ogden, H. W., 'The geographical basis of the Lancashire cotton industry', *Journal of the Manchester Geographical Society*, 43 (1927), 14–26.

[7] Rodgers, H. B., Altrincham—a town of the Manchester Conurbation, *Town Plann. Rev.*, 23 (1952–1953), 190–5.

[8] Bruton, F. A. (ed.), *The Roman fort at Manchester* (Manchester, 1909), is a full account.

[9] Redford, A., *The history of local government in Manchester*, vol. 1 (London, 1939), 15–18.

[10] *Ibid.*, I, 15.

[11] Taylor, E. G. R., in Darby, 376.

[12] *Ibid.*, 366.

[13] *Ibid.*, 410, 414 (J. N. L. Baker).

[14] *Ibid.*, 414.

[15] Defoe, 670.

[16] *Ibid.*, 675.

[17] *Ibid.*, 677.

[18] *Ibid.*, 596.

[19] Ogden, H. W., *op. cit.*, 18–26.

[20] Ogden, H. W., *op. cit.*, 14.

[21] *Manchester and district regional planning proposals* (1945), 73–6.

[22] Aikin, J., *A survey of the counties of Lancashire, Cheshire, Derybshire, West Riding of Yorkshire and the northern part of Staffordshire* (London, 1797), 147.

[23] Young, A., *A six months tour through the North of England* (London, 1770), III, 251–71.

[24] Aikin, *op. cit.*, 166.

[25] Love, B., *Hand-book of Manchester* (1842), 35.

[26] Everett, J., *Manchester Guide* (Manchester, 1840), 183.

[27] Jackman, 371.

[28] Priestley, 32–6.

[29] *Ibid.*, 435.

[30] Aikin, *op. cit.*, 203.

[31] Redford, A., *Manchester merchants and foreign trade* (Manchester, 1934), 178.

[32] Everett, *op. cit.*, 188–94.

[33] Bruton, F. A., *A short history of Manchester and Salford* (Manchester, 1924), 187.

[34] *Ibid.*, 187.

[35] *Ibid.*, 187.

[36] *Ibid.*, 188.

[37] *Ibid.*, 189.

[38] *Ibid.*, 189.

[39] Millward, R., *Lancashire* (London, 1955), 72–93.

[40] Census 1851, Population Tables I, vol. II, 12–17, 36–45.

[41] Poor Law Commissioners, Reports 1835, App. B, 11, report from J. P. Kay, 183.

[42] Census 1851, Population Tables, I, vol. II, Div. VIII, 40, 42.

[43] Census of Ireland 1841, lxxxciii–lxxxix.

[44] Calculated from material in Census of 1851.

[45] Census 1851, Population Tables I, vol. II, Div. VIII, 15.

[46] Information from 6 in. to 1 mile maps, 1848.

[47] Ashton, T. S., *Economic and social investigations in Manchester 1833–1933* (London, 1934), 2.

[48] Information drawn from 6 in. to 1 mile maps, 1848.

[49] Census 1861, vol. I, 556, 572–5. *Ibid.*, 1871, II, Div. VIII, 385–8, 399–403.

[50] Census 1851, Population Tables I, vol. II, Div. VIII, 42. *Ibid.*, 1871, II, Div. VIII, 402.

[51] *Ibid.*, (as 50).

[52] *Ibid.*, 1851, Population Tables I, vol. II, 42: *ibid.*, 1901, Lancaster 55.

[53] *Ibid.*, 1871, II, Div. VIII, 402: Baker, H., 'On the growth of the commercial centre of Manchester, movement of population and pressure of habitation—Census decenniad 1861–1871,' *Trans. Manchr. statist. Soc.* (1871–1872), 90–3, 105: Martin, R., 'Sanitary progress and its obstacles in Manchester', *Trans. Manchr. statist. Soc.* (1874–1875), 99.

[54] Census 1871, II, Div. VIII, 401: Baker, H., *op. cit.*, 105.

[55] Redford, A., *Manchester merchants and foreign trade* (Manchester, 1934), 217–28: Henderson, W. O., *The Lancashire cotton famine 1861–1865* (Manchester, 1934), 1–27, 35–47, 118.

[56] Daniels, G. W., and Jewkes, J., 'The comparative position of the Lancashire cotton industry and trade', *Trans. Manchr. statist. Soc.* (1926–1927), 57–93.

[57] Local information. There are numerous papers on the Ship Canal in *Trans. Manchr. statist. Soc.*, but the main source is Leech, T. B., *History of the Manchester Ship Canal from its inception to its completion* (London and Manchester, 1907).

[58] Census 1951, Report . . . conurbations, xlix.
[59] Simon, Shena D., *A century of city government Manchester 1838–1938*: (London, 1938), 284–302.
[60] *Ibid.*, 290–2.
[61] Census 1891, vol. II, 806.
[62] Simon, S. D., *op. cit.*, 297. An excellent review of housing is given in Redford, A., *History of local government in Manchester*, vol. 2 (1940), 403–22; vol. 3, (1940), 226–68.
[63] L.I.D.A., no. 5. *The spinning area*, (Manchester, 1950), 7, 28–30.
[64] Thesis of J. Shaw, B.A., Oldham: a town of the Industrial Revolution: The *White Paper on Slum Clearance 1955*, Cmd. 9593, stated that 11,169 houses in Oldham, 26 per cent of the whole, were unfit for habitation.
[65] Stocks, Mary, *Fifty years in Every Street* (Manchester, 1945), 86–7.
[66] Redford, A., *History of local government in Manchester*, vol. 3, 248–53.
[67] Census 1931, Chester Part I, 14.
[68] Census 1951, Lanchashire 2.
[69] *Ibid.*, 1951, 2–3.
[70] *Ibid.*, 1951, Report . . . conurbations, 81.
[71] Nicholas, R., *City of Manchester Plan* (1945), 175–7.
[72] Local information.
[73] Cmd. 9559 (1955), 71: Cmd. 193 (1957), 42.
[74] Cmd. 9876 (1956), 50.
[75] Chorley, K., *Manchester made them* (London, 1950), is an account of Alderley Edge rich in social history.
[76] Census 1951, Report . . . conurbations, maps at end, xliv (Div. V).
[77] Newspaper report, e.g. *Manchester Guardian*, February 18, 1958, 'Three towns ready for amalgamation'—in this case Ashton, Dukinfield and Stalybridge. Four neighbouring towns were interested but not convinced of the wisdom of joining a 'combine'—Audenshaw, Denton, Hyde, Mossley.
[78] Fawcett, 103.
[79] Retail 2, 5–6.
[80] Taylor, R. P. and E., *Rochdale Retrospect* (1956), is an excellent account of the town.
[81] Census 1951, Lancashire 75: Cmd 9559 (1955), 144.
[82] Census 1851, Population Tables I, vol. II, Div. VIII, 64 6.
[83] Census 1871, vol. I, xviii–xxxii.
[84] Census 1891, vol. II, 803, 806: Census 1901, Lancaster 24, 27, 31.
[85] *Ibid.*, 1891, 806.
[86] Census 1911, vol. I, Administrative areas, 177, 179, 181.
[87] Census 1931, Lancaster Part I, 23.
[88] Redford, A., *op. cit.*, vol. 2, 315–16, 322.
[89] Census 1911, vol. I, Administrative areas, 177, 181.
[90] *Ibid.*, 76–80: Census 1921, Lancaster, 27.
[91] Census 1911, vol. I, Administrative areas, 78: Census 1931, Chester Part II, 14.
[92] Census 1891, vol. II, 802: 1901, Chester 13: 1911, vol. I, 77: 1931, Chester Pt. I, 14.
[93] Census 1901, Chester 14.
[94] *Ibid.*, 12: 1911, vol. I, Administrative areas, 76: 1931, Chester Pt. II, 9.
[95] *Ibid.*, 1931, Chester Pt. II, 12.
[96] Census 1901, Lancaster 20.
[97] *Ibid.*, 26.
[98] *Ibid.*, 37, 38, 40.
[99] *Ibid.*, 21.
[100] Census 1931, Lancaster Part II, 6–7.
[101] *Ibid.*, 14.

[102] Census 1931, Lancaster Part II, 12.

[103] *Ibid.*, 10.

[104] *Ibid.*, 8.

[105] *Ibid.*, 1931, Lancaster Part I, 22; Part II, 8.

[106] *Ibid.*, Part II, 9, 11, 13, 14.

[107] Bateson, H., *Centenary history of Oldham* (Oldham, 1949), 226 ('sooner or later the inevitable march of progress will override parochial prejudice and complacency').

[108] Census 1931, Chester Part I, 14; Part II, 14.

[109] *Ibid.*, 1921, Chester 17: 1951, Cheshire 16.

[110] *Ibid.*, 1901, Chester 14: 1931, Chester Part II, 8, 10.

CHAPTER 6

[1] Fawcett 103–5, 111–12.

[2] *Ibid.*, 104.

[3] Census 1951, England and Wales, Report . . . conurbations, lxxvi–xcii, 210–58.

[4] Gaskell, E. C., *Life of Charlotte Brontë* (1857), Everyman, 2–3.

[5] Chorley, K. C., 'Cities of the Pennines' in *Hills and Highways* (London, 1928), 209–10.

[6] Defoe II, 600.

[7] *Ibid.*, 601.

[8] *Ibid.*, 602.

[9] Crump, W. B., and Ghorbal, Gertrude, *History of the Huddersfield woollen industry* ,Tolson Memorial Museum, Huddersfield (1935), 16.

[10] *Ibid.*, 82.

[11] Heaton, H., *The Yorkshire woollen and worsted industries* (Oxford, 1920), 299–300.

[12] *Ibid.*, 288.

[13] *Ibid.*, 283, 289.

[14] *Ibid.*, 289.

[15] Parsons, E., *The civil, ecclesiastical, literary, commercial and miscellaneous history of Leeds, Bradford, Wakefield, Dewsbury, Otley and the district within ten miles of Leeds* (London, 1834), gives an excellent account of the towns named and of others.

[16] Heaton, *op. cit.*, 1360–81.

[17] Parsons, E., *op. cit.*, 217–18.

[18] Parsons, E., *op. cit.*, 218: Crump, W. B., and Ghorbal, Gertrude, *op. cit.*, 80: Jackman, I, 371: Priestley, 340–4, 531–2.

[19] Priestley, 84–6.

[20] *Ibid.*, 120–5.

[21] Parson, E., *op. cit.*, 428–9: Crump, W. B., and Ghorbal, Gertrude, *op. cit.*, 80–2.

[22] Crump, W. B., and Ghorbal, Gertrude, *op. cit.*, 17.

[23] *Ibid.*, 19.

[24] *Ibid.*, 19.

[25] Smith 25.

[26] Heaton, H., *op. cit.*, 286–8.

[27] *Ibid.*, 289.

[28] Dodd, G., *Textile manufactures of Great Britain* (London, 1851), 93–123.

[29] Census of 1851, Div. IX, Yorkshire West Riding 24–33.

[30] Parsons, E., *op. cit.*, 254, 279.

[31] *Ibid.*, 254, 399: Crump, W. B., and Ghorbal, Gertrude, *op. cit.*, 102–10: Dodd, G., *op. cit.*, 120.

[32] Parsons, E., *op. cit.*, 428–33.

[33] *Ibid.*, 428, 431–2.

[34] Dodd, G., *op. cit.*, 120.

[35] Parsons, E., *op. cit.*, 253, 449, 452.

[36] *Ibid.*, 438.

[37] *Ibid.*, 443.

[38] *Ibid.*, 443–4.

[39] *Ibid.*, 253.

[40] *Ibid.*, 254.

[41] *Ibid.*, 254.

[42] *Ibid.*, 253: Dodd, G., *op. cit.*, 123.

[43] Dodd, G., *op. cit.*, 122.

[44] *Ibid.*, 93.

[45] Thanks are due to G. M. Harrap, B.A., for the use of his unpublished thesis on Ossett and Horbury.

[46] Fawcett 103–4.

[47] Census 1931, West Riding and York C.B., Part II, 1940, 5–16.

[48] Census 1921, Yorkshire 55.

[49] Census 1931, West Riding, Part II, 16.

[50] Census 1891, Div. IX, 85; 1901, Co. of York 38; 1931, West Riding Part I, 25; Part II, 7.

[51] Census 1921, Co. of Yorkshire 54, 55; 1931, Part I, 24–5.

[52] Census 1891, Div. IX, 92; 1931, Part II, 14.

[53] Census 1901, Co. of York 50; 1931, Part II, 14.

[54] Census 1931, Yorkshire Part II, 8.

[55] Census 1911, Yorkshire 374; 1931, Yorkshire Part II, 9.

[56] Census 1911, Yorkshire 386; 1931, Yorkshire Part II, 8: 1951, West Riding, 22.

[57] Census 1911, Yorkshire 374.

[58] Beaver, S. H., in Stamp, L. D., *The land of Britain, Part 46, Yorkshire West Riding*, (1941), 128.

[59] Census volumes, esp. 1851, 1901 and 1951, Report . . . conurbations.

[60] Census 1951, Report . . . conurbations, xcii.

[61] *Ibid.*, lxxxiv.

[62] Census 1871, vol. II, 439 40.

[63] *Ibid.*, 440.

[64] *Ibid.*, 440.

[65] Census 1851, Population Tables I, vol. II, Div. IX, 31.

[66] Census 1871, vol. II, 440.

[67] *Ibid.*, 440.

[68] *Ibid.*, 438.

[69] Census 1851, Population Tables I, vol. II, Div. IX, 100–1.

[70] Fawcett 104, 105.

[71] Census 1951, Occupations, 352–3.

[72] Smith 433.

[73] Fawcett 107–9, 111–12.

[74] Local information and thesis of J. W. Sanderson, B.A., on Wakefield.

[75] Local information.

[76] Housing memorandum from Medical Officer of Health, Leeds.

[77] Dickinson, R. E., 'The regional functions and zones of influence of Leeds and Bradford', *Geography*, 15 (1929–1930), 548–57.

[78] Retail 6–7.

[79] *Huddersfield Official Handbook*, 11.

[80] Retail 6–7.

CHAPTER 7

[1] Report of the Royal Commission on local government in the Tyneside area (1937), Cmd. 5402, 55.

[2] Fawcett 112.

[3] Mess, H. A., *Industrial Tyneside* (London, 1928), 18–19.

[4] Defoe II, 659–60.

[5] *Ibid.*, II, 660; Nef, J. U., *The rise of the British coal industry* (London, 1932), 207.

[6] Philbin, P., 'A geographical analysis of the sea-salt industry of north-east England', *Scot. geogr. Mag.*, 51 (1935), 22–8. Mr. Philbin shows that brine evaporation was practised at numerous places on the British coasts.

[7] Smailes, A. E., 'Population changes in the colliery districts of Northumberland and Durham', *Geogr. J.*, 111 (1938), 223.

[8] Smailes, A. E., 'The development of the Northumberland and Durham coalfield', *Scot. geogr. Mag.*, 51 (1935), 204.

[9] Defoe II, 661.

[10] Quoted in Nef, J. U., *op. cit.*, 257.

[11] Smailes, A. E., 'Early industrial settlement in north-east England', *Advanc. Sci. Lond.*, 6, no. 24 (1950), 326.

[12] Nef, J. U., *op. cit.*, 9. 21.

[13] Nef, J. U., *op. cit.*, 25; Smailes, *op. cit.*, in note 11.

[14] Nef, J. U., *op. cit.*, 350–1.

[15] Poole, G., and Raistrick, A., B.A. North-eastern 88.

[16] Smailes, A. E., *op. cit.* in note 11, 330.

[17] Philbin, P., *op. cit.* in note 6, 26–8. Causes included the development of rock-salt mining in Cheshire after 1670, and the discovery of a copious salt spring at Birtley, Co. Durham, at the end of the eighteenth century. 'There were only five pans at South Shields in 1820, and probably one at North Shields'.

[18] Guthrie, J., *The river Tyne: its history and resources* (Newcastle and London, 1880), 37; Smailes, *op. cit.* in note 11, 328; B.A. North-eastern 167–8 (in article on Chemicals by Hill, B. P., and Clemo, G. R.).

[19] Guthrie, *op. cit.*, 36; British Association, *A history of the trade and manufacture of the Tyne, Wear and Tees* (1863), 113–14.

[20] B.A. North-eastern 135.

[21] North-east Development Board, *A survey of industrial features on the north-east coast* (1936), 111.

[22] *North-east Coast Industrial Survey* (1932), 279.

[23] *Ibid.*, 21.

[24] B.A. North-eastern 135–6.

[25] *Ibid.*, 137–8.

[26] *Ibid.*, 143.

[27] *Ibid.*, 147.

[28] *Ibid.*, 147–8.

[29] *Ibid.*, 161–6.

[30] *Ibid.*, 167–8.

[31] *Ibid.*, 169–70.

[32] Ministry of Labour—Reports of investigation into the industrial conditions in certain Depressed Areas (1934), Cmd. 4728, 82–3.

[33] *Ibid.*, 83.

[34] *Ibid.*, 106.

[35] Report of the Royal Commission on local government in the Tyneside area (1937), Cmd. 5402, 54.

[36] Guthrie, *op. cit.*, 45.

[37] *Ibid.*, 60–1.

[38] *Ibid.*, 66.

[39] Tomlinson, W. W., *The North Eastern Railway: its rise and development* (Newcastle and London, 1914), 241.

[40] *Ibid.*, 438–9, 449–50, 463–82.

[41] *Ibid.*, 484, 525, 606.

[42] *Ibid.*, 506.

[43] *Ibid.*, 500. See also Cleveland-Stevens, E., *English railways—their development and their relation to the state* (London, 1915), 28, 222–4.

[44] Guthrie, *op. cit.*, 76–90.

[45] *Ibid.*, 102.

[46] *Ibid.*, 111.

[47] *Ibid.*, 122.

[48] *Ibid.*, 138–83.

[49] Tomlinson, *op. cit.*, 579, 666.

[50] *Ibid.*, 612.

[51] *Ibid.*, 580.

[52] *Ibid.*, 633.

[53] *Ibid.*, 685.

[54] B.A. North-eastern 149.

[55] Census 1871, Div. X, 493.

[56] Census 1851, Northumberland 23.

[57] Census 1871, Div. X, 493.

[58] Census 1851, Northumberland 25.

[59] Census 1871, Div. X, 493.

[60] Census 1901, Northumberland 20.

[61] Census 1871, Div. X, 492–3.

[62] Census 1851, Durham 23.

[63] Census 1871, Div. X, 492.

[64] North-east Development Board, *Survey, op. cit.*, 1936, 28–9.

[65] Cmd. 5402 (see note 1); Mess, *op. cit.* in note 3.

[66] Census 1851, Durham 68–9.

[67] Report of the Commissioners appointed to report and advise upon the boundaries and wards of certain boroughs and corporate towns in England and Wales (1837), Part II, sections on Newcastle and Gateshead.

[68] Ashworth 38.

[69] *Cf.* note 67.

[70] Cmd. 5402 (note 1), 19.

[71] *Ibid.*, 20.

[72] *Ibid.*, 21; Census 1911, Northumberland 247.

[73] Cmd. 5402, 23.

[74] Census 1911, Northumberland 259; Census 1931, Northumberland Part 2, 7.

[75] Cmd. 5402, 22; Census 1931, Northumberland Pt. 2, 7.

[76] Cmd. 5402, 22.

[77] Cmd. 5402, 24; Census 1931, Northumberland Pt. 2, 8.

[78] Cmd. 540, 27.

[79] *Ibid.*, 32; Census 1931, Durham Pt. 2, 12.

[80] Cmd. 5402, 31; Census 1931, Durham Pt. 2, 9.

[81] Cmd. 5402, 29; Census 1931, Durham Pt. 2, 10.

[82] Cmd. 5402, 18; Census 1931, Durham Pt. 2, 10.

[83] Cmd. 4728 (see note 32), 87–8.

[84] Mess, *op. cit.*, 164–8.

[85] Co. Borough of Gateshead, *Annual Report of the Public Health Department for the year 1953*, 1–5.

[86] Retail 3–4, 7.

[87] B.A. North-eastern has two valuable articles on urban geography by M. R. G. Conzen, 75–83, 191–7.

[88] Mess, *op. cit.*, 29, 165–6.

[89] Census 1951, Housing, 81, 87–8, 100–1.

[90] Information on recent industrial growth is given in *Tyneside Story*, published by Tyneside Industrial Development Board, n.d., and *Industrial Estates*, published by the North-east Trading Estates Ltd., Team Valley, Gateshead (n.d., c. 1953 and 1957) and personal information.

[91] Census 1951, Report . . . conurbations, 312.

[92] Mess, *op. cit.*, 18–23.

CHAPTER 8

[1] Census 1851, Population Tables, vol. I, xlv–li, lxxxiii–lxxxiv.

[2] *Ibid.*, xlvi.

[3] *Ibid.*, lxxvi–lxxvii.

[4] *Public health and social conditions—Statistical memoranda and charts prepared in the Local Government Board relating to Public Health and Social Conditions*, Cmd. 4671 (1909), 18: *The Public Health Act 1875*, 38 and 39, Vict. Cap. 55 with short explanatory notes by J. V. Vesey Fitzgerald (London, 1876).

[5] Cmd. 4671, 18.

[6] *Ibid.*, 19, 77–80: Lipman, V. D., *Local government areas 1835–1945* (Oxford, 1949), 167–79.

[7] These include Cole, G. D. H., *Local and regional government* (London, 1947); Finer, H., *English local government* (London, 1933); Laski, H. (ed.), *A century of municipal progress* (London, 1935); Lipman, V. D., *op. cit.*; Robson, W. A., *The development of local government* (London, 1931, 1948).

[8] These places became 'urban' under the provisions of the Local Government Act 1858, to avoid the inclusion of their parishes in the Highway Districts formed under the Highway Act of 1862. Some such places had less than 100 inhabitants. Second Report of the Royal Commission on Local Government (1928), Cmd. 3213.

[9] Census 1851, Population Tables, vol. I, lxxiv.

[10] Royal Commission on local government reports: First (1927), Cmd. 2506: Second (1928), Cmd. 3213: Final (1929), Cmd. 3436.

[11] Smailes, A. E., 'The urban hierarchy in England and Wales', *Geography*, 29 (1944), 41–51: 'The urban mesh of England and Wales', *Pub. Inst. Brit. Geogr.*, 11 (1946), 87–101.

[12] Ashworth 15–16.

[13] Census 1851, vol. I, xlv–xlvii.

[14] *Ibid.*, 1851, xlvi–xlvii.

[15] Dickinson, R. E., *City, region and regionalism* (London, 1947), 53–62.

[16] Census 1951, vol. I, xlvii.

[17] *Ibid.*, xlvii–xlviii, xlix–xlx.

[18] *Ibid.*, xlvii.

[19] Census 1951, England and Wales General Tables, 9.

[20] Vince, S. W. E., 'Reflections on the structure and distribution of rural population in England and Wales, 1921–1931, *Pub. Inst. Brit. Geogr.*, 18 (1952), 53–76.

[21] Census 1851, vol. I, xlvii–xlviii.

[22] Gilbert (1948), 173–4.

[23] Details of changes for each county are given in Part II of each 1931 (Census) volume.

[24] Gilbert (1948), 184–98, including a map of the 1945 White Paper, Local

government in England and Wales during the period of reconstruction, Cmd. 6852.

[25] Cmd. 9559 (1955), 26.

[26] *Ibid.*, 29.

[27] Local government: area and status of local authorities in England and Wales (1956), Cmd. 9831.

[28] Fawcett 100–1.

[29] Gilbert, B.A. Oxford 172.

[30] *Ibid.*, 168.

[31] Census 1951, Glamorgan 1.

[32] Fawcett 107–9.

[33] Gilbert (1954), 17–21.

[34] Census 1921, Glamorgan 1.

[35] Daysh, G. H. J., Symonds, J. S., and others, *West Durham* (Oxford, 1953), 87–112.

[36] Geddes 16–19.

[37] Fawcett 100.

[38] Osborne, R. H., 'Population concentrations and conurban tendencies in the middle Trent counties, *East Mid. Geogr.*, 2 (1954), 30–7.

[39] Census 1851, vol. I, xlvi–xlvii.

[40] Gilbert (1939), 28–31.

CHAPTER 9

[1] Thanks are due to T. F. Pears, B.A., for the use of his unpublished thesis on Carlisle.

[2] Personal communication from Mr. F. J. Donnelly.

[3] *Industrial Estates*, pub. North Eastern Trading Estates, n.d., 25.

[4] *Ibid.*, 25, 29, 32.

[5] *Ibid.*, 32, 48, 237–8.

[6] *Ibid.*, 25, 233, 237–8.

[7] B.A. North-eastern 135, 154, 173.

[8] British Iron and Steel Federation, *Steel on the North East coast* (July, 1955): Smith 324–8; Stamp, L. D., and Beaver, S. H., *The British Isles* (London, 1954), 361–2, 369, 376–9. An excellent social survey is Glass, Ruth (ed.), *The social background of a Plan—a study of Middlesbrough* (London, 1948).

[9] B.A. North-eastern, 162–3.

[10] Gilbert (1948), 193, and map opp. 175.

[11] Ashworth 45; Gilbert (1939), 22–3.

[12] British Association 1922, *Handbook to Hull and the East Riding of Yorkshire*, ed. T. Sheppard: Brown, R. N. Rudmose in Ogilvie, 308: de Boer, G., 'The evolution of Kingston-upon-Hull', *Geography*, 31 (1946), 139–46: Lutyens, E., and Abercrombie, P., *A plan for the city and county of Kingston-upon-Hull* (London and Hull, 1945).

[13] Valuable material has been drawn from the thesis of Miss B. M. Waddington, B.A., on Doncaster.

[14] Defoe II, 598.

[15] Census 1901, York 52: 1911, Yorkshire W.R. and York C.B., 383–4: 1921, Yorkshire 54: 1031, Yorkshire W.R. 6, 8, 15, 25.

[16] Cmd. 9559 (1955), 29.

[17] B.A. Sheffield, esp. 162 (map), 166–7. It is noted that so far no suitable site has been found for an airport: Brown, R. N. Rudmose, 'Sheffield: its rise and growth', *Geography*, 21, 1936, 175–84.

[18] Brown, R. N. Rudmose in Ogilvie, 296–7.

[19] Hunt, A. J. in B.A. Sheffield, 228–42: *Sheffield Re-planned*, n.d., 30.

[20] Census 1851, Population Tables I, vol. I, cv.

[21] Millward, R., *Lancashire* (London, 1955), 72, 74–6: L.I.D.A., *The Furness area* (Manchester, 1948).

[22] L.I.D.A., *The weaving area* (Manchester, 1949) and thesis of K. Wallwork, M.A., on the towns of the Calder–Darwen valley.

[23] Smith 497–8.

[24] L.I.D.A., *op. cit.* in note 22, 13, 15, 26.

[25] *Ibid.*, 6–15, 22–8.

[26] L.I.D.A., *The spinning area* (Manchester, 1950), 14, 15, 16, 19–21.

[27] L.I.D.A., *The Lancashire coast area* (Manchester, 1951), 13: Millward, R., *op. cit.*, 98–103: Curnow, W. I., 'The growth of Blackpool as a health and holiday resort', in British Association Scientific Survey (1936), 74–84.

[28] L.I.D.A., *The Lancashire coast area*, 25.

[29] Millward, R., *op. cit.*, 103.

[30] L.I.D.A., *The Lancashire coast area*, 10, 30–1: Gilbert (1954), 21–5, 30, 241–3.

[31] L.I.D.A., *op. cit.*, 28.

[32] *Ibid.*, 6, 12.

[33] Gilbert (1954), 18–19, 25, 242–3.

[34] Millward, R., *op. cit.*, 102–3. Bailey, F. A., 'The origin and growth of Southport'. *Town Plann. Rev.*, 21 (1951) 297–317.

[35] Census 1951, Report . . . workplace, 109. Southport had 2,541 workers in Liverpool and 1,033 in Manchester.

[36] L.I.D.A., *op. cit.*, 12, 20.

[37] Census 1921, Lancaster 27.

[38] Geddes 31–5.

[39] L.I.D.A., *The coal/chemical area* (Manchester, 1950), 23.

[40] Historical aspects are treated in Barker, T. C., and Harris, J. R., *A Merseyside town in the Industrial Revolution—St. Helens 1750–1900* (Liverpool, 1954): L.I.D.A., *op. cit.*, 38. But is St. Helens on Merseyside?

[41] Millward, R., *op. cit.*, 18–20.

[42] *Ibid.*, 50–1.

[43] Note in *Arch. Rev. Lond.*, 118 (1955), 305–11.

[44] Retail 5–6.

[45] L.I.D.A., *The coal/chemical area*, 18–20.

[46] Census 1951, Report . . . workplace, 109.

[47] *Ibid.*, 109.

[48] *Ibid.*, 110, 117, 118.

[49] L.I.D.A., *The coal/chemical area*, 25–8.

[50] B.A. Merseyside, 283–4.

[51] Retail 2.

[52] Chaloner, W. H., *The social and economic development of Crewe* (Manchester, 1950).

CHAPTER 10

[1] Census 1951, County reports: Willatts, E. C., and Newson, E. C., 'The geographical pattern of population changes in England and Wales, 1921–1951', *Geogr. J.*, 99 (1953), 431–50.

[2] Powell, A. G., 'The 1951 Census: (2) An analysis of population changes in Leicestershire', *East Mid. Geogr.*, 3 (1955), 3–15.

[3] *Ibid.*, 3–4.

[4] Moisley, H. A., 'The industrial and urban development of the North Staffordshire conurbation', *Pub. Inst. Brit. Geogr.*, 17 (1951), 151–65 (an admirable study): Shrapnel, M., 'City of six Town Halls', *Manchester Guardian*, 17 March 1954.

[5] *Manchester Guardian*, 17 November 1954, 'Water in the church, but the baths run dry'.

[6] Wise, M. J., 'Some notes on the growth of population in the Cannock Chase coalfield', *Geography*, 36 (1951), 235–48 and 'The Cannock Chase region', B.A. Birmingham 269–88.

[7] Glaisyer, Janet, Brennan, T., Ritchie, W., and Florence, P. C., *County town—a civic survey for the planning of Worcester* (London, 1946), 26, 43–59, 193–229.

[8] Addison 116–19; Ashworth 39; theses of D. A. Lewis, M.A., on Leamington and P. A. Morton, B.A. (Warwick).

[9] Burns, W., 'The Coventry Sociological Survey: results and interpretation', *Town Plann. Rev.*, 25 (1954), 128–43: a debt is owed to Miss Janet M. Storer, B.A., for the use of her thesis on Coventry.

[10] Jackson, E. A., unpublished B.A. thesis on Nuneaton.

[11] McAllister, J., B.A., thesis on the Swadlincote district.

[12] Chandler, T. J., 'Communications and a coalfield: a study in the Leicestershire and South Derbyshire coalfield', *Pub. Inst. Brit. Geogr.*, 23 (1957), 163–73.

[13] Edwards, K. C., 'The East Midlands: some general considerations', *East Mid. Geogr.*, 1 (1954), 3–12.

[14] *Ibid.*, 11.

[15] Smith, B., B.A. thesis on Chesterfield has been used here.

[16] *East Mid. Geogr.*, 5, 1956, 37–8, note by E. M. Rawstron.

[17] Lee, K. G., unpublished B.A. thesis on Mansfield has much useful information.

[18] Osborne, R. H., 'Population concentrations and conurban tendencies in the middle Trent counties', *East Mid. Geogr.*, 2 (1954), 30–7: Powell, A. G. 'The 1951 Census: an analysis of population changes in Derbyshire', *ibid.*, 2 (1954), 13–23 and 'The 1951 Census: (3) an analysis of population changes in Nottinghamshire', *ibid.*, 4 (1955), 29–42.

[19] Census 1951, Report on usual residence and workplace, 61: Vollans, E. C., 'Derby: a railway town and regional centre', *Pub. Inst. Brit. Geogr.*, 15 (1949), 93–112.

[20] Osborne, R. H., *op. cit.*, 33.

[21] Edwards, K. C., 'Some location factors in the development of Nottingham', *East Mid. Geogr.*, 5 (1956), 3–9. See also Large, D. C., 'Nottingham: its urban pattern', *ibid.*, 6 (1956), 35–41 and Weekley, I. G., 'Service centres in Nottingham', *ibid.*, 41–6.

[22] Edwards, K. C., *op. cit.*, 7 and Johnston, W. B., 'The East Midlands and post-war development in manufacturing', *East Mid. Geogr.*, 4 (1955), 3–18.

[23] Edwards, K. C., *op. cit.*, 7–9.

[24] Powell, A. G., 'The 1951 Census: (2) an analysis of population changes in Leicestershire', *East Mid. Geogr.*, 3 (1955), 8–10.

[25] Stamp, L. D., and Beaver, S. H., *The British Isles* (1954), 678–80.

[26] Census 1951, Report . . . workplace, 125–6.

[27] Edwards, K. C., 'Geographical patterns in Lincolnshire', *Geography*, 39, (1954), 78–90; and 'Lincoln: a geographical excursion', Geographical Association (Lincoln, 1953).

[28] Healey, Pamela, and Rawstron, E. M., 'The brickworks of the Oxford Clay Vale', *East Mid. Geogr.*, 4 (1955), 48.

[29] Halford, W., and Wright, H. M., *Cambridge planning proposals* (Cambridge, 1950).

[30] East, W. G., in Darby, 495, 498.

[31] B.A. Norwich, esp. 19–21, 89–100.

[32] *Ibid.*, 102–4.

[33] Harris, C. D., 'Ipswich, England', *Econ. Geogr.*, 18 (1942), 1–12: Stamp, L. D., and Beaver, S. H., *op. cit.*, 426.

[34] Census 1951, Report . . . workplace, 78–9.

[35] Thesis of D. M. Ray, B.A., on Watford.

[36] Census 1931, Essex Part II, 11.

[37] Bird, J., *The geography of the port of London* (London, 1957), 108–14, 147, 154.

[38] *Ibid.*, 114, 144, 146.

[39] Hewett, R. W., *Maidstone: official charter brochure 1549–1949*.

[40] Gilbert (1954), 4–5.

[41] Census 1951, Occupation Tables, 304.

[42] Census 1951, Report . . . workplace, 188, 189.

[43] Brookfield, H. C., 'Worthing: a study of a modern coastal town', *Town Plann. Rev.*, 23 (1952), 145–62.

[44] Beckit, H. O., 'The South-east Midlands', in Ogilvie, 142.

[45] Gilbert (1947) 1–22: B.A. Oxford, esp. 121–31, 141–73.

[46] Sharp, T., *Oxford replanned* (London, 1948), 213.

[47] Gilbert, E. W., 'Reading: its position and growth', *Transactions of the South-eastern Union of Scientific Societies* (1934), 81–90.

[48] *City of Portsmouth Development Plan, Report of the Survey*, n.d., but after 1950.

[49] Gilbert (1954) 20; Stamp, L. D., and Beaver, S. H., *The British Isles*, 1954, 680–5: Ford, P., *Work and wealth in a modern port* (London, 1934), 25–57.

[50] Gilbert (1954) 21–3: Ashworth 42–3: Young, D. S., *The story of Bournemouth* (London, 1957), esp. pp. 50–177.

[51] *The borough of Swindon, official handbook 1952–1953*, and information from the Town Clerk.

[52] *Gloucester Official Guide*, n.d.

[53] Addison 112: Thesis of J. K. Noyes, B.A., and local information. Since the 1951 census there has been a large increase of population in both Gloucester and Cheltenham, with building on a substantial scale between the two towns.

[54] Defoe 432–4 suggests thst a visit to Bath had many attractions besides the pursuit of health: see Addison 58–73, 131–3, 144–7.

[55] Various aspects of the historical geography are treated in Darby. There are some distinguished contributors on the history of the city and district in B.A. Bristol. Two pioneer geographical papers are Jones, S. J., 'The growth of Bristol —the regional aspects of city development', *Pub. Inst. Brit. Geogr.*, 11 (1946), 57–83: and 'The cotton industry in Bristol', *ibid.*, 13 (1948), 61–79.

[56] Gilbert (1949), 2, 28.

[57] Shorter, A. H., 'The site, situation and functions of Exeter', *Geography*, 39 (1954), 250–61.

[58] Shorter, A. H., and Woodley, E. T., 'Plymouth: port and city', *Geography*, 32 (1937), 293–306.

[59] Geddes 37.

[60] Bowen, E. G. (ed.), *Wales, a physical, historical and regional geography* (London, 1957) includes much of general interest on industrial Wales and an excellent chapter by G. M. Howe, 'The South Wales coalfield', 353–400. A predepression work is Rider, S. W., and Trueman, A. E., *South Wales* (London 1929), esp. 77–99, 126–7, 145–70. Population history has been treated in numerous papers, notably Thomas, B., 'Migrations of labour into the Glamorganshire coalfield (1861–1911)', *Economica*, London, 10 (1930), 275–94.

[61] Thomas, T. M., 'Wales: land of mines and quarries', *Geogr. Rev.*, 46 (1956), 59–81 is an excellent summary article. See also Board of Trade, *An industrial survey of South Wales made . . . by University College of South Wales and Monmouthshire* (H.M.S.O., 1932) and the later *Second Industrial Survey of South Wales* (Cardiff, 1937), made by the National Industrial Development Council.

[62] Census 1931, Glamorgan 1: 1951, 1: Monmouthshire 1951, 2.

[63] Information on recent industrial development is given in National Industrial Development Council of Wales and Monmouthshire, Cardiff, Wales and Monmouth (n.d. but *c.* 1954) and in *Achievement*, published by Wales and Monmouthshire Industrial Estates Ltd., *c.* 1954.

[64] Williams, D., *A history of modern Wales*, London, 1950, esp. 213–45. See also John, A. H., *The industrial development of South Wales 1750–1850* (Cardiff, 1950).

[65] Chappell, E. L., *History of the port of Cardiff* (Cardiff, 1939), 74–6.

[66] *Ibid.*, 59: Williams, D., *op. cit.*, 192–3.

[67] Rider, S. W., and Trueman, A. E., *op. cit.*, 133–5.

[68] *Ibid.*, 135–6.

[69] *Ibid.*, 136–43: Chappell, E. L., *op. cit.*, 83–105.

[70] Thomas, B., *op. cit.* (in 60), 276–7.

[71] *Ibid.*, 284.

[72] Report of the Royal Commission on Merthyr Tydfil, Cmd. 5039 (1935), 8–10.

[73] *Ibid.*, 17.

[74] Williams, D., *op. cit.*, 226, 239–40.

[75] See note 63. Acknowledgement is made also to three former Manchester students for the use of their B.A. theses on parts of the Rhondda valleys— Muriel E. Edwards, A. J. Evans and G. C. Woosnam. There is also useful background material in Ministry of Labour, *Report of investigations into the industrial conditions on certain depressed areas*, Cmd. 4728 (1934), 132–88 and Lloyd, T. A., and Jackson, H., *South Wales Outline Plan 1949* (published for the South Wales . . . Development area).

[76] Rider, S. W., and Trueman, A. E., *op. cit.*, 50, 144–52, 160–2: Chappell, E. L., *op. cit.*, 48–130: Council for Wales and Monmouthshire, *Report on the South Wales ports*, Cmd. 9359 (1955), 5–13.

[77] Rider, S. W., and Trueman, A. E., *op. cit.*, 77–99, 126–7, 148–51: Bowen, E. G. (ed.), *op. cit.*, 205–7, 213, 216–18, 365–6, 389–98: Cmd. 9359, *op. cit.*, 15. See also Williams, D. T., *The economic development of Swansea and of the Swansea district*, Pamphlet 4 of the Social and Economic Survey Swansea and District (1940): this is an admirable detailed work published by the University of Wales Press Board on behalf of the University College of Swansea.

[78] Cmd. 9359 (1955) 14.

CHAPTER 11

[1] Census of Great Britain, 1951 Sample Tables Part 2.

[2] Census of Scotland 1951, Vol. 1, Parts 2, 15, 21 and 27, and Vol. 2.

[3] Fawcett 104, 112.

[4] Geddes 17–19.

[5] *Lanarkshire and its Industries* (1955), 7. Published by McKenzie, Vincent & Co. Ltd.

[6] *Industrial Guide to Glasgow* (*c.* 1953), 50, and *Glasgow Industrial Guide* (1955), 53. Published for the Corporation of Glasgow by John Menzies & Co. Ltd.

[7] *Old Statistical Account*, Glasgow (1793), Vol. 5, 502.

[8] *Ibid.*, Paisley (1793), Vol. 7, 73.

[9] Grant, I. F., *The Economic History of Scotland* (1934), 241.

[10] *Old Statistical Account*, Glasgow (1793), Vol. 5, 504.

[11] *Ibid.*, Old Monkland, 1793, Vol. 7, 386–8.

[12] *Ibid.*, Glasgow, Vol. 5, 489–90.

[13] *Ibid.*, Glasgow, Vol. 5, 587.

[14] Marwick, J. D., *The River Clyde and the Clyde Burghs* (1909), p. 179, quoting Smiles' 'Lives of the Engineers'.

[15] *New Statistical Account* (1845), Vol. 6, 198.

[16] Marwick, J. D., *op. cit.* Appendices 1, 2, and 3.

[17] *New Statistical Account*, Vol. 6, pp. 696–8.

[18] *Ibid.*, p. 148.

[19] Cleland, J., *The Rise and Progress of the city of Glasgow* (1840), p. 27.

[20] Grant, I. F., *op. cit.*, 251.

[21] *New Statistical Account*, Old Monkland, Vol. 6, 659.

[22] *Ibid.*, Vol. 6, 664, and Vol. 7, 561–2. See also O'Dell, A. C., 'A Geographical Examination of the Development of Scottish Railways', *Scot. Geogr. Mag.*, Vol. 55 (1939), 130 and 145.

[23] *New Statistical Account*, Vol. 6, 205–6.

[24] Grant, I. F., *op. cit.*, 257.

[25] *Ibid.*, 260.

[26] O'Dell, A. C., *op. cit.*, 131–2.

[27] Oakley, C. A., *The Second City* (1946), 209.

[28] Grant, I. F., *op. cit.*, 261.

[29] Marwick, J. D., *op. cit.*, 205–226.

[30] *Ibid.*, appendices 1, 2 and 3.

[31] O'Dell, A. C., *op. cit.*, 131–2.

[32] Oakley, C. A., *op. cit.*, 158–9.

[33] Pratt Paul, W. M., in *Industries of Dunbartonshire and Forth and Clyde Canal*, 1955, 59. Published by McKenzie, Vincent & Co. Ltd.

[34] Oakley, C. A., *op. cit.*, 157–8.

[35] Oakley, C. A., in Meikle, H. W. (ed.), *Scotland* (1947), 80.

[36] O'Dell, A. C., and Houston, J. M., in Daysh, G. H. J. (ed.), *Studies in Regional Planning* (1949), 63.

[37] Abercrombie, P., and Matthews, R. H., *The Clyde Valley Regional Plan* (1949), Appendix 10, 369.

[38] *Paisley official Guide* (1955), 23, and *Renfrewshire County Handbook* (*c.* 1947), 59.

[39] *The Scottish Industrial Estates* (*c.* 1956), 69–105.

[40] *The Scotsman*, 12 October 1956.

[41] Webster, Alexander, *An account of the number of people in Scotland in the year one thousand seven hundred and fifty-five.* Typewritten copies, Edinburgh, 1921.

[42] *Clyde Valley Regional Plan*, *op. cit.*, 7.

[43] Cleland, J., *op. cit.*, 11.

[44] *New Statistical Account*, Old Monkland, Vol. 6, 667.

[45] *Old Statistical Account*, Glasgow, Vol. 5, 511.

[46] Oakley, C. A., *op. cit.*, 249–50.

[47] *Encyclopaedia Britannica* (14th edition, 1929), Vol. 10, 397.

[48] Oakley, C. A., *op. cit.*, 250.

[49] *Clyde Valley Regional Plan*, *op. cit.*, 174.

[50] Grieve, R., *The Clyde Valley—a Review* (reprinted from the Town and Country Planning Association, Scottish Section 1954), 5.

[51] *Ibid.*, 17.

[52] *Corporation of the City of Glasgow—Written Statement as modified by the City of Glasgow Development Plan Approval Order* (1954), 20.

[53] Grieve, R., *op. cit.*, 12–14.

[54] *The Scotsman*, 19 September 1956 and 9 February 1957.

[55] Grieve, R., *op. cit.*, 14.

[56] Snodgrass, C. P., in *Scientific Survey of South-eastern Scotland*, British Association Handbook (1951), 137.

[57] Saunders, L. J., *Scottish Democracy, 1815–1840: the Social and Intellectual Background* (1950), 81–2.

[58] Abercrombie, P., and Plumstead, D., *A Civic Survey and Plan for Edinburgh* (1949), 15.

[59] *Ibid.*, map 3.

[60] *Ibid.*, 83.

[61] Census of Scotland, 1951, Vol. I, Pt. 1, 7.

[62] Mackenzie, H., *The Third Statistical Account of Scotland*, Vol. 4 (Aberdeen, 1953), 26–7.

[63] *Ibid.*, 43–59.

[64] *Ibid.*, p. 18.

[65] *Old Statistical Account*, Vol. 19 (1797), 170.

[66] Mackenzie, H., *op. cit.*, 123, 129.

[67] *Ibid.*, 83.

[68] *Ibid.*, 129–33.

[69] Lythe, S. G. E., 'The Origin and Development of Dundee: a study in Historical Geography', *Scot. geogr. Mag.*, Vol. 54 (1938), 352–6: Mackie, R. L., in *Dundee, British Association Souvenir Guide* (1947), 15–22.

[70] Industry and Employment in Scotland (1952), Cmd. 8797, 14–20.

[71] Strawhorn, J., and Boyd, W., *The Third Statistical Account of Scotland*, Vol. 1 (1951), Ayrshire, 530–47.

[72] *Ibid.*, p. 533.

[73] *Ibid.*, p. 530.

[74] *Ibid.*, p. 539.

[75] *Ibid.*, pp. 567–70.

[76] *Prestwick, The Official Guide*, pp. 28–31, 46–51.

CHAPTER 12

[1] Best, R H., and Ward, T. J., *The Garden Controversy*, Studies in rural land use, Report no. 2, Wye College, Ashford (1956). Out of fairness to the authors of this work one must acknowledge their careful economic arguments, of which only the conclusions are noted here.

[2] Census 1851, Population Tables 1, xxii.

[3] *Ibid.*, 1851, Population Tables 1, Div. IX, 27, 29, 33, 37. Cases of decrease of population, due for example to the decline of mining, are also noted.

[4] Report of Royal Sanitary Commission I (1871), Cmd. 281, 25.

[5] Briggs, A., *History of Birmingham*, vol. II (Oxford, 1952), 141.

[6] Robson, W. A. (ed.), *Great Cities of the World—Their Government, Planning and Politics* (London, 1954), 64–70.

[7] Manchester and District Town Planning Advisory Committee (Manchester 1926), produced maps for a far wider area than the conurbation.

[8] Local Government: Areas and status of local authorities in England and Wales, 1956, Cmd. 9831, 9, 14.

[9] John, A. H., *The Industrial Development of South Wales, 1750–1850* (Cardiff, 1950), 98.

[10] Manchester and District Town Planning Advisory Committee (Manchester, 1926).

[11] Walker, G., 'The growth of population in Birmingham and the Black Country between the wars', *University of Birmingham Historical Journal*, I (1947–1948), 158–79.

[12] Fawcett 100.

[13] *The New Survey of London Life and Labour*, vol. 6 (London, 1934), 141.

B B *

[14] Baker, H., 'On the growth of the commercial centre of Manchester . . . 1861–1871', *Trans. Manchr. statist. Soc.* (1871–1872), 90–3.

[15] Report (Improvements and Town Planning Committee) on the preliminary draft proposals for post-war reconstruction in the City of London (1944), 1.

INDEX

383